Philosophy of Religion

Philosophy of Religion

Second Edition

Norman L. Geisler
and
Winfried Corduan

Wipf and Stock Publishers
EUGENE, OREGON

Wipf and Stock Publishers
199 West 8th Avenue, Suite 3
Eugene, Oregon 97401

Philosophy of Religion
Second Edition
By Geisler, Norman and Corduan, Winfried
Copyright© January, 1988 Geisler, Norman and Corduan, Winfried
ISBN: 1-59244-134-3
Publication Date: January, 2003
Previously published by Baker Book House, January, 1988 .

To
all our students,
whose thought-provoking questions
have occasioned the reflection
so necessary to the pursuit
of truth

Contents

Preface

It has been said that Western philosophy has "carried the burden of God." Despite attempts earlier this century to eliminate God from the philosophical arena, philosophy of religion has emerged again as a prime topic in contemporary thought. Numerous books have been published on the topic, but few have been satisfyingly positive from a theistic viewpoint.

The pressing questions on the contemporary scene are four. First, is there any basis in reality for a religious experience? Men have experiences they describe as religious, but is there a real transcendent object of these experiences (e.g., God)? Or, is the object purely illusory or entirely imaginary? Secondly, is there any basis in reason for belief in God? Can the existence of God be proved or disproved? Is there any validity to the theistic arguments? Thirdly, whatever the basis in experience or reason for belief in God, is it even possible to speak meaningfully of a transcendent Being? What significance do words have when they are torn from their empirical rootage and applied to some transcendent Being beyond the world? Finally, in view of the claim that there is a good and powerful Being beyond this world, how does one account for evil? If God is good, why did he allow this plague of evil? And if he is powerful, why does he not overcome it?

Many theists have written on these topics. But apart from anthologies, there are few texts available that attempt to answer these questions from a theistically positive philosophical perspective. It is our conviction that piecemeal critiques of nontheisms will not suffice. The theist must enter the arena with a positive and comprehensive case of his own. It is in this spirit that we have surveyed the field of issues and presented arguments for classical theism.

PART 1 ✳

GOD AND EXPERIENCE

GUIDING QUESTIONS

1. What is a religious experience?
2. What are characteristics and dimensions of religious experience?
3. Can there be a religious experience without an object of experience?
4. Can one test the truth claims arising out of religious experience?

RECOMMENDED COLLATERAL READING

William James, *The Varieties of Religious Experience*. New York: Mentor, New American Library, 1958.

Rudolf Otto, *The Idea of the Holy*. Translated by J. W. Harvey. New York: Oxford University Press, 1967.

Paul Tillich, *The Dynamics of Faith*. New York: Harper Torchbooks, 1957.

1 ✴

The Nature of Religious Experience

Philosophy of religion concerns itself with difficult questions, many of which revolve around sorting out positions on some clearly delineated topics (e.g., Does God exist?). The question before us in part 1 of this book is, What is religious experience? A philosophy of religion that does not answer the question may lose itself in fascinating arguments that may be irrelevant. Religion is an experiential issue, not a merely intellectual one.

In order to get underway, we shall attempt two equally difficult tasks. First we shall give a brief analysis of the meaning of experience. This analysis will be followed by a section on the meaning of religion. Then we will contrast religious experience with moral, aesthetic, and purely secular experience. With those preliminary considerations, we will be able to undertake the more detailed expositions of the subsequent chapters.

The Meaning of Experience

By experience is meant the consciousness or awareness that individuals have. Experience is the awareness of a subject but not necessarily a mere subjective awareness. That is, all experience is subjective in that it is something that subjects or individuals have. However, not all experience is purely subjective; there are objective referents for at least some experiences. Experience is the state of consciousness of an individual who is aware of something as other whether or not it really is other.

This point carries the weight of commonsense understanding. When I experience, I experience something. However, in philosophical circles that point is far from undisputed. Recently a number of writers have criticized this notion. Steven T. Katz, for example, maintains that an experience and the object of it cannot be separated.[1] He bases his contention on the fact that the supposed intended object always determines the nature of the experience. Thus a strict

---

1. Steven T. Katz, "Language, Epistemology, and Mysticism," in *Mysticism and Philosophical Analysis,* ed. Steven T. Katz (New York: Oxford University Press, 1978), pp. 22–74. See also the reply by Peter Byrne, "Mysticism, Identity and Realism: A Debate Reviewed," *International Journal for Philosophy of Religion* 16 (1984): 237–44.

trichotomy between the subject, the object, and the experience that unites them would not be warranted.

However, this view of things is counterintuitive and factually inaccurate. No modern philosophy has attempted to reduce ontology to subjectivity as has phenomenology. But even in a phenomenologically reduced state, supposedly there are three components: the transcendental ego, the noemata (the objects of knowledge), and noesis (the act of intentionally knowing the noemata). All experience, no matter how it is labeled, includes such aspects.

The question of whether these aspects are ontologically distinct or not makes no difference as to whether they are what is experienced. Of course, experience may be an awareness of one's self, or self-awareness. But even here there is at least a psychological distinction between the self that is the subject of the awareness and the self of which it is aware.

Experience may be viewed in two ways—generally and specifically. Experience in general is the totality of consciousness like that of being alive. A specific experience focuses on a given aspect or moment within the whole of one's consciousness, such as a certain event in one's life. Or, the difference, respectively, is like that between the awareness of being in a state of marriage and getting married (i.e., the consciousness of taking a wife in the ceremony of marriage). In this study we will be concerned primarily with religious experience in general rather than with specific religious experiences, for two reasons. First, experience in general is the backdrop and basis for particular experiences, just as vision is the general faculty that makes it possible to focus on this or that particular object. Secondly, religious experience in general is more readily available to people in general. Not everyone has had a special religious experience, such as a mystical experience. But, as we shall argue subsequently, religious experience in the general sense is both more readily available to, and more understandable by, people in general. This will be made more explicit once religion is defined. However, we must first distinguish different levels of experience.

The most basic level of experience may be called primary awareness. It is the basic unreflective consciousness an individual has. Secondary awareness is the consciousness of being conscious; it is being aware of the fact that one has awareness.[2] Unlike humans, animals give no evidence of this secondary awareness. Within this secondary awareness are many activities such as remembering, reflecting, relating, and reasoning. All of these presuppose or build upon primary awareness.

The study of religious experience undertaken here will treat both kinds of awareness. It will recognize, however, that primary awareness is fundamen-

2. Michael Novak makes a similar distinction between primary and secondary awareness. See *Belief and Unbelief* (New York: Macmillan, 1965), pp. 72–75.

tal to secondary awareness, even though secondary awareness may be necessary for reaching primary awareness. Furthermore, it is recognized that in order to get at the religious awareness of other people one does not have direct access to either their primary or their secondary awareness. In order to understand the religious experiences of others one must depend on their expressions of their experiences. In brief, expressions of experience must be studied to understand the experiences behind these expressions, and secondary experience must be studied in order to understand the primary experience behind it. And primary religious experience in general (as opposed to special religious experience) will be the primary center of concern. Special religious experiences may be used to illustrate a focusing or intensifying of the experience that is more generally available for persons. But precisely what is a religious experience?

The Meaning of Religion

Attempts to define religion have generally not gained universal acceptance.[3] In fact, it is almost impossible to provide a general definition of religion that does justice to most world views to which we refer as religious. Zen Buddhism involves a notion of transcendence apart from belief in gods, but no clear-cut code of morality. On the other hand, Confucianism emphasizes morality, but its commitment to divine realities is only peripheral. Thus a definition that would center on either morality or gods will not do justice to either religion, let alone a third religion such as Islam, in which both a God and morality are stressed.

But this restriction does not constitute a serious problem for the philosophy of religion, for religion interests the philosopher because of the phenomena of belief in gods and acceptance of morality. A religion without such features is not any less a religion, but it will be of less interest to the student of philosophy of religion. A theoretical religion in which there is no transcendence, no God, no morality, and no experience would simply have no relevance to the matters which usually concern philosophers of religion.

Thus we can make our definition somewhat narrower than all the data demand and still be able to deal with religions as unique among world views. We can also help ourselves with a Wittgensteinian notion of "family resemblance." That is, no two religions have all of the same characteristics (obviously), but to varying degrees all religions exhibit typical characteristics.

---

3. Wilfred C. Smith wrote: "It is perhaps not presumptuous to hold that no definition of religion so far proposed has proven compelling, no generalization has come anywhere near to Adequacy." *The Meaning and End of Religion* (New York: New American Library of World Literature, 1964), p. 16.

The vast majority of definitions of religion include at least one common element: awareness of the Transcendent. They differ, of course, in what kind of awareness is involved and what is meant by the Transcendent. We will begin with what appears to be common to most definitions and then attempt to discover what must be characteristic of an awareness of the Transcendent to make it qualify as a distinctive experience to which we may give the title *religious*.

In at least two senses religious experience may involve transcendence. First, transcendence may be the process of overcoming the conditions of one's finitude or frustrations. This may also be called self-transcendence.[4] Transcendence may also be the object of religious experience (the Transcendent). It is in this latter sense that we are primarily concerned with religious transcendence in this study.

It should be pointed out that the Transcendent is not intended to be equivalent to the Christian view of God. God as defined by Western theisms is one (specific) form or way of viewing the Transcendent. What is meant by the Transcendent is a much broader, more general, and less specific notion that includes pantheistic as well as theistic, personal as well as impersonal, religious views. Brahman of Hinduism, Nirvana of Buddhism, the Tao of Taoism, Friedrich Schleiermacher's All, Rudolf Otto's Numen, and Paul Tillich's Being beyond being are all ways of viewing the Transcendent. In short, forms of transcendence are found in deism, finite godism, panentheism, and even atheism.

The Transcendent not only has many descriptions but also may have many dimensions. It need not be viewed as being "above"; it may be thought of as a transcendence in "depth." Then too, it may be the transcendent "origin" or even the "center" or "goal" of one's religious experience. In brief, we do not intend here to narrow or limit the meaning of the Transcendent to any particular direction or dimension.

"Transcendent" means two things. First, something is transcendent if it goes beyond or is more than one's immediate consciousness. In this sense the subconscious is transcendent, for it goes beyond one's immediate consciousness and yet one is somehow aware that it is there.[5] The transcendental ego is also an example,[6] for we are conscious of it, but we are conscious that it

---

4. But self-transcendence can be misleading in a religious context if it is taken to mean transcending by one's self or on one's own. A religious experience involves a sense of dependence, and it cannot in the same way involve an attitude of complete independence from anything beyond man.

5. William James calls the subconscious the hither side of the Transcendent, but it is definitely beyond the individual's conscious self. See *The Varieties of Religious Experience* (New York: Mentor, New American Library, 1958), p. 508; cf. p. 232.

6. Peter Koëstenbaum develops this point in an excellent summary of a phenomenological

is beyond our consciousness.[7] Even other selves are transcendent, for we are conscious of them, but conscious of them as being beyond ourselves. Immanuel Kant's *noumenon* is transcendent, for he somehow knows that the noumenon is there, even though he cannot say what it is.[8] Further, it is more than what is experienced in the way that the whole is greater than its parts (e.g., there is a wholeness, structure, or relationship missing when the parts are scattered). In a similar way a word or sentence is more than letters (a unity of meaning not in the parts taken separately), or a painting is more than the pigment and colors. That is, something is transcendent if there is more in it than meets the eye. If there is a depth or perspective that is more than the empirical experience of it, then it transcends the empirical.[9]

Second, something is transcendent in a religious sense if it is believed to be ultimate. The Transcendent is the object of a total commitment—that for which one would make even the supreme sacrifice. The Transcendent is the object of ultimate concern because it is thought to be ultimate or final. It is that More in view of which one sees no need of more. It is the Beyond beyond which one seeks no more beyonds. Examples of such commitment outside of religion are difficult to find, but to some degree the patriot's "my country, right or wrong," or the moralist's "duty for duty's sake," or an artist's commitment to absolute Beauty are examples. (A fascinating example of this last attitude is provided by the main character in *My Name Is Asher Lev* by Chaim Potok. Asher's artistic compulsion makes him break with all the structures of his environment—family, society, and religion.) It is, as Tillich said, the Ultimate to which one makes an ultimate commitment.[10] Anything less than a total commitment is less than a religious experience. But more about this later (in chap. 2). For now, let us see how a religious experience differs from other kinds of experiences.

---

approach to religion, "Religion in the Tradition of Phenomenology," in *Religion in Philosophical and Cultural Perspective*, ed. J. Clayton Feaver and William Horosz (Princeton, N.J.: Van Nostrand, 1967), pp. 186–93.

7. We are not here arguing for the existence of the subconscious, the transcendental ego, or other minds. We are simply saying that if they exist, they would be real examples of what we mean by transcendent. If they do not exist, they would be merely possible examples.

8. See Immanuel Kant, *The Critique of Pure Reason*, trans. Lewis W. Beck (New York: Bobbs-Merrill, 1956), p. 273, where he says, "On the contrary, it itself limits sensibility by applying the term *noumenon* to things in themselves (things not regarded as appearances). But in so doing it at the same time sets limits to itself, recognizing that it cannot know these noumena through any of the categories, and that it must therefore think them only under the title of an unknown something."

9. See Ian T. Ramsey, *Religious Language* (New York: Macmillan, 1963), pp. 42–50.

10. See Paul Tillich, *Ultimate Concern*, ed. D. MacKenzie Brown (London: SCM, 1965), pp. 7, 8, 11, passim.

Religious Experience Distinguished from Other Experiences

Two or three kinds of experiences are sometimes closely associated with religious experience—the moral, the aesthetic, and more recently, the secular. Distinguishing these will aid in understanding what characterizes a religious experience.

Religious Experience in Contrast to Moral Experience

Since a religious experience is similar to a moral experience and since some thinkers tend to equate them, a few words of clarification are in order. Kant's definition of religion as "the recognition of all duties as divine commands" falls into this general category. Bishop Butler said that religion and morality "closely resemble" each other.[11] Ian T. Ramsey calls them "close logical kinsmen" with "great affinities,"[12] and suggests this is why they have so often had the same friends and the same enemies in the history of philosophy. R. B. Braithwaite distinguishes them only in theory, not in practice, arguing, "Unless religious principles are moral principles, it makes no sense to speak of putting them into practice. A moral belief is an intention to behave in a certain way: a religious belief is an intention to behave in a certain way (a moral belief) together with the entertainment of certain stories associated with the intention in the mind of the believer."[13] Erich Fromm believes that "the difference between the religious and the ethical is to a large extent only an epistemological one, though not entirely so."[14]

Even those who see a difference between religion and morality tend to stress their inseparability. Tillich wrote, "Morality is intrinsically religious, as religion is intrinsically ethical."[15] Henri Bergson contended that "originally [i.e., among the primitives], the whole of morality is custom; and as religion forbids any departure from custom morality is coextensive with religion."[16]

Despite the interrelationship and seeming inseparability of religion and morality, they involve clearly differing experiences. As John Dewey observed, "The religious attitude signifies something that is bound through imagination to a *general* attitude. This comprehensive attitude, moreover, is much

11. As quoted by Ramsey, *Religious Language*, pp. 32, 33.

12. Ramsey, *Religious Language*, pp. 34, 42.

13. R. B. Braithwaite, "Religious Statements as Ethically but not Factually Significant," in *The Existence of God*, ed. John H. Hick (New York: Macmillan, 1964), pp. 241, 250.

14. Erich Fromm, *Psychoanalysis and Religion* (New Haven: Yale University Press, 1959), p. 93. He does admit that "there is a factor common to certain kinds of religious experience [the mystical] which goes beyond the purely ethical. But it is exceedingly difficult if not impossible to formulate this factor of religious experience" (p. 94).

15. Paul Tillich, *Morality and Beyond* (New York: Harper and Row, 1963), p. 15.

16. Henri Bergson, *The Two Sources of Morality and Religion*, trans. R. A. Audra and C. Brereton (New York: Doubleday, 1935), p. 123.

broader than anything indicated by 'moral' in its usual sense."[17] William James summed up the difference by arguing that morality accepts the yoke of the universe, but religion welcomes it; religion is not a mere Stoic submission to the universe, but a love of it. Morality calls for obedience, said James, but religion calls for volunteers.[18] Schleiermacher offered a further distinction when he contended that morality is a person's duty to the universe; religion is his dependence on it.[19] Even in dependence there is a kind of duty, only it is a more basic duty than moral duty.

Perhaps no one has drawn the distinction between a moral duty and a religious duty more sharply than Søren Kierkegaard in his famous panegyric on Abraham.[20] The ethical, said Kierkegaard, expresses one's universal duty, but the religious says that "the individual as the particular is higher than the universal." This can also be expressed by saying that "there is an absolute duty toward God for in this relationship of duty the individual as an individual stands related absolutely to the absolute." Or, to summarize Kierkegaard, an ethical experience responds to the moral law; a religious experience responds to the moral Lawgiver himself. The moral law says, "Thou shalt not kill"; God told Abraham, "Sacrifice your son Isaac." In this situation, either

17. John Dewey, *A Common Faith* (New Haven: Yale University Press, 1934), p. 23. However, in the final analysis Dewey's definition of religion turns out to be one's broad moral goal, which hardly shows that there is a basic difference between them.

18. James, *Varieties of Religious Experience*, pp. 41–45.

19. Friedrich Schleiermacher, *On Religion: Speeches to Its Cultured Despisers*, trans. John Oman (New York: Ungar, 1955), pp. 275ff.

20. Buber said Kierkegaard rejected this sharp distinction in his later works. "Our rejection can be supported by Kierkegaard's own teaching. He describes 'the ethical' as 'the only means by which God communicates with man' (1853). . . . The ethical no longer appears here, as in Kierkegaard's earlier thought, as a 'stage' from which a 'leap' leads to the religious, a leap by which a level is reached that is quite different and has a different meaning; here it dwells in the religious, in faith and service. This ethical can no longer mean a morality belonging to a realm of relativity, time and again overtaken and invalidated by the religious; it means *essential* acting and suffering in relation to men, coordinated with the essential relation to God" (*The Writings of Martin Buber*, ed. Will Herberg [New York: World, 1956], p. 78). But if this were so, it would necessitate a reversal of virtually everything Kierkegaard said about Abraham, and this is difficult to believe. Kierkegaard often closely identified the ethical and the religious, particularly when he was contrasting them with the aesthetic. But since he did not anywhere clearly repudiate the sharp distinctions between the ethical and the religious made in *Fear and Trembling*, it seems best to interpret these other isolated statements (that seem to identify the ethical and the religious) in the light of the clear distinction he did make between them and nowhere clearly repudiated. See Søren Kierkegaard, *Fear and Trembling*, trans. W. Lowrie (New York: Doubleday, 1954), p. 78, where he wrote, "The ethical is the universal, and as such it is again the divine. One has therefore a right to say that fundamentally every duty is a duty toward God; but if one cannot say more, then one affirms at the same time that properly I have no duty toward God. Duty becomes duty by being referred to God, but in duty itself I do not come into relation with God. Thus it is a duty to love one's neighbor, but in performing this duty I do not come into relation with God but with the neighbor whom I love."

the religious is above the ethical, or Abraham, far from being the great hero of faith, is a murderer. Thus, we are "wrong in not protesting loudly and clearly against the fact that Abraham enjoys honor and glory as the father of faith, whereas he ought to be prosecuted and convicted of murder." In reality, Abraham had to transcend the ethical in order to do the religious. This does not mean the ethical is destroyed by the religious; rather, it is merely dethroned by it. The ethical is a necessary prerequisite to the religious; one cannot be religious unless one is first ethical. However, the religious is a higher relationship of duty to God in view of which even the ethical must give way. "Abraham, by a religious act of faith, overstepped the ethical and possessed a higher *telos* outside of it, in relation to which he suspended the former." In this state of absolute duty to God, "the ethical is reduced to a position of relativity" to the point that "love to God may cause the knight of faith to give his love to his neighbor the opposite expression to that which, ethically speaking, is required by duty." The religious is higher than the ethical as the individual is higher than the universal, or as the concrete is over the abstract, or as the response to the person of God takes precedence over response to mere propositions about God. That is to say, morality is a human's responsibility in this world; religion is his response to revelation from beyond this world. The former calls for duty, the latter for worship.[21]

Furthermore, it may be added that religion differs from morality because the latter can point out weaknesses or sin but only the former can help a person transcend them. That is, religion is higher than ethics because a feeling of grace is higher than a sense of guilt. Morality tells a person what he ought to do; religion can help him do it. The former provides the transcendent norm; the latter can give the motivation and power for transcending.

In brief, a religious experience differs from an ethical experience in several ways: its commitment is broader in scope; its commitment is different in kind; its object is of a higher order; and its object alone has the power to overcome and unify. Let us take a closer look at each of these. First, a religious commitment is broader than a moral one since the former is a whole commitment of the whole person to the whole universe.[22] That is, it is a commitment of the person as a whole, including his nonmoral aspects of being (meditating) and acting (such as knowing, art, and play). Secondly, even if one defines the moral more broadly so as to include the whole man, a moral commitment would still differ from a religious commitment in that the moral experience as such involves merely the sense of what one should do; a religious experience goes beyond this, being characterized by what the person

21. All of the preceding quotes appear in Kierkegaard, *Fear and Trembling*, pp. 66, 90, 78, 65, 69, 80.
22. See chapter 2 on this point.

wills to do. Morality is a matter of duty; religion is a matter also of desire. Further, a religious experience has a higher object than a moral experience. For morality is a person's commitment to other persons; religion is his commitment to what goes beyond them to the Transcendent. Finally, only a religious experience can bring complete unity into one's life. Failure in morality can produce guilt; only religion can provide grace to overcome both failure and guilt. One's moral shortcomings call for a religious overcoming. The duality within the human being calls for a unity beyond him.

There is no need to be long concerned with whether morality flows from religion or religion flows from morality, or whether they are separate streams.[23] Their close historical and logical connections would seem to preclude the latter. As to the former question, Schleiermacher's suggestion is helpful: "Specific actions follow only from specific impulses. Religion is not a specific impulse, so no specific actions can follow from it. Religion produces action only as a sum of activity flows from a sum of feeling, viz., as that which reflects the inner unity of the spirit. But," he continues, "while a man does nothing from religion, he should do everything with religion. Uninterruptedly, like a sacred music, the religious feelings should accompany his active life."[24]

As Tillich indicated, "If the moral imperative were derived from religion in the traditional sense of the word, secular ethics would have to sever any ties with religion, for it rejects direct dependence on any particular religion."[25] There is certainly a danger in tying ethics to specific religious beliefs, as Sigmund Freud rightly noted. For if these religious beliefs are rejected—and people are prone to reject them—then one has lost his basis for morality.[26] However, if one means that morality flows from the far more extensive, if not universal, attitude of humans called the religious, then Freud's objection loses its force.

Religious Experience in Contrast to Aesthetic Experience

There is also a close connection between religion and art. Alfred North Whitehead contends that religion and play have the same origin in ritual.

23. Tillich wrote in this regard: "The question of moral motivation can be answered only transmorally. For the law demands, but cannot forgive; it judges, but cannot accept. Therefore, forgiveness and acceptance, the conditions of the fulfillment of the law, must come from something above the law, or more precisely, from something in which the split between our essential being and our existence is overcome and healing power has appeared." *Morality and Beyond*, p. 64.

24. Schleiermacher, *On Religion*, pp. 57–59.

25. Tillich, *Morality and Beyond*, p. 30.

26. Sigmund Freud, *The Future of an Illusion*, trans. W. D. Robson-Scott (New York: Doubleday, 1957), pp. 62–64.

"This is because ritual is the stimulus to emotion, and an habitual ritual may diverge into religion or into play, according to the quality of the emotion excited. . . ." He also observed, "In the modern world, a holy day and a holiday are kindred notions."[27] Otto noted that the sacred and the sublime are similar in two ways: both are inexplicable and both have the dual character of humbling yet exalting the beholder.[28] In fact, the two experiences are so similar that an aesthetic experience may be used to evoke a religious one, as Otto observed.[29] Tillich noted that the religious may even appear in a painting that has no religious content in the traditional sense.[30]

How, then, can we differentiate between these two closely associated experiences? Schleiermacher put his distinction this way: all science is the existence of things in the human; art is the existence of the human in things. But both art and science are dependent on the universal existence of all things in the Infinite. Or, to say it another way, science is speculative, art is practical, and religion is intuitive.[31]

The problem with this distinction is that an aesthetic experience can be intuitive too, as Plotinus points out. That is, art as a practice (e.g., man making something beautiful) is no doubt distinguishable from religion as a feeling or awareness of the Absolute. But what about one's awareness of absolute Beauty; is this kind of aesthetic experience distinguishable from a religious awareness of the Absolute? For example, in Plotinus there is that absolute Beauty (the "One" or "Good") which is experienced as ultimate and is identified with "God." It is beyond all sensible and even intellectual beauty and can be known only in a mystical union with it. If by the term *aesthetic experience* one refers to this kind of ultimate intuition, then it would seem that Schleiermacher's distinction between aesthetics and religion would not hold.

Kierkegaard, in a more radical distinction, views the aesthetic, moral, and religious dimensions as three ascending levels or stages of life.[32] The aesthetic level is that of feeling; the ethical, of deciding; and the religious, of existing. The aesthetic stage represents the routines of life, the ethical gives rules for life, and the religious gives a revelation to life. Whereas the first is self-centered and the second is law-centered, the last is God-centered. Aesthetics

27. Alfred North Whitehead, *Religion in the Making* (New York: World, 1960), p. 21.

28. Rudolf Otto, *The Idea of the Holy*, trans. J. W. Harvey (New York: Oxford University Press, 1967), pp. 44, 45.

29. For example, darkness (as in temples) can evoke a mystical effect; silence can provoke a spontaneous reaction to a numinous presence; and emptiness, by doing away with the "this" and "here," can draw attention to the "wholly other." Ibid., pp. 72, 73.

30. Tillich, *Ultimate Concern*, p. 6.

31. Schleiermacher, *On Religion*, pp. 39, 275–84.

32. These three levels are represented respectively by three of his works, *Repetitions* (the aesthetic), *Either/Or* (the ethical), and *Fear and Trembling* (the religious), and the overall view of these dimensions in *Stages on Life's Way* (New York: Harper and Row, 1954).

represents a life without choosing; morality, a choosing of life; religion, the choosing of God. From the aesthetic to the moral is a leap[33] from being spectator to being participator in life, a leap from personal whims to universal norms, from mere deliberation to decision, from being controlled by life to being in control of life. The further leap from the ethical stage to the religious is a leap from the objective realm of abstract, universal moral code to the subjective realm of concrete, particular conduct, from the essential order to the existential, from propositions about God to the person of God. Briefly, then, aesthetics is something one has; religion is something one is. The former is impersonal; the latter is personal. Aesthetics is something one knows; religion is something one lives. One grips the aesthetical dimension of life, but the religious grips him.

But even Kierkegaard's radical distinction would not do to differentiate what Plotinus meant by an experience of absolute Beauty from what Schleiermacher meant by a religious experience. Both are ultimate; both are absolute. Perhaps the simplest way to resolve the problem is to say that for Plotinus there is no distinction between a religious and an aesthetic experience of absolute Beauty; in fact, they are identical for him.[34] However, there remains the question of whether this is the normal and customary meaning of an aesthetic experience. At least on the lower levels (sensual, intellectual) of aesthetic experience there is a marked difference between the religious and the aesthetic experiences; the former is ultimate, the latter is not. These lower aesthetic experiences may lead to the higher religious experience, but they are not identical.

In another attempt to distinguish them, Otto contends that an aesthetic experience can be used to evoke a religious experience, even though the two experiences differ in kind. An aesthetic experience is a sense of the sublime; a religious experience is an awareness of the sacred or holy—a numinous experience. And even though there is a hidden relation between the sacred and the sublime, these two experiences differ in kind and not merely in degree.[35] Although Otto does not clearly draw out his distinctions, he seems to imply that the difference between them is that of a sense of grandeur on the one hand and a vision of God on the other; like the difference between viewing the Grand Canyon and seeing a holy God (as in Isaiah's vision in the Old Testament). As A. E. Taylor put it, if William Shakespeare walked into

---

33. Each stage is separated by a crisis of despair and is spanned only by a "leap of faith." Lower levels are not destroyed, only dethroned, by higher levels, and attainment is no guarantee of permanence. Kierkegaard, *Fear and Trembling*, p. 80.

34. However, there is certainly a distinction in Plotinus between an aesthetic experience on either a sensual or intellectual level and this highest intuitive experience. See *Six Enneads* (Chicago: Encyclopedia Britannica Press, 1952), 1.6.6, 9; 5.5.12.

35. Otto, *Idea of the Holy*, pp. 65, 106.

the room we should stand, but if Jesus Christ walked into the room we should kneel.[36] The former could occasion an aesthetic experience; the latter would provide a religious encounter. Aesthetics involves a sense of wonder and amazement; religion involves a sense of worship and adoration.

But how can one say they differ in kind unless it can be shown what the difference is? In response, we would suggest two differences. First, the object of an aesthetic experience, at least in the ordinary sensual or intellectual sense, is not ultimate, whereas the object of a religious experience is ultimate. And in the Plotinian sense of an intuitive experience of absolute Beauty, one is actually describing religious experience in its aesthetic dimension. Second, the nature of an aesthetic experience (even in the Plotinian sense of absolute Beauty) is different from a religious experience. Even if the object of both is considered to be one and the same Absolute, nevertheless the attitude of the religious person toward it differs from that of the artist. The artist as such has only an attitude of wonder and admiration toward the Absolute, whereas the religious person has a spirit of worship and adoration toward it. The artist is drawn by it, but the religious person is also repelled by it. As Otto observed, there is a sense of fear as well as fascination. That is, the religious person not only is devoted to the ultimate but also senses his dependence on it. Furthermore, the artist has an attitude of contemplation; the religious person an attitude of complete commitment. That is, the former remains detached from ultimate beauty whereas the latter is aware of his dependence on the ultimate.

Religious Experience in Contrast to Purely Secular Experience

We need to distinguish between humanistic and secular experience. An experience need not be secular or nonreligious simply because it is humanistic. Both Fromm's and Dewey's views are humanistic and yet both qualify as religious.

In Fromm's view, what he calls a humanistic religion (in contrast to an "authoritarian" religion) qualifies under our definition as religious. For the higher human self, which he calls God, does indeed transcend the individual and is considered ultimate; that is, one is ultimately committed to it.[37] Likewise, Dewey's form of humanism is essentially religious. He said, "Any activity pursued in behalf of an ideal end and against obstacles and in spite of threats of personal loss because of conviction of its general and enduring value is religious in quality."[38] The ideal goal is transcendent and the conviction of it and commitment to it are total.

If this is so, then one may ask just what type of humanistic experience would not qualify as a religious experience. A nonreligious or purely secular

36. A. E. Taylor, "The Argument from Religious Experience," in John Hick, ed., *The Existence of God* (New York: Macmillan, 1964) p. 159.

37. Fromm, *Psychoanalysis and Religion,* pp. 37, 49, 60.

38. Dewey, *Common Faith,* p. 27.

experience would be one in which either no transcendent Other exists beyond the individual, or, if there is such, the individual would not be totally committed to it. The fact that purely secular experiences are difficult to find is testimony to how incurably religious man is. Even Freud's god of human reason, which he calls *Logos*,[39] is not identified with the individual's rational powers and thus qualifies as a transcendent. Likewise, the projected human "self," which Ludwig Feuerbach says men (falsely) consider to be God, is not the individual human being but human nature in general; that is, universal or generic humanity.[40] Of course, he does not consider it to be real, nor does Dewey hold his ideal goal to be real. Nevertheless, it is beyond the individual and it is considered ultimate by the religious person. Therefore, it qualifies as an object of religious experience.

The first way in which one may be irreligious is to refuse to recognize any kind of transcendence whatsoever. This said Wilfred C. Smith, is what characterizes contemporary secularity.[41] That is, a completely immanent, this-worldly outlook that is unable (or unwilling) to transcend in any direction is essentially nonreligious. As Martin E. Marty put it, "Secularism permits no transcendent. . . . It is self-contained, self-explanatory, self-enclosed."[42] Or as Thomas J. J. Altizer wrote, "If there is one clear portal to the twentieth century, it is . . . the collapse of any meaning or reality being beyond the newly discovered radical immanence of modern man, an immanence dissolving even the memory or the shadow of transcendence."[43] There are several possible reasons for this failure to comprehend the Transcendent: it is "dead" (Altizer); our language about it is "dead" or meaningless (van Buren); it is "eclipsed" by conceptualizations about it (as Buber said); or it is "silent" or hiding (Beckett).

But there is a radically immanent, irreligious stance taken by some contemporary people not only because of the inability to discover the Transcendent but also because of an unwillingness to make a total (or even a partial) commitment to it. This unwillingness is the second characteristic of a nonreligious experience. There are many reasons some people would refuse to commit themselves to the Transcendent, even if it were there: it is deemed unworthy of their devotion;[44] a person considers himself mature enough to

39. Freud, *Future of an Illusion*, p. 88.

40. Ludwig Feuerbach, *The Essence of Christianity*, trans. George Eliot (New York: Harper and Row, 1957), p. 7.

41. Smith, *Meaning and End of Religion*, p. 127.

42. Martin E. Marty, *Varieties of Unbelief* (New York: Doubleday, 1964), p. 138.

43. Thomas J. J. Altizer, *The Gospel of Christian Atheism* (Philadelphia: Westminster, 1966), p. 22.

44. Ivan, in Dostoevsky's *The Brothers Karamazov*, reflects this attitude. Ivan leaves the impression that even if God were known to exist, he would never surrender to God because of the injustice he has done to man.

function without the Transcendent;[45] and the individual desires to honor himself as ultimate.[46]

In brief, a person may be irreligious or purely humanistic in two ways: first, because he is unable to see a Transcendent, and second, because he is unwilling to submit to it. In either event, his experience would fall short of being adequately religious.

The Universality and Reality of Religious Experience

In actual practice, few if any people have attained a state of complete secularity. Most secular experience is still quasireligious. Tillich argued that all persons have an ultimate commitment; even atheists have a center of their personality, a unifying core of concern.[47] Others, like Otto, have argued only for the universality of the capacity for religion, just as people have a universal capacity for song or art even if they never sing or paint.[48] Mircea Eliade amply illustrates the thesis that the modern person with all of his secularity has not completely extricated himself from the religious. The secular person, for example, has been unable to shake himself from certain quasireligious myths. Nudism's nostalgia for Eden, Communism's desire for the Golden Age, and the aesthetic attempt to escape time via the novel or the theater all indicate humanity's unshakable religious heritage.[49]

Whether the religious consciousness is only potentially universal or whether it is actually so is moot. What is demonstrable from both believer and nonbeliever is that humankind as a whole has been incurably religious. Even Freud acknowledged that what Schleiermacher called religious (the feeling of cosmic dependence) was indeed a universal experience.[50] Literary existentialists like Franz Kafka and Samuel Beckett reflect also the modern person's longing for God. Beckett's *Waiting for Godot* is a reflection of Martin Heidegger's phrase *waiting for God*. Jean-Paul Sartre's designation of

45. Fromm states this well: "If mankind is able to produce enough to feed all men, it does not need to pray for daily bread. Man can provide that by his own effort." *Psychoanalysis and Religion*, p. 104.

46. Ayn Rand's philosophy of selfishness is as clear an example of this as one can find. "By the grace of reality and the nature of life, man—every man—is an end in himself, he exists for his own sake, and the achievement of his own happiness is his highest moral purpose." *For the New Intellectual* (New York: New American Library, 1961), p. 123.

47. Tillich, *Ultimate Concern*, p. 106; *The Dynamics of Faith* (New York: Harper Torchbooks, 1957), p. 105.

48. Otto, *Idea of the Holy*, pp. 116ff.

49. Mircea Eliade, *The Sacred and the Profane*, trans. Willard R. Trask (New York: Harcourt, Brace and World, 1959), pp. 202ff.

50. Freud, *Future of an Illusion*, p. 52. However, Freud was unwilling to call the feeling of absolute dependence a religious feeling. Not this feeling but what a man does with it is the essence of religion, according to Freud.

the fundamental human project as the desire to be God is an even clearer indication of the essentially religious character of the human. To be human means to reach toward being God. "Man makes himself man in order to be God," he wrote.[51] Walter Kaufmann repeats the same point even more dramatically, claiming, "Man is the ape that wants to be God. . . ."[52] In view of all of this, it seems safe to claim some kind of universality for religious experience.

The more serious question does not relate to the universality but to the reality of religious experience. Sartre considered the whole project to realize God to be fundamentally absurd. Freud was less definitive but perhaps equally discomforting to religious experience when he described it as an illusory wish for a cosmic Comforter. "We say to ourselves," wrote Freud, "it would indeed be very nice if there were a God who was both creator and benevolent providence. . . , but at the same time it is very odd that this is all just as we should wish it ourselves."[53] The reality of God is suspect because it is an illusory wish, like the proverbial pot of gold at the end of the rainbow. We will suspend judgment on Freud's thesis until we have examined more thoroughly the characteristics and dimensions of religious experience. For now, it will suffice to say that the mere universality of religious experience is by no means a guarantee of its reality or a sure indication of its unreality. Human experiences reveal that some desires can be fulfilled and some cannot. Which class religion falls into will have to be determined by some criteria other than the experience itself.

51. Jean-Paul Sartre, *Being and Nothingness* (New York: Washington Square, 1966), p. 766.

52. Walter Kaufmann, *Critique of Religion and Philosophy* (New York: Doubleday, 1961), p. 354.

53. Freud, *Future of an Illusion*, pp. 57–58.

2 ✻

The Characteristics of Religious Experience

Before we are ready to evaluate religious experience, we need to further describe its core. Two generalizations will become clear. First, in order to be religious, an experience must involve awareness of the Transcendent. It is a realm needed by the person and it must be beyond and other than the person. Secondly, the experience is not truly religious until the person makes an ultimate commitment to the Transcendent.

Religious Experience Involves an Awareness of the Transcendent

There have been many attempts to define religion. Most of these definitions have at least one common element: that religion involves an awareness of the Transcendent. That a religious experience involves the Transcendent is held not only by theists and pantheists but by many atheists as well. The dimensions and definitions of the Transcendent differ, but a religious experience nonetheless involves the Transcendent.

Some have contended that there is little or no cognitive content common to all descriptions of religious experience, but few if any have denied that there is a transcendent dimension that is thought to go beyond the individuals having the experience.[1] Those who believe the Transcendent has a reality of its own beyond the human have identified it with the Universe or All (Schleiermacher), the Numinous or Holy (Otto), the Wholly Other (Kierkegaard), Being itself or the Being beyond being (Tillich), the Transcendental Ego (Koëstenbaum), and numerous other realities, personal and impersonal, pantheistic, deistic, or theistic. On the other hand, those who deny its objective reality often admit nonetheless that belief in the reality of the Transcendent is characteristic of religion. Some identify it (at least in part) with the individual's subconscious (James), the collective subconsciousness of individuals (Jung), the collective consciousness of the group (Cornford), the projection of

---

1. It does not seem possible to know that something is without having at least some general notion as to what it is. For example, one may know that there are other persons without being able to define precisely what is meant by a person; however, one would need to have a general idea such as "speaking somethings."

28

human imagination (Feuerbach), the person's absurd project to become self-caused (Sartre), the illusory object of a universal neurosis (Freud), a person's higher or ideal self (Fromm), the imaginative unity of human values (Dewey), and so on. But whatever the description or name for the Transcendent, there is something (real or not) which goes beyond the individual in which or by which he transcends his finite conditions.

Let us now explicate further the meaning of this awareness. First we will provide some linguistic help, by means of paradigms, toward understanding the nature of the Transcendent. Then, after having argued for the universal need for such an experience, we can show that implicit in the notion of the Transcendent is its otherness from the finite person. Further, it is possible to isolate some unity within the diversity of religious awareness. Finally, this section will close with a defense of the idea that the Transcendent represents a different realm or being. One must remember throughout, however, that this discussion is based on the perceptions of the religious person. Judgment on the question of truth is deferred.

Some Paradigms for the Meaning of Transcendence

We are speaking of a religious experience as an awareness of the Transcendent; that is, as that which goes beyond the conditions of man's finite circumstances. To make this possible we need to assign meaning to the use of the term *transcendent*. In order to elucidate what is meant by this term we will follow the suggestion of Antony Flew: that of giving some paradigm cases or examples from experience.

Paul M. van Buren focused the problem when he wrote, "The difficulty of speaking about 'transcendence,' 'ground and end of all things,' or some other oblique phrase substituted for the word 'god' . . . simply begs the empiricist's question. . . . In a secular age, what would that 'more' be? It is our inability to find any empirical linguistic anchorage for that 'more' that has led to our interpretation [that all God-language or its equivalent is dead]."[2]

Since van Buren confessed regard for Ian T. Ramsey's approach to this question, we will begin with illustrations Ramsey used to explain what is meant by more, beyond, or transcendence. These are what Ramsey calls discernment situations. He lists a series of discernment situations, which are ordinary empirical situations that suddenly "come alive" when the "ice breaks" or the "light dawns," or that take on "depth"; for example, when a judge suddenly recognizes the accused as his long-lost lover, when "eye meets eye," when it dawns on one that the twelve lines on a paper have the "depth" of a cube, when a formal party takes on warmth and a "new dimension," or

---

2. Paul M. van Buren, *The Secular Meaning of the Gospel* (New York: Macmillan, 1963), pp. 79, 197–98. Cf. p. 84.

after someone splits his dinner jacket. In each case, something more is revealed than what is seen in the empirical facts alone—the situation has a "depth of dimension" that goes beyond the sensory.

According to Ramsey, metaphors and verbally odd words have the same disclosure power.[3] For examples of verbally odd words, he uses nicknames that evoke personal response (e.g., "sweetheart" vis-à-vis "Elizabeth"). Ramsey also finds some tautologies ("I am I," "duty for duty's sake," or "love for love's sake") to be significant and revelatory of more than they seem to say linguistically. In fact, he finds first-person language ("I-language") and moral language to be the key to "God-language," in that both are verbally odd; both are straightforward but strained, and both gain their meaning in use.[4] That is the way moralists speak of a sense of duty and religion speaks of a sense of the unseen. Both are literally and logically odd but are far from being completely nonsensical. On the contrary, odd words and metaphors by their very similarity-with-a-difference can generate insight in the way two pictures, rather similar but in some points significantly different, can lead to the apprehension of depth in a 3-D viewer. Another example is first-person subjectivity. That is, "I" cannot be exhausted by all that is said about "me"; "I" am more than everything that can be objectively said about me; subjectivity transcends objectivity.[5] As Michael Novak indicates, even an empiricist "is more of a mystery to himself than his theory allows him to recognize, and every time he acts he uses the first awareness his theory neglects."[6]

Other illustrations of what is beyond the purely empirical experience could be developed, such as the sense in which Immanuel Kant's noumenon or thing-in-itself is beyond the phenomenon or thing-for-me,[7] or the way in which the so-called transcendental ego is beyond the empirical ego. Or the beyond or more may be illustrated by the way the unity of a sentence is more than the words that constitute it or the way the whole is greater than its parts.

The Need for Self-Transcendence

Religious experience involves the need to transcend the unalterable displeasures of life. In this sense Peter Koëstenbaum was right in describing religion as "man's effort to do something about the desperate condition of his own

---

3. In fact, Ramsey goes so far as to say, "What is not verbally odd is void of disclosure power." *Models and Mystery* (London: Oxford University Press, 1964), p. 69.

4. Ian T. Ramsey, *Religious Language* (New York: Macmillan, 1963), pp. 42–50.

5. Ramsey, *Models and Mystery*, pp. 10, 41.

6. Michael Novak, *Belief and Unbelief* (New York: Macmillan, 1965), p. 74.

7. Immanuel Kant, *The Critique of Pure Reason*, trans. Lewis W. Beck (New York: Bobbs-Merrill, 1956), p. 273.

finitude."[8] For that matter, Sigmund Freud was correct in depicting religion as the human search for a cosmic Comforter to help him cope with the fearful eventualities of life. Also accurate was Rudolf Bultmann's definition: "human longing to escape from this world by the supposed discovery of a sphere above this world."[9] There seems to be little reason to dispute Walter Kaufmann when he said, "Religion is rooted in man's aspiration to transcend himself. . . . Man is the ape that wants to be a god. . . . Whether he worships ideals or strives to perfect himself, man is the God-intoxicated ape."[10] Or as Jean-Paul Sartre put it, man's project is to become God.[11] In this sense, one may say that a human is the being who is characterized by his need for self-transcendence.[12]

Other humanistic definitions of religion evidence the inclusion of this characteristic feature. John Dewey's pursuit of general and enduring ideals despite threats of personal loss is definitely an aspiration for self-transcendence.[13] Even Erich Fromm's self-labeled humanistic religion admits the need for self-transcendence. Religious experience "in this kind of religion," he writes, "is the experience of oneness with the All, based on one's relatedness to the world as it is grasped with thought and with love."[14] With this stress on self-transcending love,[15] Paul Tillich's statement agrees. He wrote, "*Agape* is a quality of love, that quality which expresses the self-transcendence of the religious element in love."[16] All the religions of love, then, are illustrative of the human attempt to transcend the conditions of hate and disunity found in this world. Love, said Koëstenbaum, is an a priori category by which the religious person unifies his world and overcomes the opposing otherness and attains self-fulfillment.[17] Whether it is viewed as love or some

8. Peter Koëstenbaum, "Religion in the Tradition of Phenomenology," in *Religion in Philosophical and Cultural Perspective*, ed. J. Clayton Feaver and William Horosz (Princeton, N.J.: Van Nostrand, 1967), p. 182.

9. See Rudolf Bultmann, *Kerygma and Myth*, ed. Hans W. Bartsch (New York: Harper and Row, 1953), 1:26ff.

10. Walter Kaufmann, *Critique of Religion and Philosophy* (New York: Doubleday, 1961), pp. 354, 355, 359.

11. Jean-Paul Sartre, *Being and Nothingness* (New York: Washington Square, 1966), pp. 762, 766.

12. Tillich said, "Human potentialities are powers that drive toward actualization. Man is driven toward faith by his awareness of the infinite to which he belongs, but which he does not own like a possession. This is in abstract terms what concretely appears as the 'restlessness of the heart' within the flux of life." *The Dynamics of Faith* (New York: Harper Torchbooks, 1957), p. 9.

13. See John Dewey, *A Common Faith* (New Haven: Yale University Press, 1934), p. 27.

14. Erich Fromm, *Psychoanalysis and Religion* (New Haven: Yale University Press, 1959), p. 37.

15. See Erich Fromm, *The Art of Loving* (New York: Harper and Row, 1956), chap. 1.

16. Paul Tillich, *Morality and Beyond* (New York: Harper and Row, 1963), p. 40.

17. Koëstenbaum, "Religion in the Tradition of Phenomenology," pp. 210ff.

other force, religious experience characteristically involves some means by which a person can self-transcend, or go beyond his own frustrating limitations.

The Necessity of the Transcendent Other in Religious Experience

Not only is it acknowledged that religious experience involves the Transcendent, but also it is recognized that the Transcendent as Other is essential to a religious experience. Ludwig Feuerbach contended it is essential that the religious person *believes* God is really out there, for he would not worship any object as the ultimate Other if he knew it to be nothing but himself.[18] Indeed, if there is to be any kind of experience, there must be at least a mental distinction (if not an actual difference) between the one which is aware and that of which he is aware. Even in the experience of self-awareness there is a distinction between the "I" and the "me." It is difficult to see what the word *experience* (or awareness, consciousness) could mean if there were absolutely no distinction between the "I" (finite individual) and the "Thou," that is, the Transcendent. As Koëstenbaum points out, religion is an I-Thou, not an I-I, relation.[19] That is, there is no meaning left to the word *experience* if there is an absolute merging of the individual and the Transcendent.[20] And even if it is possible to effect an ontological merging of "the human being" and "God" (though most mystics probably refer to psychological, not ontological, merging), this state could hardly be called one of awareness or consciousness (which is what we mean by experience).

If experience by its very nature will involve an "other," then it follows that religious experience must also involve something beyond or transcendent. Wilfred C. Smith summed it up well when he wrote, "What they have in common lies not in the tradition that introduces them to transcendence, nor in their faith by which they personally respond, but in that to which they respond, the transcendence itself."[21]

The Unity of Meaning of the Transcendent

The point of general agreement among scholars is that religions have a great diversity of experience and expression and little if any unity of content.

18. Ludwig Feuerbach, *The Essence of Christianity*, trans. George Eliot (New York: Harper and Row, 1957), pp. 13, 30 n. 1.

19. Koëstenbaum, "Religion in the Tradition of Phenomenology," pp. 204, 205.

20. In view of this, if the attainment of Nirvana is taken to mean the loss of all awareness, then it would not be a religious experience. It would be the "experience" of losing all experience.

21. Wilfred C. Smith, *The Meaning and End of Religion* (New York: New American Library of World Literature, 1964), p. 173.

With regard to the first point, Friedrich Schleiermacher argued that multiplicity, far from being bad for religion, is necessary for the complete manifestation of religion.[22] William James suggested that plurality in religious experience is necessary to fit the plurality of human needs.[23] Tillich thought that we should not pretend an identity where there is a fundamental difference in the whole experience and attitude such as that between Western and Eastern religions (e.g., as to their views on history as cyclical versus linear).[24] Nor did he feel that they should be mixed, for "a mixture of religions destroys in each of them the concreteness which gives it its dynamic power."[25]

Having said this, however, is not to deny any possibility of identifying a common meaning to religious experience. Dewey was not far from the truth when he argued that there is little if any specifiable content of value that is common to all religions.[26] However, this conclusion can be misleading, for it discourages the effort to find and define the elements that are common to most if not all religious experiences.

The analysis of James reveals a greater appreciation for the common elements of religious experiences. He suggested that all religions have the following three characteristics in common: "1) that the visible world is part of a more spiritual universe from which it draws its chief significance; 2) that union or harmonious relation with that higher universe is our true end; [and] 3) that prayer or inner communion with the spirit there-of—be that spirit 'God' or 'law'—is a process wherein work is really done, and spiritual energy flows in and produces effects, psychological or material, within the phenomenal world."[27] Concerning the basic "creed" or cognitive content of all religions, James contended that it is twofold: an uneasiness or sense that something is wrong about us as we naturally stand; an awareness that we are saved from this wrongness by making proper connection with higher powers.[28]

Religion and the Transcendent

Not only does religious experience involve a process of transcending or self-transcendence but also it implies a dimension or sphere that is called the

22. Friedrich Schleiermacher, *On Religion: Speeches to Its Cultured Despisers*, trans. John Oman (New York: Ungar, 1955), p. 213.

23. William James, *The Varieties of Religious Experience* (New York: Mentor, New American Library, 1958), pp. 326, 368, 477.

24. Paul Tillich, *Ultimate Concern*, ed. D. Mackenzie Brown (London: SCM, 1965), pp. 152, 153.

25. Paul Tillich, *Christianity and the Encounter of the World Religions* (New York: Columbia University Press, 1963), p. 96.

26. Dewey, *Common Faith*, pp. 7–11.

27. James, *Varieties of Religious Experience*, p. 475.

28. Ibid., p. 498.

Transcendent. That is, if the religious aspiration to go beyond is to be realized, then there must be a beyond in which or by which this can occur. To some this is a personal God; to others it is an impersonal Force. For some, it is attainable in this life; for others, it is sought in another life. For many, it is the essence of reality; for some, it is an illusive dream sought in another life. But in every religious experience there is a transcendent dimension of one kind or another in which the transcending occurs.

As will be shown later (in chap. 3), this transcendence can and does have many dimensions and descriptions. But in each case a Transcendent is always involved in religious experience. Many of the definitions of religion make this explicit. The *Oxford English Dictionary*, for example, calls religion a "recognition on the part of man of some higher unseen power. . . ." All definitions that use any form of the words *God* or *gods* clearly recognize that there is a transcendent realm germane to religious experience. What is not as obvious, however, is that those forms of religion that do not have any such divine Being nevertheless have a Transcendent of their own. That is, the word *transcendent* is not to be limited to personal theistic concepts nor even to pantheistic or impersonal modes of describing the ultimate object or goal of religious aspiration. Nor is it to be limited to what is commonly called the supernatural.[29] In point of fact, by "Transcendent" we do not mean any or all of the particular conceptual ways of describing God. Rather, by "Transcendent" is meant the supposed reality that is beyond all of these ways of designating it. It includes the Hindu Brahman, the Taoist Tao, the Buddhistic Nirvana, Tillich's Being beyond being, Schleiermacher's Universe, Otto's Holy, and so on.

Even among those who deny the reality of the Transcendent there is still an admission that religion involves such an alleged reality. Sartre, for example, uses the word *God* repeatedly[30] and characterizes the person as one whose fundamental project is to become God.[31] Fromm is willing to retain the word *God* as the symbol of the Transcendent, providing it is recognized that he speaks of the higher human values. He said, "In humanistic religion God is the image of man's higher self, a symbol of what man potentially is or ought

29. For many moderns this term implies a false bifurcation of reality. Dewey felt strongly that the concept of a "supernatural" religion is a hindrance to the religious experience. See *Common Faith*, pp. 27, 28. Tillich said antisupernaturalism is fundamental to all his thinking. *Ultimate Concern*, p. 158. See also his *Systematic Theology* (Chicago: University of Chicago Press, 1951), vol. 1, on reason and revelation. For an evaluation of the modern antisupernatural trend see Norman L. Geisler, *Miracles and Modern Thought* (Grand Rapids: Zondervan, 1982).

30. See Jean-Paul Sartre, *The Words*, trans. B. Frechtman (New York: Braziller, 1964), pp. 18, 97, 173, 178, 185, 188, 190, 193, 227.

31. Sartre, *Being and Nothingness*, p. 776.

to become. . . ."[32] Although Feuerbach categorically denies any reality other than human behind the term *God,* he not only uses it but also recognizes that it is essential to religion to believe that there is a transcendent God. Even though, for Feuerbach, consciousness of God is really only consciousness of the human being himself, nevertheless man is not directly aware of this. On the contrary, he said, "Ignorance of it is fundamental to the peculiar nature of religion."[33] God is really nothing but the projection of humanity's own nature, but the religious person is not aware of this and that is why he worships this projection as God.[34] However, the present concern is not whether the Transcendent is real. Rather, the concern here is with the fact that religious experience seems always to involve a transcendent dimension.

To sum up, a religious experience is not only one of self-transcendence but one that involves a transcendent realm by which or in which the transcending is made possible or toward which it is directed. That is, in order to go beyond, there must be a Beyond (real or imagined) toward which or in which the religious experience moves.

However, we cannot remain only on this level of cognitive awareness. For the religious person, the Transcendent not only discloses itself, but also evokes a response from the individual. And this response must have certain definite characteristics in order to be truly religious. Let us return to Ramsey's paradigms, which we mentioned earlier.

Certainly a discernment situation that discloses more than the empirical eye can see is not automatically an experience of religious transcendence. That is to say, when the twelve lines on a paper take on "depth," the viewer does not thereby worship the cube. Nor when a dinner jacket splits does it "disclose" God. Indeed, there seems to be a missing dimension of transcendence that causes these experiences to fall short of being religious. There must be something to the meaning of More.

Religious Experience Involves a Total Commitment

The missing element is found in total commitment. A religious experience involves something beyond a mere disclosure, something unconditional and ultimate; something to which persons are willing to commit themselves with utter loyalty and devotion. That is, it involves not only an awareness of the transcendent but an awareness of it as ultimate and as demanding an ultimate commitment.

32. Fromm, *Psychoanalysis and Religion,* p. 41.
33. Feuerbach, *Essence of Christianity,* p. 13.
34. Feuerbach said men come gradually to recognize that they have been worshiping themselves; hence, "what was at first religion becomes at a later period idolatry." Ibid.

In Ramsey's words, the Transcendent must be something to which one is willing to give a "total commitment" before it qualifies as religious. Commitment situations, he said, have a claim on a man and yet leave him in exercise of his free will. The patriot's "my country right or wrong" or one's all-absorbing devotion to his favorite hobby are examples of total commitment. Combining the two sets of illustrations, Ramsey argues that a religious experience of the unseen or beyond is one that involves both discernment of that which goes beyond the mere empirical facts of the situation and at the same time evokes from the individual a total commitment to it.[35]

In a hobby one is totally committed to only part of the universe (e.g., to coin collecting); in mathematics, on the other hand, one is only partially committed to the whole universe (i.e., the commitment to given axioms is loose because other axioms are possible, but it is a commitment to apply these axioms everywhere). In religion one gives a total commitment to the whole universe.[36]

What Ramsey is getting at with his phrase *total commitment,* Tillich called ultimate concern. He said, "The fundamental concept of religion is the state of being grasped by an ultimate concern, by an infinite interest, by something one takes unconditionally seriously, that for which one would be willing to suffer or even die." Ultimate concern has both a subjective and an objective side. Subjectively, it indicates that the subject or individual is being unconditionally serious about something; objectively, it refers to the object of our ultimate concern for which Tillich reserves the name *God.*[37]

Tillich further argued that every person has an ultimate concern, because without a center of concern there would be no integrating center to one's personality. "Such a state," he said, "can only be approached but never fully reached, because a human being deprived completely of a center would cease to be a human being."[38] This ultimate concern, which all people have, provides the unity and depth to all other concerns a person has and with them to his whole personality.

Of course not every ultimate concern is about something that is really ultimate. "Perhaps the ultimate was once actually the parents. . . . Later another ultimate, perhaps a loved one, girl or boy, liberates us from this."[39] But since a person's faith is inadequate if his whole existence is determined by something less than ultimate, he must always try to break through the limits of finitude and to reach the ultimate itself.[40] For to commit oneself ultimately to something that is not ultimate is idolatry. This is why Tillich at times even

35. Ramsey, *Religious Language,* pp. 19ff.
36. Ibid., pp. 35–41.
37. Tillich, *Ultimate Concern,* pp. 7, 8, 30, 11.
38. Ibid., pp. 105, 106.
39. Ibid., p. 183.
40. Tillich, *Dynamics of Faith,* p. 57.

rejects the words *God* or *Being* as ultimates and speaks of the "God beyond God" or the "Being beyond being," since the former terms imply limitations to some. Hence, experience is religious if it involves an ultimate commitment, but it is not adequately religious unless that to which it is committed is really ultimate.

Perhaps the most common way of describing what Tillich called an ultimate commitment is by the term *worship*. An individual responds to something with a total concern because of the worth he sees in it. This is called worship because it is a response to the worth-ship of the object. In this sense, then, worship is the attitude of admiration and acceptance of the ultimate worth of the Transcendent of which it is aware. Worship in the narrower sense of specific prayer need not be an essential element in religious experience. But in the broader sense of an implicit acknowledgment of the ultimate worth of the object of its devotion or commitment, worship is at the very heart of a religious experience.

Schleiermacher described a religious experience of the Transcendent as a "feeling of absolute dependence."[41] By that he meant a sense of creaturehood or an awareness that one is not independent from, but dependent upon, the All or the Universe. It is a sense of existential contingency, a life dependent on the infinite whole.[42] Rudolf Otto agreed but felt that the sense of creaturehood resulted from one's awareness of the Numen rather than being the basis of it.[43] Even Freud concurred that men have this sense of dependence, although he did not wish to identify it with religious experience.[44] Nonetheless, there is general agreement on the fact that people do have such a sense of dependence, concern, or commitment that we have called religious experience. Tillich called it an ultimate concern for the Ultimate. For Schleiermacher it was depending for one's all on the All. Ramsey saw it as a total commitment to the Total. But in essence all of these are the same.

These descriptions reveal that a religious experience involves at least two fundamental factors: an awareness of the Transcendent, and a total commitment to it as ultimate. There are many different ways the Transcendent has been conceptualized and expressed, but these are the two basic factors in the religious experience itself.

Furthermore, to say the Transcendent must be viewed as ultimate does not mean that it is ultimate.[45] Idolatry is always a real possibility for the religious.

41. Friedrich Schleiermacher, *The Christian Faith,* trans. H. R. Macintosh and T. S. Stewart (Edinburgh: T. and T. Clark, 1928), pp. 12, 19, passim; *On Religion,* pp. 275ff.

42. Schleiermacher, *On Religion,* p. 39.

43. Rudolf Otto, *The Idea of the Holy,* trans. J. W. Harvey (New York: Oxford University Press, 1967), pp. 9–11.

44. Sigmund Freud, *The Future of an Illusion,* trans. W. D. Robson-Scott (New York: Doubleday, 1957), p. 52.

45. This is not to say that these are all the factors there ought to be in a religious experience.

However, it is difficult to see how something can deserve the description *object of religious experience* if it is not at least viewed as ultimate by the devotee. Nor does the Ultimate have to be static to be ultimate. A commitment to a Hegelian dialectic as the divine unfolding itself in history is an example of a dynamic ultimate. Nor is Dewey's definition of "God" as the imaginative goal of all human values to be excluded from the category of the ultimate. In other words, something does not have to be permanent and unchangeable to qualify as a religious ultimate. If a person is completely committed to the sum total of human "progress" or "achievement," then it is a religious ultimate for him. All that is necessary for a transcendent to qualify as religious is that it be something final and supreme, something beyond appeal and irrevocable. It must be something capable of evoking a complete commitment, utter loyalty, or ultimate concern on the part of an individual. The question as to whether or not there is anything really ultimate and/or really worthy of an ultimate commitment must wait until the various dimensions of transcendence have been examined. Meanwhile the religious individual must remind himself that the mere fact that he has an ultimate commitment to something he feels is really ultimate and ultimately real does not guarantee either the reality or the ultimacy of the object of his worship. Even the fact that man has an essential need to transcend is not proof of the reality of the religious experience. As Sartre contended, the whole fundamental project of self-transcendence may be impossible or absurd.[46] Or, as Feuerbach argued, the projection of what people call God may be nothing more than an objectification of the best in humanity. God may be a projection of man that is necessary for the progress of humanity. Perhaps a human being cannot see the good that is in himself unless he objectifies it into another whom he calls God. Maybe, as Feuerbach contended, the Transcendent is necessary only ideologically but not ontologically. This thesis will be examined subsequently. But first, a more complete analysis of the various dimensions of religious experience is called for.

It does not mean that all that is necessary for an adequate or efficacious religious experience is an ultimate commitment to something beyond man that he thinks (or feels) is ultimate. First, as we indicated in chapter 1, the religious person ought to be concerned with the reality of the transcendent, even though some appear to be content with it as an ideal or to hold it merely as if it were true. Secondly, it is questionable whether an ultimate commitment is adequate if it is a commitment to something that is less than ultimate. However, we are not here discussing what a religious experience ought to be in order to be satisfactory but what in fact it is in the experience of religious men. See chapter 5 for a discussion of the adequacy of religious experience.

46. Sartre eventually came to temper his earlier atheism, saying, "I needed God, He was given to me, I received Him without realizing that I was seeking Him. . . . Whenever anyone speaks to me about Him today, I say, . . . 'Fifty years ago, had it not been for that misunderstanding . . . there might have been something between us.'" *Words*, pp. 102–3.

Religious experience is universal. It involves two basic elements: an awareness of the Transcendent and a total commitment to the Transcendent. Further, since a person has a fundamental desire to transcend himself and since it is not possible to go beyond oneself unless there is a Beyond (ideal or real) toward which man can transcend, then we may conclude that the Transcendent is necessary to the fulfillment of man's fundamental drive to transcend. And since this transcendent thrust in its most basic dimension is what we call religious experience, then for better or for worse, religion is essential to humanity. If this is not a proven fact, it is at least a thesis with not only theistic and pantheistic subscribers but also great atheistic subscribers.

3 ✳

The Dimensions of Religious Experience

Religious experience involves two basic factors: an awareness of a transcendent Other and a commitment to it as having ultimate worth. By this commitment to the Transcendent, a person is able to transcend himself. And since he has a fundamental desire to transcend, the religious experience of self-transcendence is germane to his very existence as a human. The person must transcend but he cannot transcend unless there is a Transcendent beyond himself by which he can transcend himself. This, of course, does not mean that all persons will believe in a theistic God. There are other ways and directions to transcend than the particular way that has been conceptualized in Western theisms. The purpose of this chapter is to describe these other dimensions of transcendence. In viewing religious experience in its broader and multiple dimensions, two results are desired: first, a more comprehensive understanding of what constitutes a religious experience; second, a correction of the mistaken tendency to disregard an experience as nonreligious simply because it does not fit a given type of transcendence.

In an attempt to fulfill these two purposes, we offer the following typology of religious transcendence: transcendence toward the Beginning; transcendence toward the Highest; transcendence toward the Outermost (Circumference); transcendence toward the End; transcendence toward the Innermost (Center); transcendence toward the Depth (Ground); transcendence in a Circle. In brief, the major directions of religious transcendence have been backward, upward, outward, forward, inward, downward, and in a circle.

We shall see that the quest for transcendence is a universal human characteristic, including even those who would confess to only a secular world view. This aspect of the subsequent description will become crucial when we argue for the reality of the Transcendent (chap. 4).

Transcending Toward the Beginning

One of the earliest directions in which the religious person reached toward the Transcendent was backward. There was a quest to go back to a beginning or point of origin and discover the Source of religious aspirations. According to Mircea Eliade, this is the characteristic feature of the primitive religious experience. Our discussion will begin with Eliade's analysis.

Eliade's Myth of Origins

For Eliade, the Transcendent is called the Sacred and this world the profane. The Sacred is the opposite of the profane. Manifestations of the Sacred he calls a hierophany, which is always something Wholly Other than the profane world.

Since time is cyclical for the preliterate, it is recoverable in ritual. That is, mythical time can be made present by repetition in ritual of the original act of the gods. Religious time, then, is continuous and periodically present by means of rites. In contrast to Christianity, which radically changed the concept of religious time by asserting that it unfolds (via the incarnation of Christ) in history, preliterate "mythical time" is not so.[1] By this ritualistic reenactment of creation the participant becomes contemporaneous with the time of origin, which is a kind of eternal present.[2] In this way, the religious person reveals that his desire for transcendence is really in the direction of the original paradise. This "myth of the eternal return," said Eliade, "did not paralyze ancient religious man. It is not a retreat from responsibility but an assuming of it in the creation of the cosmos. It is not for them a retreat to the dream world but a return to the real world, the original world."[3] It is a kind of retrospective transcendence.

"The myth," said Eliade, "relates a sacred history, that is, a primordial event that took place at the beginning of time, ab initio."[4] It is the revelation of a mystery, a recital of what the gods did at the beginning. The function of myth is to fix the paradigmatic model for all significant human activity. Living a myth, then, implies a genuinely religious experience. The religiousness of this experience is due to the fact that one reenacts the creative deeds of the supernatural.[5] By repeating the myth, a person remains in the "sacred" or "real," and by continual reactivation of the original gestures of the gods the human sanctifies his world. To forget to reenact the myth is "sin," for it is through ritual and myth that the person is in contact with the Transcendent. Only by reactualizing the myth does he have hope. That is, by eternal repetition there is eternal recovery.[6]

1. See Mircea Eliade, *The Sacred and the Profane*, trans. Willard R. Trask (New York: Harcourt, Brace and World, 1959), pp. 108–12.

2. Mircea Eliade, *Myth and Reality*, trans. Willard R. Trask (New York: Harper and Row, 1963), p. 13.

3. Eliade, *The Sacred and the Profane*, pp. 92–94.

4. Ibid., p. 95. Cf. *Myth and Reality*, pp. 5, 6.

5. Eliade, *Myth and Reality*, p. 19.

6. Eliade, *The Sacred and the Profane*, pp. 98, 99, 101. Cf. *Myth and Reality*, pp. 144, 145.

The religious life assumes the following basic form: the belief that there is an absolute reality that transcends the world but is manifest in the world; life has a sacred origin and a human being realizes his potential in the degree to which he participates in it; gods created the world, the history of which is preserved in myths; by imitation of the gods a person reactualizes sacred history and keeps close to the gods. A nonreligious person, on the other hand, is characterized by his refusal of transcendence and his acceptance of the relativity of reality or even doubt of its meaning. No such people, said Eliade, are known in archaic cultures; only in modern Western society has "profane" man fully developed.[7]

Eliade's view may be summed up this way: Religion is the paradigmatic solution for every existential crisis not only because it can be indefinitely repeated, but also because it is believed to have a transcendent Origin, thus enabling a human being to transcend personal situations and finally gain access to the world of spirit. The symbols of the religious person are able to "open up" the universe to him. To be sure, the secular human has many symbols, but none of them are any more than private and partial mythologies that are not experienced by the whole person. None of them are paradigmatic provisions for retrospective transcendence; they do not take the "profane" person back to the transcendent origin of all things.[8] For the primitive person, the meaning of the world was gained through the myth of origin or cosmogony. Its function is to reveal models and thereby to give meaning to the world and to human life. Through myth, the world can be apprehended as an intelligible and significant cosmos.[9]

The Limitations of Transcending Backward

What Eliade describes is one form of religious transcendence, a retrospective kind. The mistake would be, however, to consider this the only way one may have a religious experience. If retrospective transcendence via myths or origin were the only way to transcend, then few people except preliterates have been religious. Furthermore, were transcendence possible only via a backward movement to the mythical origin, then Greek philosophy would have spelled the end to mythical religion. In fact Greek philosophy opened up the way for a new dimension of transcendence, for the Greek philosophers too were interested in origins, but they replaced cosmogony with a cosmology.[10]

7. Ibid., pp. 202, 203.
8. Ibid., pp. 210, 211.
9. Eliade, *Myth and Reality*, pp. 144, 145.
10. As Eliade points out, this attitude is not exclusive to archaic societies: "The desire to know the origin of things is also characteristic of Western culture." *Myth and Reality*, p. 76.

Both are answers to the question of origins, but the latter is an attempt to go beyond the myth and find an *archē* or absolute point of beginning by reason. Eliade said that the Greeks attempted to go beyond mythology as divine history and to reach a primal source, to identify the womb of Being. "It was in seeking the source, the principle, the *archē*, that philosophical speculation for a short time coincided with cosmogony; but it was no longer the cosmogonic myth, it was an ontological problem." That is, "the 'essential' is reached, then, by a prodigious 'going back'—no longer a *regressus* obtained by ritual means, but a 'going back' accomplished by an effort of thought. In this sense it could be said that the earliest philosophical speculations derive from mythologies. . . ."[11] So the earliest philosophic speculations are derived from mythologies: the *mythos* and the *logos* find their common source in an attitude which is religious; that is, the desire to know the answer to the question of origins.

However, the Greek philosophers effected a radical change in the religious myths they inherited. For one thing, instead of viewing them in an emotional or involved way, they looked on them in a rational and detached manner. "A representation of the world-order which had once been a mystery, fraught, in its earlier days, with awful emotion and serious practical consequences, is now put forward as a rational theory, which anyone who can understand it is free to take or leave."[12] But the rationalization was not complete. There were not only remnants of religious thought in Greek thought; there was also a breaking out in a new dimension of transcendence. This can be seen most clearly in the way that Greek rationalism culminated in Plotinian mysticism.

Transcending Toward the Highest

The idea of transcending upward by leaving the lower world of shadows and images and ascending to the world of pure forms above is present already in the thought of Plato.[13] However, the concept is both more explicit and more clearly religious in the thought of Plotinus.

For Plotinus, all things proceed from the One and all things return to it, for all plurality presupposes a prior unity.[14] "Anything existing after the First must necessarily arise from that First," he wrote. Since the One is an absolute unity, all emanations that flow from it must be something less than pure simplicity. In fact, they form with the One a triplicity of unity in a descending order toward greater multiplicity. After the primary unity (the One) there is a

11. Ibid., pp. 111, 112.

12. F. M. Cornford, *From Religion to Philosophy* (New York: Harper and Row, 1912), p. 50.

13. See particularly Plato's famous cave analogy in *Republic* 7.

14. Plotinus, *Six Enneads* (Chicago: Encyclopedia Britannica Press, 1952), 3.8.9; 5.3.15.

secondary unity (One-Many, called Nous or Intellect) and a tertiary unity (One-and-Many, called World Soul).[15]

The first movement in Plotinian thought is that from unity to multiplicity. This continues to the bottom of the chain of emanation where Matter is, which is the most multiple of all, having the least possible unity. Matter is the place where unity takes its last stand against chaos. It is the place where the whole process of emanation from absolute simplicity (the One) peters out. Furthermore, the farther something is from unity, the less reality it has, for divergence from unity involves a corresponding divergence from reality. In other words, the farther down the emanation extends, the greater is the multiplicity and the less is the reality. And at the very bottom one finds the evil of almost total multiplicity and an almost complete lack of reality, which Plotinus calls Matter or Non-Being. By contact with this matter the lower phase of the individual soul of a person is contaminated. Therefore, the soul must purify itself of this proliferation and begin to ascend toward higher and higher unity.[16]

The second great movement in Plotinian philosophy is the return upward from multiplicity to a higher unity. Human beings must be careful lest by continually drenching themselves in the multiplicity of matter, they become irretrievably fragmented and absolutely evil. But, fortunately, as people wander in this foreign land of evil they have a natural homesickness for the fatherland of good. That is, being unsatisfied in the multiplicity of evil, they are pulled together by a higher unity. Since the move from unity to multiplicity is outward and downward, the move up toward greater unity again will be inward and upward.[17]

The first step in the move upward toward higher unity is *from the sensible to the intellectual*. It begins in the realm of sense, where one is "busy about many things." Looking at the multiple images of sensation, a person recognizes in them a unity which, as a fugitive, has entered the realm of matter. So as one beholds the unity below, one is impelled to pursue the images of sensation to their higher source. That is to say, the sensible images point upward from their own multiplicity to a higher unity; the roads of the many lead to the one. But the road that leads upward first leads inward. The human being has an intellectual unity that is greater than sensation. The inner unity of his intellect is greater than the outward multiplicity available through his bodily senses.[18]

The next step in the ascent toward greater unity moves *from the intellectual to the intuitional*. Since every particular thing has a unity of its own to

15. Ibid., 5.4.1; 5.3.15; 5.1.8.
16. Ibid., 2.4.11; 1.8.7; 6.2.5; 1.8.3; 1.8.5; 1.2.4.
17. Ibid., 1.8.13; 4.8.4; 1.6.7.
18. Ibid., 1.3.4; 1.6.2–8; 6.9.11; 1.3.6.

which it may be traced, as one mounts upward from sensation, he must come first to the immediate unity for soul, which is found in the intellectual realm called Nous. Here the intellect joins in a higher unity where knower becomes identical with the known.[19] However, even in the intellectual realm there is this basic duality of knower and known and the multiplicity of Forms or Ideas by which things are known. Hence, it is necessary for the one seeking absolute unity to press upward, beyond intellectual knowledge to an intuition of absolute Simplicity.

In this final stage in one's vertical transcendence one finds oneself *alone with the Alone.* For "the Supreme is not known intellectually." Hence, one wishing to contemplate what transcends the Intellectual attains contemplation of it by putting away all that is of the intellect. "Knowledge of the One comes to us neither by science nor by pure thought . . . but by a presence which is superior to science . . . for science implies discursive reason and discursive reason implies manifoldness. He then misses the One and falls into number and multiplicity." To know the Supreme, one must merge with the Supreme and become one with it, center coinciding with center. Just as one must become godlike and beautiful if one cares to see God and Beauty, so one must become one with the One if he is to know the One. The soul must put away all multiplicity, sensible and intellectual, so that "alone it may receive the Alone."[20] At this point one's vertical transcendence is realized, when he has reached the Top of the pyramid in which the many beings meet in an absolute simple source of all Being. He has transcended upward to the Highest.

So in Plotinus the Greek rationalization went beyond itself, beyond reason, and returned to its religious roots. As Emile Bréhier said, the Greek yearning for philosophical unity had fulfilled itself in the mystical unity; mysticism had completed rationalism.[21] But the religious transcendence involved in this mystical union is not the same as for prephilosophical humanity. There are no myths for Plotinus. It is not a question of origin but of unity; not a search for what is at the Beginning but for what is at the Top. That is, transcendence is not retrospective but vertical. And, furthermore, transcendence is no longer supernatural but natural for Plotinus, a fact which the neo-Platonic Christians would find some difficulty in reconciling with divine grace.[22] A representative critical reaction to this form of transcendence will be included with the next section.

19. Ibid., 5.3.4.
20. Ibid., 6.7.35; 5.5.6; 6.9.4 (Katz's translation); 6.9.10; 1.6.9; 6.7.34.
21. Emile Bréhier, *The Philosophy of Plotinus,* trans. Joseph Thomas (Chicago: University of Chicago Press, 1958), p. 162.
22. Even Augustine was still sorting out the neo-Platonic incompatibilities with his Christian philosophy at the end of his life, as the many modifications and revisions of his "Platonism" in his *Retractions* reveal.

Transcending Outward or Toward the Beyond

Mystics have not always limited the direction of their transcendence to the upward; sometimes it is broadened to the "outward" realm. That is, the religious person presses beyond himself by reaching to the outermost limits of his being. God or the Transcendent is found at the uttermost extremity of human experience.

The Circumference of All Things

According to Meister Eckhart, "God is an infinite sphere whose center is everywhere and whose circumference is nowhere."[23] By this he meant that there are no boundaries to God and that from any center man can transcend outward to God and yet never reach a limit. Speaking of the Transcendent in terms of a limitless sphere indicates that the movement of transcendence is outward from oneself in any direction. God is found at the infinite circumference of life, and a person must transcend outward from himself in order to reach God.

Using similar analogies, Nicholas of Cusa described God as the greatest possible circle with the smallest possible curvature. In brief, God is the "coincidence of opposites."[24] It is in this regard that transcending outward to the circumference is also at the same time a transcending inward toward the center. The Beyond is also the Within, toward a Center.

Perhaps the most general way of describing this dimension of transcending outward is to call it the Beyond or the Out There. The religious person functioning in this dimension finds it necessary to move from within himself to beyond himself. He transcends away from his own center to what surrounds him and for which he can find no limits. The Transcendent is out there and he attempts to reach it by going beyond himself. It is neither up nor down as such but merely out and away from himself.

Reaction to the God Up There or Out There

Some thinkers have not been content with the idea of vertical transcendence, since they feel that it too involves a mythological view of the universe. Contrary to what the Greek philosophers did in seeking the reality of the logos in the mythos, these contemporary thinkers have denied any reality in the mythos. Rather, they have sought a reality behind the myth, by stripping the myth of its historical trappings to get at the ontological truth. Rudolf

23. Cited in Armand A. Maurer, *History of Medieval Philosophy* (New York: Random, 1960), p. 418.
24. Nicholas of Cusa, *De docta ignorantia* 1.13.

Bultmann's thought provides a good example of this reaction to the God up there or out there.

Bultmann contended, for example, that "the whole conception of the world which is presupposed in the preaching of Jesus as in the New Testament generally is mythological." By this he meant the conception of the world as being structured in three stories, heaven, earth, and hell; the conception of the intervention of supernatural powers in the course of events; and the conception of miracles. According to Bultmann, "These mythological conceptions of heaven and hell are no longer acceptable for modern men, since for scientific thinking to speak of 'above' and 'below' in the universe has lost all meaning. . . ."[25]

In this mythological structure it would be necessary to speak of God as up there or out there.[26] In this sense Bultmann's "demythology" would oppose even the concept of vertical transcendence. "To demythologize," said Bultmann, "is to reject not Scripture or the Christian message as a whole, but the world-view of Scripture. . . ." It is "to deny that the message of Scripture and of the Church is bound to an ancient world-view which is obsolete. . . . Therefore, it is mere wishful thinking to suppose that the ancient world-view of the Bible can be renewed."[27]

However, demythologizing does not mean a rationalizing of the Christian message, Bultmann assured us. "Not at all! On the contrary, demythologizing makes clear the true meaning of God's mystery." It is to seek the "deeper meaning which is concealed under the cover of mythology."[28] He held that "the purpose of demythologization is not to make religion more acceptable to modern man by trimming the traditional Biblical texts, but to make clearer to modern man what the Christian faith is." What "I am fighting against is just this fixation of God as an objective entity. . . . Therefore my attempt to demythologize begins, true enough, by clearing away the false stumbling blocks created for modern man by the fact that his world view is determined by science."[29] What Bultmann rejected is the objectification mythology implies. In this sense, modern science can be as guilty as ancient mythology.[30] In

25. Rudolf Bultmann, *Jesus Christ and Mythology* (New York: Charles Scribners Sons, 1958), pp. 15, 20; cf. pp. 36, 38. See Norman L. Geisler, *Miracles and Modern Thought* (Grand Rapids: Zondervan, 1982), chap. 6.

26. John A. T. Robinson, *Honest to God* (Philadelphia: Westminster, 1963), pp. 11ff.

27. Bultmann, *Jesus Christ and Mythology*, pp. 35, 36, 38.

28. Ibid., pp. 43, 18.

29. Rudolf Bultmann, "The Case for Demythologization," in Karl Jaspers and Rudolf Bultmann, *Myth and Christianity* (New York: Noonday, 1958), pp. 59, 50.

30. "Mythical thinking is just as objectifying as scientific thinking, for instance, when the former represents the transcendence of God in terms of remoteness in space [way up there]. . . ." "For all human world-views objectivize the world and ignore or eliminate the significance of the encounters in our personal existence." Bultmann, *Jesus Christ and Mythology*, p. 61 n. 1; p. 83; cf. p. 62.

brief, to demythologize means to deobjectify. It is in this respect somewhat the reverse of the Greek rationalization.

What does one discover in demythologizing the biblical concept of the God up there? According to Bultmann, one discovers "the transcendence and hiddenness of God as acting." This is because "the invisibility of God excludes every myth which tries to make God and His action visible; God withholds Himself from view and observation." That is to say, "man's life is moved by the search for God because it is always moved, consciously or unconsciously, by the question about his own personal existence." Of course, "the question of God and the question of myself are identical," wrote Bultmann. But, "from the statement that to speak of God is to speak of myself, it by no means follows that God is not outside the believer," he reminded us. "Thus, the fact that God cannot be seen or apprehended apart from Faith does not mean that He does not exist apart from faith." What this does show, said Bultmann, is that God cannot be objectified.[31]

From this it is clear that Bultmann's demythologization of vertical transcendence, of the God up there, is by no means to be construed as a negation of all transcendence. To be sure, "for scientific thinking to speak of 'above' and 'below' in the universe has lost all meaning, but the idea of the transcendence of God . . . is still significant," he wrote.[32] There is a "God" or "Transcendent." He is active in human personal, existential experience. He does in some sense exist apart from humanity, but he does not exist up there.

If God does not exist up there, then where is he to be found? In which direction does a human transcend in a religious experience? In brief, the answers are respectively "in Christ" and "forward." Bultmann believes that God is revealed in Christ and that "it has become more and more clear that the eschatological expectation and hope is the core of the New Testament preaching throughout. Today," he writes, "nobody doubts that Jesus' conception of the Kingdom of God is an eschatological one—at least in European theology and, so far as I can see, also among American New Testament scholars." What Bultmann finds, then, in New Testament eschatology "is not simply the idea of transcendence as such, but of the importance of the transcendence of God, of God who is never present as a familiar phenomenon but who is always the coming God, who is veiled by the unknown future." In brief, "this, then, is the deeper meaning of the mythological preaching of Jesus—to be open to God's future which is really imminent for every one of us . . . ; to be prepared, because this future will be a judgment on all men who have bound themselves to this world and are not free, not open to God's future."[33]

31. Ibid., pp. 83, 84, 53, 70, 72.
32. Ibid., p. 20.
33. Ibid., pp. 13, 22–23, 31–32.

From Bultmann's demythological rejection of the upward dimension of transcendence, then, one is led naturally to consider more seriously the view of eschatological transcendence. As the Greek rationalization made retrospective transcendence obsolete, so also demythologization makes vertical transcendence untenable for some modern people. Hence, there is a turn in a new direction, that of transcending forward.

Transcending Toward the End

Only on the view that history is going somewhere is it possible to conceive of transcending forward toward the end or eschaton. For if history is not moving toward an ultimate end or goal, then a person cannot transcend in that direction. Such a linear view of history is unknown to ancient and Eastern ways of thinking. For the archaic societies, Eliade pointed out, time is mythical and not historical.[34] However, with the Hebrew prophets appears the first clear indication that there is an end or goal for time, that is, a culmination or climax toward which human events are moving.[35] Even more decidedly clear is this point in the New Testament. As Eliade observed, Christianity radically changed the nature of time by sanctifying it through the incarnation of Christ.[36]

The Death of God

G. W. F. Hegel wrote that God is dead[37] and Friedrich Nietzsche took it seriously.[38] And Thomas J. J. Altizer drew out the religious implications for

34. Eliade, *The Sacred and the Profane*, pp. 72, 112.

35. A recent historian wrote, "The Hebrews broke sharply with all these prevailing conceptions of time and history. Instead of recurring events, they saw a series of distinct episodes, each involving a unique intervention by Yahweh, unrepeatable and irreversible. Instead of circular patterns, they saw history moving in a straight line toward the fulfillment of divine purpose." Trygve R. Tholfsen, *Historical Thinking: An Introduction* (New York: Harper and Row, 1967), p. 43.

36. Eliade, *The Sacred and the Profane*, pp. 72, 112.

37. Hegel, in *The Phenomenology of Spirit*, near the beginning of the section on "Revealed Religion," wrote that unhappy consciousness "is the bitter pain which finds expression in the cruel words, 'God is dead.'" *The Philosophy of Hegel*, ed. Carl J. Friedrich (New York: Modern Library, 1953), p. 506.

38. Henry D. Aiken wrote, "Hegel said, but Nietzsche believed, that 'God is dead.'" *The Age of Ideology* (New York: Mentor, 1956), p. 206. Nietzsche's famous passage comes from his *Joyful Wisdom*, no. 125, where the Madman cries out, "Do we not hear the noise of the grave-diggers who are burying God? Do we not smell the divine putrefaction?—for even gods putrefy! God is dead! God remains dead! And we have killed him!" See *The Portable Nietzsche*, ed. Walter Kaufmann (New York: Viking, 1954), pp. 95–96.

this in a kind of eschatological transcendence. In fact, Altizer contends that Nietzsche was the first radical Christian.[39]

When Altizer says God is dead he does not mean that God has always been dead (i.e., that there never was a living God) or that the idea or word *God* has ceased to be effective today (as van Buren said),[40] or that God is merely hidden from man's view (as Buber held). For "every man today," Altizer wrote, "who is open to experience knows that God is absent, but only the Christian knows that God is dead, that the death of God is a final and irrevocable event. . . ."[41] He feels that too many thinkers have been attracted by Martin Buber's idea of the "eclipse" of God. "God is not simply hidden from view, nor is he lurking in the depths of our unconscious or on the boundaries of our infinite space. . . ."[42] We must confess, he adds, that "the death of God is so to speak an actual and real event, not perhaps an event occurring in a single moment of time or history, but notwithstanding this reservation an event that has actually happened both in a cosmic and in a historical sense."[43]

When did God die? God died in the incarnation of Christ. "To know that God *is* Jesus," Altizer remarked, "is to know that God himself has become flesh: no longer does God exist as transcendent Spirit or sovereign Lord. . . ." Why? As spirit becomes the word this empties the speaker of himself and the whole reality of spirit becomes incarnate in its opposite. That is, "if Spirit truly empties itself in entering the world, then its own essential or original Being must be left behind in an empty and lifeless form." Or, to put it another way, if Christ is identical with God, then heaven was emptied of its God when Christ came to earth.[44]

Further, God died not only in a general sense by becoming incarnate, that is, by entering the realm of flesh (and thus leaving the realm of Spirit), but also in a specific sense when Christ died on the cross. "Yes, God dies in the Crucifixion: therein he fulfills the movement of the Incarnation by totally emptying himself of his primordial sacrality." In fact, "only in the Crucifixion, in the death of the Word on the Cross, does the Word actually and wholly become flesh." And "the Incarnation is only truly actually real if it effects the death of the original sacred, the death of God himself."[45] Finally, God died in

39. Thomas J. J. Altizer, *The Gospel of Christian Atheism* (Philadelphia: Westminster, 1966), p. 25.

40. Altizer lists ten different senses of "God is dead" in *Radical Theology and the Death of God* (New York: Bobbs-Merrill, 1960), pp. x–xi.

41. Altizer, *Gospel of Christian Atheism*, p. 111.

42. Altizer, *Radical Theology*, pp. 125–26.

43. Altizer, *Gospel of Christian Atheism*, p. 103.

44. Ibid., pp. 67, 68 (Altizer admits to a Hegelian interpretation here). See pp. 62–69, 80, 69, 92.

45. Ibid., pp. 113, 54, 90, 86, 153, 149, 82, 83.

history, in modern times, as the realization of his death worked its way out in Western culture.

How does the incarnation effect the "death" of God? To understand this, said Altizer, one must speak of God as a dialectical process rather than as an existent Being. That is, "progressively but decisively God abandons or negates his original passivity . . . becoming incarnate both *in* and *as* the actuality of world and history." In fact, to the extent that the Christian Word fails to negate its original form it cannot be a forward-moving process or a progressive descent into the concrete. That is to say, "only a sacred that negates its own unfallen or primordial form can become incarnate in the reality of the profane." To cling to a transcendent and wholly other God is a denial of the historical reality of the incarnation. For "dialectically, everything depends upon recognizing the meaning of God's total identification with Jesus and of the understanding that it is God who becomes Jesus and not Jesus who becomes God."[46] God must die in the incarnation, for God is a historical and dialectical process which can come to realization only by negation.

Is transcendence totally lost, then, in the immanence of the incarnation and death of God? Certainly what we have called retrospective and vertical transcendence are eliminated by Altizer. For "as the result of a total movement from transcendence to immanence, we must be freed from every attachment to transcendence, and detached from all yearning for a primordial innocence." That is, "the Crucifixion embodies and makes finally real a divine movement from transcendence to immanence. . . ." So then "the Christian who wagers upon a totally incarnate Christ must negate every form and image of transcendence, regardless of what area of conciousness or experience in which it may appear." In fact, it is suicidal for the contemporary Christian to cling to transcendence, since both guilt and repression result from clinging to a transcendent God. Above all, said Altizer, theology must abandon a religious form, wholly and consistently repudiating the religious quest for the primordial sacred. Unless it does, theology will remain bound to a primordial or transcendent Word and thereby it will remain closed to the present and human actuality of history. In brief, "the death of God abolishes transcendence, theology making possible a new and absolute immanence, an immanence freed of every sign of transcendence."[47]

However, regardless of the very categorical sound of Altizer's statements, he does not eliminate all dimensions of religious transcendence. He repudiates retrospective and vertical transcendence but does not eliminate eschatological transcendence; in fact, his own view involves a kind of eschatological transcendence. He wrote, "An incarnate Word embodying a real

46. Ibid., p. 83.
47. Ibid., pp. 136, 139, 143, 145, 77, 154.

transfiguration of Spirit into flesh cannot be sought in a heavenly beyond, nor can it be reached by a backward movement to primordial time; it is only in the actual and contingent processes of history that Spirit becomes flesh."[48] What Altizer is saying is that a human being cannot transcend backward or upward; he must transcend in the forward movement of history.

Like Bultmann, Altizer argued that the New Testament concept of the kingdom of God is decidedly eschatological, that the believer must remain open to the future. Said Altizer, "Radical faith is a total response to the actual presence and the forward movement of God in history." As a distinctively Christian form of faith it "must ever be open to new epiphanies of the Word or Spirit of God, epiphanies that will not simply be repetitions of the original manifestation of God . . . truly new epiphanies whose very occurrence either effects or records a new actualization or movement of the divine process."[49] It is this forward movement of Christianity that distinguishes it from other movements of transcendence. "Yet such a forward movement cannot culminate in an abolition of the opposites by returning to a primordial Beginning. Like its analogue in the prophetic faith of the Old Testament, it must be grounded in an eschatological End. . . ." That is, a person "must move forward beyond the death of a primordial or original sacred to an eschatological *coincidentia oppositorum* that reconciles and unites the sacred and the profane." So any authentically kenotic (self-emptying) movement of incarnation must be a continual process of Spirit becoming flesh, of eternity becoming time, or of the sacred becoming profane. However, this does not mean that the sacred becomes and remains the profane, thus ending the forward transcendence. For the movement of the sacred into the profane is inseparable from a parallel movement of the profane into the sacred. "Consequently, a consistently Christian dialectical understanding of the sacred must finally look forward to the resurrection of the profane in a transfigured and thus finally sacred form."[50] Just what this "transfigured" form or "new epiphany" will be is not known nor is it important for present purposes. What is significant is to observe that the radical Christian has an eschatological hope; that when the Transcendent could no longer be discovered in the realm up there but rather came down here in human history, it keeps moving forward. In brief, transcendence is not dead for Altizer. The traditional backward and upward forms of it are dead, but the forward direction is open.

48. Ibid., pp. 45, 46, 156. See also his *Radical Theology*, p. 150.

49. Altizer, *Gospel of Christian Atheism*, pp. 105, 84.

50. Altizer, *Radical Theology*, pp. 150, 151, 152, 155. Of course this does not mean that the whole Christian life is merely anticipatory. While he is waiting for the new epiphany, the Christian must go out into the world in seeking Jesus.

The Secularization of Christianity

While the radical theologians await the transcendent future, the Christian life must be lived in the present without a Transcendent. God is dead and so is any transcendent equivalent. All theology must be transformed into anthropology. God cannot be found beyond the world but only in other persons. God is loved only by loving others. Jesus led the way when he said, "As you did it to one of the least of these my brethren, you did it to me" (Matt. 25:40). All present theology and ethics is immanentistic. The only transcendence is eschatological.

Even theological language is nontranscendent. Paul M. van Buren denied meaning to any kind of theological language. "Today," he wrote, "we cannot even understand the Nietzschian cry that 'God is dead!' for if it were so, how could we know? No, the problem now is that the word 'God' is dead."[51] In brief, atheism is not only theological in that God died (Altizer) and ethical in that we must live as though God were dead (Bonhoeffer), but it is semantical as well in that we cannot even speak meaningfully of God or the Transcendent. The transcendent language of the past is dead and the theological talk of the present is meaningless unless it is translated into immanent, anthropomorphic language arising out of empirical experience.[52] The result is the thoroughgoing secularization and immanentizing of religion. For the Christian, "God" can be known only in the man Jesus who said, "He who has seen me has seen the Father" (John 14:9).

So then, statements about transcendence must be translated or understood in terms of immanence; statements about God must be translated into statements about human beings. In this way religion can be secularized by being humanized; that is, by being understood in purely human terms. But if one must look inward for an understanding of the Transcendent, it is only natural that people would explore the center or depth of human experience.

Transcending Toward a Center

The Primitive Mythical Center of Life

Looking inward for a divine center of human existence is not new in the history of religious experience. Eliade noted that preliterate religions speak of the manifestation of the Sacred at the center of the cosmos. This center serves as a doorway or gateway to God. At this center the altar of the temple is built and around it the primitive man orients his life. This "opening" is considered

---

51. Paul M. van Buren, *The Secular Meaning of the Gospel* (New York: Macmillan, 1963), pp. 64–68, 83, 84, 103.
52. Ibid., pp. 103, 196, 147.

the "Center of the World" and the organizing of one's life around it is called cosmosizing, that is, forming a microscopic creation. It is the place where the primitive mythology is repeated.[53] In short, the religious person seeks to situate himself at the center of the world where the Sacred breaks through. Herein is the place of transcendence.

The Mystical Center of the Universe

As was noted earlier, the mystics often speak of God as the Center of all things. Eckhart called God the "infinite sphere whose center is everywhere." Plotinus spoke of God as a Center in whom the human centers himself as he becomes one with the One. For in the mystical union a person goes beyond himself; "he is merged with the Supreme, sunken into it, one with it: centre coincides with centre. . . ."[54] Just as one circle becomes identical with another when their centers are identical, so the person goes beyond himself and merges with God when he finds his center in the Center of the universe by mystical union.

Alan Watts stylizes the Eastern tradition of the infinite with a diagram: a circle in which all finite entities, located along the circle at various distances from each other, are exactly the same distance from the center. But the radii "represent a relation of immediate presence in space and time alike, and must be imagined as having no spatial and temporal length."[55] Thus all finite reality is simultaneously and immediately present to the infinite.

The Center in the Divine Milieu

Pierre Teilhard de Chardin attempts to avoid both a primitive mythology and medieval mysticism and yet preserve a transcendent Center which he calls the divine milieu. God, he says, "reveals himself everywhere . . . *as a universal milieu*, only because he is *the ultimate point* upon which all realities converge. . . . No object can influence us by its essence without our being touched by the radiance of the focus of the universe. . . . This focus, this source, is thus everywhere. . . . It is *precisely because* he is the centre that he fills the whole sphere." Hence, "however vast the divine milieu may be, it is in reality a *centre*. It therefore has the properties of a centre, and above all the absolute and final power to unite (and consequently to complete) all beings

53. Eliade, *The Sacred and the Profane*, pp. 10ff., 30, 45, 52, 65.
54. Plotinus, *Enneads* 5.9.10.
55. Alan Watts, *The Supreme Identity: An Essay on Oriental Metaphysic and the Christian Religion* (New York: Random, 1972), pp. 54–55.

within its breast. In the divine milieu all the elements of the universe *touch each other* by that which is most inward and ultimate in them."[56]

Since God is the Center of the universe, a person should transcend in that direction. Chardin urges, "Let us leave the surface, and, without leaving the world, plunge into God. . . . Let us establish ourselves in the divine *milieu.*" However, one must not lose himself in the Center. Rather, he must seek "*to be united* (that is, to become the other) *while remaining oneself.*" This distinction, says Chardin, marks off the true Christian mystic from counterfeits. Furthermore, for the Christian, "the immense enchantment of the divine milieu owes all its value in the long run to the human-divine contact which was revealed at the Epiphany of Jesus. If you suppress the historical reality of Christ, the divine omnipresence which intoxicates us becomes, like all other dreams of metaphysics, uncertain, vague, conventional—lacking the decisive experimental verification by which to impose itself on our minds, and without the moral authority to assimilate our lives into it." So, however far we may be drawn into the divine Center opened to us by Christian mysticism, "we never depart from the Jesus of the Gospels."[57] In short, we transcend toward the divine Center which is focused in the historical Christ.

Transcending Toward the Depth or Ground

Another way to transcend within one's experience is to go to the depth or ground of one's experience. Transcendence in depth is by no means new. Mystics have long sought the Divine in the depth of their own souls. The Bible speaks of God as the foundation of the believer's life (Ps. 18:2; 1 Cor. 3:11). However, there is a definite connection between this modern transcendence in depth and the rejection of the other dimensions of transcendence, such as the Transcendent up there or out there.

Robinson's God Within

Various influences in the contemporary world have converged to direct the religious person downward in search for the Transcendent. First, the stress on immanence is obvious in the thought of all the secular theologians. Then, the inapplicability of objective or empirical language about God leads naturally to a search for a more subjective approach. Also, the very fact that two of the traditional forms of transcendence (retrospective and vertical) have been so emphatically rejected left little option for those who viewed the world with a

56. Pierre Teilhard de Chardin, *The Divine Milieu: An Essay on the Interior Life* (New York: Harper Torchbooks, 1960), p. 114.

57. Ibid., pp. 116, 117.

"modern mind." But since people are incurably religious and must transcend, if they cannot transcend backward or upward, then they may try transcending downward in depth.

John A. T. Robinson led a reluctant revolution in the direction of depth transcendence. Echoing Bultmann, he argued that God can no longer be conceived as being up there at the top of a three-story universe. He can no longer be thought of as the "Most High" who on occasion "comes down" to us or the one to whom some people are "caught up." Robinson said we must drop the primitive concept of a "Sky god" or "High god" as well as the equally false mental image many modern people have of "an Old Man in the sky." Nor can the outmoded, prescientific conception of a God up there be replaced with the equally unacceptable one of a God out there. That is, God is not beyond outer space. Such a crude projection of God has been destroyed with the coming of the space age, Robinson argued. Hence, this spatial way of picturing God is more of a stumbling block than an aid to belief in God today.[58]

However, Robinson makes it clear that his intent is not to replace a transcendent God with a pantheistic and purely immanent one. "On the contrary, the task is to validate the idea of transcendence for modern man." What Robinson proposes, following Paul Tillich, is to reject the symbolism of a God of "height" for one of "depth" in order to make religious language more relevant. For the word *deep* means more than the opposite of high; it also means the opposite of shallow. This is why "height" so often signifies unconcern while "depth" denotes concern, for a remote God cannot really be involved. It should be further noted that "this is not just the old system in reverse, with a God 'down under' for a God 'up there.'" God is not another being but is the "depth and ground of all being" (as Tillich said).[59]

So then, "theological statements are not a description of 'the highest Being' but an analysis of the depths of personal relationships . . . it is saying that God, the final truth and reality of 'deep down things,' *is* love." And furthermore, Robinson wrote, "If statements about God are statements about 'ultimacy' of personal relationships, then we must agree that in a real sense [Ludwig] Feuerbach was right in wanting to translate 'theology' into 'anthropology.'" This does not mean, of course, that God is nothing but humanity personified, as Feuerbach would have it, for this would lead to the deification of man. Rather, as Buber said, "Every particular *Thou* is a glimpse through to the eternal *Thou*." That is, it is between human and human that we meet God, but not (as Feuerbach said) that man is God.[60]

58. Robinson, *Honest to God*, pp. 11–17.
59. Ibid., pp. 44, 54, 130, 44, 45–48.
60. Ibid., pp. 49–53.

For Robinson the necessity of the Transcendent within human experience "lies in the fact that our being has depths which naturalism, whether evolutionary, mechanistic, dialectical or humanistic, cannot or will not recognize." That is, "the man who acknowledges the transcendence of God is the man who *in* the conditioned relationships of life recognizes the unconditional and responds to it in unconditional personal relationship." In other words, "God, the unconditional, is to be found only in, with and *under* the conditioned relationships of life: for he *is* their depth and ultimate significance."[61] And as Tillich observed, to speak of the Transcendent in this sense means that within itself the finite world points beyond itself.[62]

In brief, Robinson is suggesting that in view of the obsolescence of a transcendence in height people may profitably speak of a transcendence in depth. That is, if it is not possible to speak of the Transcendent up there, people may speak of the transcendent depth in here.

God and the Subconscious

Speaking of the God within the depth of human experience is neither new nor without problems. It was a natural way to describe God even before the Freudian elaboration of a subconscious depth to human experience. However, since Sigmund Freud, there has been the temptation to consider the subconscious either identical with or closely associated with the Transcendent because it is beyond, mysterious, and a realm over which human beings allegedly have no conscious control. Rather, in some way it controls them.

Eliade, for example, said that the unconscious displays the structure of a private mythology. Further, he contends "not only that the unconscious is 'mythological' but also that some of its contents carry cosmic values. . . . It can even be said that modern man's only real contact with cosmic sacrality is effected by the unconscious, whether in his dreams and his imaginative life or in the creations that arise out of the unconscious."[63]

William James also closely associates the subliminal and the supreme. He argues that the spontaneous source of religious conversion is the subconscious. For James, the source or root of a religious experience is not important: "If the *fruits for life* of the state of conversion are good, we ought to idealize and venerate it, even though it be a piece of natural psychology." James does not say that the source of conversions is *purely* natural, that the subconscious *is* God. He admits that "the reference of a phenomenon to a sublimal self does not exclude the notion of the Deity altogether," for "it is

61. Ibid., pp. 54, 55, 60.

62. Paul Tillich, *Systematic Theology*, 3 vols. (Chicago: University of Chicago Press, 1957), 2:8.

63. Eliade, *Myth and Reality*, p. 77.

logically conceivable that *if there be* higher spiritual agencies that can directly touch us, the psychological condition of their doing so *might be* our possession of a subconscious region which alone should yield access to them." That is, James does not deny that there is more meant by "God" than the subconscious; what he did say is that the Transcendent is at least "the subconscious continuation of our conscious life."[64]

But it is precisely this close association of the Transcendent with the human subconsciousness that raises anew the question of the reality basis for religious transcendence. For if one admits that sudden religious conversions can be explained on a purely natural basis and that there are no unmistakably unique characteristics of so-called supernatural conversions; if one admits that there is in the subconscious a transcendent realm of spontaneous power capable of transforming lives,[65] then one cannot help but wonder whether the subconscious is all that is meant by the Transcendent.

Indeed, Carl Gustav Jung took a position like this. In Jung's depth psychology the unconscious, as he prefers to call it, is populated by certain symbols, archetypes, which recur throughout all of humanity. Their presence reveals a collective unconscious, to which Jung ascribes purely natural origin. These archetypes occur most frequently in works of art and in dreams as well as in religious imagery. The archetypes have no fixed meaning or significance, but they usually represent certain aspects of human psychology. The symbol of God in Jung's thought represents an idealization of one's self-image. Thus to know self is to know God and vice versa.[66]

And even those who do not make this identification are sometimes haunted by the possibility that there might be no more to the Transcendent than what transcends the consciousness of individual men (i.e., the subconsciousness of the race). But since we take it that the term *reality* implies independence of the subconsciousness of human beings, whether individual or collective, this raises afresh the question of how to test the reality of the Transcendent.

Transcending in a Circle

Transcendence by Eternal Recurrence

It is commonly but wrongly thought that atheists admit no form of transcendence. Atheism, it is said, is a denial of all transcendence. That this is not

---

64. William James, *The Varieties of Religious Experience* (New York: Mentor, New American Library, 1958), pp. 232, 237; cf. pp. 265, 508.

65. Ibid., pp. 233–37.

66. "The self . . . is a God-image, or at least cannot be distinguished from one." Carl Jung, "Aion: Researches into the Phenomenology of the Self," in *The Portable Jung*, ed. Joseph Campbell (New York: Viking, 1971), p. 162.

the case can be shown from the writings of well-known atheists (see chap. 4). Nietzsche is a case in point. No one appears to be more anti-God and against all forms of religious transcendence than Nietzsche. "God is dead! God remains dead!" was his cry.[67] Elsewhere Nietzsche exhorted, "I beseech you my brothers, remain faithful to the earth, and do not believe those who speak to you of other worldly hopes!"[68] God is "the formula for every slander against this world . . . the deification of nothingness, the will to nothingness pronounced holy."[69]

But despite the categorical sound of Nietzsche's pronouncements against God, Nietzsche could not avoid the need to transcend. In a letter (July 2, 1885) Nietzsche complained of the unbearable solitude of a life without God. "My life now consists in the wish that it might be otherwise," he wrote.[70] Conceptually, Nietzsche never accepted any kind of theism or even pantheism. But existentially he moved inescapably toward replacing the traditional forms of self-transcendence with one of his own. This substitute form of transcendence was called "willing the eternal recurrence of the same state of affairs." He says that "eternal recurrence" is superior to the loss of God because it is this-worldly and man-centered. It is the only way of overcoming complete nihilism. Since everything is in flux and since time is cyclical, the only way a person can overcome the utter vacuity of life is to will the return of the same state of affairs eternally. This life, then, is more than something fleeting; it is something eternally reappearing. Thus, in contrast to all religions that despise this life as something fleeting, eternal recurrence is really the "religion of religions."[71] In short, the eternal Center is replaced by the eternal Cycle; the transcendence outward toward an infinite circumference is replaced by transcendence around a never-ending circle. Linear time transcending toward an ultimate End is replaced by cyclical time transcending within its own eternal Circuit.

Transcendence by Eternal Absurdity

Albert Camus sees a form of religious transcendence in all existential philosophies, for they "without exception suggest escape, . . . they deify what crushes them and find reason to hope in what impoverishes them. That forced hope is religious in all of them. It deserves attention." So "the absurd becomes god (in the broadest meaning of this word) and illuminates everything." But Camus, on the contrary, does "not want to found anything on the

---

67. Nietzsche, *Joyful Wisdom*, p. 168.
68. Nietzsche, *Thus Spoke Zarathustra*, p. 125.
69. *The Portable Nietzsche*, pp. 585, 586.
70. Ibid., p. 441.
71. Ibid., pp. 364–65.

incomprehensible." Rather, says he, "I want to know whether I can live with what I know and with that alone."[72] He does not wish to negate God but neither does he desire to appeal to God. He knows of no meaning beyond that which a man gives to life and in fact is a rebel against any alleged superior meaning. Life is absurd and the absurd does not lead to God.

In view of the ultimate absurdity of the world, Camus admits that suicide is the primary philosophical problem. However, he concludes that suicide is wrong because it would abolish a person's freedom and conscious revolt against any ultimate meaning. Only by living can one keep the absurd alive and resist any final resolution of the problem. Life is lived all the better if it has no meaning. In fact, life is meaningless; the myth of Sisyphus, wherein a man was condemned forever to roll a stone up a hill only to have it return so that he could roll it up again, exemplifies this idea. At this point Camus's resignation to absurdity looks very much like Nietzsche's eternal recurrence. That is, the human being transcends himself by rebelling against nihilism in the eternal affirmation of the cyclical nature of his absurd life. To be sure, there is no God to help in the transcendence or to console a person either by giving a superior meaning to his life or by aiding him via an immortal escape from it. Nonetheless, there is a self-initiated and self-effected form of transcendence that seeks to overcome the otherwise nihilistic demands of an absurd universe. Eternal rebellion against supernatural meaning in support of the recurrent absurdities of life becomes the replacement for God. There is no God who transcends absurdity and there is no reason to make absurdity into God. However, by willing the eternal absurdity of life one can transcend personal nihilism. And in this sense Camus, too, is committed to a kind of circular transcendence.

Religious experience always involves transcendence. This transcendence has taken at least seven directions: among the primitives transcendence was backward to the Origin; the neo-Plotinians transcended upward to the highest possible reality; and other mystics sometimes transcend either outward or inward. But due to demythologization, many modern religious people have been unable to transcend in these traditional directions and have transcended either forward to the final End or downward to the Ground of all that is.[73] Others, who deny religion, nevertheless transcend in a circle.

72. Camus, *The Myth of Sisyphus* (New York: Knopf, 1969), pp. 24, 30, 40, 41.

73. No attempt has been made to categorize Eastern religions on this sevenfold typology, but since they have no linear view of history eschatological transcendence is ruled out. More primitive forms tend to fit Eliade's transcendence toward origin or center. The more sophisticated forms of Hinduism and Buddhism fit the transcendence toward the height or depth types.

Three important observations emerge from this analysis. First, religious experience has many dimensions. It is much broader than theism. Second, humans are incurably religious. When one way to transcend is cut off, people find another. When fully religious ways are not possible, then quasireligious means are devised, as is evidenced in secularized societies (e.g., Communistic societies). For better or for worse, in reality or illusion, a human being must transcend. If traditional religious symbols or myths are incapable of evoking an experience of ultimate transcendence, new ways are created. The sacred or secular history of humanity supports the thesis that by nature a person has an irresistible urge to transcend himself. And even those who see no ultimate meaning or religious significance in their form of transcendence admit nonetheless that they too seek to transcend fundamental nihilism.

Third, one of the basic differences between those who see religious significance in their transcendence and those who do not lies in the question of the reality of the transcendent dimension or direction toward which self-transcendence moves. The truly religious person seeks reality. And the honest unbeliever refuses to take meaning or consolation from what he believes to be devoid of either ultimate meaning or discoverable reality. The residual question, then, is whether or not the Transcendent that goes beyond the person (in whatever direction) is real. This is the subject of the next chapter.

4

Testing the Reality of Religious Experience

The reality of religious experience is not axiomatic. Simply because the religious devotedly believe there is a Transcendent does not guarantee the reality of it. Illusion is a fact of life and religion is not immune to it. The data of religious experience, like the data of any other kind of experience, must be critically examined. And the unexamined religious life is no more worth living than any other kind of life.

This chapter will confront the question of the reality of the Transcendent. The discussion will proceed along the following lines. First, we will describe once more the basis of religious experience. Then, by listening to the strictest critics, we will delineate what may or may not count as reality. The chapter will conclude with an argument that religious experience does meet those criteria and thus has a basis in reality.

The Nature of Religious Experience

Before examining the reality basis for religious experience, it would be well to review what is meant by religious experience.[1] Religious experience has been taken in the broad sense of an awareness of the Transcendent and not in the narrow sense of specific religious experiences such as mystical experiences. Not that special religious experiences are not considered to be legitimately religious, for in a sense they may be even more intensely religious than the other kind. That is, there may be a heightened or more highly concentrated awareness of what is sensed in the religious experience in general. But the reason for limiting our analysis to religious experience in the broad sense is that it seems to be available to a much broader group of persons who have not had these special religious experiences.

The Awareness of the Transcendent

One of the fundamental factors in a religious experience is an awareness of something that lies beyond the individual, that is, a Transcendent. We have

1. See chapter 2 for a fuller treatment of the nature of religious experience.

seen that the individual religious person always senses a More or Beyond. That is, he always feels that there is something beyond himself that is more ultimate than himself. He is convinced that there is an All or Whole of which he is only a "part" and on which he is dependent.

Now this Transcendent takes on various dimensions and descriptions in different religious experiences. In some, it is viewed as the transcendent Origin which can be reached by going back via myths of origin (Eliade). Others view it as the transcendent Top or point of absolute Unity which can be approached only by going upward in a vertical transcendence (Plotinus). Other mystics view the Transcendent as either a Center or a Circumference (Eckhart, Cusa). Still others consider the Transcendent to be the ultimate End of a forward or eschatological transcendence (Altizer). And, finally, there is the religious experience that transcends toward the ultimate Depth (Robinson) or the attempt to transcend in a circle (Nietzsche). But whatever the direction taken by religious experience or the description given to the Transcendent, the religious experience always involves a dimension or Object toward which the individual transcends.

A Total Commitment to the Transcendent

Not only does religious experience always involve a consciousness of a transcendent object but it also involves a total commitment to that object as ultimate. Simple awareness of it does not render the experience religious; submission to it is necessary. For, as the Ultimate, it demands an ultimate commitment; a partial commitment will not suffice. To qualify as religious, one's commitment must be total. Partial commitments and concerns are not enough; there must be an ultimate concern.

Of course, if one is completely committed to this Transcendent, it is because one sees worth in it—ultimate worth. And it is in this sense that a religious experience is one of worship, because of what the religious person feels to be the worth-ship of the transcendent Object. That is, he worships It because he finds It completely worthy of his complete adoration.

Also implied in a total commitment is a sense of absolute dependence on the Object of religious experience. For one would not need to be totally committed to it if one felt that one could live independently of it. It is basic to the religious experience that one feels a sense of utter dependence on what one considers the Ultimate. The religious person feels that he cannot transcend completely without the aid of the Transcendent.

The Challenge to the Reality of Religious Experience

There is no reason to doubt that people have religious experiences. What is subject to question is the basis in reality for such experiences. In order to decide this issue we must determine first what is meant by "reality." Then we can lay down some basic considerations of verifying reality. Our conclusions on what is properly considered real are crucial for the final argument. To prove religious experience to be true on the basis of less demanding standards would be easier, but it would not be satisfying.

The Meaning of Reality

Several things are *not* meant by reality. After we see what is not meant by the word *reality* (the first four points that follow), then we can more fully appreciate the problem of trying to determine the reality of the Transcendent. The last two points attempt to provide a more positive characterization of the meaning of "reality."

1. *Reality is more than a subjective condition of human experience.* That people have experiences which they feel are ultimate and religious no one can reasonably doubt; not the experiences but their reality basis is in question. The problem is compounded by the fact that in many religious and mystical experiences there seems to be no sure way to separate the hallucinatory from the real. As Henri Bergson noted, even the great mystics have recognized this fact and have warned their disciples about it.[2] There is always the possibility that one's religious experience can be explained on a purely psychological level.[3] There is no question that religious experience is subjective; if it were not, it would not be an experience, for all experience is subjective. The important question is: Is it more than subjective? As even religious persons admit, "There cannot be any important sense in which God is *for me* unless there is some real and objective sense in which *God is,* irrespective of my belief or my lack of belief."[4] Religious transcendence must be more than a subjective condition in religious experience before it should be called "real."

2. *Reality is more than a projection of human imagination.* Further, religious transcendence is not real if, as Ludwig Feuerbach argued, it is nothing but a projection of human nature, an objectification of man that he calls God. Feuerbach wrote, "The nature of God *is nothing else* than an expression of the nature of feeling," for "the object of any subject is *nothing else* than the subject's own nature taken objectively." But the object of religion is not real if a person makes it. If what he thinks is God is actually nothing but an unconsciously worshiped projection of the best in his own human nature, then it is

---

2. Henri Bergson, *The Two Sources of Morality and Religion,* trans. R. A. Audra and C. Brereton (New York: Doubleday, 1935), p. 229.

3. See William Sargant's *Battle for the Mind* (London: William Heinemann, 1957), in which he explains religious experience in a behavioristic way, comparing it to Pavlov's conditioned response.

4. Elton Trueblood, *Philosophy of Religion* (New York: Harper and Row, 1957), p. 34.

grossly misleading to call that projection real. If consciousness of God is no more than unwitting self-consciousness, if while adoring God one is worshiping nothing but his own nature,[5] and if every advance in religious thinking is nothing but an advance in self-knowledge, then certainly it is a meaningless use of words to call it real. As Karl Marx wrote, "Man, who looked for the superman in the fantastic reality of heaven and found nothing there but the *reflexion* of himself, will no longer be disposed to find but the *semblance* of himself, the non-human [*Unmensch*] where he seeks and must seek his true reality."[6] That is, a person is a reality seeker. Should he discover that religion is but a projection of his own imagination, he will turn to the human reality instead of worshiping the mirror that reflects it, for there is reality.

3. *Reality is more than an object of wish-fulfillment.* Sigmund Freud contended that religion is an illusion, not in the sense that it is necessarily untrue, but because it resulted mainly from a wish that there be a God. "An illusion," he said, "is not the same as an error, it is indeed not necessarily an error. . . . It is characteristic of the illusion that it is derived from men's wishes." He differentiates an illusion from a delusion, which is necessarily false, whereas "the illusion need not be necessarily false, that is to say, unrealizable or incompatible with reality." However, the reality of religion is highly suspect first because of the primitive (ignorant) period in which it arose, and then because of the specious, inauthentic ground upon which men justify it. Furthermore, it is suspect because of its very nature as an illusion, namely, that human wishes play a dominant role in its motivation. "We say to ourselves," wrote Freud, "it would indeed be very nice if there were a God who was both creator and a benevolent providence, if there were a moral world order and a future life, but at the same time it is very odd that this is all just as we should wish it ourselves."[7] In view of this, we hold as minimal to the definition of real that it be more than an illusion in Freud's sense. That is, it must be more than something men wish, or even deeply wish, to be so; it must actually be so, apart from their wishes.

4. *Reality is more than a subconscious force in human experience.* William James somewhat sidestepped the basic issue when he defined the hither side of the Transcendent in terms of the subconscious. He wrote, "Whatever it may be on the *farther* side [and that is the crucial question], the 'more' with which in religious experience we feel ourselves connected is on its

---

5. Ludwig Feuerbach, *The Essence of Christianity*, trans. George Eliot (New York: Harper and Row, 1957), pp. 9–12, 13, 12, 29.

6. Karl Marx and Friedrich Engels, *On Religion*, introduction by Reinhold Niebuhr (New York: Schocken, 1964), p. 41.

7. Sigmund Freud, *The Future of an Illusion*, trans. W. D. Robson-Scott (New York: Doubleday, 1957), pp. 52–53, 53, 40–50, 54, 57–58.

hither side the subconscious continuation of our conscious life."[8] The farther side is a matter of what James called over-beliefs which he personally justified on pragmatic grounds.[9] However, the concern here is not with how James justified the farther side of transcendence but whether there really is a farther side. Certainly one should not consider the hither side or "subconscious continuation of our conscious life" to be the Transcendent of which the religious man speaks. There would be no difficulty in saying, as James admits is possible, that the subconscious is the doorway to the divine,[10] that the ultimate transcendence that people call God works in and through the subconscious. But to identify the Transcendent with the subconscious means we cannot call it real in a meaningful sense of the word.

It seems undeniable that certain subconscious patterns of mental activity and symbolism occur and have depths of meaning not always obvious to the consciousness of the individual in whom they occur.[11] In view of this fact, people cannot help but wonder whether the object of their religious experience is anything more than a product of subconscious symbolism. Nor will it suffice to do as Carl Gustav Jung did and call the collective subconscious the real, for, as Erich Fromm observed, this does not in itself show that the Transcendent is more than a mass delusion.[12] As Alfred North Whitehead indicated, to move toward the dark recesses of the subconscious is to surrender finally any hope of a solid foundation for religion.[13] If by the reality of ultimate transcendence one does not mean something more than the human subconscious, whether individual or collective, it seems inadvisable to call it real.

5. *Reality means to have an independent existence*.[14] If the Transcendent is to be more than a mere subjective experience, more than mere human imagination, more than what people deeply wish to be true (an illusion), more than the realm of human subconsciousness, then it must mean that which has an independent existence of its own.[15] That is, the Transcendent

8. William James, *The Varieties of Religious Experience* (New York: Mentor, New American Library, 1958), p. 502.

9. William James, "The Will to Believe," in *Pragmatism, and Other Essays* (New York: Washington Square, 1963), pp. 193–213.

10. Ibid., pp. 232, 237, 265.

11. Ninian Smart, *The Religious Experience of Mankind* (New York: Charles Scribner's Sons, 1969), p. 16. Even though Sartre strongly denounced Freud's view of subconscious determination in his *Existential Psychoanalysis*, he admitted to a "depth of consciousness" that would not necessarily conflict with the assertion of Smart.

12. Erich Fromm, *Psychoanalysis and Religion* (New Haven: Yale University Press, 1959), p. 15.

13. Alfred North Whitehead, *Religion in the Making* (New York: World, 1960), p. 120.

14. The word *existence* is not meant here to imply that the Transcendent has to be *a* being to be real. The verbal forms *existing* and *be-ing* are better.

15. This does not mean that nothing dependent can exist; it can have a dependent existence

must mean that which exists outside of the minds of the people who conceive it and outside the experience(s) of the people who experience it. For it is certainly not proper to attribute to the Transcendent a reality of its own if it exists only in the consciousness of finite individuals. That is to say, if the Transcendent is dependent on the consciousness of others for its reality, then it seems unfitting to attribute to it an independent existence of its own.

By "real" we mean something like a material object (something that exists outside of a mind) as opposed to the existence of a number (which exists only in a mind). This is not to say that only material objects can be real, for minds or spirits can be real too. But this is to say that the Transcendent will not be considered real unless it has an existence of its own outside of the reality of other things that exist, including human minds.

6. *Reality means to have an objective existence.* Another way to describe what is meant by "real" is to say that it refers to what has an objective existence. By "objective" we do not mean that something is merely an object (of a mind) or objectified, for in both of these senses something is not real. Rather, by "objective" we mean what is not merely the objectification made by a subject but what is itself a subject or thing. In common usage today (due to the influence of Idealism) "objective" means "real in itself" and "subjective" means "not having an independent existence of its own."[16]

So when we say that "real" means to have an objective existence, we mean objective in the modern sense. To claim that the Transcendent is objectively real is not to say that it is a mere object or objectification of a mind, for then it would not have an independent existence of its own. In brief, then, the question about the reality of the Transcendent is whether the Transcendent object of religious experience has an independent and objective existence apart from the subjective and mental states in the religious persons who sense it.

The Need for Verification

The reality of religious experience is not axiomatic. Deception and illusion are possible, and hence there must be some means of determining whether there is a basis in reality for religious experience. But lest the need for verification be taken as self-evident, one must address Søren Kierkegaard's objection about attempts to demonstrate the reality of God.

(dependent on the Universe of God) and yet exist independently (i.e., separately from other things). That is, everything except a necessary existence would in some way be a dependent existence. But things that are dependent ultimately for their existence can still have (relatively speaking) an independent or separate existence of their own.

16. Cf. Martin Heidegger, "The Problem of a Non-Objectifying Thinking and Speaking in Contemporary Theology" in *Philosophy and Religion*, ed. Jerry H. Gill (Minneapolis: Burgess, 1968), p. 62.

For Kierkegaard the very need to give evidence for God reveals that one has already rejected him. It is like asking one's wife to prove her identity before loving her. The whole attempt to verify God's presence is ridiculous. "For if God does not exist it would of course be impossible to prove it; and if he does exist it would be folly to attempt it. For at the very outset," Kierkegaard continues, "in beginning my proof, I will have presupposed it, not as doubtful but as certain. . . , since otherwise I would not begin, readily understanding that the whole would be impossible if he did not exist." One does not prove Napoleon's existence from his deeds. "His existence does indeed explain his deeds, but deeds do not prove his existence, unless I have already understood the word 'his' so as thereby to have assumed his existence." Likewise, "in the beginning of my proof [for God] I presuppose . . . that the God exists, so that I really begin by virtue of confidence in him." One is not led to God by reason; only a leap of faith brings one to God. The need for proof already reveals a lack of faith in God. And the believer who attempts to prove God knows that he has really begun with God. For "deepest down in the heart of piety lurks the mad caprice which knows that it has itself produced the God."[17] God is present to the believer from the beginning, and God cannot be proven to the unbeliever. Verification is unnecessary.

These arguments are not without merit. They have been echoed by Alvin Plantinga with his contention that belief in God is "properly basic." What Plantinga means is that there are certain beliefs for which it is possible, but foolish, to require verification; for example, "I exist," or "there is a past." One is entitled to hold them without having to provide a further account. The belief that there is a God is included among them. It is so central to the believer that it would be folly to ask him for its foundation—the belief itself is the hub of the believer's world view.[18] Nonetheless, the unbeliever wanting to have reason to believe ought not to be stymied by a believer's intransigent response. In short, if belief in God is "properly basic," then there must be some rational justification for placing it in this category.

An important distinction can help build a bridge between the verificationists and the fideists: there is a difference between the basis for believing that there is a God and the basis for believing in God. One needs evidence to know that there is a God, but one needs faith to commit oneself to the God that the evidence indicates is really there. To illustrate: it would be an insult to one's wife to demand reasons for loving her. But it is not an insult to her to demand that one have evidence that it is really she (and not a neighbor's wife) before one kisses her. Likewise, one must have some evidence that there is an

17. Søren Kierkegaard, *Philosophical Fragments*, trans. David F. Swenson (Princeton: Princeton University Press, 1967), pp. 49, 50, 53, 56.

18. Alvin C. Plantinga, "The Reformed Objection to Natural Theology," *Christian Scholar's Review* 11 (1982): 187–98.

ultimate reality before one makes an ultimate commitment to it. Once one has sufficient evidence to believe that there really is an ultimate value, there is no reason one should not believe in it for its own sake and not because of the evidence. It is unworthy of God (if there is a God) to believe in him for the sake of the evidence. If there is an ultimate value in the universe, then it ought to be believed in for its own sake. On the other hand, it would be unworthy of a reasonable creature to not examine the evidence that there is an ultimate value before he makes an ultimate commitment to it. Verification demands that one look before one leaps, that he makes sure that a woman is his wife before he embraces her, and that one is assured God is there before one believes in him for his own sake.

Verifying the Reality of Religious Experience

There is no question that human beings have what we have called a religious experience (i.e., that people sense a basic need for God). Both theists and atheists have confessed to a feeling of absolute dependence, an ultimate commitment, a sense of contingency. The crucial question is this: Is there really a God to fulfill the need that people sense? The answer in part emerges from a closer analysis of the sense in which men need the Transcendent.

The argument will proceed in the following way. We will show what it means to speak of the human need for the Transcendent. We find this need expressed, even by those who deny the Transcendent, in such varied terms as a sense of absolute dependence, being-unto-death, and an existential need for God. On the basis of the universal attestations to this need we can then conclude that the possibility of fulfilling the need—the Transcendent—is real.

The Need for the Transcendent

It is well known that Freud analyzed the human need for religion as purely psychological. Religion grows out of the illusory wish to have a Father-Protector. It is an infantile neurosis of humankind. The evils of the world spawn the desire for a cosmic Comforter. As Freud noted, anyone with a sense for reality will be discontent to believe in God simply because he wishes God to be there. "Man cannot remain a child forever; he must venture at last into the hostile world. This may be called 'education to reality'!"[19]

THE SENSE OF ABSOLUTE DEPENDENCE

But while Freud denied this psychological wish as a basis for religion, he did not deny that people have what we have described earlier as a religious

19. Freud, *Future of an Illusion*, pp. 88–89.

experience. Indeed, Freud himself had a religious experience in the sense in which we have defined it. Freud did not deny that there is "a sense of man's insignificance and impotence in the face of the universe. . . ."[20] Freud admitted that even the scientific person "will have to confess his utter helplessness and his insignificant part in the working of the universe; he will have to confess that he is not the centre of creation. . . ."[21] Science can never overcome a human's finitude or sense of cosmic contingency. Unlike primitive religion, science can aid human beings in controlling the forces of the world instead of personifying them into gods and befriending them. But nothing can alter the fact that the human is and feels dependent on the Universe.

Now Friedrich Schleiermacher takes this sense of cosmic need to be the essence of religion. Not just any feeling of dependence is religious. But a sense of absolute dependence is religious, for in religion one surrenders his all to the All. He engages in a whole-soul dependence on the Whole. All individuals have this feeling of absolute dependence but not all describe it the same way. And not all persons refer to its object by the name *God*. Nevertheless, the experience is universal and the fact of dependence is inescapable.[22] So, like Freud, Schleiermacher recognizes the human need of the All, his dependence on the Universe. Unlike Freud, Schleiermacher is willing to call this experience religious. What the experience is called is not important, but the fact of the experience is significant. People are dependent, contingent creatures, and both believers and nonbelievers recognize it. There is a need for what transcends the person, for the Transcendent. Just what this Transcendent is called, how it is characterized, and whether it is real or imagined is not the question here. People do sense a need for some Transcendent, whether it is really there or not.

HUMANITY'S BEING-UNTO-DEATH

There are other indications that humans needs the Transcendent. Martin Heidegger characterized human life as "being-unto-death." We find ourselves "thrown" into a world as though on a one-way, downhill track toward death. The evidence of this objectless fear of death or nothingness is our "anxiety." I am, but I need not be and will not be. The person asks himself, "Why is there something rather than nothing at all?" Further, why am I, and why am I going to not be? All of these questions evidence human ontological dependency, man's need for a grounding for his being.[23] The person finds

20. Freud does not wish to call this feeling of dependence a religious feeling. Religion for Freud is what a man does in response to this feeling, as a remedy against it; ibid., p. 57.

21. Ibid., p. 88.

22. See Friedrich Schleiermacher, *On Religion: Speeches to Its Cultured Despisers*, trans. John Oman (New York: Ungar, 1955), pp. 37, 47, 50.

23. See Martin Heidegger, *Being and Time* (New York: Macmillan, 1967), pp. 290–311.

himself thrust into a world, facing nothingness, without a ground for his being.

Paul Tillich began at this point and posited, beneath a human's being, a Ground of Being. Beyond the immediate there is an Ultimate that is the object of our ultimate concern. Finite being is ungrounded; it needs a Ground for its being. This need for a grounding for finite being is man's ultimate concern and is found only in an ultimate Ground. Anything less than an ultimate Ground for an ultimate concern is inadequate, says Tillich. For a finite object of unconditional loyalty—whether it is one's mother, one's country, or whatever—is idolatry. Humans need an ultimate Ground for their ultimate concerns; anything less is inadequate and idolatrous. The problem, however, is not with the inadequacy of the Ground for a human's being but with its reality. Does the need for God as an ontological grounding of one's being imply that there really is such a grounding?[24]

THE EXISTENTIAL NEED FOR GOD

Further testimony that persons at least need God, whether God is there or not, comes from the French atheist, Jean-Paul Sartre. In his autobiography Sartre confessed, "I needed God, He was given to me, I received Him without realizing that I was seeking Him." Furthermore, continued Sartre, "I reached out for religion, I longed for it, it was the remedy. Had it been denied me, I would have invented it myself."[25] Although this youthful quest for God seems psychologically based, Sartre's mature philosophy makes it clear that humans have more than a psychological need for God.

There is in the person as human being a fundamental, existential need for God. Sartre wrote, "To be man means to reach toward being God. Or if you prefer, man fundamentally is the desire to be God."[26] Man's fundamental project in life is to be God. That is, he seeks to be self-determined or self-caused. The person is nothingness desiring Being; he is freedom wanting determination; he is the "Being-for-itself" which seeks to be the "Being-in-itself." The very existence of a person cries out for God to give it definition and essense. Of course, the whole project is absurd for Sartre. For how can a person transcend himself and discover himself? How can the uncaused become self-caused? How can the free become determined? The human being is a thrust toward the Transcendent, but there is no Transcendent there. The individual is an empty bubble on the sea of nothingness. The whole human

24. See Paul Tillich, *Ultimate Concern*, ed. D. Mackenzie Brown (London: SCM, 1965), pp. 43–46.

25. Jean-Paul Sartre, *The Words*, trans. B. Frechtman (New York: Braziller, 1964), pp. 102, 97.

26. Jean-Paul Sartre, *Being and Nothingness* (New York: Washington Square, 1966), pp. 762, 766.

project is an abortive ontological quest. Humanity has a fundamental and essential need for God, but there is no God to fulfill this need. Nevertheless, Sartre makes an important admission. Persons do need God and the need is more than psychological; it is a fundamental existential need.

Other Expressions of the Human Need for the Transcendent

Sartre was not alone in expressing the human need for God. Samuel Beckett's *Waiting for Godot* is reminiscent of Heidegger's phrase *waiting for God* and reflects a craving of contemporary man to hear from God. Likewise, the novels of Franz Kafka express the lonely person's unsuccessful attempts to be in communication with some meaningful cosmic otherness beyond oneself.[27] Walter Kaufmann is more pointed in his acknowledgement of the human need for the Transcendent: "Man is the ape that wants to be god. . . . Religion is rooted in man's aspiration to transcend himself. . . . Whether he worships idols or strives to perfect himself, man is the God-intoxicated ape."[28] Even Friedrich Nietzsche found life unbearable without God. Speaking of Dante and Spinoza, he wrote: "Of course, their way of thinking, compared to mine, was one which made solitude bearable; and in the end, for all those who somehow still had a 'God' for company. . . . My life now consists in the wish that it might be otherwise with all things that I comprehend, and that somebody might make *my* 'truths' appear incredible to me. . . ."[29] In short, Nietzsche found his atheism unbearable. Sartre, too, complained of the seeming unlivability of his position, declaring that "atheism is a cruel and long-range affair."[30]

The experience of these atheists is reminiscent of the skepticism and agnosticism of David Hume and Immanuel Kant. Hume confessed that when he could no longer bear his own skeptical thoughts he would leave them for a game of backgammon. (Arthur Schopenhauer found his release in art.) Kant, after he had allegedly demonstrated the impossibility of arriving at God rationally, found it practically necessary to postulate a God to make sense out his moral life.[31] That people generally, if not universally, manifest a need for the Transcendent seems incontestable. The sense of contingency, the feeling of cosmic dependence, the need to believe in some sort of Transcendent is apparently present in all men. The residual but most essential question is this:

27. See William Barrett, *Irrational Man* (New York: Doubleday, Anchor Books, 1958), p. 63.

28. Walter Kaufmann, *Critique of Religion and Philosophy* (New York: Doubleday, 1961), pp. 354, 355, 359.

29. Friedrich Nietzsche, *The Portable Nietzsche,* ed. Walter Kaufmann (New York: Viking, 1954), p. 441.

31. Immanuel Kant, *The Critique of Pure Reason,* trans. Lewis W. Beck (New York: Bobbs-Merrill, 1956), pp. 525ff., 630ff.

Is there any basis in reality for this God-need which both believers and nonbelievers have confessed to having?

The Possibility of Fulfilling the Need for the Transcendent

Some people have stopped short in the search for a reality basis for religious experience because they have judged in advance that the project is hopeless. This seems a bit abortive. For if humans, both believers and nonbelievers, have expressed such a deep-seated need for God, then surely one is cruelly unjust to oneself to give up in despair before one has searched diligently for an answer. Indeed, upon examination, all of the alleged disproofs of the possibility of there being a transcendent Reality have failed.[32] One of the basic reasons for their failure is this: It is extremely difficult to rule out in advance, a priori, the possibility of the existence of something. Pure logical disproofs of God are no more successful than purely logical proofs for God. And before one judges, a priori, that it is impossible for God to exist, one should consider more seriously the possibility that God could exist.

The momentousness of the question of the reality basis for religious experience makes it even more imperative that one not dismiss in advance the possibility of God's existence. If the need for God is even half as great as even the nonbelievers have indicated, then the question of God's reality is worth pursuing. Especially is this true in view of human expectations. Humans expect that there are ways of fulfilling their basic needs. They anticipate that there are solutions to their problems. Science is predicated on this expectation, as is social activity. Dismissing as impossible what people sense so deeply as a basic need is like saying there are no mothers simply because a particular child is bereaved. Likewise, individual and local failures to find a reality basis for religious experience cannot be transformed into universal impossibilities. On the other hand, the mere fact that a child desires a fairyland is not in itself a guarantee that one really exists. Human desires and needs must be subject to verification. Psychological desire alone is an insufficient ground for establishing the reality of something.

Establishing the Reality of the Transcendent

There have been many attempts to establish rationally the existence of God or a Transcendent. These will be discussed later. Here it is not a question of proof or rational demonstration. Rather, it is a matter of experiential verification. Is there any way to test the alleged reality of the object of religious experience from an experiential point of view? The problem is this:

32. See chapter 5 for a fuller discussion of this point.

How can one use experience to test experience? People do experience the need for God. But that experience is not its own proof. And how can another experience support the reality of religious experience when religious experience cannot support its own reality?

The circle is not as vicious as it seems. For there is a premise based on experience that can provide an answer, namely this: What human beings really need really exists.

This premise is based on distinguishing between two kinds of human needs: needs that are perceived but not real, and needs that are perceived and real (for which the possibility of fulfillment will also exist). The former kind constitutes needs that individuals might ascribe to their lives on the basis of particular circumstances. Someone "needs" money; another one "needs" a vacation. A child may believe he "needs" ice cream. But they lack the universality of such real human needs as those for food, drink, affection, sex, and exercise. Since these needs are part of what is essential to any fulfilled human life, the potential for their fulfillment must also exist (though the need may not actually be fulfilled in every case). Hence what human beings really need really exists.

This premise is based on human experience in two ways. First, it is in accord with basic human expectations. Experience teaches us that people do expect that there are answers to their problems, that there are fulfillments of their needs. Persons do in practice assume that the universe is not ultimately irrational. Even though people have sometimes thought differently, nevertheless they have lived as though the universe is meaningful. Hume and Kant could not live their theoretical skepticism, nor can anyone else. Nietzsche wrote of the discomforting nature of his atheistic life. Sartre spoke of the cruelty of his attempt to be consistently atheistic. John Cage held that the universe operates through blind impersonal chance and composed his music by tossing coins. However, when it came to his hobby of mushroom hunting, he wrote, "I became aware that if I approached mushrooms in the spirit of my chance operations, I would die shortly. . . . So I decided that I would not approach them in this way!"[33] People cannot lead a life built on total absurdity. A totally meaningless life is contrary to human expectation.

There is a second confirmation from human experience for the principle that real human needs can be fulfilled. Experience shows that even though basic human needs are not always actually fulfilled in the case of given individuals, often these needs actually are fulfilled. To illustrate, simply because a man is dying of thirst in a desert does not mean that he will find an oasis. His particular needs may go unfulfilled. However, to assume that the

33. See Francis Schaeffer, *The God Who Is There* (Downers Grove: Inter-Varsity, 1968), pp. 71–74.

whole world is a spiritual desert in which people thirst for God and that there is no God anywhere to fulfill that need is quite another matter. That people die of thirst in no way proves no water is to be found anywhere. Or, to put it positively, the fact that people need water and expect it to be somewhere obtainable indicates that there really is water somewhere. Basic human expectations and experience lead people to believe that if they need water, then there is water somewhere. If people need food, then there is food to be found. And even though some people die of thirst and hunger, water and food do exist to fulfill human needs. It is contrary to both human expectation and human experience to suppose that what people really need is really not there to fulfill that need. It is in opposition to a person's very fiber as human to ask him to believe that there is thirst and no water, that there are males but no females, that there are sucklings and no mothers' breasts, that there is the need to be loved and no love anywhere to fulfill that need. Some people may think that needs are real but cannot be fulfilled; few people (if any) will really believe it, and no person can consistently live with that belief.

We may conclude, therefore, that what humans really need really exists. From this it would follow that there really is a God or Transcendent. For it was argued earlier, from both believer and nonbeliever, that people really need God. There is that sense of contingency and dependence, that need for transcendence within a person that cries out for fulfillment. And if people really need the Transcendent, then there must be a Transcendent somewhere to fulfill that need, even if some people do not find it. To believe otherwise would conflict with both human expectations and human experience. For just as some people have claimed satisfaction from hunger through food and some have had the need to be loved fulfilled through marriage, so others have experienced the fulfillment of their need for God through a spiritual experience. Not only does the need for God show that there is a God somewhere to satisfy that need, but the fulfillment of the need for God in some people indicates that an experience with this God is actually achieved.

But could not the sense of religious fulfillment be a mere illusion? Is it not possible that all religious persons are being deceived? Admittedly, this is a logical possibility, for no contradiction has been shown in affirming that the universe is completely deceiving people. It is possible that all of life is mocking humanity, saying, "You have this need for God and you think there is a God and that he is fulfilling your need, but you are completely wrong." It is logically possible that the world is braying at us like a malevolent demon, mocking our very needs and even the sense of their fulfillment. From the standpoint of mere experience we must admit that this is all possible, but it certainly is not believable. The position that humanity has needs that are not fulfilled is unbelievable because it goes against the very grain of human hopes and of human history. People do expect that there are real objects of their real needs. And people have found by experience that these needs have often been fulfilled. The problem with atheism is that it admits the human need to transcend but allows no object to fulfill this need. This is an existential cruelty.

We may reverse the tables on unbelief and say that to deny the reality of the Transcendent is unbelievable. For it must assume that one of humanity's most basic needs is being completely mocked by the world, leaving people with the real need for God but without a real God who can fulfill that need. Further, the denial of the reality of the Transcendent entails the assertion that not only some people have been deceived about the reality of God but that indeed all religious persons who have ever lived have been completely deceived into believing there is a God when there really is not. For if even one religious person is right about the reality of the Transcendent, then there really is a Transcendent. It seems much more likely that such self-analyzing and self-critical men as Augustine, Blaise Pascal, and Kierkegaard were not totally deceived than that total skepticism is right. It is simply unbelievable that every great saint in the history of the world, and even Jesus Christ himself, was completely deceived about the reality of God.[34] Unless it is true that no person in the history of the world has ever really been truly critical of his religious experience, then it follows that the reality of God has been critically established from human experience. Experience—hard, critical experience—indicates that people are not being totally deceived. There is a reality basis for at least some religious experience. And hence there is a God (or Transcendent) to fulfill the human need to transcend.

---

34. See Trueblood, *Philosophy of Religion*, pp. 146ff.

PART 2 �֎

GOD AND REASON

GUIDING QUESTIONS

1. Is it possible to give a rational demonstration of God's existence?
2. What are the strengths and flaws of the teleological, moral, ontological, and cosmological arguments as they have been expressed historically?
3. How does the cosmological argument based on existential causality avoid the problems of other versions of the cosmological argument?

RECOMMENDED COLLATERAL READING

Anselm, *Proslogion* in *Basic Writings*. Translated by S. N. Deane. 2d ed. LaSalle, Ill.: Open Court, 1962.

C. S. Lewis, *Mere Christianity*, part 1. New York: Macmillan, 1953.

William Paley, *Natural Theology: Selections*. Edited by Frederick Ferré. Indianapolis: Liberal Arts, Bobbs-Merrill, 1963.

Thomas Aquinas, *Summa Theologica*, volume 1, question 2, articles 1–3; and *Summa contra Gentiles*, chapters 1–11. Available in many editions.

5 ✳

The Function of Theistic Proofs

Most theists object to resting the case for the reality of God on the level of experience alone. First, at best the conceptual content of the Transcendent is minimal. Not much (if anything) is known via unanalyzed experience about the nature of such a reality. Second, it seems to them that only reason can transcend the subjectivity of pure experience. Third, the argument from experience is not a rational demonstration such as the one many theists offer for their belief in God. For these reasons, theists have offered rational proofs for their belief that there is an objective basis for their religious experience.

In this chapter we will first use a summary by Peter Koëstenbaum to expound on some modern objections to theistic proofs. Then we will respond to those objections.

The Modern Attitude Toward Proofs for God

From at least the time of Plato on, philosophers have offered proofs for the existence of God. Traditionally, these rational arguments have been categorized into four basic kinds of arguments with variations within each. Proponents of the teleological argument (from *telos*, design or purpose) have reasoned from the apparent design within the world to the need of an intelligent Designer of the world. Those who espouse the cosmological argument (from *cosmos*, world) have generally begun with the existence of the finite world or some condition within the cosmos, such as change, and argued that there must be a behind-the-world Cause or sufficient reason to explain the existence of this kind of world. Because it is based on causality, this argument is sometimes called aetiological (from *aetios,* cause). (Some philosophers have offered an anthropological argument, which concludes that because humans exist, there must be an intelligent cause of rational beings such as humans are. But these arguments are similar to causal arguments and may be subsumed under cosmological arguments.) The ontological argument (from *ontos*, being) is based on the idea that the very concept of an absolutely perfect Being or necessary Being demands that such exist. The moral argument, although it did not begin as a proof for God,[1] has evolved into a rational argument that contends the moral law of the universe requires that there be a moral Lawgiver behind it.

Not all proponents of these arguments have offered them as rational demonstrations or proofs in the strict sense. But many have defended one or another of these arguments as rationally inescapable. Certainly most theists have felt that their theistic argument is more reasonable than any other alternative.

The attitude of nontheists toward theistic proofs, as well as those who believe in God on nonrational grounds, has been understandably different from that of the theists. Furthermore, some theists believe that their belief in God is rational, though they do not ground it in proofs. Some of these nonproof theists are often among the most vocal objectors to proofs and sometimes join with antitheists in their objections.[2] Koëstenbaum summarized succinctly some of the basic objections to theistic proofs when he wrote, "The arguments are logically invalid, epistemologically defective, and axiologically misplaced."[3] We may perhaps expand the list of objections to five.

Proofs Are Psychologically Unconvincing

Rational proofs for God are generally unpersuasive to outsiders. Martin E. Marty noted that "apologists know that proof is convincing only when people are already predisposed to believe."[4] Others have pointed out that the most persuasive force for religion "is not rational theology but mystical theology, not the principle of objectivity but of subjectivity, not the clear . . . arguments of Aquinas but the record of the tormented inner experience of Augustine, Pascal, Kierkegaard, which are found most appealing."[5] The reason for this, William James suggested, is that human needs go deeper than the rational. In fact, the rational nature of a person is impressed with argu-

---

1. Kant devised this view as a practically necessary postulate in view of the fact that God could not be proven to be rationally necessary and yet that man's moral life demanded that he live as if there is a God.

2. For example, Gordon H. Clark states of David Hume: "It may be that his conclusions are validly drawn from his premise; he may be perfectly correct in arguing that the existence of God cannot be demonstrated on the basis of sensory experience. And if this is so, Christians should thank him for pointing out a procedure that ends only in embarrassment for them." *Religion, Reason, and Revelation* (Nutley, N.J.: Craig, 1961), p. 39.

3. Peter Koëstenbaum, "Religion in the Tradition of Phenomenology," in *Religion in Philosophical and Cultural Perspective,* ed. J. Clayton Feaver and William Horosz (Princeton, N.J.: Van Nostrand, 1967), p. 178.

4. Martin E. Marty, *Varieties of Unbelief* (New York: Doubleday, 1964), p. 209.

5. Michael Novak, *Belief and Unbelief* (New York: Macmillan, 1965), p. 105.

ments only after his feelings have been impressed. That is, experience is more convincing than logic because the rational nature of a human being is at best secondary as compared with his private, inner life.[6] In other words, a person finds reasons for something because he already believes it; he does not believe it because he already has reasons for it. Psychological persuasion precedes rational demonstration. Proofs are psychologically unconvincing because they tend to be academic and formal; they often do not touch people where they live. John Dewey, commenting on theistic proofs, said, "The cause of the dissatisfaction is . . . that they are too formal to offer any support to religion in action."[7] In other words, a rational proof does not meet human existential needs. Rational proofs like the mathematical proofs are cold and do not call for a commitment of the whole person. As Ian T. Ramsey pointed out, "There are no placard-bearers in mathematical departments with legends like 'There'll always be a Euclid,' or 'Prepare to meet thy Riemann today.' "[8] Likewise, there is little tendency for most moderns to join the cause of an uncaused Cause or to be deeply moved by Aristotle's unmoved Mover. In brief, even if rational proofs for God were valid, they seem not to be vital; they seem too speculative to mean much for our practical life. And even if the arguments could "prove" God, they leave many unpersuaded. For what value is it to have been rationally driven to the theistic waters from which one is unconvinced that he should drink?

Proofs Are Logically Invalid

Not only are theistic proofs psychologically unpersuasive to the modern mind, but also they are widely considered to be logically invalid. As Walter Kaufmann argued, "Can we prove God's existence with a valid argument in which God does not appear in any of the premises?" For "clearly, if God does not appear in any of the premises, he will not appear in the conclusion either: if he did, the argument would have to be invalid."[9] That is, logically, the conclusion can be no broader than the premises. If one begins with God in the premises, one has already begged the question. And if one does not begin with God in the premises, there is no logically valid way to come up with God in the conclusion, Kaufmann insists.

This same objection may be put in another way. The cosmological argument says: Every finite thing is caused; the world is finite; therefore, the world

6. William James, *The Varieties of Religious Experience* (New York: Mentor, New American Library, 1958), pp. 72, 73.

7. John Dewey, *A Common Faith* (New Haven: Yale University Press, 1934), p. 11.

8. Ian T. Ramsey, *Religious Language* (New York: Macmillan, 1963), p. 37.

9. Walter Kaufmann, *Critique of Religion and Philosophy* (New York: Doubleday, 1961), p. 169.

has a cause.[10] But in this form of the argument the word *cause* in the conclusion seems to have a different (broader) meaning than it has in the premise. For in the premise it means finite cause and in the conclusion it is supposed to mean an infinite Cause (God). From a logical standpoint, this seems to be a "four-term" fallacy.

Another way of alleging the logical invalidity of theistic arguments was put briefly by David Hume, who contended that "whatever we conceive as existent, we can also conceive as nonexistent. There is no being, therefore, whose nonexistence implies a contradiction. Consequently there is no being whose existence is demonstrable."[11] That is, it is not rationally inescapable to conclude the existence of God, since it is also logically possible to posit the opposite of whatever is said to exist.

This argument is directed particularly at the ontological argument, which Immanuel Kant held was basic to all the other proofs for God. For no argument, Kant argued, can conclude that God necessarily exists, unless it demonstrates that God is a necessary Being. "But experience can only show us that one state of things, often or at most commonly follows another, and therefore affords neither universality nor necessity."[12] So the only nonexperiential argument that could possibly show that the existence of God is necessary is the argument for a necessary Being (i.e., the ontological argument). This ontological argument, however, is not rationally inescapable, since it is not contradictory to reject it. For, Kant said elsewhere, "to posit a triangle, and to reject its three angles, is self-contradictory; but there is no contradiction in rejecting the triangle together with its three angles."[13] In brief, it is argued that the other theistic arguments are based on the ontological argument and the ontological argument is logically invalid.

Proofs Are Epistemologically Defective

At the core of this criticism is the notion that, even if there is a God, one cannot have such knowledge rationally. Epistemology is the study of knowledge or giving an account for beliefs we hold as true. This criticism says that no rational account can be given for the supposed truth of the belief that God exists.

10. Allan B. Wolter, *The Transcendentals and Their Function in the Metaphysics of Duns Scotus* (St. Bonaventure, N.Y.: The Franciscan Institute, 1946), p. 44.

11. David Hume, *Dialogues Concerning Natural Religion*, ed. Norman Kemp Smith (Indianapolis: Bobbs-Merrill, 1962), pt. 9.

12. Immanuel Kant, *Prolegomena to Any Future Metaphysics*, introduction by Lewis W., Beck (New York: Liberal Arts, Bobbs-Merrill, 1950), p. 62.

13. Immanuel Kant, *The Critique of Pure Reason*, trans. Lewis W. Beck (New York: Bobbs-Merrill, 1956), p. 502.

The most influential advocate of this view was Kant. Kant's epistemology is his transcendental method, which proceeds along two steps: defining what constitutes true knowledge and deriving those elements or conditions of knowledge that make knowledge possible and certain. Kant supplied the first part by referring implicitly and explicitly to the rise of scientific knowledge in his day, particularly to the vast gains made by Newtonian science. Such knowledge has two main characteristics: it begins with an empirical origin and it endows itself with the apparent certainty of mathematics.

Kant, in trying to model all knowledge on the Newtonian pattern, identified the following components of true knowledge as he considered it. First there is an a posteriori element—an empirical intuition, which is the reception of a manifold of sense data. This intuition is unified by the a priori contributions of the human makeup: the forms of space and time and the pure concepts of the understanding that make categorical judgment possible.

These latter categories (e.g., causality, unity, particularity) have sometimes been used to construct a metaphysics, including arguments for the existence of God. But it is here that Kant saw an essential mistake. The categories are not in themselves objects of knowledge; they are merely constituents or facilitators of knowledge. To turn them into objects of knowledge has three disastrous results.

First, it assumes that we have direct knowledge of something for which we are not entitled to such a claim. For example, it expects us to know things apart from our knowledge of them. Kant expressed this contention in several ways. He said that we can know only phenomena and not noumena; also he said that we cannot know a thing-in-itself. The meaning is the same.

Second, it opens the door to the contradictions that inevitably follow when pure reason is being given free rein. Kant schematized these as the antinomies of pure reason.

Third, it has caused people to feel confidence in arguments for God's existence that can in fact be shown to be invalid, as Kant thought he had demonstrated. In Kant's words, "Through concepts alone, it is quite impossible to advance to the discovery of new objects and supernatural beings [as in the ontological argument]; and it is useless to appeal to experience, which in all cases yields only appearances."[14] In brief, we can know only the thing-to-us (the phenomena), not the thing-in-itself (noumena). We know the way things appear to be but not how they really are.

Proofs Are Ontologically Inadequate

Another sophisticated critique of theistic proofs grows out of some of the previous criticisms. It argues that even if one could devise a rational proof for

14. Ibid., p. 530. See also on this point F. H. Parker, "Traditional Reason and Modern Reason," *Philosophy Today* 7 (1963): 235–44.

God, it would not necessarily follow that God really existed. It argues that even if it were rationally necessary to conclude that there is a God, it does not follow from this that God really exists. For there is always the possibility that the rationally inescapable is not real. Perhaps the way people must think is not the way things really are.

The basis of this reaction to theistic proofs may be traceable to Kant's contention that people must act and think as if there is a God. On one interpretation of this it could be argued that God does not really exist, but it is necessary to think that he does exist in order to have unity in one's thoughts. Whether or not Kant actually took this position, it is at least a possibility that a theistic proof could be logically valid even if there were no God. Norman Malcolm offered an ontological proof for God but said of it, "I can imagine an atheist going through the argument becoming convinced of its validity, acutely defending it against objections, yet remaining an atheist. . . ."[15]

But how can something be rationally inescapable without being ontologically so? Those who object that the theistic arguments do not really prove God exists could argue in the following way. In order to defend the proposition that the rationally inescapable is real, the theist would have to prove that the principle of noncontradiction, which is at the base of all rational arguments, is necessarily true of reality. But the traditional defense of this principle is that it cannot be denied without affirming it; therefore, it must be so.[16] For one must assume that the very statement (or thought) by which one denies the principle of noncontradiction is itself noncontradictory; otherwise the very denial is meaningless. But all this really proves is that the principle of noncontradiction is inescapable; it does not prove that it is true of reality. That is, for one to say that it is unavoidable is not the same as affirming that it is ontologically so. For even though one cannot affirm it to be false, one can believe it to be false. Furthermore, the argument goes, even though it cannot be demonstrated to be false, it might still be false.[17]

Arguing in this same vein, C. I. Lewis suggests, "if we should be forced to realize that nothing in our experience possesses any stability . . . that denouncement would rock our world to its foundations," and "yet such a world-shaking event is still quite possible . . . simply because, on this view, not even the law of non-contradiction is necessarily true of the real world."[18]

15. Norman Malcolm, "Anselm's Ontological Argument," in *The Existence of God,* ed. John H. Hick (New York: Macmillan, 1964), p. 67.

16. See Aristotle, *Metaphysics* 4.4.1006a, in *Basic Works of Aristotle,* ed. R. McKeon (New York: Random, 1941).

17. F. H. Parker, "The Realistic Position in Religion," in *Religion in Philosophical and Cultural Perspective,* ed. J. Clayton Feaver and William Horosz (Princeton, N.J.: Van Nostrand, 1967), pp. 86ff.

18. C. I. Lewis, *Mind and the World Order* (New York: Charles Scribner and Sons, 1929), p. 306.

Proofs Are Axiologically Misplaced

Even though Kant gave up any rational proofs for the existence of God, he did hold that it is morally necessary to posit God. This shift from what is rationally necessary to what is morally required signals another shift in the modern attitude toward rational proofs for the existence of God. Kant argued, for instance, that moral duty demands that people seek the highest good (the summum bonum), which is the union of virtue and happiness. But this is not possible in this life, since doing one's duty does not always bring one the maximum of happiness. "Thus God and a future life are two postulates which, according to the principles of pure reason, are inseparable from the obligations which that same reason imposes upon us."[19] Kant felt that by connecting God with a person's concrete moral values rather than his abstract reason a person would have a more valuable orientation for his religious convictions. This is why Kant could say, "I inevitably believe in the existence of God and I am certain that nothing can shake this belief, since my moral principles would thereby be themselves overthrown, and I cannot disclaim them without becoming abhorrent in my own eyes."[20]

Not all modern religious thinkers agree with Kant about the need to posit God in order to secure the fulfillment of human moral duty. However, many have followed Kant's basic axiological orientation by relating their religion to basic moral values. And in view of this the value of rational proofs is seen to be secondary at best. James, for example, contended that the modern person wants to know what will be the "cash value" of religion in his life and world.[21] Søren Kierkegaard took a more radical position, arguing that it is folly even to attempt to prove the existence of God.[22] Michael Novak's view is not quite so extreme but it reflects this same axiological reorientation toward proofs. "A formal argument for the existence of God is not of much use in the life of one who is trying to decide between belief and unbelief." For "there are many layers of point of view, inquiry, and new horizons to come through before one can understand the formal argument."[23] That is, there may be a secondary (or tertiary) role or value for a formal rationalization of one's experience of God. But to consider a rational proof to be the prime importance in one's religious experience is a misplacement of values.

---

19. Kant, *Critique of Pure Reason*, p. 639.
20. Ibid., p. 650.
21. James, *Varieties of Religious Experience*, pp. 433, 435.
22. Søren Kierkegaard, *Philosophical Fragments*, trans. David F. Swenson (Princeton: Princeton University Press, 1967), pp. 49ff.
23. Novak, *Belief and Unbelief*, p. 130.

Relating to the Modern Attitude Toward Proofs

The modern attitude toward theistic proofs is not without some justification. It does have a corrective value for theism. And any theist who desires to be relevant cannot avoid heeding these criticisms. On the other hand, the current distaste for demonstration must not deter theists from stating the full force of their case. No retreat to fideism is necessitated by the modern reaction against attempts to support the existence of God by reason. Philosophical substantiation of beliefs is as essential for contemporary persons as it was for their predecessors. Let us examine the modern attitude toward proofs, hoping to gain some clarification of the whole theistic enterprise.

Proof or Persuasion?

The statement that proofs are not psychologically persuasive is generally misleading and often flatly wrong. If it is true that people are never swayed by proof, we must assume that there is no intellectual integrity among scientists and great thinkers. It is asking too much to expect one to believe that mathematicians are not persuaded that the Pythagorean theorum is correct when they see the demonstration. One's credulity is stretched beyond limits to hold that chemists and physicists are not convinced by what they can demonstrate in the laboratory, even if they believed otherwise before the experiments. Why, then, should we believe that philosophers are never persuaded by rational demonstrations?

The relationship between an individual's total beliefs and the force of evidence is a complex one. There can be no doubt that we do hold many beliefs, even religious ones, apart from direct rational evidence. Thomas Aquinas himself pointed out that it is a good thing that we do not have to have rational proofs for belief in God. Otherwise very few people would believe that he exists, since most of us would be prevented from believing by limitations of intellect or disposition.[24] Many modern philosophers from Hume on have elaborated on our propensity to hold beliefs for nonrational (perhaps cultural) reasons. Nonetheless, to say that rational proof does not play as maximal a role as maybe René Descartes thought is far from allowing it no role at all.

A description of belief systems in which the role of evidence is minimized has been given us by W. V. O. Quine. According to Quine's analysis each person carries a web of beliefs that are mutually interdependent. Basic questions of truth, including ontological ones, are settled by appealing to the function that a belief carries out in the system as a coherent whole. External

24. Saint Thomas Aquinas, *Summa contra Gentiles*, trans. the English Dominican Fathers (London: Burns, Oates and Washbourne, 1923), 1.4.

modification occurs rarely, and Quine argues that it is, "where rational, pragmatic."[25] That looks like a very small concession, but it is sufficient for our purposes. Even Quine does not rule out persuasion on the basis of rational (albeit pragmatic) grounds. And few philosophers are as stingy as Quine is with permitting evidence.

Furthermore, even if it were true that people always believed in God apart from evidence, it still would not follow that they believed against evidence. Certainly their own testimony is to the contrary.

Most people do not live by leaps of faith into the absurd. They live and move on the sufficiency of the evidence. And what is true of their everyday life is not entirely untrue of their religious life—with one difference which will be discussed in a moment. Theists have not usually come to believe that there is a God because they think this is the most unreasonable view they could hold. On the contrary, theists almost always believe their position is most reasonable. Tertullian's alleged "I believe because it is absurd" is untrue. Indeed, Tertullian never said *absurdum* (contradictory); he said *ineptum* (foolish).[26] He was speaking not of the grounds for belief in God but of the mystery of the crucifixion of Christ which the apostle Paul said was "foolishness" to those who do not believe (1 Cor. 1:18–31). And Christians who do believe in God or Christ without any reasons are acting contrary to the command of Peter "to make a [reasoned] defense *(apologia)*" for their faith (1 Peter 3:15). Most theists believe in God because they have been persuaded by evidence that it is most reasonable to do so. So there must have been some reasons that persuaded them of this position.

It is true that proofs do not always persuade. This is no doubt part of the modern reaction to proofs. But two factors here should not be overlooked. First, a proof for God as such, if it is successful, leads a person only to believe that there is a God and not necessarily to believe in that God. A person may decide not to believe in (i.e., commit himself to) the God which the evidence indicates is really there. Second, disbelief does not always indicate disproof. Persuasion is not a purely intellectual matter; it is a volitional matter as well. Why is it that some great minds were not convinced by theistic arguments (Nietzsche, Sartre, Russell, et al.)? Granting that there are theistic proofs known by nonbelievers, there are several possibilities as to why they reject these arguments. First, some atheists do not accept any kind of proof. Second, some do not allow the kind of arguments for God which they would allow for other areas of life. Third, some nonbelievers choose not to commit themselves to God, despite the fact that the evidence indicates he is there. Only a psycho-

---

25. W. V. O. Quine, *From a Logical Point of View*, 2d rev. ed. (Cambridge: Harvard University Press, 1961), p. 46.

26. See Tertullian, *On the Flesh of Christ*, chap. 5 in *The Ante-Nicene Fathers*, ed. Philip Schaff (Grand Rapids: Eerdmans, 1956), 3:525 n. 10.

logical and spiritual analysis could indicate what is the cause in each particular case. The point here is that their lack of persuasion is not necessarily a fault of rational proofs as such; it is a result of persons' own choice. In order for a proof to be persuasive there must be a cooperation of the will with the mind. If one is unwilling to look at a proof, unwilling to accept any proof, unwilling to accept the validity of a proof as applied to God, or unwilling to accept the God the proof concludes, then one will not be persuaded by theistic arguments. On the other hand, persons of good will who are seeking the truth will be persuaded by good reasoning. And it is up to the theist to supply these good reasons.

Proofs and Logical Validity

The question of the formal validity or invalidity of theistic proofs can be determined only by a careful and detailed analysis of the proofs. This will be attempted in the next two chapters. Any final decision as to their validity must await that discussion. Meanwhile, we must content ourselves with four observations. First, a formal invalidity in some theistic proofs does not mean that there are no formally valid proofs. Second, even if no theist has stated a formally valid proof, it does not follow that it cannot or will not ever be done. (There was a time when no living persons could state a valid formula for splitting an atom.)

Third, it must be kept in mind that even something as fundamental as logical validity is not purely objective.[27] It rests on the decision made by the philosopher as to which system to follow. For example, does the statement "All unicorns are invisible" imply the statement "Some unicorns are invisible"? A medieval logician would have said yes, but under a modern Boolean understanding of logic, the answer would be no, since here universal statements are considered to be only hypothetical.

Furthermore (and fourth), we must remind ourselves that not all rationally acceptable demonstrations need to take the form of a valid deduction. Who would question my belief that I exist or that my wife loves me just because I fail to supply him with a valid deduction or even a standard induction? But I am not without evidence for those beliefs, nor am I irrational in counting it as evidence. The human mechanisms for marshaling and evaluating evidence go beyond formal logic. This point was made clear by C. S. Peirce with his concept of abduction in the natural sciences. Our contention is not intended

27. For example, "All three-sided figures are triangles; this is a triangle; therefore, this is a three-sided figure" is formally invalid but actually so. It is formally invalid because it affirms the consequent. But we know it is actually so. Hence, there must be some other way to show its validity.

to be a premature apology for unsuccessful proofs, but a reminder that what ultimately counts is actual truth, not formal validity.

Are All Theistic Proofs Epistemologically Defective?

As persuasive as is Kant's argument that all theistic proofs are epistemologically defective (and as stylish as it has been to repeat his conclusions), the argument is at best arbitrary and probably wrong. If one follows Kant's argument as stated, then Kant has made his case. But his argument rests on an unfounded assumption: that all true knowledge is modeled after the empirical/mathematical knowledge of Newtonian science. To grant Kant this assumption is to clinch his case for him, but it is also arbitrary. It excludes a priori those other kinds of knowledge which Kant does not like, but which others see as true. Kant's conclusion follows only after he has done radical amputational surgery on the body of human knowledge.

Even Kant cannot consistently mean what he says. As A. J. Ayer put it, "How can [Kant] tell what are the boundaries beyond which the human understanding may venture, unless he succeeds in passing them himself?"[28] Or as Wittgenstein said, "In order to draw a limit to thinking, we should have to think both sides of this limit."[29] In brief, there is no way to deny that our knowledge can reach reality unless our knowledge has already reached it. Consistent agnosticism is self-defeating.

Kant established a dichotomy between phenomena and noumena. He denied us access to the noumena. Critics of Kant have frequently made the counterassertion that we can reach the noumena from phenomena after all. The point, however, is that the dichotomy itself is an unfounded assumption that is best dispensed with.

Hence, it is not possible to demonstrate in advance that all theistic arguments are epistemologically defective. Each argument must be evaluated on its own basis. The possibility is open that reality can be known. Indeed, this has been one of the most persistent assumptions in the history of philosophy. Men have been and still are in the pursuit of reality. Any reasoning that would eliminate this possibility a priori is not only self-defeating but also runs against the major current of the philosophical pursuit.

Is the Rationally Inescapable Real?

Is it so that one could rationally demonstrate the existence of God and yet God not really exist? This objection to theistic proofs is built on the assump-

28. A. J. Ayer, *Language, Truth, and Logic* (New York: Dover, 1946), p. 34.
29. Ludwig Wittgenstein, *Tractatus Logico-Philosophicus*, trans. D. F. Pears and B. F. McGuinness (London: Routledge and Kegan Paul, 1961), preface.

tion that what is rationally inescapable is not necessarily ontologically so. Three things should be said here. First, the admission that the theistic arguments are rationally inescapable could be taken as a triumph for theism. For whatever is rationally inescapable ought to be accepted as true by the rational mind. If theism is rationally inescapable, then surely the atheist is not being rational in rejecting it.

Second, even if no argument could be devised to prove the premise that the conclusion of a rationally inescapable argument is true, it can still be argued that such a premise is a basic, if not necessary, assumption of human thought. It is humanly necessary to operate on the premise that reality is not contradictory, even if reality is not that way. People think the way they must think. And if they must believe that reality cannot be otherwise than the way they must think about it, then it matters little if reality can be otherwise than this. For if it is inescapable to affirm that a rationally inescapable conclusion is true, then we cannot go beyond that and may as well content ourselves with the belief that this is so.

But this brings us to a third point. To argue that logically necessary conclusions about reality are not true is to deny that logic (or reason) is applicable to reality.[30] As to the question, Does logic apply to reality? there are three possible answers. First, it cannot be true; second, it may or may not be true; third, it must be true. These exhaust the possibilities.

To affirm that logic does not apply to reality is self-defeating. For the statement that logic does not apply to reality purports to be a noncontradictory statement (otherwise it is meaningless). But it is a statement about reality. And as a noncontradictory statement about reality it cannot thereby inform us that reality must be contradictory. For to claim that the only noncontradictory position cannot be true is to affirm that a contradictory position must be true. To say that reality cannot be noncontradictory is to claim that it is contradictory. But the sentence "Reality must be contradictory" is contradictory, for it assumes that reality is not contradictory in order to make that statement about reality.

The second alternative, that reality may or may not be contradictory, is more subtle, but it turns out to be meaningless. For to affirm that reality may be contradictory is to say that it is possible that the law of noncontradiction does not apply to reality. What makes the sentence meaningless is that there is no meaning to the word *possible*, unless the law of noncontradiction does apply to reality. Obviously the sentence "It is possible that reality may be contradictory" does not mean that it is logically possible for reality to be contradictory, for this is precisely what it assumes is not the case. For it

30. See Norman L. Geisler, "The Missing Premise in the Ontological Argument," *Religious Studies* 9, no. 3 (September 1973): 289–96.

admits that it is logically necessary to think of reality as noncontradictory, as do all three positions. Further, the statement is not that reality may be thought of as contradictory, for it is readily admitted that it cannot be so thought. Rather, the statement is that reality may be contradictory. This is an ontological statement and not a purely logical one. It is intended as a description about the actual state of affairs and not merely about a possible state of affairs. But if it is a statement about reality, then it makes no sense. In order to make sense it must at least be noncontradictory. But it is clearly contradictory. For if it is a noncontradictory statement about reality, then it cannot at the same time inform us that reality may be contradictory. If reality were contradictory, then the statement would be contradictory, and surely contradictory statements must be rejected, whatever one does with contradictory reality. If reality is not contradictory, then the statement is contradictory, since it alleges that reality may be contradictory. And if it is a contradictory statement about reality, then it is obviously an untrue statement, for contradictory statements are untrue. Hence, the statement "Reality may be contradictory" is self-defeating. For it is either contradictory or not. If it is contradictory, then it is clearly untrue. If it is not contradictory, then it implies that reality is not contradictory, for it is a statement about reality. But if reality is not contradictory, then the statement cannot be true, for it claims that it is possible for reality to be contradictory when reality is actually not contradictory.

If, then, there are only three possible positions that can be affirmed and two of them are either contradictory or self-defeating, then the other position must be true. The other position is this: "Reality cannot be contradictory." But if reality cannot be contradictory, then the law of noncontradiction does apply to reality, which is what we set out to show.

The usual objection to this kind of argument is that it uses the law of noncontradiction to prove that the law of noncontradiction is true. It is saying that there are only three logically possible positions and two of them turn out to be logically contradictory; hence, it is logically necessary to conclude that the third one is correct. Actually, it is charged, one has simply used the necessity of logic to prove the necessity of logic. What has this proven except that it is rationally inescapable for us to think that the rationally inescapable conclusions are true?

This objection is not quite true. First, we have not used the law of noncontradiction as the basis of the proof of the law of noncontradiction. We have used noncontradiction in the proof but not as the proof. Anyone using any kind of meaningful argument must employ the law of noncontradiction, because there is simply no way to make meaningful assertions without the law of noncontradiction. Everyone must agree that the principle of noncontradiction is at least linguistically or humanly necessary for meaningful statements and arguments. It is one thing to use noncontradiction in the process of a proof (and we all must use it if we are to make sense), but it is quite another thing to use it as the basis of the proof. The basis of our proof was not the law of noncontradiction but self-stultification. It is not that no other position is conceivable but that no other position is affirmable. It is conceivable that nothing is real (i.e., that nothing exists). But it is not affirmable that nothing is real (or exists), for one cannot deny one's own reality (or existence) without assuming it. Hence, since something is real, it is necessary to affirm that it is not impossible. What is rationally inescapable to affirm is real.

Our basis for holding that the rationally inescapable is real is that the other positions turn out to be nonpositions because they are meaningless or self-destructive. The view that logic applies to reality is undeniable. The only meaningful and affirmable position is that "logic must apply to reality." Since no other position is affirmable and this one is affirmable (i.e., noncontradictory), then it must be true that rationally inescapable conclusions about reality are true. The basis for this argument, then, is the undeniability of the statement that logic applies to reality, or more properly, to statements about reality. Since no other position is consistently affirmable, then this one must be true. Hence, the theist need not be concerned about showing that God's nonexistence is inconceivable but only that (granting something exists) it is unaffirmable. After all, what the theist seeks is not mere rational inconceivability but existential undeniability. That is, the theist seeks a necessary Being, not a necessary Thought at the end of his argument.

Are Proofs Axiologically Misplaced?

Is there any value to theistic proofs? If so, is this not often a misplaced value? What precisely is the value of proofs and where do they fit into the total religious experience? These questions are too weighty for anything more than a summary treatment here. Perhaps an illustration will help. Suppose we come upon a man drowning on an overcast day. We respond to his cry for help by reminding him that his whole way of life in this world depends on an invisible sun beyond the clouds and that he would never have been alive, nor even able to cry for help, were it not for the sun's support of his whole way of life. In desperation he replies, "That is irrelevant, man! Don't give me philosophy about what makes life possible. Throw me a rope; I need help." Who is right? Obviously both parties are right and for different reasons. The drowning man is right about his immediate need, but ultimately the man on the shore is correct about the source and support of life itself.

Theists find themselves in a similar difficulty. True, we should not spend our time throwing out mere theoretical arguments to people whose existential dilemma calls for an immediate response. Persons on skid row need food and love, not theistic arguments. On the other hand, theists must never allow men's immediate needs to rule out any consideration of the more ultimate problems of life. Changing the illustration will help to express the point. What if the man on the shore had replied by saying, "I will throw you this rope. Hold onto it and I will pull you in." But the drowning man replied, "No, I do not trust ropes. I fell from one when I was young. Give me a life jacket." But there is no life jacket, and the only way one has of saving him is the rope. At this point one must prove to the man that holding the rope will be effective or at least reason with him to try it. The point is this: reasoning can be important even for a person's immediate, existential needs, as well as for ultimate needs. One's evaluation of his here-and-now needs can be strongly influenced by reasoning. If there is a God who loves all people, then this is important data which could significantly affect a person attempting suicide, if he could only be convinced of it. Likewise, the evidence supporting the existence of God can have an important influence on those who see no value in life. And theists would be disregarding basic values to ignore completely all the reasons for God and spend their time in helping men who need God but find it unreasonable to believe in him.

Proofs can play a practical role, indeed a crucial one. For if people really need God, then only God can really supply that need. And if only God can supply people's need and they are not convinced there is a God to supply that need, then the persons' basic spiritual needs will go unfulfilled. Proofs are not necessarily axiologically misplaced. It is as essential that people be convinced that there is a God before they trust in him as it is that a groom be convinced that there is a bride standing at the altar with him before he says, "I do."

The modern reaction to theistic proofs has been basically negative and skeptical. Rational proofs are widely considered to be psychologically unconvincing, logically invalid, epistemologically defective, ontologically inadequate, and/or axiologically misplaced. These criticisms are not totally lacking in justification, particularly for theistic arguments that would make God's nonexistence rationally inconceivable. The theist, however, may attempt to show the undeniability of God's existence and the practical relevance of this truth to the practical needs of men. Minimally, the theist must not retreat to fideism. Reasonable people do not adopt a position because it is the most unreasonable alternative, and they are not likely to make an exception in the case of theism. Religious experience reveals that human beings need God, and if reason can aid in assuring persons that there is a God to fulfill that need, so much the better. If, on the other hand, the theistic arguments turn out to be unreasonable, then there may be a God, but no good reasons for believing God exists have been provided. Only a thorough examination of the arguments can decide which is the case.

6 ✳

Teleological and Moral Arguments

Classically, there have been four kinds of attempts to establish the existence of God. These have been called the teleological, moral, ontological, and cosmological arguments, denoting their differing starting points in design, the moral law, the idea of a necessary Being, and the existence of a world. In this chapter we will examine the basic argumentation related to the first two of these arguments, beginning with the teleological argument and following with the moral argument. We shall first look at a simple standard example of each argument. Then we will move through a series of criticisms and fortifications of the argument until we reach a disposition concerning it. The thesis of this chapter is that neither argument is without value, but that both arguments need further support. Specifically, both arguments are dependent on the logic and essential content of the cosmological argument.

Teleological Proofs and Problems

The teleological argument for God's existence begins with the apparent design in the world. In essence, it argues that this apparent design is evidence of an intelligent Architect of the world.

Paley's Watchmaker

One of the most popular forms of the argument was given by William Paley (1743–1805), the archdeacon of Carlisle. Paley insisted that if one found a watch in an empty field, one would rightly conclude that it had a watchmaker because of its obvious design. Likewise, when one looks at the even more complex design of the world in which we live, one cannot but conclude that there is a great Designer behind it. Let us put the argument in summary form.[1]

---

1. See Donald R. Burrill, ed., *The Cosmological Arguments: A Spectrum of Opinion* (New York: Doubleday, Anchor Books, 1967), pp. 165–70. (Earlier forms of the teleological argument are found in Socrates [see Xenophon's *Memorabilia*. 1.4.4ff., Plato [*Phaedo*], Philo [*Works of Philo*] 3.182, 183.33, and Aquinas's [*Summa Theologica* 1.2.3] "fifth way.")

1. A watch shows that it was put together for an intelligent purpose (to keep time).
   a. It has a spring to give it motion.
   b. It has a series of wheels to transmit this motion.
   c. The wheels are made of brass so that they do not rust.
   d. The spring is made of steel because of the resilience of that metal.
   e. The front cover is of glass so that one can see through it.
2. The world shows an even greater evidence of design than a watch.
   a. The world is a greater work of art than a watch.
   b. The world has more subtle and complex design than a watch.
   c. The world has an endless variety of means adapted to ends.
3. Therefore, if the existence of a watch implies a watchmaker, then the existence of the world implies an even greater intelligent Designer (God).

Cleanthes' Greater Machine Maker

In David Hume's *Dialogues Concerning Natural Religion*, the theist Cleanthes offers a similar form of the teleological argument:[2]

1. All design implies a designer.
2. Great design implies a great designer.
3. There is great design in the world (like that of a great machine).
4. Therefore, there must be a great Designer of the world.

The argument extends beyond Paley's on several points. First, Cleanthes uses other illustrations of design than that of a watch or a machine. The human eye, male-female relation, a book, and a voice from heaven are all used to illustrate design. Second, he makes it clear that the teleological argument is an argument from analogy, insisting that like effects have like causes. Third, Cleanthes alludes to chance as an improbable explanation that a distinct voice from heaven could have been an accidental whistling of the wind. Finally, he insists that whatever irregularities there are in nature do not affect the argument. Rather, these are the exception that establishes the rule.

Thereby Hume anticipated some of his own criticisms, thus making his final case all the stronger. However, Hume did not do justice to Paley's argument so much as he did to his own creation, Cleanthes. John Stuart Mill concentrated on the aspect of the method of analogy for his critique. We shall follow this critique and then study a rejoinder by Stuart C. Hackett on this point.

2. Ibid., pp. 171–76.

Mill's Objection to the Watchmaker Argument

John Stuart Mill (1806–73) objected to Paley's form of the argument from analogy and then offered what he thought was a better one. His objection is not a destruction of but a weakening of the argument. It runs as follows:[3]

1. Paley's argument is built on analogy—similarity in effect implies similarity in cause.
2. This kind of analogy is weaker when the dissimilarities are greater.
3. There is a significant dissimilarity that weakens this argument.
   a. Watches imply watchmakers only because, by previous experiences, we know that watches are made by watchmakers, not by anything intrinsic in the watch.
   b. In like manner, footprints imply human beings, and dung implies animals only because previous experience informs us that this is so, not because of any intrinsic design in the remains.
4. Therefore, Paley's argument is weaker than he thought.

After criticizing Paley's form of the teleological argument, Mill offered what he considered to be a stronger expression of it. It is built on Mill's inductive "method of agreement." This argument was the weakest of Mill's inductive methods but he considered the teleological argument to be a strong form of this kind of induction. Mill began with the organic rather than the mechanical aspect of nature.

1. There is an amazing concurrence of many diverse elements in a human eye.
2. It is not probable that random selection brought these elements together.
3. The method of agreement argues for a common cause of the eye.
4. The cause was a final (purposing) cause, not an efficient (producing) cause.

But Mill admitted that evolution, if true, diminishes the strength of even this stronger form of the teleological argument. For much of what appears to be design is accounted for in evolution by the survival of the fittest.

Hackett's Rejoinder on Analogy

Stuart C. Hackett would take issue with Mill on the question of whether the method of analogy inherently weakens the argument. He states his argument in terms of the following three premises:[4]

3. Ibid., pp. 177–84.
4. Stuart C. Hackett, *The Reconstruction of the Christian Revelation Claim: A Philosophical and Critical Apologetic* (Grand Rapids: Baker, 1984), p. 106.

1. All composites that involve the relation of complex means so as to produce a significant result are composites of whose cause purposive intelligence is an indispensable aspect.
2. The space-time universe is a composite in which complex means are so related as to produce significant results.
3. Therefore, the space-time universe is a composite of whose cause purposive intelligence is an indispensable aspect.

Certainly this argument proceeds by analogy, since the space-time universe is placed alongside all other apparently similar composites. But Hackett asserts that this feature can hardly be considered a flaw. He states, "Granted that the reasoning involves analogy, nevertheless it should be pointed out that virtually all reasoning about matters of fact involves analogy, . . . so that the rejection of the analogical principle would be virtually tantamount to rendering all factual reasoning spurious."[5]

The weakness of dissimilarity as shown in Mill's third premise has been attacked several times. As Hackett also points out, however, the similarity for the analogy does not lie in the production of the artifact, but in its features that lead us to draw conclusions on its production.

Alvin Plantinga, though not himself a proponent of the teleological argument, also showed that this criticism is not as forceful as it appears. The universe is unique in many different ways, but in crucial ways it surely bears sufficient resemblance to other things so that we cannot immediately rule out inductive analogies.[6]

Still, Mill leaves us with the possibility that apparent design is only the result of natural selection. We must now examine that point more closely.

Russell's Evolutionary Disproof

Bertrand Russell later offered a disproof of the teleological argument from evolution:[7]

1. The adaptation of means to end in the world is either the result of evolution or else the result of design.
2. This adaptation is the result of evolution.
3. Therefore, this adaptation is not the result of design.

5. Ibid., p. 104.

6. Alvin Plantinga, *God and Other Minds: A Study of the Rational Justification of Belief in God*, Contemporary Philosophy series (Ithaca, N.Y.: Cornell University Press, 1967), pp. 97–107.

7. See Bertrand Russell, *The Basic Writings of Bertrand Russell*, ed. Robert E. Egner and Lester E. Denonn (New York: Simon and Schuster, 1957), p. 589.

If adaptation can be accounted for by the survival of the fittest, there is no need to invoke design to explain it, Russell argued.

Russell's argument does not follow, for there is no logical reason why adaptation cannot be the result of both evolution and design. Furthermore, one need not grant that natural selection can explain all adaptation.[8] And if natural selection cannot explain all apparent design, it gives some force to the design argument. Hence, Russell's argument does not disprove the teleological argument; at best it only forces a modification in the argument.

Hume's Skeptical Alternatives to Teleology

The most famous critique of the teleological argument comes from Hume. Although many scholars feel it is Hume's own view, he placed in the mouth of a skeptic, Philo, two responses to the teleological argument. The first is based on the assumption that there is design in nature and argues that the God indicated by this design assumed that design would be at best[9]

1. different from human intelligence, since human inventions differ from those of nature.
2. finite, since the effect is finite (and the cause is like the effect).
3. imperfect, for there are imperfections in nature.
4. multiple, for the creation of the world is more like the cooperative building of a ship.
5. male and female, for this is the way humans generate.
6. anthropomorphic, for his creatures have eyes, ears, noses, and other physical traits.

The best one could conclude from assuming there is design in the world is that the world arose from something like design. At worst, the world may be the crude product of some infantile god(s) or the inferior result of some senile deity or deities.

The second argument of Philo does not assume that there is design in the world. It insists that it is possible that the world arose by chance. The argument may be stated as follows:[10]

1. The apparent order in the world resulted from either design or from chance (but not both, for they are mutually exclusive).
2. It is entirely plausible that the world resulted from chance.
   a. It is possible that the universe of matter in motion is eternal.

8. See Norman L. Geisler and J. Kerby Anderson, *Origin Science: A Proposal for the Creation-Evolution Controversy* (Grand Rapids: Baker, 1987).
9. See Burrill, *Cosmological Arguments*, pp. 184–91.
10. Ibid., pp. 191–98.

b. In an infinity of chance operations every combination will be realized.
c. Combinations that best fit will tend to perpetuate themselves once they happen.
d. What does not fit tends to move around until it, too, settles down.
e. Hence, the present "ordered" arrangement of the universe may be the result of pure chance.

Philo adds two other new points to the overall development of the teleological argument and alternatives. First, he insists that animal adaptation cannot be used to prove that animals must be designed, for they could not survive unless they did adapt to their environs. One cannot use what could not have been otherwise as an evidence of intelligent planning. However, Philo admits that it is difficult to explain extra organs not needed for survival, such as two eyes or two ears. Noting that the design theories have problems and absurdities, Philo suggests suspending judgment on the whole question of whether there is a God.

Plantinga agrees with these critiques from Hume.[11] He allows that there might be a "smidgin of evidence" for design in the universe, but then argues that it is virtually impossible to go on and draw inferences from that bit of insight to the existence or nature of God as designer.[12]

We already saw that in Russell's argument the methodology is no longer analogy so much as a disjunction (albeit an invalid one). The groundwork for this shift in method was laid by Hume in the arguments by Philo. From this point on, any argument on either side needs to reckon with the choice between a cosmic designer or a chance production. And to make this kind of argument work, it is not enough to simply endorse one's own view. A disjunctive argument works by negation. Thus it becomes necessary to show that the argument of the other side is insufficient. For example, the teleological theist would have to show not only that the existence of God explains design in the world, but also that the world did not come about by chance.

Taylor's Anticipatory Design

It seemed obvious enough that the survival of the teleological argument hinged upon its ability to handle both the evolutionary and chance alternatives. This is precisely what A. E. Taylor hoped to accomplish with his argument based on the apparent advanced planning within nature. Let us summarize his argument.[13]

11. Plantinga, *God and Other Minds*, pp. 107–11.
12. Alvin Plantinga, *God, Freedom, and Evil* (New York: Harper Torchbooks, 1974), p. 84.
13. In Burrill, *Cosmological Arguments*, pp. 209–32.

1. Nature reveals an anticipatory order; that is, it plans for its own preservation.
   a. Bodily need for oxygen is anticipated by membranes that provide it.
   b. Many insects deposit eggs where food is available for their babies to eat it.
   c. A cat's movements are prospectively adapted to capture its prey.
2. Nature's advanced planning cannot be accounted for by physical laws alone (for there are countless ways electrons could run), but they do move in accord with the advanced planning of preserving the organism.[14]
   a. This is true in healthy and unhealthy organisms (e.g., antibodies).
   b. On the basis of physical laws alone, misadaptations would be as probable as adaptations.
   c. Unless we retreat to the absurd, there must be something more than physical laws to account for the indefinitely high improbabilites involved.
3. Mind or intelligence is the only known condition that can remove these improbabilities against life emerging despite these improbabilities.
   a. The human mind is direct evidence of anticipatory adaptation.
      1) Humans plan ahead. (Aged people make wills.)
      2) No jury considers a man guilty of first-degree murder unless he anticipated the result of his actions.
   b. Even scientists who reduce anticipation to complicated reflex action do not live that way themselves.
      1) They write books in hope that others will read them.
      2) They vote in hope that it will provide for a better future.
4. The mind or intelligence that explains anticipatory adaptations cannot be explained as a result of evolution, for
   a. Mind is not a life-force that resulted from evolution and then took over and captured lifeless matter (since the advanced planning which gave rise to mind can only be explained as a result of Mind).
      1) We use tools which other minds make, but some mind had to make the tool to begin with.
      2) Likewise, the fact that mind can use nature as a tool assumes that the process of nature that produced mind is itself intelligently directed.

14. This point, which would have to assume some ontogenetic development in science, is a controversial one. It has been made more recently as the anthropic principle (that the universe is amazingly preadapted to the eventual appearance of humanity). For if there were even the slightest variation at the moment of the big bang, the conditions for human life would not have been possible. See Bill Durbin, "A Scientist Caught Between Two Faiths: Interview with Robert Jastrow," *Christianity Today* 26, no. 13 (Aug. 6, 1982), p. 17.

    b. The very appearance and persistence of species is impossible without preparatory adaptation of the environment.

      1) With different chemicals, life would not have been possible.

      2) With the right chemicals and different conditions, life would not be possible.

    c. Therefore, either prospective adaptation is meaningless or else there is a Mind beyond man that is guiding the whole process.

5. Darwinian natural selection cannot explain the advance planning evident in nature, for

    a. The fittest are not necessarily the best; the most stupid sometimes survive (e.g., a drunk in an accident).

    b. Even mutations imply design, since to make evolution work, mutations

      1) must not be random and impartial but occur in trends, implying design;

      2) must be not small and gradual but large and sudden, indicating design.

    c. Darwinism does not explain, but merely presupposes, life with a preparatory environment.

    d. The human mind cannot be explained by survival of the fit or adaptation to its environment, for

      1) there is no reason these adjustments should produce foresight in man;

      2) the human mind does not adapt to the environment but transforms it.

    e. Therefore, if mind was not totally produced by nature, then it must have been active in the producing of nature (since nature indicates advanced planning explainable only by intelligence).

Taylor admits that objections can be leveled against the teleological argument. He contends, however, that they do not affect the basic argument but are applicable only to certain unjustifiable assumptions that have sometimes been connected with the argument. The teleological argument itself, at least as based on the design apparent in the anticipatory adaptations of nature, is valid.

Clark: Design and Thermodynamics

Another attempt to substantiate the teleological argument in view of the possibility that the apparent order is only a "happy accident" is typified by R. E. D. Clark. He argues against chance by using the second law of thermodynamics:[15]

15. R. E. D. Clark, *The Universe: Plan or Accident?* (London: Paternoster, 1949).

1. Whatever had a beginning had a Beginner.
2. The universe had a beginning (as evidenced by the second law of thermodynamics).
   a. The universe is "running down" and hence cannot be eternal.
   b. The second law applies to the whole universe so far as we know.
   c. A "rewinding" of the universe on its own is not probable (for there is no scientific way to explain this).
3. Therefore, the universe had a Beginner.
4. This Beginner must be
   a. intelligent, since he engaged in advanced planning, and
   b. moral, because he obviously valued creation.

Since intelligence and morality are characteristic of personality, the Beginner of the universe must be personal. He may be more than personal, but he cannot be less than personal.

In essence the teleological argument has now taken this form:

1. The universe resulted either from design or from chance.
2. It is highly improbable that it resulted from chance.
3. Hence, it is highly probable that the universe was designed.

The high improbability of a chance happening is due to the fact that there is not, as Hume's Philo assumed, an eternity of time in which to realize the ordered arrangement in which things now find themselves. There are only so many billions of geological years for things to take their present arrangement. As someone else put it, the chances that the universe happened by chance is about that of the chances that Webster's unabridged dictionary resulted from an explosion in a printing shop. In Hackett's words, "I conclude that the notion of chance simply does not provide any rationally plausible explanation of the significant order in the universe, and that therefore the principle of purposively directed activity provides an overwhelmingly more reasonable explanation."[16]

A Loophole in the Argument Against Chance

Of course the proponents realize (and opponents stress) that it is still possible that the universe happened by chance, even though there is only a limited duration of time for such an occurrence. The chances that one will get two sixes when he rolls two dice is one in thirty-six, but this does not mean that it will actually take thirty-six rolls to get two sixes. One may get it on the first roll. Likewise, the a priori odds against the universe happening by chance

16. Hackett, *Christian Revelation Claim*, p. 106.

alone are immense. Nonetheless in actual fact (a posteriori) it may have happened that way, although the chances are incomprehensibly remote.

Julian Huxley, an archdefender of evolution, estimated that at the known rate of helpful mutations over the known time scale the odds against evolution happening by pure chance alone were three million zeros (fifteen hundred pages of zeros) to one.[17] Huxley felt, however, that natural selection was the process that overcame these stupendous odds. But from the teleologist's point of view, natural selection functions as a kind of supreme intelligence, deciding with apparent foresight at thousands of points against thousand-to-one odds. What but intelligent advance planning could possibly make the right selection so consistently against such overwhelming odds?

Tennant: Filling in the Loophole of Chance

Perhaps the gravest objection to the teleological argument comes from the chance hypothesis: that the design in the knowable universe may be only a temporary and fragmentary episode in the history of the whole universe (a kind of oasis of design in the much wider desert of chance). F. R. Tennant replies to this alternative by pointing out that it is conceivable but highly improbable because[18]

1. The mere possibilities of the unknowable (or unknown) world cannot be used to refute the probabilities within the knowable world.
2. There is no evidence to support the thesis that the knowable world is a lie to the unknowable world.
3. The knowable universe is not isolated from the unknowable but is interwoven and interdependent with it.
4. Thermodynamics makes completely random development unlikely.
5. Chance reshuffling of matter by mechanical forces cannot explain the origin of mind and personality.
6. The qualitative greatness of human values in the oasis of the knowable world outweigh the quantitative immensity of the unknowable world.

After attempting to plug the alleged loophole in the teleological argument, Tennant offers his own revised form based on what he calls a wider teleology: the conspiration of innumerable cases to produce and maintain by united and reciprocal action a general order of nature (and not merely this or that particular design within the world). The value in arguing that nature as a whole is designed is, according to Tennant, that such an argument is not susceptible to many of the criticisms to which the "narrow" teleology is open.

17. Julian Huxley, *Evolution in Action* (New York: Harper and Brothers, 1953), p. 46.
18. F. R. Tennant in *The Existence of God*, ed. John H. Hick (New York: Macmillan, 1964), pp. 120–36.

For instance, a wider teleology does not demand that every detail of the process be foreordained. A purposeful process may produce as a by-product some inevitable evils. (For example, a by-product of lakes to enjoy is that some persons will drown in them.) Tennant sees six areas in which the world reflects its wider teleology:

1. adaptedness of thought to thing (the thinkability of the world),
2. adaptedness of the internal part of organic beings,
3. adaptedness of inorganic nature to purposeful ends,
4. adaptedness of nature to man's aesthetic needs,
5. adaptedness of the world to human moral goals, and
6. adaptedness of world process to its culmination in man with rational and moral status.

The conspiration of all the parts and processes of the world to produce the human value it has places beyond any reasonable doubt the fact that the world was planned.

William Lane Craig agrees that "cosmic considerations have also breathed new life into the argument from design."[19] The same is true of recent biological considerations which show a strong analogy (actually, mathematical identity) between the genetic code in living organisms and that of a human language produced by intelligence. Leslie Orgel noted that "living organisms are distinguished by their *specified complexity*. Crystals . . . fail to qualify as living because they lack *complexity;* random mixtures of polymers fail to qualify because they lack *specificity*."[20] In this light, Paley's argument can be restated:

1. Living cells are characterized by their specified complexity.
   a. Crystals are specified but not complex.
   b. Random polymers are complex but not specified.
   c. Living cells are both specified and complex.
2. A written language has specified complexity.[21]
   a. A single word repeated over and over is specified.
   b. A long series of random letters has complexity.
   c. A sentence has specified complexity.
3. Uniform experience informs us that only intelligence is capable of regularly producing specified complexity.
4. Therefore, it is reasonable to assume that living organisms were produced by intelligence.

Two things should be noted about the teleological argument in this form. First, it is based on the scientific principle of regularity. The cause of an event

19. William Lane Craig, *Apologetics: An Introduction* (Chicago: Moody, 1984), p. 73.

20. Leslie Orgel, *The Origins of Life* (New York: Wiley, 1973), p. 189, emphasis added.

21. See Hubert P. Yockey, "Self organization origin of life scenarios and information theory," *Journal of Theoretical Biology* 91, 1 (July 7, 1981): 13–31.

is that which can regularly produce that event. Second, as applied to the origin of life, this argument is based on the Humean principle of uniformity: that constant conjunction of antecedent and consequent factors is the basis for attributing causal connection. Paley clearly accepted this Humean principle and used it in his argument:

> Wherever we see marks of contrivance, we are led for its cause to an *intelligent* author. And this transition of the understanding is founded upon uniform experience. We see intelligence constantly contriving; that is, we see intelligence constantly producing effects, marked and distinguished by certain properties. . . . We see, wherever we are witnesses to the actual formation of things, nothing except intelligence producing effects so marked and distinguished in the same manner. We wish to account for their origin. Our experience suggests a cause perfectly adequate to this account . . . because it agrees with that which in all cases is the foundation of knowledge—the undeviating course of their experience.[22]

Therefore, contrary to current wisdom, Hume did not answer Paley in advance. Rather, Paley based his argument on the principle of uniformity (constant conjunction) that he borrowed from Hume. Thus, he argued that since intelligence is the only cause constantly joined with design (such as in a watch), then intelligence is the most reasonable cause to postulate for nature that manifests this same kind of design. Paley was, of course, unaware of microbiology, so he did not foresee how his argument would be strengthened by the discovery of specified complexity in DNA.

In view of the rediscovered principle of uniformity (constant conjunction) as a basis for the teleological argument, a new critique to the chance alternative suggested by Hume emerges: it is contrary to the principle of constant conjunction laid down by Hume himself. That is, chance is not a rational explanation on Hume's own grounds, since a rational person should posit as a cause only that which is constantly conjoined to the effect. But the only cause constantly conjoined to specified complexity (such as is found in living things) is intelligence. Hence, only intelligence (not chance) should be posited as the cause of life.

In brief, rational or scientific thinking is not based on chance occurrences but on constant conjunction. Hence, to posit a nonintelligent natural force as a cause of specified complexity, one must show how it constantly conjoined to a purely natural nonintelligent cause. This has not been done. In fact, purely naturalistic explanations of the origin of life have been demonstrated to be implausible.[23]

22. William Paley, *Natural Theology* (Trenton, N.J.: D. Fenton, 1824), 37.
23. See Charles B. Thaxton, Walter L. Bradley, and Roger L. Olsen, *The Mystery of Life's Origin* (New York: Philosophical Library, 1984). Even biologically interesting chemicals (such as amino acids), which are as far from a living cell as a few words are from a volume of an

Kant: Ontological Defects in the Teleological Argument

Immanuel Kant exemplified a general feeling toward the teleological argument. He neither offered a disproof of God nor suggested a complete disregard of the teleological argument.[24] Kant did, however, insist that the teleological argument is inconclusive. For,

1. The teleological argument is based on experience of design and order in the world.
2. But experience never provides us with the idea of an absolutely perfect and necessary Being. For,
   a. If God is only the highest in an actual chain of experienced beings, then a higher is possible.
   b. And if God is separate from this chain, then he is not being based in experience. (And we have thereby left the experiential basis for the argument and imported an invalid ontological argument from pure thought).[25]
3. Hence, a necessary Being cannot be proved from design in the world.
   This is not to say, however, that there is no force to the teleological argument. Kant, too, was impressed when he looked at the stars. When he put this experience in logical form it took this shape:
   a. There is everywhere in the world clear indication of intentional arrangement.
   b. The fitness of this arrangement is foreign to the things themselves (they possess this order contingently, not spontaneously).
   c. Hence, there is a sublime and wise cause (or causes) that arranged the world.
   d. That this cause is one may be inferred from the reciprocal relation of the parts to the whole universe in a mutual fit, forming a unified whole.

The argument, of course, is not conclusive but it does have value. The teleological argument, while not proving a creator, does indicate an architect. Since the cause can only be proportioned to the effect, the architect is only a very great being and not an all-sufficient being. The argument at best yields only the highest cause which is not a sufficient basis of religion. The step from the highest actual cause indicated by experience to the highest possible cause

---

encyclopedia, result only when there is illegitimate intelligent intervention (as in Urey's and Miller's experiments). Hackett makes a strong case for the teleological argument, but only after he has argued that the world is an effect with God for its cause. Serious questions, such as those brought up by Kant and Ducasse, will ultimately lead us to look for an argument behind the teleological argument. Kant says it is the ontological, whereas Ducasse looks for the cosmological argument.

24. See the next chapter for Kant's objection to the ontological argument.
25. Burrill, *Cosmological Arguments*, pp. 199–207.

demanded by pure reason is an unjustifiable ontological leap. Kant concluded that theists using the teleological argument to prove the existence of God made a desperate leap from the soil of experience to fly in the thin air of pure possibility without even admitting that they left the ground.

Ducasse: Cosmological Problems in the Teleological Argument

According to C. J. Ducasse, the teleological argument suffers from several other defects.[26]

1. First, it does not prove a perfect creator.
    a. The design in the world is not perfect, and it needs only an imperfect cause to explain it (man is just as capable of judging what is not purposeful as what is purposeful).
    b. Evil, waste, and disease all show lack of purpose.
2. Further, designers can be inferior to what they design (microscopes, steam shovels, and computers all have powers their inventors do not).
3. Finally, the teleological argument has the same defects as the cosmological argument, namely,
    a. If the world needs a designer then so does that designer, ad infinitum.
    b. But if everything is caused (according to the principle of sufficient reason), then there can be no first cause.

Ducasse offers what he considers a more plausible alternative to the teleological argument:

1. The most economical explanation is probably the correct one.
2. The world is more economically explained by a purposeless craving within man (Schopenhauer) than by some intelligence beyond the world.
    a. It is simpler, since it is located in man and not dependent on causes beyond the world.
    b. It explains things as well as God does (e.g., the eye is a purposeless craving for sight which is never satisfied).
3. Therefore, it is more probable that the world is the result of a purposeless craving (than of intelligent design).

This argument is far from definitive. It is open to challenge at several points. First, is the principle of economy or simplicity appropriately applied to the question of the cause of the universe? (Hume's skeptic argued against applying it, and skepticism cannot have it both ways.) Does it not really beg the question by assuming that the best cause will come from within the universe but not beyond it? Second, even granting that the simplest explana-

26. Ibid., pp. 234–39.

tion is the best, is a purposeless craving really the simplest explanation? (It appears far more obscure and complicated in some respects.) Third, how can a purposeless craving result in purposeful activity? How can the effect be greater than the cause?

In Hume's *Dialogues* Philo was the skeptic, Demea was the pantheist, and Cleanthes was the theist defending the teleological argument. Offering a summary at the conclusion, Hume said, "I confess that, upon a serious review of the whole, I cannot but think that Philo's principles are more probable than Demea's; but that those of Cleanthes approach still nearer to the truth."[27] It seems that this is correct. It seems necessary to grant some weight to the teleological argument. However, in accord with the criticisms of Hume, Kant, and others, it seems necessary to admit that the teleological argument as such falls short of a demonstrative proof of an absolutely perfect God. In particular, we conclude that the teleological argument as such

1. makes it probable but not certain that there is some kind of intelligence behind the design manifested in the world (chance is possible though not probable);
2. favors the unity of this cause since this world is really a uni-verse, not a multiverse;
3. does not demand as such that this cause be absolutely perfect;
4. does not ipso facto explain the presence of evil and disorder in the world;
5. is dependent on the cosmological and moral arguments to establish these other aspects of a theistic God;
6. is really a causal argument from effect to cause, only it argues from the intelligent nature of the effect to an intelligent cause.

This last point is important. For if the principle of causality cannot be supported, then admittedly one cannot insist that there must be a cause or ground of the design in the world. Design might just be there without the need for any cause. Only if there is a purpose for everything can it follow that the world must have a Purposer behind it. The teleological argument depends on the cosmological argument in this important sense that it borrows from it the principle of causality. As can be readily seen from every form of the design argument, the underlying assumption is that there needs to be a cause for the order in the world. Deny this and the argument fails,[28] for the alleged design (if uncaused) would be merely gratuitous or given.

27. Ibid., p. 189. Many believe this is not Hume's personal view.
28. See chapter 8.

Moral Arguments and Objections

Another basic approach to the existence of God is the moral one. At first it was not used as a rational argument but as a practical postulate. Later forms of this approach, however, have been presented as bona fide attempts to establish God's existence by rational argumentation. Once again we shall proceed by way of back-and-forth argumentation, moving from proponents of the argument to its critics as a way of developing all of the issues involved. We will include in this section a brief discussion of the innovative argument advanced by Hans Küng.

Kant: Positing God out of Moral Necessity

Kant categorically rejected any theoretical proofs for the existence of an absolutely perfect or necessary Being. He did, however, offer in their place a God that must be practically posited in order to make sense of our moral experience. This is not a rational demonstration for Kant but a practical presupposition. His reasoning runs like this:[29]

1. Felicity (happiness) is the desire of all human beings (what they want).
2. Morality (the categorical imperative) is the duty of all persons (what they ought to do).
3. Unity of these two is the greatest good (summum bonum).
4. The summum bonum ought to be sought (since it is the greatest good).
5. The unity of duty and desire (which is the greatest good) is not possible by finite human beings in limited time.
6. But the moral necessity of doing something implies the possibility of doing it (ought implies can).
7. Therefore, it is morally (i.e., practically) necessary to postulate
   a. deity to make this unity possible (i.e., the power to bring them together) and
   b. immortality to make this unity achievable (i.e., the time beyond this life to do it).

Kant's moral postulate may be stated in another form, which is somewhat more simplified:

1. The greatest good is that all persons have happiness in harmony with duty.
2. All persons ought to strive for the realization of the greatest good.
3. What persons ought to do, they can do.

29. From Kant's *Critique of Practical Reason* (bk. 2, chap. 2, sect. 5), in *Existence of God,* pp. 137–43.

4. But persons are able to realize the greatest good neither in this life nor without God.

5. Therefore, it must be assumed that there is a future life and God to achieve the greatest good.

There are several obvious objections to this as a proof for God's existence. The postulate was not offered as a proof by Kant. And, as he said, it is in no sense rationally necessary. It is only practically required in order to make sense of one's moral experience. Further, if, against Kant's intentions, it is construed as a rational proof, then it has several loopholes. It is possible that the summum bonum is not achievable. Many philosophies have held that it is not. Further, it is possible that ought does not imply can. Some theologians (e.g., Luther) have held that people are indeed incapable of living up to God's moral requirements of them. Some have challenged the premise that duty and desire cannot be achieved in this life. One's duty may be to do the desirable or pleasurable thing, as hedonists and utilitarians contend. Finally, some have argued that the postulate only calls for one to live as if there is a God and an immortal state. That is to say, Kant's argument necessitates only the conclusion that one must live as though there were a God. Kant does not contend that the moral experience demands one postulate that there really is a God. These objections will suffice to show that, despite Kant's intents, the argument by no means demands that one conclude that there really is a God.

Rashdall: Positing God Is Rationally Necessary

However, what Kant did not do with the moral argument, others did. Hastings Rashdall, beginning with the objectivity of a moral law, argues that there must be an absolutely perfect moral Mind.[30]

1. An absolutely perfect moral ideal exists (at least psychologically in our minds).
2. An absolute moral law can exist only in an absolute mind, because
   a. Ideals can exist only in minds (thoughts exist only in thinkers).
   b. Absolute ideas exist only in absolute minds (not in individual minds).
3. Hence, it is rationally necessary to postulate an absolutely perfect mind as that in which the absolute moral ideal exists.

In support of the objectivity of the absolute moral idea Rashdall offers the following arguments:

1. Morality is generally understood as objectively binding.
2. The mature mind understands morality as being an objective obligation.

30. Ibid., pp. 144–52.

3. Moral objectivity is a rationally necessary postulate [something cannot be judged as better or worse unless there is a standard of comparison].
4. Objective moral ideals are practically necessary to postulate.

If the moral law is objective and independent of individual minds, then it must reside in a Mind that exists independently of finite human minds. It is rationally necessary to postulate such a Mind to account for the objective existence of the moral law.

Sorley: An Expansion of the Moral Argument

The moral argument rests heavily on the objectivity of the moral law, a premise that has not gained universal recognition. It is understandable, then, that the proponents of the argument would offer an expanded defense of this point. W. R. Sorley does precisely this in his statement of the moral argument.[31]

1. There is an objective moral law independent of humans' consciousness of it and despite their lack of conformity to it, as evidenced by the facts that
   a. Persons are conscious of such a law.
   b. Persons acknowledge its claim on them even while not yielding to it.
   c. Persons admit its validity is prior to their recognition of it.
   d. No finite mind completely grasps its fullness.
   e. All finite minds together have not reached complete agreement on its meaning nor conformity to its ideal.
2. But ideas exist only in minds.
3. Therefore, there must be a supreme Mind (beyond all finite minds) in which this objective moral law exists.

Sorley is arguing that since there exists a moral law superior to, prior to, and independent of, all finite minds, then there must be a supreme Mind from which this objective moral ideal is derived.

Further, Sorley notes an important difference between the argument from natural law and the moral law argument. Natural laws can be explained as part of the observational universe (having only formal necessity). Not so with the moral law. Being prescriptive on the world and not merely descriptive of the world, the moral law cannot be considered part of the scientific universe. It is more than the way nature is and more than what people do; it is what human beings ought to do whether they are doing it or not. And since this moral ought, unlike a natural law, is beyond the world, it cannot be consid-

---

31. See Sorley, "The Moral Argument," in *Philosophy of Religion: A Book of Readings*, ed. George L. Abernathy and Thomas A. Langford, 2d ed. (New York: Macmillan, 1968), pp. 201–11.

ered a formal part of the universe. The moral law calls for an explanation beyond the natural world, for it comes from beyond the observable universe. It is a prescription on man's activity which is not descriptively reducible to man's activity.

Trueblood: Further Refinement of the Moral Argument

Elton Trueblood adds some significant dimensions to the moral argument, though his formulation falls generally in the tradition of Rashdall and Sorley. Trueblood formulates the argument in the following way:

1. There must be an objective moral law; otherwise
   a. There would not be such great agreement on the meaning of it.
   b. It would follow that no ethical disagreements have ever occurred (each person being right from his own perspective, if there is no objective view).
   c. No moral judgment has ever been wrong (each being subjectively right).
   d. No ethical question could even be discussed (there being no objective meaning to any ethical terms).
   e. Contradiction would result (since opposites could both be right).
2. This moral law is beyond individual persons and beyond humanity as a whole.
   a. It is beyond individual persons, for they often sense a conflict with it.
   b. It is beyond all humanity, for they collectively fall short of it and judge the progress of the whole race by it.
3. This moral law must come from a moral Legislator because
   a. Law has no meaning unless it comes from a mind (only minds emit meaning).
   b. Disloyalty makes no sense unless it is to a person.
   c. Truth is meaningless unless it is a meeting of mind with mind.
   d. Hence, duty to and discovery of moral law makes sense only if there is a mind or person behind that moral law.
4. Therefore, there must be a moral personal Mind behind the moral law.

Lewis: Further Expansion of the Moral Argument

In recent years the moral argument has gained a wider hearing and reception through the writings of C. S. Lewis. His argument falls in the tradition of Rashdall and Sorley but incorporates additional aspects of Lewis's own thought. Here is a summary of his reasoning:[32]

32. C. S. Lewis, *Mere Christianity* (New York: Macmillan, 1953), chaps. 1–5.

1. There must be a universal moral law, or else
    a. Disagreements would make no sense (as we assume they do).
    b. All criticisms are meaningless (e.g., "The Nazis are wrong").
    c. Promise and treaty keeping are unnecessary.
    d. We would not make excuses for breaking the moral law.
2. This moral law cannot be herd instinct, or else
    a. The stronger impulse would always win, which it does not (for the moral law sometimes sides with the weaker impulse).
    b. We would always be acting from instinct, which we do not. We sometimes act for instinct to bolster the weaker impulse (e.g., to help someone in trouble).
    c. Some instincts would always be right, which they are not (even mother love and patriotism are sometimes wrong).
3. This moral law cannot be mere convention, because
    a. Not everything learned is a mere social convention (e.g., math is learned through, but is not based on, society; it is valid independent of society).
    b. Judgment about the moral progress of a society makes sense only if the basis of that value judgment is independent of human society.
    c. Variations in value judgments are largely factual, not moral (e.g., witches are no longer treated as murderers, not because murder is now right but because as a matter of fact witches are not thought to be murderers).
4. The moral law cannot be identified with a law of nature, since
    a. The moral law is not a descriptive "is" but a prescriptive "ought."
    b. Situations equally factually inconvenient differ morally (e.g., a man who gets the seat I want in a bus because he was there first versus the man who jumped in front of me to get it).
    c. Sometimes factually more convenient situations are morally worse than those less convenient (e.g., a man who accidentally trips me is not wrong as is a man who tries to trip me but fails).
    d. Factually convenient situations can be wrong (e.g., a betrayal of one's friend).
    e. To argue that something is factually convenient to the whole race does not explain why I should do it when it does not pay me (unless I am under some universal moral obligation to do it, despite the fact that it is not desirable to me).
5. The moral law cannot be mere fancy because
    a. We cannot get rid of it even though we would sometimes like to do so.
    b. We did not make it; it is impressed upon us from without.
    c. Value judgments would be meaningless without it.
6. The person is the key to understanding this moral law because

    a. He has information that is more than merely descriptive (the prescriptive "ought" cannot be derived from a mere descriptive "is").

    b. The source of this moral law must be more like a human (mind) than nature (law). Moral laws come from minds, not from matter.

    c. The source of the moral law cannot be merely part of the (descriptive scientific) universe any more than an architect is part of the building he makes.

7. Therefore, there is an absolutely perfect power outside of humankind which is more like mind than anything we know, since

    a. It gives us moral commands.

    b. It is very much interested in our behavior (i.e., in the keeping of these commands).

    c. If it were not absolutely good, then all moral effort would be futile in the long run (e.g., we may be sacrificing our lives for the vain cause of "right" unless there is really an absolute "right").

    d. This source of all right must be absolutely good, for the standard for all good cannot be less than completely good himself).

Before concluding this argument, Lewis offered a critique of Bergson's creative evolution which would account for the presence of the moral law as a kind of immanent Life-Force within nature. This, said Lewis, has the comfort of believing in God (as opposed to a blind force) without the cost of believing in God (in terms of one's responsibility to a moral Being beyond this world). This view, wrote Lewis, is the greatest achievement of wishful thinking in the world. Furthermore, if the Life-Force can strive and purpose, then it is really a Mind after all, which is precisely what the moral argument contends.

Russell: Moral Disproof of God

Russell offered a kind of moral disproof of God. It is brief and to the point:[33]

1. If there is a moral law, either it results from God's fiat or it does not.

2. If it results from God's fiat, it is arbitrary (and then God is not essentially good).

3. If it does not result from God's fiat, God too is subject to it (and if God is subject to it, then God is not ultimate; the moral law is).

4. So, either God is not essentially good (because he is arbitrary about what is right and wrong) or else God is not ultimate (because there is a moral law to which even he is subject).

33. Bertrand Russell, *Why I Am Not a Christian* (New York: Simon and Schuster, 1957), p. 590.

5. But neither an arbitrary God nor a less than ultimate God is worthy of an ultimate commitment (i.e., neither is religiously worthy).

6. Therefore, there is no God (who is worthy of religious devotion).

This argument is put in dilemma form and hence the theistic alternatives will reply to that form. First, some theists (following Ockham) have admitted that the moral law flows from the will of God but deny that this is arbitrary and wrong. If God's will is the ultimate, then what God wills is the ultimate basis for all right and wrong. Others (following Aquinas), have insisted that it is a false disjunction. The moral law flows from the nature of God by way of the will of God. God's will is subject to God's nature, which nature is the basis for the moral law. And God is subject to his own nature. Of the two alternatives the latter seems a more plausible alternative for a theist. Either one would invalidate Russell's disproof.

Usually the fact of evil and injustice in the world is not used as a categorical disproof for an absolutely perfect God, but merely as lending probability that such a God does not exist.[34] However, on occasion, such a disproof is offered. To qualify as a disproof of the theistic God, an argument need not demonstrate that no God exists but merely that no absolutely perfect God could exist. Thus any argument that could prove a God finite in love or justice would be a disproof of traditional theism. Most arguments for a finite God do not claim to be demonstrative and hence would not qualify as disproofs of an infinitely perfect God. Some antitheists, however, seem to feel that an absolutely perfect God can be ruled out on moral grounds.

Bayle: The Basic Form of the Dilemma

Pierre Bayle's (1647–1706) famous dilemma gives the basic logical form of the moral argument against God. According to his formula,[35]

1. Evil exists.
2. An omnipotent God could destroy evil.
3. A benevolent God would destroy evil.
4. Therefore, since evil is not destroyed, then either
   a. God is omnipotent and hence malevolent in some way, or
   b. God is benevolent and hence impotent in some way, or
   c. God is both malevolent and impotent, or
   d. There is no God at all.

For several reasons, most nontheists have not pressed the argument as a definitive disproof. First, it is possible that God is doing something to destroy

---

34. The problem of evil and God will be treated fully in chapters 14–17.

35. See E. Beller and Lee M. Beller, Jr., eds., *Selections from Bayle's Dictionary* (Princeton: Princeton University Press, 1952), pp. 157–83.

evil. Second, it is possible that there is some greater good in permitting evil. Third, it is possible that what seems to be evil is part of a larger picture of good. Fourth, it is possible that it would be in some way contradictory to God's nature and/or man's free choice to destroy evil, and even an omnipotent being cannot do the contradictory. Finally, it is possible that God is all-perfect but not all-powerful. If so, the problem of evil is explained and the perfection of God is retained, since he would destroy evil if he could. These logical possibilities notwithstanding, there are still some who would insist that the logic of injustice lends itself to a kind of disproof of God.

Camus: Theism Is Contrary to Humanitarianism

The literary expression of this argument is forcefully articulated in Albert Camus's *Plague*. Speaking of a plague brought by rats into the city of Oran before the Second World War, Camus insists that[36]

1. Either one must join the doctor and fight the plague or join the priest and not fight the plague.
2. Not to join the doctor and fight the plague would be antihumanitarian.
3. To fight the plague is to fight against God who sent it.
4. Therefore, if humanitarianism is right, theism is wrong.

Thus, if humanitarianism is right, there cannot be an all-loving God. And if there is some kind of God, he must be worked against, since he is the cause of evil. Since other arguments against theism follow this basic form, let us examine them first before looking at the theistic objections to the argument.

Other Forms of the Moral Argument Against God

In response to John H. Hick's defense of theism,[37] Ronald Puccetti argued that[38]

1. There are instances of innocent suffering.
2. An all-wise, all-powerful, all-good God would not allow innocent suffering.
3. Therefore, such a God does not exist.

Puccetti anticipates objections from the theistic point of view concerning premise 2. In support of this premise Puccetti argues that it is not necessary to

---

36. See Albert Camus, *The Plague*, trans. S. Gilbert (New York: Modern Library, 1948), pp. 115–23, 201–7.

37. See John H. Hick, *Evil and God of Love* (New York: Harper and Row, 1966).

38. Ronald Puccetti, "The Loving God—Some Observations on John Hick's *Evil and the God of Love*," *Religious Studies* 2, no. 2 (1966): 255ff.

prove that God's nonexistence is logically necessary. It is sufficient to point out that theistic attempts to give reasons for innocent suffering always are inconsistent with the nature of such a God. That is, it is not logically impossible for there to be both a God and innocent sufferers, but it is practically impossible. For to say God is all-good, even though he allows innocent suffering, is like saying one does not know of any good reason that Adolf Eichmann should have killed all those Jews, nor may a reason ever be found. But he believes there is a good reason for his doing so because he believes him to be a morally good man. Puccetti's argument takes this form:

1. Any view for which one can supply no plausible reason is a practically (though not logically) impossible position.
2. The theist can supply no plausible reason why an all-wise, all-powerful, all-loving God should allow the innocent to suffer.
3. Therefore, it is practically impossible that there is such a God.

Theists have responded in several ways to this argument. First, it does not logically disprove an all-perfect God, since it admits that it is logically possible that such is compatible with innocent suffering. Second, innocent suffering is not the same as unrewarded and unredeeming suffering. The former is not necessarily incompatible with theism; the latter is. Third, it is possible that no suffering is purely innocent. There is always some fault, not of God, involved in human suffering. Fourth, there are plausible explanations as to why God permits innocent suffering.[39] The second and fourth answers seem to offer the most hope out of the dilemma for theism. Their plausibility would invalidate the argument against an all-perfect God. Fifth, even if no theist knows of a plausible reason for all suffering, it is still possible that there is one. At best, innocent suffering does not prove God is dead but only that theists are ignorant of the true reason for innocent suffering. Sixth, if the theistic God exists, there is a good explanation for all suffering. For such a God is infinitely good. But an infinitely wise God has a reason for everything, and an infinitely good God has a good reason for everything. Hence, if God exists there is a good reason for all suffering, even if we do not know what that reason is.

J. L. Mackie has summarized the basic logic of the moral argument against God:[40]

1. An all-powerful God could eliminate evil and an all-loving God would stop it.
2. There is evil in the world that is not being eliminated.

39. The plausible theistic alternatives are offered in chapters 15 and 16.
40. See. J. L. Mackie, "Evil and Omnipotence," in Nelson Pike, ed., *God and Evil: Readings on the Theological Problem of Evil* (New York: Prentice-Hall, 1964).

3. Therefore, either there is
   a. no God with both attributes, or
   b. no God who is all-powerful, for he cannot stop evil, or
   c. no God who is all-loving, for he will not stop evil.

Of course, here too it is possible for a theist to challenge the assumption that God is not trying to eliminate evil or that evil is not being defeated nor will be defeated. Further, it is always possible that the evil in the world is somehow necessary to a greater good in the world. Unless these possibilities can be eliminated, the attempt at a moral disproof of God fails.

One last attempt to disprove God by moral argument must be examined. H. J. McCloskey's argument may be put in this way:

1. Either we should work to eliminate all suffering or we should not.
2. If we should not work against all suffering, then the moral law is wrong (for it declares it our moral duty to work to eliminate all suffering).
3. If we should work against suffering, then theism is wrong (because God's existence is not justifiable unless suffering is justified as a condition to a greater good).
4. But the moral law is right (we should work to eliminate all suffering).
5. Therefore, theism is wrong (i.e., an absolutely perfect God does not exist).

It would appear that theists would want to grant premises 1, 2, and 4 but not the conclusion (5). If so, the theist would ask for proof of premise 3. McCloskey would provide the following proof for premise 3:[41]

1. The theist is morally obligated to promote the greatest good.
2. The greatest good cannot be achieved by eliminating suffering, for
   a. If the necessary condition for achieving something is eliminated, then the possibility of achieving that something is eliminated.
   b. Eliminating evil would (according to theism) eliminate the necessary condition for achieving a greater good.
   c. Hence, the greatest good cannot be achieved by eliminating suffering.
3. Therefore, the theist is morally obligated in accord with his own thesis not to work to eliminate all evil.

The whole case against God from the moral unjustifiability of suffering can be more briefly stated:

1. If suffering is justifiable, then it is wrong to work to eliminate it.
2. It is not wrong to work to eliminate suffering (it is right to do so).
3. Hence, suffering is not justifiable.

41. H. J. McCloskey, "God and Evil," in ibid.

4. But if evil is not justifiable, then the theistic God does not exist.
5. For God's existence is incompatible with unjustifiable suffering.
6. But there is unjustifiable suffering (premise 3).
7. Therefore, the theistic God cannot exist.

In this final form of the moral argument against God it becomes obvious that if the conclusion is to be denied, the theist must reject the major premise. The theist may hold that what causes suffering (namely, sin) is wrong and thus work to eliminate the cause. But to work merely against the result of sin without attacking its cause is futile. The theist does not believe that all pain as such is good; otherwise he should refuse pain pills. But the theist may contend that permitting suffering (without promoting it) as the condition to a greater good is not wrong for God, since God can achieve a greater good by permitting it than not. That is, the theist may insist that God is working against suffering and evil, and he desires us to do so as well, even though God knows that the presence of evil is a condition for a greater good. This solution is at least possible (its plausibility will be discussed later in chapters 16 and 17), and as such it invalidates any moral disproof of God.

Two final observations are in order. First, moral disproofs of God all appear to be doomed to failure, for in order to establish that there is really some injustice in the world that militates against God, they must assume some standard of justice beyond the world by which the situation is judged to be unjust (i.e., not-just). In fact, in order for the antitheist to affirm that the situation is ultimately unjust, he must assume an ultimate standard of justice.[42] In short, he proves too much by trying to disprove too much. For an ultimate Justice is what theists claim to be the nature of God. Hence, the antitheist's disproof can backfire into an argument for God. This leads to the second observation. Even if the antitheist insists that an ultimate standard of justice is not to be identified with God but perhaps with something like the Platonic Good, nonetheless he has granted a major premise in the theistic argument—the objectivity of the moral law—and leaves for the theist to establish only the premise that ultimate moral laws imply an ultimate moral Lawgiver.

Küng: Exercising Fundamental Trust

The Roman Catholic theologian Hans Küng has developed an argument that does not easily fit into any traditional category, but is perhaps best treated here because it involves the essential question of affirming a meaningful reality and thereby also affirming its creator. In many ways, however, the argument is as much cosmological as moral.

---

42. Lewis makes this point in *Mere Christianity*, pp. 45, 46.

Küng first presented this argument briefly in *On Being a Christian*[43] and then expanded it into book-length form in *Does God Exist?*[44] In outline form, the argument is this:

1. Traditional defenses of God's existence are inadequate.
   a. Both rationalistic proofs and fideistic appeals fall short of being convincing for the contemporary person.
   b. The concept of God presented in ancient metaphysical terms may no longer be acceptable.[45]
2. Modern atheism is not rationally defensible, but neither is it rationally refutable.
3. For thinkers such as Friedrich Nietzsche atheism has given way to nihilism, denial of a meaningful reality—saying no to reality.
4. Human beings find themselves constantly confronted by the threat of nihilism. One must make a choice whether to affirm reality or to deny it.
5. As we affirm meaningfulness, we can say yes to reality and exercise fundamental trust.
6. Reality does not show itself to be self-grounded.
7. We must make a choice whether to see reality as grounded in something ultimate or not.
8. We can say yes to God as the ground of reality.

It is important to recognize the logical pattern that Küng's argument assumes. It does not follow the traditional structure of a deductive argument. Thus it is certainly not an Aristotelian syllogism, nor a truth-functional deduction, such as modus ponens. We have here no given premise that, upon proper investigation, yields a necessary conclusion. Küng goes to great lengths to demonstrate that such deductive techniques are entirely out of place.[46] There are no absolute principles from which such an argument could begin, and there is no guarantee that a deduced conclusion is in fact the best one, he claims.

Instead, Küng appeals to the power of the will. He is asking us to make a choice—a fundamenal choice with regard to reality and the meaning of life. But neither is Küng simply asking for a fideistic decision. We may and must use our reason, but we must recognize that on such questions reason can never be the final authority.[47]

43. Hans Küng, *On Being a Christian,* trans. Edward Quinn (Garden City, N.Y.: Doubleday, 1976), pp. 55–79.

44. Hans Küng, *Does God Exist? An Answer for Today,* trans. Edward Quinn (New York: Vintage, 1981).

45. See Hans Küng, *Menschwerclung Gottes* (Freiburg: Herder, 1971). For a critique, see Winfried Corduan, "Hegelian Themes in Contemporary Theology," *Journal of the Evangelical Theological Society* 22 (1979): 351–61.

46. Küng, *Does God Exist?* pp. 3–41.

47. Ibid., 42–125.

Thus, from the logical point of view, Küng presents us with a disjunctive argument. It is a radical disjunction; God cannot both exist and not-exist; reality cannot both be and not-be meaningful. And we must deny one half of the disjunction and affirm the other. Which one to affirm is a complex matter. It involves, in addition to purely rational reasons, the axiological, moral, and psychological factors that go into the construction of a complete world view.

Much can be (and has been) said of Küng's argument (which spans 702 pages, not counting the notes). Some brief comments must suffice here.

The argument pulls together all of the foregoing discussion. It is driven by the question whose answer constitutes the initial premise of the moral argument: Can we affirm an ordered meaningful reality?

Stripped of all explanatory material, the bones of the argument are cosmological. The argument will work only if in fact the reality we affirm is an effect from God as its cause.

As Küng has deliberately structured the argument, it is still possible to rationally say no. We are not compelled by anything but our own ultimate choice to exercise fundamental trust and affirm God. For Küng the existence of God is not rationally inescapable. To affirm him is not irrational, but neither is atheism. Thus Küng appeals not only to our reason, but also to our moral faculties and even to our survival instinct. Consequently, as a rational argument his case may not be convincing to an atheist, since he or she may still choose to reject. Indeed, as Nietzsche said, "God degenerated into the *contradiction* of life, instead of being its transfiguration and eternal yes!"[48] The atheist can still put the shoe on the other foot.

Several summary comments may now be stated. First, no rationally inescapable moral proofs for God have been offered, for it is still logically possible (however improbable) that there is no objective moral law (it may be merely a psychological projection or a social convention), or that there is an objective moral law but no moral Lawgiver behind it. That is, this may be a universe with an objective moral standard (apart from God) to which, God (if he exists) does not measure up. Secondly, neither has any definitive moral disproof of God been offered. It is always possible (and shown to be plausible by further argument) that evil is being permitted for a greater good. Thirdly, the theistic case is not complete until it demonstrates the plausibility of evil being a condition for a greater good. Fourthly, when the antitheistic argument is pressed too far, it either backfires into an argument for God (i.e., for ultimate Justice, which the theist identifies with God) or at least grants a major premise in the theist's argument (an objective moral law). Fifthly, even

48. Friedrich Nietzsche, "The Antichrist," in *The Portable Nietzche,* ed. Walter Kaufmann (New York: Viking, 1954), p. 585.

granting an objective moral law, the theistic argument depends on a premise borrowed from the cosmological argument (that laws need causes [law-givers]). This is not true in an absurd universe or one in which the law of causality does not apply. In brief, whatever weight the moral argument possesses is derived from the causal premise used in the cosmological argument. So we must await the exposition of the cosmological argument to see if there is a firm basis for the moral argument.

7 ✤

Ontological Arguments

It has been suggested in the previous chapter that no rationally inescapable proofs or disproofs of God have been presented from either moral or teleological experience. Indeed, some (following Kant) would argue that the only hope for a theistic proof is to leave the realm of experience and enter the sphere of pure reason. Such is precisely what the ontological argument purports to do. Its proponents have sometimes argued that the existence of God is more necessary than the conclusions of mathematics. René Descartes wrote, "As for me, I dare well to boast of having found a proof of God's existence which I find entirely satisfactory, and by which I know God exists, more certainly than I know the truth of any geometric proposition."[1] As in the previous chapter, we shall trace this argument through its history of defense and critique. It will become evident that perhaps none of the theistic proofs has engendered as much affection on the one hand and outright hostility on the other hand.

The ontological argument has had a fascinating history from Anselm to the present. Most of its proponents have held it to be rationally inescapable once one grants the mere idea of a perfect or necessary Being. Anselm of Canterbury (1033–1109) is the author of the argument (which was labeled ontological by Kant, who thought it to have an ontological invalidity in it). For Anselm it was more of a "proof from prayer," for he came upon it by meditating on the concept of a perfect being, the Christian God.

Anselm's First Ontological Proof

It is now widely held that Anselm actually offered two forms of the ontological argument. The first one was this:[2]

1. God is by definition that than which nothing greater can be conceived. (This definition is understood by both believers and unbelievers.)

---

1. Descartes, in a letter to Mersenne, Nov. 25, 1630. See Ralph M. Eaton, ed., *Selections* (New York: Charles Scribner and Sons, 1927), p. 33.
2. The whole discussion between Anselm and Gaunilo is found in *The Ontological Argument: From Anselm to Contemporary Philosophers*, ed. Alvin Plantinga (Garden City, N.Y.: Doubleday, Anchor Books, 1965), pp. 3–27.

2. It is one thing to exist in the understanding only and another thing to exist both in the understanding and outside the understanding (e.g., a painting existing only in the painter's mind as opposed to one both in his mind and on canvas).

3. It is greater to exist both in the understanding and outside the understanding than in the understanding only.

4. Therefore, God must exist both in the understanding and outside the understanding (i.e., in reality). If he did not, then we could conceive of One who did, which would be greater. But God by definition (agreed upon by both believer and unbeliever) is the greatest Being conceivable. Hence, God must exist.

This form is the way Anselm presented the argument. It conceals what later analysts feel is a hidden premise. In order to reveal this premise the argument can be stated this way:

1. Whatever can be affirmed (predicated) of the most perfect Being possible (conceivable) must be affirmed of it (otherwise, by definition, it would not be the most perfect Being possible).

2. It is possible to affirm a real existence (outside of our minds) of the most perfect Being possible.

3. Hence, a real existence of the most perfect Being possible must be affirmed.

The same argument can be put in a negative form:

1. Nothing possible can be denied of the most perfect Being possible (conceivable).

2. Real (extramental) existence is possible for the most perfect Being possible.

3. Therefore, real existence cannot be denied of the most perfect Being possible.

In brief, when one begins to think or meditate on the concept of an absolutely perfect Being, it is literally inconceivable that such a Being could not exist.

Anselm's Second Form of the Ontological Proof

In repeating his argument, Anselm gave what some feel is a second form of the ontological argument. In summary,

1. It is logically necessary to affirm of a necessary Existent what is logically necessary to the concept of such a Being.

2. Real existence is logically necessary to the concept of a necessary Existent.

3. Hence, it is logically necessary to affirm that a necessary Existent really exists.

The same argument in negative form is this:

1. It is logically impossible to deny what is necessary to the concept of a necessary Existent (for it would be contradictory to say that it is not necessary that it is necessary).
2. Real existence is logically necessary to the concept of a necessary Existent.
3. Therefore, it is logically impossible to deny real existence of a necessary Existent.

The difference between the arguments is that the first form of Anselm's argument is based on predicability of existence to an absolute perfect Being and the second form is based on the inconceivability of the nonexistence of a necessary Being. The first form appears to be subject to some criticism to which the second is not, such as Kant's criticism that existence is not a predicate (see the discussion that follows).

Anselm's Debate with Gaunilo

A fellow monk, Gaunilo, was not convinced that Anselm's argument was undeniable. The ensuing debate will help clarify the Anselmian argument. First, we will give Gaunilo's objection and then Anselm's answer:

Objection 1: The argument is built on the false premise that whatever exists in the mind must also exist in reality outside the mind.

Answer 1: The argument does not apply to just any being but to only one Being, an absolutely perfect Being (which for Anselm would also have to be a necessary Being, since if it lacked necessity, it would not be absolutely perfect).

Objection 2: If God's nonexistence were really inconceivable, then no one could doubt his existence. But people do doubt and even deny it; there are atheists.

Answer 2: People can doubt or deny God's nonexistence, but they cannot conceive of God's nonexistence. God's nonexistence is affirmable but not conceivable.

Objection 3: We cannot even form the concept of the most perfect being possible. It is only a series of words with no empirical reference or meaning.

Answer 3: We do understand what the word *God* means as is evidenced by six facts: it is a common, familiar word; our faith and conscience provide content for it; conceptions do not have to be in terms of sensible images—

abstract concepts are possible; God can be understood indirectly, the way the sun is understood from its rays; we can form the concept of the most perfect by working from what is less than perfect to the perfect and from there to what is most perfectly possible; and those who deny that they can conceive of God must have some conception of what they are denying.

Objection 4: The existence of God can no more be inferred from the idea of a perfect Being than the existence of a perfect island can be inferred from the mere idea of a perfect island.

Answer 4: The existence of an island cannot be inferred from its idea because it is not an absolutely perfect Being that by its very nature cannot be lacking in anything. The idea of an island may lack existence, but an absolutely perfect Being cannot lack anything, especially being.

Objection 5: God's nonexistence is no more inconceivable than my own nonexistence. I can conceive of my own nonexistence, and I can conceive of God's, too.

Answer 5: This is not so. The nonexistence of everything except a necessary Being is conceivable. Granted that I do exist, I cannot affirm that I do not exist. It is conceivable that I might never have existed. This is not the case with a necessary Being. If it is possible for a necessary Being to exist, then it is necessary that it exist. Its nonexistence is inconceivable.

Objection 6: God's existence must be proved before we can discuss his essence. Otherwise there is no basis for saying he *is* the most perfect Being possible.

Answer 6: This is not so. We can compare ideal characteristics before we know if they are real.

Finally, Anselm charged that Gaunilo's objections and restatements of Anselm's argument reveal that Gaunilo misunderstood the argument. Gaunilo thought the argument was this:

1. God is the greatest of all beings.
2. It is greater to exist in reality than merely in the understanding.
3. Therefore, God must exist in reality (or else he would not be the greatest).

This, said Anselm, confuses the greatest actual Being with the greatest Being possible. The correct argument says only that the greatest possible or conceivable Being must exist. Anslem claimed that Gaunilo missed this fundamental distinction and hence missed the central point of the argument.

It appears to us that Anselm won the debate. Gaulino did misunderstand the argument and Anselm did satisfactorily answer his objections. This is not to say that the Anselmian argument is valid. Other objections have been leveled at Anselm's ontological proof.

Aquinas's Objection to the Ontological Argument

Another medieval monk objected to Anselm's argument. Thomas Aquinas understood Anselm to be saying this:[3]

1. God is by definition that than which nothing greater can be conceived.
2. What exists actually and mentally is greater than what exists only mentally.
3. Therefore, God must exist actually (for once the sentence "God exists" is understood, it is seen to be a self-evident proposition).

Aquinas's objections to the argument are three. First, not everyone understands the term *God* to mean "that than which nothing greater can be conceived." Second, even if God is understood this way, it does not prove that God exists actually but only mentally. Thus the alleged proof of God's existence really presupposes it. Third, the proposition "God exists" is self-evident in itself but is not self-evident to us. We cannot know God's essence (as a necessary Being) directly, but only indirectly through his effects in creation. Hence, the only way we can arrive at God's existence is through the existence of creatures (a posteriori) and not by a direct intuition of that existence (a priori) via a pure conception of it.

Aquinas's objection grows out of the difference of his realistic epistemological starting point (in experience) from Anselm's idealistic one (in thought). In this respect Aquinas was more Aristotelian and Anselm was more Platonic. Other than this, it appears to many that Aquinas does not appreciate the full force of the Anselmian argument when it is stated apart from the alleged Platonic context. Aquinas, too, had the concept of a necessary Being and yet he did not seem to appreciate that Anselm argued that this very concept (however one arrives at it) logically demands that one affirm that such a Being really exists.

Descartes's Formulation of the Ontological Argument

Eleventh-century history repeats itself with some new advancement in the ontological argument in the seventeenth century. Descartes, too, has two forms of the ontological argument. And, like Anselm with Gaunilo, he held polemics with the priest Caterus.[4] The second form of Descartes's arguments runs this way:

3. Ibid., pp. 28–30.
4. Ibid., pp. 31–49.

1. It is logically necessary to affirm of a concept whatever is essential to the nature (definition) of that concept (e.g., a triangle must have three sides).
2. Existence is a logically necessary part of the concept of a necessary Existent (otherwise it could not be defined as a necessary *Existent*).
3. Therefore, it is logically necessary to affirm that a necessary Existent does exist.

Briefly stated, if God by definition cannot *not* exist, then he must exist. For if it is impossible to conceive of a Being which cannot *not* exist as nonexistent, then it is necessary to conceive of such a Being as existing. Descartes's first form of the ontological argument is as follows:

1. Whatever we clearly and distinctly perceive of something is true. (Clarity and distinctness are the guarantee that there is no falsehood in a thing.)
2. We clearly and distinctly perceive that the conception of an absolutely perfect Being necessitates the existence of that Being.
   a. It is impossible to conceive of an absolutely perfect Being as lacking anything.
   b. But if an absolutely perfect Being does not exist, then it would lack existence.
   c. Hence, it is clear that the concept of an absolutely perfect Being necessitates its existence.
3. Therefore, it is true that an absolutely perfect Being cannot lack existence (i.e., it must exist).

Descartes was careful to qualify his argument to avoid misdirected criticism of the sort Anselm received from Gaunilo. Descartes insisted on the following propositions:

This argument applies only to an absolutely perfect or necessary Being. Any other being can be conceived not to exist. Only a necessary Being cannot be conceived as not existing.

It is not necessary for anyone to think of God, but if and when he does begin to think of God, he must conceive of God as necessarily existing. Any conception of a necessary Existent as not existing is contradictory.

To conceive of God as a necessary Being is not imaginary but necessary, for God alone is the Being whose essence necessitates his existence; it is impossible to conceive of two or more supremely perfect beings. There can be only one completely perfect being possible; and there is an infinite number of other properties in God that one cannot change by imagination. The concept of a necessary Being must be what it is and it cannot be otherwise. Hence, the concept of a necessary Being cannot be the product of one's imagination.

The Debate Between Caterus and Descartes

Caterus the priest agreed with Aquinas against Descartes that the ontological argument proves only a conceptual but not a real existence of God. Further, he contended, by way of illustration, that the complex of words *existent lion* is conceptually necessary as a complex, but this does not prove that a lion must exist. One must look to experience for the existence of a lion and not to any necessary concept about a lion.

Descartes replied by insisting that Aquinas refuted an argument that Descartes did not hold namely, that existence is concluded from the meaning of the word *God*. Descartes then repeated the argument he did hold in several different forms. The following is Descartes's first restatement of the argument:

1. Whatever we clearly and distinctly perceive is true.
2. We clearly and distinctly perceive that the concept of a necessary Existent necessitates that it exists.
3. Therefore, it is true that a necessary Existent necessarily exists.

The second restatement by Descartes is as follows:

1. Whatever is of the essence of something must be affirmed of it.
2. It is of the essence of God that he exists (for by definition his essence is to exist).
3. Therefore, existence must be affirmed of God.

The third restatement in response to Caterus was this:

1. God's existence cannot be conceived of as only possible but not actual (for in such case we would not be thinking of him as God, that is, as a necessary *Existent*).
2. We can conceive of God's existence (it is not a contradictory concept).
3. Therefore, God's existence must be conceived of as more than possible (as actual).

Other Reactions to Descartes's Proofs

Certain other seventeenth-century philosophers reacted to Descartes's ontological argument negatively. They restated his argument:

1. If it is not contradictory that God exists, then it is certain that he exists.
2. It is not contradictory that God exists.
3. So, it is certain that God exists.

In view of this new form of the argument, these philosophers offered two objections which (if true) would invalidate Descartes's conclusion. The first is that the minor premise can be doubted or denied. Hence, the argument does not necessarily follow. Second, Descartes admitted that his idea of God was inadequate. But if it is inadequate, then it is unclear. And if it is unclear, then, on Descartes's own definition of truth as "clear and distinct" ideas, it is untrue.

Descartes replied to each point. First, God's existence is noncontradictory in whichever of the two senses one takes it. If noncontradictory means *whatever does not disagree with human thought,* it is clearly noncontradictory. For we have not attributed to him anything but what human thought necessitates that we attribute to him. If noncontradictory means *what cannot be known by the human mind,* then no one can know anything, let alone God's existence. Such a definition would overthrow all human thought (which is impossible). Second, even if our concept of God is inadequate, it does not follow that it is contradictory, since all contradiction arises from a lack of clarity, and we clearly see that God must be a necessary Being. Descartes further implied that what we do not clearly see does not destroy what we do clearly see. Since we do clearly see that there is no contradiction in the concept of a necessary Being, the argument follows. For this is all that is necessary to support the disputed minor premise of the argument.

The Debate Between Gassendi and Descartes

A skeptic, Pierre Gassendi, also took issue with Descartes's ontological argument, saying that it confuses existence with a property. Gassendi made seven points.

God need not exist any more than a triangle must exist, since the essence of each can be thought of apart from its existence.

Existence is not a property either for God or for triangles. Rather, existence is that in the absence of which there are no properties or perfections. What does not exist has no perfections and what does exist has perfections, but existence is not one of them.

Descartes begs the whole question by not listing existence as part of the triangle's meaning (he does list existence as part of God's definition).

Essence and existence can be distinguished only in thought, not in reality, whether we are speaking of Plato or of God. Hence, we must conclude that either Plato exists necessarily (if essence and existence are identical) or else God does not necessarily exist (if essence and existence are not identical).

We are just as free to think of God as not existing as we are to think of Pegasus as not existing.

We know triangles have 180 degrees only by demonstration, not by assumption. We need the same kind of demonstration that existence must belong to God, not merely the assumption that it does. Otherwise we could prove that anything exists.

Descartes did not really prove that nonexistence is incompatible with God. But unless Descartes can demonstrate that God's existence is not logically impossible, he cannot argue that God's existence is logically necessary.

In his reply to Gassendi, Descartes stressed four points.

Existence is a property (like omnipotence) in the sense that it is attributable to something. And necessary existence is a necessary property of a necessary Being, because it belongs to God's essence alone.

We cannot compare triangles and God on the question of necessary existence, for existence has a different relation to triangles (a contingent one) that it has to a necessary Existent.

In view of this, it is not begging the question to include existence among the attributes of a necessary Existent.

Finally, existence and essence cannot be separate in God as they are in all other things, for he would not be God if his existence were not necessary.

One important qualification emerged from this discussion. It is this: the logical inescapability of the ontological argument depends on demonstrating the logical impossibility of there being a contradiction in affirming the existence of a necessary Being. For if it is possible that the concept of a necessary Being is logically contradictory, then the existence of God cannot be affirmed as logically necessary. This point was clearly perceived by Gottfried Wilhelm Leibniz, who offered a proof to remedy the situation.

Leibniz's Consideration of the Ontological Argument

Sensing that the basic ontological argument was valid but that it was necessary to demonstrate that the concept of God was not contradictory, Leibniz restated the argument thus:[5]

1. If it is possible for an absolutely perfect Being to exist, then it is necessary that it exist, for
   a. By definition an absolutely perfect Being cannot lack anything.
   b. But if it did not exist, it would be lacking in existence.
   c. Hence, an absolutely perfect Being cannot be lacking in existence.
2. It is possible (noncontradictory) for an absolutely perfect Being to exist.
3. Therefore, it is necessary that an absolutely perfect Being exist.

5. Ibid., pp. 54–56.

In support of the crucial minor premise Leibniz gave this argument:

1. A perfection is a simple and irreducible quality without any essential limits.
2. Whatever is simple cannot conflict with other irresolvably simple qualities (since they differ in kind).
3. And whatever differs in kind with another cannot conflict with it (since there is no area of similarity in which they can overlap or conflict).
4. Therefore, it is possible for one Being (God) to possess all possible perfections.

Even defenders of the ontological arguments do not agree that Leibniz has really proven the compatibility of all possible attributes in God.[6] Norman Malcolm saw two problems with the argument. It assumes that some qualities are essentially "positive" and others "negative," whereas this may not be the case. Some qualities may be positive in one context and negative in another. Further, Leibniz wrongly assumes that some qualities are intrinsically simple, contrary to Ludwig Wittgenstein, who showed that what is simple in one conceptual system may be complex in another. A third objection may be added. Leibniz's argument depends on the validity of the principle of the actual identity of what is conceptually indiscernable. There is a move from the conceptual to the actual that is open to challenge.

Spinoza's Ontological Proof

Like Descartes, his contemporary Benedict Spinoza held that the existence of God was mathematically demonstrable. He wrote, "We cannot be more certain of the existence of anything, than the existence of a being absolutely infinite or perfect—that is, of God." And, like Descartes, Spinoza felt that this certainty was derived from the ontological proof. Spinoza's statement of the argument is this:[7]

1. There must be a cause for everything, either for its existence or for its nonexistence.
2. A necessary Being (God) necessarily exists, unless there is a cause adequate to explain why he does not exist.
3. There is no cause adequate to explain why a necessary Being does not exist,
   a. For that cause would have to be either inside God's nature or outside of it.
   b. But no cause outside of a necessary Existent could possibly annul it.

6. Ibid., pp. 156ff.
7. Ibid., pp. 50–53.

   c. And nothing inside a necessary Existent could annul it (there cannot be anything inside a necessary Being denying it is a necessary Being).

   d. Hence, there is no cause adequate to explain why a necessary Being does not exist.

4. Therefore, a necessary Being necessarily exists.

It would seem that the usual objection could be leveled at Spinoza's proof, plus at least one more objection. One may object to the first premise which affirms that "there must be a cause for nothing." Not only is this premise without proof but it would seem to be contradictory. The law of causality demands only that "there must be a cause for something." It seems quite unusual to insist on a cause for nothing. Spinoza's defense of the premise is in the statement "The potentiality of nonexistence is a negation of power. . . ." But nonexistence is already a negative and a negation of nonexistence would be an affirmation of existence. However, this would leave the traditional basis for the ontological argument and would begin with existence. This is precisely what Spinoza does in his second form of the argument:

1. Something necessarily exists (to deny this one would have to affirm that something exists, namely, himself).
2. This necessary Existence is either finite or infinite.
3. It is possible for this necessary Existence to be infinite.
4. There must be a cause as to why this is not an infinite existence.
5. No finite existence can hinder this being an infinite Existence (and to say that an infinite Existence hinders its own infinite existence is contradictory).
6. Therefore, this must be an infinite Existence (God).

There are two important things to note about Spinoza's arguments. First, he borrows from the cosmological argument the premise that something exists, thus leaving a strictly a priori proof, as he admits. Second, the conclusion of Spinoza's argument is not the theistic God of Descartes and Leibniz but a pantheistic God. For this infinite Existence is absolutely one; there are not in addition to it many finite substances or creatures. What theists call creatures Spinoza views as merely modes or moments in this one infinite Substance—God.

The Objections of Hume and Kant

David Hume laid down what has become a standard objection to the ontological proof as well as to other alleged proofs for God's existence. It has this basic logical form:

1. Nothing is rationally demonstrable unless the contrary implies a con-

tradition (for if it leaves open any other possibility, then this position is not necessarily true).

2. Nothing that is distinctly conceivable implies a contradiction (if it were contradictory, it would not be distinctly conceivable; if it is impossible, it cannot be possible).

3. Whatever we conceive to exist we can also conceive as nonexistent (the existence or nonexistence of things cannot be ruled out conceptually).

4. There is no being, therefore, whose nonexistence implies a contradiction.

5. Consequently, there is no being whose existence is rationally demonstrable.

In essence, Hume reasons that no argument for God is rationally inescapable, because it always contains premises that can logically be denied. The conclusions always lack logical necessity, because the premises always admit of other logical possibilities. Both friend (Malcolm) and foe (Gassendi) have already admitted that there are other logical possibilities than that in which the ontological argument would conclude. According to this, the ontological argument fails to be a rational demonstration in the strict sense.

Kant's Critique of the Ontological Proof

It was Immanuel Kant who named the argument ontological, since he thought it made an illicit transition from the sphere of pure thought to that of reality (from *eidos* to *ontos*). Kant had several objections to the argument which he felt were fatal to the whole theistic cause.[8] First, he objected to the fact that we have no positive concept of a necessary Being. God is defined only as that which cannot *not* be. Further, necessity does not apply to existence but only to propositions. Necessity is a logical, not an ontological, qualifier. There are no existentially necessary propositions. Whatever is known by experience (which is the only way existential matters are knowable) could be otherwise. Next, what is logically possible is not necessarily ontologically possible. There may be no logical contradiction in the necessary existence but it still may be actually impossible. Then, there is no contradiction involved in rejecting both the idea and the existence of a necessary Being. Likewise, there is no contradiction in rejecting the triangle along with its three-sidedness. Contradiction results in rejecting one without the other. Finally, existence is not a predicate, as though it were a perfection or property that could be affirmed of a subject or thing. Existence is not a perfection of an essence but a positing of that perfection. Kant implies the following argument to support this point:

8. Ibid., pp. 57–64.

1. Whatever adds nothing to the conception of an essence is not part of that essence.
2. Existence adds nothing to the conception of an essence (i.e., no characteristic is added to an essence by positing it as real rather than as imaginary; a real dollar does not have any characteristics that an imagined one lacks).
3. Therefore, existence is not part of an essence (i.e., it is not a perfection which can be predicated of something).

If Kant's last criticism is solid, it invalidates at least the first form of the ontological argument given by Anselm. In view of Kant, Anselm's argument would really amount to this:

1. All possible perfections must be predicated of an absolutely perfect Being.
2. Existence is a possible perfection which may be predicated of an absolutely perfect Being.
3. Therefore, existence must be predicated of an absolutely perfect Being.

According to Kant's criticism, the minor premise is wrong. Existence is not a perfection that may be predicated of anything. Existence is not a predication of a characteristic but an instantation of a characteristic or thing. Essence gives the definition and existence provides an exemplification of what was defined. The essence is given in the conceptualization of something; existence does not add to this conceptualization but merely provides a concretization of it. Hence, existence neither adds nor detracts from the concept of an absolutely perfect Being. This has been a standard objection to the ontological argument since Kant.

Supposed Causes of the Ontological "Mistake"

Assuming the ontological argument is invalid, many great minds have been greatly deceived into thinking they held a rationally inescapable argument that is really invalid. There must be some reason for this deception. Opponents of the ontological argument have laid the blame at various doorsteps. Let us examine some of them.

Platonic philosophy. Following Aquinas, it has been common to pinpoint the problem in a faulty Platonic epistemology that supposes one can directly and intuitively know essences. Some claim that if we deny that one's direct and/or distinct insight into the essence of something can yield knowledge of reality and the ontological argument fails.

Metaphysical thinking. Others, since Kant, have preferred to place the blame on any kind of metaphysical thinking. They argue that "is" or "exists" has only a logical but not an ontological status. Theists are duped by the statement "God *is* a necessary Being" to suppose that the "is" really implies existence, whereas it is merely a copula or logical connective.

Confusion of cause and reason. Arthur Schopenhauer believed the confusion rested in the failure to distinguish between a cause, which demands something beyond it, and a reason, which does not demand something beyond it.[9] The reason for something can be in itself. The definition of God as an absolutely perfect and necessary Being does not require anything beyond that definition to explain it. Thus the ontological argument is "a charming joke," a kind of ontological sleight of hand. For it assumes the existence of God in the definition of God and then pretends to arrive at it in the conclusion. To use Schopenhauer's illustration, the chicken was already in the egg the theist was brooding over.

Use of a proper name. Some thinkers,[10] following Bertrand Russell, feel that the source of the ontological mistake is in the use of a proper name such as necessary Being. In the English language a proper noun signifies existence. We have been duped by the ontological implications of using a proper noun. If the proponents of the argument had used phrases like "whatever gods there are" or "whatever necessary beings there are," they would not have been deceived into thinking that there really was an absolutely perfect Being (God).

The use of the English conditional. Alvin Plantinga traced the problem to the use of the English conditional.[11] For instance, "*If* Jones is a bachelor, then he is necessarily not married" does not necessarily imply "Jones is a bachelor." There may be no Jones at all. Hence, "If God exists, then he necessarily exists" does not necessarily imply "God exists." There may be no God at all.

Findlay's Ontological Disproof of God

Whatever the cause of the error in the ontological argument, it has been widely rejected in modern times. Some have even turned the tables on it in a kind of ontological disproof of God. Such was the intention of J. N. Findlay, who argued[12]

1. God must be thought of as a necessary Being (i.e., as necessarily existing), for anything short of this kind of being would be unworthy of worship.
2. But existentially necessary propositions cannot be true (as Kant showed), for necessity is merely a logical characteristic of propositions, not of reality.

9. Ibid., pp. 65–67.
10. See Henle, in ibid., pp. 177–78.
11. Plantinga, ibid., pp. 165–66.
12. Ibid., pp. 111–22.

3. Therefore, God cannot exist.

Let us put Findlay's argument in this more simple form:

1. The only way God could exist is if he exists necessarily (any kind of existence less than necessary would make him less than God).
2. But nothing can exist necessarily (for necessity does not apply to existence but only to propositions).
3. Therefore, God cannot exist (for the only way he could exist is the very way he cannot exist).

More properly, however, the argument should be stated this way:

1. The only way a necessary Being could exist is to exist necessarily.
2. The proposition "God exists necessarily" is an existentially necessary proposition.
3. No existentially necessary proposition can be true.
4. Therefore, the proposition "God exists necessarily" cannot be true.

Now, in this latter form, the fallacies of the argument become more apparent. We will pass by the objection to premise 1 from the vantage point of finite godism (that God does not have to be conceived as necessarily existing), since the subject here is whether or not the traditional theistic conception of an absolutely perfect Being is correct. The theist would challenge the next two premises (2 and 3). First, granting for the moment that there are no existentially necessary propositions, a theist could change the proposition "God exists necessarily" to "God exists." The theist could then hold that the proposition "God exists" is a logically necessary proposition to hold.[13] In this way, necessity applies only to the proposition and not to existence, thus invalidating the criticism. Second, the theist need not grant that there are no existentially necessary propositions. Indeed, some theists have offered examples of what they consider to be existentially necessary statements. Ian T. Ramsey suggests that "I am I" is an example. Malcolm offers "There are an infinite number of prime numbers" as an example. Some feel that "Square circles do not exist" would be existentially necessary, even though it is negative in form. (If there can be negative examples, then why not positive examples? Negatives presuppose positives.) Third, still other theists, taking Anselm and Descartes literally, insist that "God necessarily exists" is a special case. It is the only existentially necessary proposition and it is not only unnecessary but impossible to give any other examples of existentially necessary propositions. Fourth, it seems, however, that the most effective way to eliminate Findlay's ontological disproof is to show that his premise is self-defeating. For the

13. See G. E. Hughes, "Can God's Existence Be Disproved?" in *New Essays in Philosophical Theology*, ed. Antony Flew and Alasdair MacIntyre (London: SCM, 1963), p. 59.

statement "There are no existentially necessary propositions" is itself an existentially necessary proposition. And if it is such, then there are existentially necessary propositions (at least there is this one, and why not others?). If it is not a necessary statement about existence, then it does not really eliminate the possibility that there could be an existentially necessary Existent. So either it does not accomplish its intended task of eliminating the possibility of existentially necessary propositions or else it defeats itself by offering an existentially necessary proposition in order to prove that there are no existentially necessary propositions.

Hartshorne's Restatement of the Ontological Proof

In its long and checkered history this venerable argument for theism has lived to see a new day. One of the most ardent defenders of the ontological argument is Charles Hartshorne. His statement and defense of the argument in full view of all the traditional criticisms is instructive. Hartshorne states the argument like this:[14]

1. The existence of a necessary being is either
   a. Impossible, and there is no example of it.
   b. Possible, but there is no example of it.
   c. Possible, and there is an example of it.
2. But premise b is meaningless (like saying there is a round square), for a necessary Being cannot be merely a possible being.
3. And premise a is not eliminated by the ontological argument as such but the meaningfulness of the term *necessary Being* is a justifiable assumption that may be defended on other grounds (see 2 below).

After pinpointing what he felt to be the basic logic of the ontological argument, Hartshorne proceeded to give the fuller elaboration of it. It may be summarized as follows:

1. All thought must refer to something beyond itself which is at least possible, since
   a. Wherever there is meaning, there must be something meant.
   b. The only thoughts that are less than possible are contradictory ones.
   c. Meaning must refer to something more than its own contents or inner consistency or else it is meaningless.
   d. The move from thought to reality is based on a prior reverse move from reality to thought.
   e. Total illusion is impossible; illusion presupposes a backdrop of reality.

---

14. See Hartshorne in *Ontological Argument*, pp. 123–35.

    f. Confusion is possible about specific reality but not about reality in general.

    g. See also the answers to objections 3 and 6.

2. The necessary existence of a necessary Being is "at least possible."

    a. There is nothing contradictory in the concept of a being that cannot *not* be.

    b. The only way to reject this is to plead a special meaning to the word *possible*. (In the usual logical sense of the word *possible* there is no contradiction in the concept of a necessary Being.)

3. With a necessary Being an "at-least-possible" existence is indistinguishable from a "possible and actual" existence. A necessary Being cannot have a "merely possible" existence (if a necessary Being *can* be, then it *must* be), for

    a. God by definition is an independent Existence and hence cannot be produced by another as "merely possible" beings can be.

    b. God is everlasting and so he could not have come into being as "merely possible" beings can come into existence.

4. Therefore, a necessary Being necessarily has both a possible and an actual existence.

Hartshorne answers at least seven different objections to his ontological argument. The objection will be stated in the answer that he gives.

Reply 1: It is not possible that God's nonexistence was always logically possible even though he actually always existed. First, this is a special pleading on the meaning of the word *possible*. In all other cases, "possible" refers to beings whose nonexistence is both logically and actually possible. Why should God be made an exception by saying that his nonexistence is actually impossible but logically possible? Further, it is not even logically possible for God to be conceived as having come into being. Indeed, by the very conception of his nature he cannot be even logically conceived as having come into existence. For it is contradictory to even think of God as being producible. By his very definition God is a necessary Being and a being so defined cannot be merely possible.

Reply 2: One cannot prove a perfect island or a perfect devil on the same premises of the ontological argument. The perfect island is not indestructible as God is. If it is made indestructible, then it becomes identical with the cosmos as the body of God [Hartshorne's view of God is not theistic nor pantheistic. It is panentheistic—the material universe is viewed as the "body" of God. But there is a transcendent pole to God that is more than his cosmic "body"]. A perfect demon is unequivocal nonsense, for it would be both infinitely responsible and infinitely adverse to all that exists; both infinitely loving and infinitely hateful toward all that is; it would be both intimately united and savagely opposed to all that exists. But such contradictory attitudes are impossible.

Reply 3: The ontological argument proves more than the mere self-consistency of the idea of a necessary Being. For all meaning has an external referent that is either possible or actual. And God by definition cannot be merely a possible being. Therefore,

1. All meaning implicitly affirms God in reference to either
   a. what he has done (called his consequent nature—God's immanence) or
   b. what he can do (called his primordial nature—God's transcendence).
2. Without God as the universal ground of meaning there would be no meaning for universals (i.e., nothing can have objective meaning unless there is a realm that is objectively meaningful).
3. We can be confused as to whether specific things exist but not as to whether God—who is the content of existence itself—exists.
4. The only way to oppose the ontological argument is to make an absolute disjunction between meaning and reality. But this kind of disjunction is meaningless (meaning and reality must meet at some point; that point we call God).

Reply 4: If existence is not a predicate, then at least the *mode* of existence is implied in every predicate. That is, when a quality is predicated of something, it is implied that that something exists either contingently or necessarily. And a necessary Being (God) cannot exist contingently.

Reply 5: The ontological argument does not make God an exception to general philosophical principles. That essence implies existence in God is not an exception to philosophical principles but a result of a consistent application of philosophical principles to different kinds of beings. God's nature implies existence and no other nature does, because in God alone there is no distinction between the possible and the actual (God is the actualization of all that is possible for him to actualize). "To say a thing might not exist is not to say there might be a thing without existence. It is rather to say that there might be existence without the thing." Existence must necessarily be; this or that existence need not be.

Reply 6: Mere thought does not produce reality, but necessary thought does. There can be no absolute disjunction between thought and reality. Thinking is a real experience, and we do think of God as possible. Hartshorne concludes, therefore, that

1. All thoughts are experiences of what is at least possible.
2. We do have thoughts about a Being which must be (i.e., a necessary Being).

3. But a necessary Being cannot be merely a possible being.
4. Therefore, a necessary Being must be more than merely possible (i.e., it must be actual).

As Hartshorne put it, "We have only to exclude impossibility or meaninglessness to establish actuality." That is, "Either God is a meaningless term or there exists a divine being." Or, to restate the argument:

1. Either the existence of a necessary Being is
   a. less than an idea (i.e., contradictory and impossible),
   b. merely an idea but not a reality, or
   c. more than a mere idea (a reality).
2. It is not less than an idea, for it is a noncontradictory concept.
3. It is not merely an idea, for it is contradictory to speak of a necessary Being as merely possible (if a necessary Being exists at all, it must exist necessarily; there is no other way it can exist).
4. Therefore, the existence of a necessary Being is more than a mere idea; it is a reality.

Reply 7: The ontological argument is not merely hypothetical; it does not assume existence. The ontological argument is *not* saying this:

1. *If* there is a necessary Being, then it exists necessarily.
2. There is a necessary Being (thus begging the whole question).
3. Therefore, a necessary Being exists necessarily.

This criticism contains the self-contradictory assumption that "if a necessary Being happens to exist as a mere contingent fact, then it exists not as contingent fact but as necessary truth." This is not the meaning of the major premise. The argument, on the contrary, is not contradictory and should be stated like this:

1. If the phrase *necessary Being* has any meaning, then what it means must actually exist (outside of the mind).
2. The phrase *necessary Being* does have a meaning (it is not contradictory).
3. Therefore, a necessary Being actually exists (outside of the mind).

In brief, the "if" does not imply the possibility of nonexistence (for a necessary existence cannot possibly *not* exist). The "if" means rather the possibility of meaninglessness. And even the possibility of meaninglessness vanishes, for unless there is a basis for meaning (God) there can be no meaning at all.

Some observations are called for at this point. First, Hartshorne rests his case heavily on the ultimate identification of the logical and the ontological, a premise disputed by others. Second, he does not really exclude the possibility that others could show the term *God* to be meaningless. It may be that someone will yet demonstrate a contradiction in the very concept of a necessary Being. If they do, the ontological arguments fail. Further, the argument rests on the assumption that there must be an objective basis for meaning in order for there to be *any* meaning. This is precisely what existentialists like Jean-Paul Sartre and Albert Camus denied. They held to a subjective basis for meaning but did not deny all meaning. Their argument is that there is no meaning "out there" in the universe except the subjective meaning one puts there. Objective absurdity would still be an option unless one considers Hartshorne has given a disproof of objective absurdity.

This leads to our final observation. There is an implied premise in all of the ontological arguments that, if true, would seem to vindicate the argument in the face of its standard criticism (that it makes an illicit transition from the logical to the ontological, from thought to reality). The premise is this: *The rationally inescapable is the real.* If defensible,[15] this would prove objective absurdity to be wrong. Indeed, if the rationally inescapable is the real and it is rationally inescapable to think of God as necessarily existing, then it would seem to follow that it is really so that God necessarily exists. But before we assume that the ontological argument has won the day we must examine another statement of it and one final criticism.

Malcolm's Restatement of the Ontological Proof

Malcolm is credited with reviving the ontological argument in a more viable form, although Hartshorne's work on it said the same thing some twenty years earlier. Malcolm did occasion a popular revival of interest in the argument, at least in the area of analytic philosophy. The first form of Anselm's argument Malcolm considers invalidated by Kant's criticism (that existence is not a predicate); the second form Malcolm believes is immune from this (or any other) criticism of which he knows. Malcolm's restatement of Anselm's first argument may be put in this manner:[16]

1. God by definition is an absolutely perfect Being possessing all possible perfections.
2. Existence is a perfection (i.e., a possible predicate for God).
3. Therefore God must possess existence (i.e., existence must be predicated of God).

The minor premise was argued by Kant to be invalid, and accordingly Malcolm rejects this form of the ontological argument as being invalid. Anselm's

---

15. See the end of chapter 4 and Norman L. Geisler, "The Missing Premise in the Ontological Argument," *Religious Studies* 9, no. 3 (September 1973): 289–96.

16. Malcolm in *Ontological Argument*, pp. 137–59.

second argument is a different argument and is not subject to Kant's criticism. Its basic logic is this:

1. The existence of a necessary Being must be either
   a. a necessary existence (a "must-be" existence),
   b. an impossible existence (a "cannot-be" existence), or
   c. a possible existence (a "may-or-may-not-be" existence).
2. But the existence of a necessary Being is not an impossible existence.
   a. No one has ever shown the concept of a necessary Being to be contradictory.
   b. There is a basis in human experience for "a greater than which cannot be thought" (e.g., the feeling of guilt or the experience of grace "a greater than which cannot be felt").
   c. Leibniz's attempt to prove that there is no contradiction fails (there may be one). We cannot show that there cannot be one. We merely know that no one has shown that there is a contradiction. And the proof stands unless or until someone shows that there is a contradiction in the very concept of a necessary Being.
3. And the existence of a necessary Being cannot be merely a possible existence, for a merely possible but not necessary existence of a necessary Being
   a. Is contrary to the very nature of a necessary Being (A "must-be" Being cannot be a "may-or-may-not-be" kind of being).
   b. A possible being would be a dependent being, and this is contrary to a necessary Being which is an independent Being by nature.
4. Therefore, a necessary Being necessarily exists.

Malcolm's argument may be put in hypothetical form:

1. If it is possible for a necessary Being to exist, then it is necessary for it to exist (for the only way a necessary Being can exist is to exist necessarily).
2. It is possible that a necessary Being can exist (there is nothing contradictory about affirming the existence of a necessary Being).
3. Therefore, a necessary Being necessarily exists.

Or, to restate the heart of the argument in categorical form:

1. A necessary Being by definition is one which cannot *not* be.
2. That which cannot *not* be, must be (for this is the logical obverse).
3. Therefore, a necessary Being necessarily must be.

It would appear that the critical premise in the argument is the one affirming that the mere possibility of a necessary Being is contradictory. Let us state again the argument with Malcolm's fuller defense of this premise.

1. The existence of a necessary Being must be either
   a. a necessary existence,
   b. a mere possible existence, or
   c. an impossible existence.
2. But it cannot be an impossible existence (there is no contradiction).
3. Nor can it be a mere possible existence, for such an existence would be
   a. a dependent existence (and a dependent existence cannot at the same time be an independent existence such as a necessary existence is),
   b. a fortuitous existence (for if God just happened to be, then he could not be a necessary Being), and
   c. a temporal existence (for if God came to be, then he would be dependent, which is contrary to his independent or necessary Being).
4. Therefore, the existence of a necessary Being is a necessary existence (i.e., a necessary Being necessarily exists).

Several observations are called for at this point. Malcolm admits that there might be a contradiction in the concept of a necessary Being and that he knows of no way to prove that there is not a contradiction there. This admission means that his "proof" is not foolproof. It is logically possible that it is wrong. Hence, the conclusion is not rationally inescapable. Thus, even granting the validity of the rest of the argument, it is not a proof in the strongest sense of the word. Furthermore, there is reason to question the validity of the rest of the argument (in premise 3). This will emerge from Plantinga's evaluation of the argument.

Plantinga's Critique of the Ontological Argument

Plantinga assesses Malcolm's ontological argument in terms of the following logical schema:[17]

1. If God does not exist, his existence is logically impossible.
2. If God does exist, his existence is logically necessary.
3. Hence, either God's existence is logically impossible or else it is logically necessary.
4. If God's existence is logically impossible, the concept of God is contradictory.
5. The concept of God is not contradictory.
6. Therefore, God's existence is logically necessary.

Here Plantinga takes issue with premise 2. God could exist without his existence being logically necessary. God's existence could be logically contingent without being ontologically contingent. Or, to put it another way,

17. Plantinga, ibid., pp. 160–71.

Malcolm equivocates on the word *possible*. Malcolm assumes that because it is not "possible" ontologically for God to be contingent is it not "possible" logically for God to be contingent. In fact, there are two meanings to the word *possible* which Malcolm overlooks. It is logically "possible" that God is a necessary Being. But it is only logically possible that this is so and not logically necessary that this is so. Our own observation here is that Plantinga is right only if the implied premise in the ontological argument is wrong, namely, "The rationally inescapable is the real." For if what is rationally inescapable must be ontologically so, then Hartshorne and Malcolm seem to make a good case against this criticism. They argue that it is logically necessary to think of God as real, since it is logically contradictory to conceive of a necessary Being as not necessarily having being. This does not mean that the ontological argument is valid. There is one final and possibly fatal criticism of it.

Plantinga continues by saying it is also logically "possible" that God never existed at all. In fact, it is logically possible that nothing ever existed, including God. But this may be only an apparent omission in the ontological argument.

Perhaps the reason that this logical possibility does not present itself as evident to the proponents of the ontological argument is that they are assuming a cosmological premise. For it seems most readily apparent to anyone existing that something does exist (himself). And if something exists, it is not true that nothing exists. And if something exists, that makes false the statement that nothing exists. But if something does exist, it is not true to affirm that nothing exists. Hence, Plantinga's criticism, that the ontological argument is unsuccessful simply because it overlooks the obvious truth that nothing exists, fails.

All the proponents of the ontological argument have to do to invalidate Plantinga's criticism is to show that something exists. This is easily accomplished by insisting that no one can deny existence without existing to make the denial. For it is actually impossible to affirm that nothing exists, since there must be someone in existence to make that affirmation. In brief, the ontological arguments based merely on predicability and inconceivability are invalid, but a third argument based on undeniability appears to evade *these* invalidities. This seems so for the simple reason that the only apparent way to invalidate the second form of the ontological argument is on the conceivability (i.e., logical possibility) of the truth that nothing exists, but this truth is not affirmable because something does exist. Hence, it is undeniable that something exists and therefore God must necessarily exist. Therefore, it would seem that a third form of the ontological argument can successfully defend itself against Plantinga's criticism.

In this revised form, however, it is not really an ontological argument but a cosmological argument. For there is a difference, as Anselm recognized in his reply to Gaunilo, between the logical possibility that nothing, including God, ever existed and the actual affirmability of the statement "Nothing, including God, ever existed" by someone who does exist. Of course, it is undeniably true that something exists, but not because it is inconceivable or logically impossible that nothing exists. It is not logically contradictory to assume that there might never have been anything in existence. Nonbeing is a logical possibility. The only way one can invalidate the logical possibility that "nothing ever was, including God" is to affirm, "Something was or is." But once one affirms the premise "Something is" and argues from that to "God is," he has left the ontological argument for the cosmological argument. He has left the a priori realm of pure reason and entered into the a posteriori domain of existence. The so-called third argument from undeniability of existence is not an ontological argument but a cosmological argument. And it needs more elaboration and defense.

After spending years studying and critiquing the ontological argument, Plantinga has proposed a version of his own, which he considers to be valid. He has provided us with several formulations, one of which can be summarized in ten steps.[18]

1. *The property* has maximal greatness *entails the property* has maximal excellence in every possible world.

This first premise establishes the argument clearly within the framework of contemporary modal logic. A possible world is any logically conceivable world. In simple terms, any time that we can close our eyes and imagine our actual world to be different in some nonabsurd way, we are conceiving of a logically possible world. Obviously the actual world is a possible world. But there are also many other possible worlds (they "are" in the sense that they are logical possibilities, not that they are actual).

Plantinga asserts that something is maximally great only if it is the best (maximally excellent) in every possible world. If it were not, it could not really be the greatest, for one could conceive of a greater one that was maximally excellent in all worlds.

2. *Maximal excellence entails omniscience, omnipotence, and moral perfection.*

With this premise Plantinga accomplishes two goals. First he defines what one would mean by saying that something is the best. Second, he structures his argument in such a way that the being whose existence he intends to demonstrate will turn out to be God.

3. *Maximal greatness is possibly exemplified.*

There is nothing self-contradictory or logically odd about the notion of maximal greatness. Hence we can stipulate a possible world in which we can

---

18. Alvin Plantinga, *The Nature of Necessity* (Oxford: Clarendon, 1974), pp. 214–15. See also Plantinga, *God, Freedom, and Evil* (New York: Harper Torchbooks, 1974), pp. 111–12.

encounter this quality. This exemplification is elaborated in premise 4, which posits a world W*, an essence E*, and the property of maximal greatness.

4. *There is a world W* and an essence E* such that E* is exemplified in W* and E* entails has maximal greatness in W*.*

In this hypothetical world W* this hypothetical essence E* has the property of maximal greatness. Now we must remember that the statement of premise 1 and that which is true of an essence would have to be true of an object bearing that essence.

5. *For any object x, if x emeplifies E*, then x exemplifies the property* has maximal excellence in every possible world.

6. *E* entails the property* has maximal excellence in every possible world.

Plantinga argues that the same relationship that is necessarily true in W* would have to be necessarily true in any other possible world. Thus he can make such a general statement concerning this essence and the property that it would entail in any possible world.

7. *If W* had been actual, it would have been impossible that E* fail to be exemplified.*

This statement is a simple component of modal logic. If something holds for any possible world, it would certainly also hold if that possible world were the actual world. Thus if the possible world under consideration were actual, then this essence with maximal excellence in every possible world would have to be real. In fact, given the preceding premises, the denial of this reality would have to be an impossibility.

8. *What is impossible does not vary from world to world.*

The differences among possible worlds are factual ones. They do not involve logical absurdities. There is no logically possible world in which circles are square or logical deductions do not follow. Logical relationships are constant over all possible worlds. Thus logical necessity or impossibility is the same in every world.

Therefore what Plantinga has said about E* in W* would have to apply to E* in every other possible world. There also it would be impossible for E* not to be exemplified. Hence,

9. *There exists a being that has maximal excellence in every world.* But then it also follows that

10. *The being that has maximal excellence exists in the actual world.*

Thus, using modal logic, Plantinga has demonstrated that God (the being with omniscience, omnipotence, and moral perfection) exists.

This is a tight and compelling argument. It avoids many of the criticisms traditionally brought against the ontological argument. But it puts into clear focus the critique we have brought against the argument in this context. This approach based on modal logic stipulates from the outset that something exists. The concept of possible worlds makes sense only in contrast to an actual world. Only if we, at least for the sake of the argument, allow that there is a reality, can the argument unfold. Further, to define a maximally perfect being in theistic terms is gratuitous (premise 2). Why could not perfection be viewed in nonmoral, nonintelligent terms?

But finally, and even more to the point, the argument in premise 4 stipulates the reality of E^* as an essence. In Plantinga's philosophy essences are not just mental concepts or words flatus vocis, but they exist in a sense as real. Hence the argument is beginning to bear faint resemblance to Descartes's argument in which he stipulates the idea of a supreme Being and then attempts to give an account thereof.[19] But that argument has also been characterized as cosmological. And the same thing may be true for Plantinga's argument. Perhaps the reason it is valid is that it has left the realm of pure ontological arguments.

Our conclusion, then, is this: the ontological argument as such is invalid. The only possible way to make it valid (if it can be made valid at all) is to assume or affirm that something exists. And once one argues, "Something exists, therefore God exists," he has really argued cosmologically. The point here is that the ontological argument by itself, without borrowing the premise "Something exists," cannot possibly prove the existence of God. For it is always logically possible that nothing ever existed and hence it is not logically necessary to affirm that God exists.

Some have suggested that our conclusion is invalid because the very concept of "nothing" is negative, and thus presupposes that something exists. If this is correct, they contend, then our contention that "it is logically possible that nothing ever existed" is wrong. This objection, however, confuses the concept of nonbeing (which does presuppose the concept of being) and a state of nonbeing that does not presuppose a state of being. We are referring to the logical possibility of the state of nothingness, not to the concept of nothingness.

Several further important conclusions emerge from this analysis of the ontological argument. No valid ontological proof has been given that makes it rationally inescapable to conclude that there is a necessary Being. On the other hand, neither has anyone made a successful ontological disproof of God, making it logically impossible that there is a God. Necessary to a valid theistic argument is the premise that "something exists or existed." If one argues that "something exists, therefore God exists," he has left the purely a priori ontological approach and has moved into an a posteriori cosmological approach. If one could somehow validate a theistic argument by importing

---

19. René Descartes, *Meditations on First Philosophy* (Indianapolis: Hackett, n.d.), pp. 23–34.

the undeniable premise that "something exists" and arguing from this that "something necessarily exists," it is still a long way from this to the one simple and absolutely perfect Being of Christian theism. It is interesting to note in this regard that three different views of God have been concluded from the same kind of ontological argument, and others feel a fourth may be inferred. Descartes and Leibniz concluded a theistic God. Spinoza argued to a pantheistic God. Hartshorne ended with a panentheistic God. Henle insisted that at best, apart from importing some kind of Platonic premise, the onto-logical argument yields polytheistic gods.[20] Even many atheists are willing to recognize the universe is somehow necessary, but in no way identify it with God. Since the positions are mutually exclusive, it follows that they cannot all be true. In order to defend theism, one must apparently go beyond the onto-logical argument. For the ontological argument alone apparently does not designate which kind of God (or gods) is found at the conclusion.

20. See Paul Henle, "A Reply by Paul Henle," in *The Ontological Argument: From Saint Anselm to Contemporary Philosophers*, ed. Alvin Plantinga (Garden City, N.Y.: Doubleday, Anchor Books, 1965), pp. 171–80.

8 ✤

Cosmological Arguments

The hope for a theistic proof has been narrowed down to the cosmo-logical argument. For it was seen (in chap. 6) that both the teleological and the moral arguments depend for what validity they have on the principle of causality which is borrowed from the cosmological argument. Further, it has been shown (in chap. 7) that the only hope for defending an ontological argument is derived from transforming it into a cosmological type of argument starting with the fact that something exists. Hence, if the cosmological argument proves invalid, the theistic proofs fail. Of course, even without rational demonstrations, belief in the God of theism may be credible and plausible. But without proofs, the object of this belief is not philosophically demonstrable.

In this chapter we provide an overview of many different versions of the cosmological argument. Again we will highlight the interaction between statement, critique, and restatement of the historical experience of this argument.

There are probably as many cosmological-type arguments for the exis-tence of God as there are aspects of the finite world from which one can argue to its cause. Whatever seemed most obvious or basic to the viewer was taken as the beginning of a demonstration that concluded with some kind of God. Plato is credited with being the first thinker to have offered cosmological-type arguments (also called aetiological arguments [from *aetios*, cause]).

Plato's Argument for a World Soul

In the *Laws* and in the *Phaedrus* Plato reasons to a first mover of the world.[1] His reasoning takes the following shape:

1. Things move (this can be established by observation).
2. Whatever moves is either moved by another (i.e., is inert) or is self-moved (spontaneous).
3. Now self-movers (called souls) are prior to non-self-movers (things that do not move themselves but must be moved by another), for the ante-cedent is logically prior to the consequent.

1. References to Plato are taken from *The Collected Dialogues,* ed. Edith Hamilton and H. Cairns Huntington (New York: Pantheon, 1941). See *Laws* 894b–897c; *Phaedrus* 245c–e.

4. Self-movers must be eternal or else there would be no motion, but
   a. there is motion, and
   b. even if motion were not eternal, only a self-mover could arise from a state of rest and begin motion;
   c. so, in either case motion must originate with self-movers.
5. There must be at least two self-movers in the universe:
   a. one mover to account for the regular motion (called good), and
   b. another mover(s) to account for the irregular motion (called evil).
6. The mover that accounts for the regular motion is called the best soul, because it is the supreme mover in the universe, God.
7. Therefore, there is a supreme soul (God) who is the self-mover of the regular (good) motion of the universe.

Thus Plato offered a proof for what he called the World Soul, the First Mover of all regular (good) motion in the cosmos.

Plato also arrives at a Demiurgos or world Former (in the *Timaeus*) and the Good (in the *Republic*) by a cosmological type of reasoning process. Plato's thinking can be elaborated into the following arguments for God.[2]

1. The cosmos would be a chaos without forms (pure stuff without any structure is shapeless).
2. Chaos (formlessness) is evil and cosmos (form) is good (by definition).
3. All forms of good in the world come from a good Former beyond the world (chaos cannot form itself into a cosmos).
4. No Former can make good forms without a Form of Good after which to pattern them.
5. The Form after which the changing sensible world is formed must be an unchanging intelligible pattern.
   a. It must be unchanging or else it could not be the pattern for the changing.
   b. It must be intelligible or else it could not be the Ideal after which the world is shaped (Ideal or Ideas are intelligible things).
6. Therefore, there is both a Former of all good (Demiurgos) and the Form of good (the Good) after which all goods are formed.

For Plato, the ultimate Good was one, because there cannot be many bests; only one can be the Best or the absolute Good by which all other goods are measured and shaped. The essence of this argument will be more influential on later theism than Plato's argument for the World Soul. Several things should be noted here. First, the Demiurgos creates by efficient causality. He is a producing cause, not merely a purposing cause. Second, his creative activity is eternal. The Former is forming from eternity; the chaos (matter) was

2. Plato, *Timaeus*, 27ff.

always there. He did not, as the Hebrew-Christian God, first bring the matter into existence and then begin to form it.[3] Third, the Good does have a quasireligious function in Plato. It is the ultimate object of truth and meditation (see *Republic*, bk. 8). Fourth, properly speaking, however, the Good is not the creating God, nor is it the personal God of Hebrew-Christian belief.

Aristotle's Unmoved Mover(s)

Plato's most famous student, Aristotle, gave further sophistication to his teacher's argument for God. In its strongest form Aristotle's cosmological argument unfolds like this:[4]

1. Things do change (this is established by observing movement, which is the most obvious form of change).
2. All change is a passing from potentiality to actuality (i.e., when a capacity is actualized, change has occurred).
3. No potentiality can actualize itself (e.g., wood cannot make itself into a chair, although it has the capacity to be made into a chair).
4. Therefore, there must be an actuality that actualizes everything that passes from potentiality to actuality (otherwise nothing would ever be actualized).
5. An infinite regress of actualizers is impossible (for the whole series would not be actualized unless there is a first actualizer).
6. This first actuality actualizes things by final causality (by drawing things to it the way a lover is drawn by his loved one).
7. There are either forty-seven (according to the astronomer Eudoxus) or fifty-five (according to Callipus) of these pure actualities (unmoved movers).
8. Ultimately, there is only one heaven and one God (for only material things can be numerically different, since matter is the principle of individuation).[5]

Several things are noteworthy about Aristotle's argument:

It introduces the question of an infinite regress of causes.
It is still struggling with a plurality of first causes.

---

3. See A. E. Taylor, *Plato: The Man and His Works* (New York: World, 1956), pp. 443–44.
4. Aristotle, *Metaphysics* 12.8.
5. Werner Yaeger believes that this passage is a later alteration by Aristotle of his own earlier plurality of gods. See *Aristotle: Fundamentals of the History of His Development,* trans. R. Robinson, 2d ed. (Oxford: Clarendon, 1934), p. 353. Plotinus later criticized Aristotle's many unmoved movers; see *Six Enneads* (Chicago: Encyclopaedia Britannica Press, 1952), 6.5.9; 5.1.9.

Unlike Plato's Demiurgos, Aristotle's First Cause is a final (purposing) cause. Neither is it the same as the efficient or producing cause (of later Christian thinkers) that brought the very cosmos into existence.

The Unmoved Mover of Aristotle was not a personal God and had no religious significance (i.e., it was not worshiped).

Aristotle's First Cause was not infinite. Only what is formless or indefinite was considered infinite to the Greeks. Aristotle's First Cause was Pure Form or Actuality. To be formless or infinite was a metaphysical insult in the context of Greek philosophy.

Neither Plato's World Soul, Demiurgos, nor Aristotle's Unmoved Mover is identical with the absolutely perfect Being of Christian theism. It will take further combination and development of these cosmological arguments of the Greeks before we arrive at the God of Christian theism.

Some of this development was accomplished by the non-Christian fountainhead of neo-Platonism, Plotinus (third century A.D.). God for Plotinus was an ineffable One who could be arrived at ultimately only by mystical meditation and not by rational demonstration. However, Plotinus's view of God did have several important influences on later theism. Plotinus identified Plato's Good as the one supreme God. This one absolutely perfect God is the source or efficient cause of all being. And this God is the object of religious worship and meditation; he does have clear religious significance. We may summarize Plotinus's thinking as follows:[6]

1. Many beings exist (this is known through both sensible and intellectual knowledge).
2. All multiplicity is based on prior unity (because multiplicity is made up of little unities [3.8.9]).
3. Ultimately, there must be an absolute unity that is the basis of all multiplicity (this follows logically from 2 [5.4.1]).
4. This absolute unity cannot be a being, because
   a. It is the source of all being, and the source of being does not need being (6.8.19).
   b. It produces being in others, and it cannot possess what it produces (6.7.15).
   c. All being involves multiplicity, and it has no multiplicity (6.2.2).
5. Therefore, there is an absolute unity (the One) beyond being which is the source of all being and multiplicity (6.8.18).

The God of Plotinus was not the God of Christian theism in several respects. First, Plotinus's God created the world ex deo (out of himself) by a necessary and emanational unfolding and not ex nihilo (out of nothing).

6. See Plotinus, ibid., for references cited.

Second, the Plotinian God was beyond all being and positive description. Finally, it possessed no perfections or characteristics in itself but had to unfold like a seed in order even to become conscious or knowing and to achieve all possible perfections which it lacked in its absolute simplicity.

Augustine's Argument from Truth

In view of the way various Greek approaches to God culminated in Plotinus, it is not difficult to see why the Platonic tradition was much more influential on Christian theism than was Aristotle. With some minor changes Augustine could use the essential elements of Platonism and expound his own Christian theism. In the exposition of his own view of God, Augustine (354–430) offered an argument for God that can be put in an a posteriori form:[7]

1. There are timeless and immutable truths.
   a. Absolute doubt is impossible (we know we are doubting).
   b. We know that we exist, that we think, and that $7 + 3 = 10$.
2. Immutable truth cannot be caused
   a. by sensible things (for the unchanging and independent cannot be caused by the changing and dependent).
   b. by finite minds (for it is independent of our minds and our minds are ruled by it).
3. Therefore, there must be a timeless and immutable Mind causing these immutable truths.

Or, to put Augustine's argument another way:

1. There are immutable truths common to all human beings (such as math, existence, and thought).
2. There must be a cause for these truths.
3. This cause must be either equal to, inferior to, or superior to our minds.
4. This cause cannot be equal to our minds, since these truths are independent of our minds and our minds are subject to them (truth does not advance with our minds but remains stable).
5. These truths cannot be inferior to our minds, since our minds are subject to them.
6. Therefore, these truths must be superior to our mutable minds.
7. Whatever is superior to the mutable is immutable.
8. Therefore, there is an immutable Mind, which is the source of these immutable truths.

The objectivity of truth is confirmed for Augustine by the fact that different people see the same truth, even though they cannot cause this truth either in

7. Augustine, *On Free Will* 2.1–15.

their own minds or in other minds. God is the inner Master who causes truth in every person's mind. Hence, whenever any person affirms truth, he is thereby (implicitly) affirming the Truth (God).

Anselm's Three Cosmological-Type Arguments

The next great Christian philosopher after Augustine was Anselm (1033–1119). Although he is most famous for his ontological argument (in the *Proslogion*), in an earlier work (the *Monologion*) Anselm offered three a posteriori proofs for God's existence. Anselm's first argument is from goodness:[8]

1. Good things exist.
2. Their goodness is derived either from many different goodnesses or from one goodness.
3. It cannot be derived from many different goodnesses, for then there would be no way to compare goodnesses and all things would be equally and unequally good (which is absurd), but as a matter of fact some things are better than others.
4. Therefore, all things derive their goodness through one good.
5. This one good is the supreme Good, since
    a. It is the good through which all other goods derive their goodness.
    b. It is good through itself alone.

The second argument is from perfection:

1. Some beings are more nearly perfect than others.
2. Things cannot be more nearly perfect unless there is a wholly perfect (by which they can be compared and judged to be more or less nearly perfect than it).
3. Therefore, there must be a most perfect Being.

The third argument, an argument from being, is the most obviously cosmological in type:

1. Something exists (the denial of this is contradictory).
2. Whatever exists, exists either through something or through nothing.
3. Something cannot exist through nothing (only nothing exists through nothing).
4. This something through which something exists is either one or many.
5. If many, then they are either mutually dependent or all dependent on one for their existence.

8. Anselm, *Monologion* 1–3.

6. They cannot be mutually dependent for their existence, for something cannot exist through a being on which it confers existence.
7. Therefore, there must be one being through which all other beings exist.
8. This one being must exist through itself (since everything else exists through it).
9. Whatever exists through itself, exists in the highest degree of all.
10. Therefore, there exists a supremely perfect Being that exists in the highest degree of all.

Several observations are pertinent here. These arguments show clearly how Christian theists transformed premises from Greek philosophy. The arguments, unlike Plato's but like Plotinus's, identify the Creator with the supreme Good. Yet, unlike Aristotle's, the arguments view God as the efficient (not final) Cause of the world. And unlike the arguments of both Plato and Aristotle, Anselm's arguments hold that this efficient Cause does not merely operate on the world of matter which is eternally there, but is the cause for the very being of everything, including matter. In brief, these Christian theistic arguments combined at least three elements: the efficient causality from Plato's *Timaeus* argument; the identification of this God with the Good of Plato's *Republic* as the supremely perfect Being; and the Hebrew-Christian concept of God as the cause of the very being (not merely the forms of being) of everything that exists.

Alfarabi's Necessary Existence Argument

The Arabian and Jewish philosophers of the Middle Ages influenced later Christian forms of the cosmological argument. The Muslim thinker Alfarabi provided the heart of later scholastic arguments by his distinction between essence and existence. Aristotle had made a logical distinction between what a thing is and that it is. But Alfarabi took this as a sign of the real distinction between a creature's essence and its existence. Implied in this real distinction is an argument for God's existence that takes this form:[9]

1. There exist things whose essence is distinct from their existence (called possible beings; that is, they can be conceived as not existing even though they do exist).
2. These beings have existence only accidentally (i.e., it is not part of their very essence to exist. It is logically possible that they might not have existed).

9. See Armand A. Maurer, *A History of Medieval Philosophy* (New York: Random, 1962), pp. 95–97.

3. Anything that has existence accidentally (and not essentially) must have received its existence from another (since existence is not essential to it, there must be some explanation as to why it has existence).
4. There cannot be an infinite regress of causes of existence (for since the existence of all possible beings is received from another, there must ultimately be a cause from which existence is received).
5. Therefore, there must be a First Cause of existence whose essence and existence are identical (i.e., who is a necessary Being and not a mere possible being), for the First Cause cannot be a mere possible being (whose essence is not to exist), since all possible beings do not explain their own existence.

In summary, if there are beings whose essence is not to exist, then there must be a Being whose essence is to exist. For the possible beings are not possible unless there is a necessary Being. There cannot be beings whose existence is received unless there is some Being from whom this existence is received. And since a being cannot give existence to another when it is dependent for its own existence on another, there must be a first Being whose existence was not given to it by another but who gives existence to all others.

Avicenna's First Cause Argument

Following Alfarabi, Avicenna formulated a similar cosmological argument that was emulated in many forms by later scholastics. Avicenna's proof is this:

1. There are possible beings (i.e., things which come into existence because they are caused to exist but would not otherwise exist on their own).
2. Whatever possible beings that do exist have a cause for their being (since they do not explain their own existence).
3. But there cannot be an infinite series of causes of being.
   a. There can be an infinite series of causes of becoming (father begets son, who begets son).
   b. But there cannot be an infinite series of causes of being, since the cause of being must be simultaneous with its effect (unless there was a causal basis for the series, there would be no beings there to be caused).
4. Therefore, there must be a first Cause for all possible beings (i.e., for all beings that come into existence).
5. This first Cause must be a necessary Being. For that which is the cause of all possible beings cannot itself be a possible being. It must be a necessary Being.

By borrowing some neo-Platonic premises and a ten-sphere cosmology, Avicenna extends his argument to prove that this necessary first Cause created a whole series of Intelligences and ten cosmic spheres controlled by them.

6. Whatever is essentially One can create immediately only one effect (called Intelligence).
7. Thinking is creating and God necessarily thinks, since he is a necessary Being.
8. Therefore, there is a necessary emanation from God of ten Intelligences (Angels) that control the various spheres of the universe and the last of which (called Agent Intellect) forms the four elements of the cosmos and by which the human mind (possible intellect) is informed of all truth.

Avicenna's God, then, was a necessary Being from whom a serial creative force of ten gods followed with absolute necessity. Unlike the Christian God who freely created and who is directly responsible for the existence of everything else that exists, Avicenna's chain of Gods is necessary and these Gods create all below them.

The famed Jewish philosopher Moses Maimonides (1135–1204) anticipated several later Christian formulations of cosmological-type arguments. He argued for a First Mover, a First Cause, and a necessary Being (like Aquinas's first three arguments) with which these arguments conclude. He insisted that the "I AM" of the Old Testament (Exod. 3:14) meant "absolute existence" and that God alone has existence absolutely and necessarily. All creatures have existence only as an "accident" superadded to their essence by their Cause.

Thomas Aquinas: Five Ways to Prove God's Existence

It can be seen that when Aquinas (thirteenth century) formulated his famous "Five Ways," he was not creating arguments that were substantially new in form. Maimonides before him had the first three arguments. Alfarabi and Avicenna had the first two proofs. Anselm had an argument for perfection similar to the fourth argument. And Aquinas's fifth proof was more of a teleological argument which men like Thierry of Chartes and William of Conches had adapted from Plato's *Timaeus* argument. Aquinas does, of course, state the arguments out of the context of his own philosophy, which is more Aristotelian than that of most of his Christian predecessors. The first four arguments of Aquinas may be summarized as follows:

1. The argument from *motion:*[10]
   a. Things do move (motion is the most obvious form of change).

10. Thomas Aquinas, *Summa Theologica* 1.2.3.

b. Change is a passing from potency to act (i.e., from potentiality to actuality).

c. Nothing passes from potency to act except by something that is in act (for it is impossible for a potentiality to actualize itself).

d. There cannot be an infinite regress of actualizers or movers (if there is no first mover, there can be no subsequent motion, since all subsequent motion depends on prior movers for its motion).

e. Therefore, there must be a first unmoved mover (a pure Act or Actualizer with no potentiality in it that is unactualized).

f. Everyone understands this to be God.

2. The argument from *efficient causality:*

a. There are efficient causes in the world (i.e., producing causes).

b. Nothing can be the efficient cause of itself (for it would have to be prior to itself in order to cause itself).

c. There cannot be an infinite regress of (essentially related) efficient causes, for unless there is a first cause of the series there would be no causality in the series.

d. Therefore, there must be a first uncaused efficient Cause of all efficient causality in the world.

e. Everyone gives to this the name of God.

3. The argument from *possibility and necessity:*

a. There are beings that begin to exist and cease to exist (i.e., possible beings).

b. But not all beings can be possible beings, because what comes to exist does so only through what already exists (nothing cannot cause something).

c. Therefore, there must be a Being whose existence is necessary (i.e., one that never came into being and will never cease to be).

d. There cannot be an infinite regress of necessary beings each of which has its necessity dependent on another because

1) An infinite regress of dependent causes is impossible (see argument 2).

2) A necessary Being cannot be a dependent being.

e. Therefore, there must be a first Being that is necessary in itself (and not dependent on another for its existence).

4. The argument from *gradation* (perfection) in things:

a. There are different degrees of perfections among beings (some are more nearly perfect than others).

b. But things cannot be more or less perfect unless there is a wholly perfect.

c. Whatever is perfect is the cause of the less-than-perfect (the higher is the cause of the lower).

    d. Therefore, there must be a perfect Being that is causing the perfections of the less-than-perfect beings.

    e. This we call God.

There seems to be a basic form behind all of these arguments with only a different starting point. Each argument begins in some characteristic of being (change, causality, contingency, and perfection respectively) and then argues to a first Cause:

1. Some dependent beings exist.
2. All dependent beings must have a cause for their dependent existence.
3. An infinite regress of existentially dependent causes is impossible.
4. Therefore, there must be a first uncaused Cause of the existence of every dependent being.
5. This independent Being is identical with the I AM of Holy Scripture (the implication is that it is impossible to have more than one absolutely necessary and independent being upon which everything else exists for its being).

Duns Scotus: Argument from Producibility

John Duns Scotus modified the cosmological argument of Aquinas in two important ways. First, he began with the *producibility* of being, not merely from produced beings. Second, he amplified the argument against an infinite regress of dependent causes. The full form of Scotus's proof is as follows:[11]

1. Some being is produced (i.e., some beings come into being).
    a. This is learned through experience (by observing beings produced), but
    b. This is true independent of experience (i.e., it would be true of beings that do not exist).
    c. It would be true even if God had not willed to create anything.
2. What is produced is producible either by itself, by nothing, or by something else.
3. But no being can produce itself (in order to cause its own existence it would have to exist prior to its own existence, and that is impossible).
4. Neither can something be caused by nothing (this is contradictory, too).
5. Therefore, being is producible only by some being that is productive (only beings can produce beings).
6. There cannot be an infinite regress of productive beings, each producing the being of the one following it, because

11. John Duns Scotus, *Philosophical Writings,* trans. Allan B. Wolter (Indianapolis: Liberal Arts, Bobbs-Merrill, 1962), pp. 39–56.

   a. This is an essentially related series of causes, not an accidentally related one,

     1) where the primary cause is more nearly perfect than the secondary one,

     2) where the secondary cause depends on the primary one for its very causality, and

     3) where the cause must be simultaneously present to the effect.

   b. An infinite series of essentially related causes is impossible, because

     1) If the whole series is dependent for its causality (every cause depending on a prior cause), then there must be something beyond the series that accounts for the causality in the series.

     2) If the infinite series were causing the effect, then there would have to be an infinite number of causes simultaneously causing a single effect, and this is impossible (there cannot be an actual infinite number in a series, for it is always possible to add one more to any number).

     3) Wherever there are prior causes there must be a prime (first) cause (one cause would not be nearer the beginning unless there is a beginning to which it is nearer).

     4) Higher causes are more nearly perfect than lower causes, and this implies a perfect Cause at the head of all of the other less-than-perfect causes.

     5) An infinite regress of causes implies imperfection (since each cause lacks the ability to explain the succeeding causes). But an imperfect series implies something perfect beyond the series as a ground for the imperfect.

7. Therefore, there must be a first productive Cause of all producible beings.

8. This first Cause of all producible beings must be one, because

   a. It is perfect in knowledge and there cannot be two beings that know everything perfectly (e.g., one would know itself more completely than the other knew it).

   b. It is perfect in will; hence, it loves itself more completely than anything else (which means that the other infinite would be loved less than perfectly).

   c. It is infinitely good and there cannot be two such, for then there would be more than an infinite good, and this is impossible since there cannot be more than the most.

   d. It is infinite in power. If there were two with infinite power, this would mean that there would be two total primary causes of the same effect, and this is impossible, since there cannot be two causes each doing all the causing.

e. Absolutely infinite cannot be excelled in perfection, since there cannot be a more perfect than the wholly Perfect.

f. There cannot be two necessary beings, for to differ, one would have to have some perfection the other lacked (if there is no real difference, they do not really differ). But whatever a necessary Being has, it must have necessarily. Hence, the one lacking what the other had necessarily would not be a necessary Being.

g. Omnipotent will cannot be in two beings, for then one could render impotent what the other wills omnipotently; even if they agreed not to hinder each other, they would still be incompatible, for each would be the total primary (and direct) cause of any given thing which they agreed should exist. But an omnipotent Cause must be total primary (and direct) Cause of what it wills (the cause agreeing to but not directly willing the effect would be only the indirect cause and hence not the direct [omnipotent] Cause of the effect).

Ockham's Reservations About the Cosmological Argument

Objections to the cosmological argument did not await the skepticism of David Hume and Immanuel Kant. William of Ockham (1290–1350) raised at least three questions that are crucial to the cosmological argument.[12] First, he denied that an essentially related infinite series of causes was impossible. He argued that it is possible that essentially related causes (such as father begetting son) need not be simultaneous causes. They could be originating causes and not conserving causes. The father is not the continued cause of the son's existence. Only if this simultaneity of the here-and-now conserving cause is added to the concept of an essentially related series of causes, argued Ockham, does it make an infinite regress impossible. For it is contradictory to affirm that there is no first Cause right now for what is right now being conserved in existence. Hence, the cosmological argument is valid only if referred to what presently exists, not for any original creation.

Further, Ockham based his knowledge of efficient causes on experience. Causality is defined as "that whose existence or presence is followed by something."[13] The distinction anticipates Hume's criticism that there is no basis in experience for making a necessary connection between cause and effect. But the inescapability of the conclusion of the cosmological argument depends on the necessity of the connection between cause and effect. Hence, Ockham has already placed his razor on the central cord of the cosmological argument.

12. William Ockham, *Philosophical Writings,* trans. Philotheus Boehner (Indianapolis: Liberal Arts, Bobbs-Merrill, 1964), pp. 129ff.
13. Quoted by Maurer, *Medieval Philosophy,* p. 270.

Finally, he held that one could not prove that there was only one God in the absolute sense of the word. Only if the unity of God is taken to mean the "most perfect" Being that actually exists can it be said that the unity of God has been proven. If, however, as Christian theists insist, the unity of God refers to the "most perfect" Being possible, then the unity of God cannot be proven in this sense, because the proposition "God exists" is not a self-evident proposition (since many doubt it and a self-evident proposition cannot be doubted), nor is the absolute unity of God known through other propositions that can also be doubted, nor is it known by experience, for experience can provide one only with the actual, not with the possible. Therefore, there is no way to demonstrate that God is absolutely one.

Descartes's A Posteriori Proof for God

Like Anselm before him and Gottfried Wilhelm Leibniz after him, René Descartes had an a posteriori theistic argument. It did not begin, however, in the certainty of sensations about the external world. It began rather with one's own mental uncertainty and doubt. Briefly stated, Descartes's proof runs as follows:[14]

1. I am doubting (and the more I doubt, the more I am sure I am doubting).
2. If I am doubting, I am thinking (for doubting is a form of thinking).
3. But doubt is an imperfect form of thinking (it lacks certitude).
4. But if I know the imperfect, then I must be aware of the perfect (since one cannot judge something as *im*-perfect [i.e., *not* perfect]) unless he knows the perfect which it is not.
5. But my imperfect mind cannot be the cause of the idea of perfection that I have (and by which I judge things to be imperfect).
6. Only a perfect Mind is an adequate cause for the idea of perfection.
7. Therefore, a perfect Mind must exist as the cause of this perfect idea.

Descartes's argument is akin to Augustine's in that both are based in what they consider to be an unquestionable truth. Then they move from there to the ultimate Truth that is the cause of this truth. The movement is a posteriori (from effect to cause); the argument is based not in finite existence, as is the usual form of the cosmological argument, but in finite thought. In this respect the arguments of Augustine and Descartes fall more in the Platonic tradition with distinct affinities to the ontological argument.

14. René Descartes, *Meditations*, trans. L. J. Lafleur (New York: Liberal Arts, Bobbs-Merrill, 1951), 3.

Leibniz: The Argument from Sufficient Reason

The most influential form of the cosmological argument in modern times arose from Gottfried Wilhelm Leibniz (1646–1716), the German rationalist. The proof is stated this way by its author:[15]

1. The entire (observed) world is changing.
2. Whatever is changing lacks within itself the reason for its own existence.
3. There is a sufficient reason for everything either in itself or else beyond itself.
4. Therefore, there must be a cause beyond this world for its existence.
5. This cause is either its own sufficient reason or else it has a cause beyond it.
6. There cannot be an infinite regress of sufficient reasons (for the failure to reach an explanation is not an explanation; but there must be an explanation).
7. Therefore, there must be a first Cause of the world that has no reason beyond it but is its own sufficient reason (i.e., the sufficient reason is in itself and not beyond itself).

Under the influence of Leibniz's disciple, Christian Wolff (1679–1754), this proof became the pattern for cosmological argument in the modern world. Wolff stated the argument in a slightly different manner:[16]

1. The human soul exists (i.e., we exist).
2. Nothing exists without a sufficient reason why it exists rather than does not exist.
3. The reason for our existence must be contained either in ourselves or else in another diverse from ourselves.
4. The reason for our existence is not in ourselves (our nonexistence is possible or conceivable).
5. So the reason for our existence must be outside of ourselves.
6. One does not arrive at a sufficient reason for his existence until he reaches a being that has within itself the reason for its own existence (if it did not, then there must be a sufficient reason for its existence beyond itself).
7. A being that has within itself the reason for its own existence is a necessary being.
8. Therefore, there must be a necessary Being beyond us that is the sufficient reason for our existence (if there is not a necessary Being

15. Gottfried Leibniz, *Monadology and Other Philosophical Essays,* trans. Paul Schreker and Anne Schreker (Indianapolis: Liberal Arts, Bobbs-Merrill, 1965), pp. 32–39.

16. See James Collins, *God in Modern Philosophy* (Chicago: Regnery, 1959), pp. 137–38.

beyond us, we would be necessary beings, having the reason for our own existence in ourselves).

9. It is logically impossible for a necessary Being not to exist (self-existence or aseity flows necessarily from the nature of a necessary Being).

10. Hence, this necessary Being is identical with the self-existent God of Scripture.

Before we turn to the criticism and reformulations of the cosmological argument, a few remarks are pertinent to the Leibniz-Wolffian formulation of the cosmological argument. It rests heavily on the principle of sufficient reason, which is usually defended as a self-evidently true analytic principle. The argument is a posteriori in form but not existential. It begins with the existence of something but then proceeds toward its conclusion with logical certainty drawn from the very nature of the concept of the necessary Being. In brief, the alleged necessity of the conclusion is based on a conceptual certainty, not an actual (existential) certainty. This is precisely the point at which the modern criticism of the cosmological argument begins. Even scholastic philosophers were highly influenced by this kind of reasoning.[17] And their reformulation of Aquinas's cosmological argument is subject to the same criticism.

Hume's Skeptical Criticisms of the Cosmological Argument

The Scottish skeptic, David Hume (1711–1776), laid down most of the fundamental criticisms of the cosmological argument to be repeated and elaborated by others. At least eight such objections are offered by Hume.[18]

1. *Only a finite cause need be inferred from finite effects.* The cause need only be adequate to the effect. And since the effect (the world) is finite, one need only posit a cause adequate enough to explain that effect. Hence, the best one could conclude from the cosmological argument is a finite God.

2. *No propositions about existence can be logically necessary.* The opposite of any proposition about experience is always logically possible. But if it is logically possible that anything known by experience could have been otherwise, then it is not rationally inescapable that it be the way it is. It follows that nothing based in experience is logically demonstrable.

3. *The words* necessary Being *have no consistent meaning.* It is always possible to conceive of anything, including God, as not existing. And whatever might not exist does not need to exist. That is, if its nonexistence is

17. See John E. Gurr, *The Principle of Sufficient Reason in Some Scholastic Systems, 1750–1900* (Milwaukee: Marquette University Press, 1959).

18. See David Hume, *Dialogues Concerning Natural Religion,* ed. Norman Kemp Smith (Indianapolis: Bobbs-Merrill, 1955).

possible, its existence is not necessary. Hence, it makes no sense to speak of something as a logically necessary Being.

4. *If "necessary Being" means only "imperishable," then the universe may be the necessary Being.* If the universe cannot be a necessary being in the sense of being imperishable, then neither can God be imperishable. Hence, either the universe is a necessary being or else God is not imperishable.

5. *An infinite series is possible.* An eternal series cannot have a cause because cause implies priority in time. But nothing can be prior in time to an eternal series. Therefore, an eternal series is possible.

6. *There is no way to establish the principle of causality.* Experience does not provide us with the necessary connections needed to establish the cause/effect relationship. Events are conjoined but never connected. Only after constant (habitual) conjoining does the mind assume that there is a cause/effect relationship. Hence, causality is built on custom. We know B occurs after A but not because of A. The sun rises after the rooster crows but not because the rooster crows. The cosmological argument is built on a post hoc fallacy.

7. *The universe as a whole does not need a cause; only the parts do.* The world as a whole does not call for a cause; only parts need causes. The whole is the explanation of the parts. The principle of sufficient reason applies only to parts within the universe but not to the universe as a whole. The parts are contingent and the whole is necessary. And the whole universe may be necessary in only a mathematically accidental sense, such as the products of 9 always use 9 (e.g., $9 \times 41 = 369$ and $3 + 6 + 9 = 18$ or 2×9).

8. *Theistic arguments convince only those who like abstract reasoning.* Only those with a "metaphysical head" are convinced by theistic arguments. Most men are too practical to be swept away with such abstract reasoning. Even the arguments that begin in experience soon fly into the thin air of pure and unconvincing speculation.

Kant's Agnosticism on Theistic Argumentation

The skeptical artillery of Hume was followed by the agnostic cannons of Kant. Their combined attack on theistic proofs is considered definitive by much of modern thought since their time. There are at least seven criticisms of the cosmological argument in Kant's writings (some of which parallel and overlap Hume's).[19]

1. *The cosmological argument depends on the invalid ontological argument.* In order to arrive at a logically necessary conclusion, the cosmological argument leaves the realm of experience with which it begins and borrows the

---

19. See Immanuel Kant. *The Critique of Pure Reason,* trans. Lewis W. Beck (New York: Bobbs-Merrill, 1956), pp. 507ff.

concept of a necessary Being. Without this ontological leap from the a posteriori to the a priori, the cosmological argument cannot complete its task.
The leap is necessary but invalid. There is no way to show that it is logically
necessary to conclude a necessary Being (one which logically cannot *not* be)
unless one leaves experience and enters the purely conceptual realm.

2. *Existential statements are not necessary.* The conclusion of the cosmological argument purports to be an existentially necessary statement. But
necessity is a characteristic of thought, not of being. Only statements are
necessary, not things or beings. The only necessity that there is resides in the
logical but not in the ontological realm.

3. *A noumenal (real) cause cannot be derived from a phenomenal effect.*
The cosmological argument illicitly assumes that one can move from an effect
in the realm of appearance (the phenomenal) to a cause in the realm of reality
(the noumenal). The thing-to-me is not the thing-in-itself. One does not know
what reality is (only that it is). Causality is merely a category of the mind that
is super-imposed on reality but is not constitutive of reality. Whatever necessity the causal connection has is made by the mind but is not found in reality.

4. *What is logically necessary is not ontologically necessary.* Flowing
from the former criticism is the implied objection that the rationally inescapable is not necessarily the real. It might be necessary to think of something as
being so when in actuality it is not so. Hence, even a logically necessary Being
would not necessarily exist.

5. *The cosmological argument leads to metaphysical contradictions.* If
one assumes that categories of thought do apply to reality and proceeds with
cosmological argumentation, then he eventuates in contradictions such as
this: there is both a first cause and there cannot be a first (both of which are
logically demanded by the principle of sufficient reason).

6. *The concept of a "necessary Being" is not self-clarifying.* It is not clear
what the meaning of "necessary Being" actually is. The concept does not
clarify itself. Without conditions no concept of necessity is possible. But
necessary Being is conceived of as having no conditions for its existence
whatsoever. Hence, the only way it could be meaningful is eliminated by its
very definition in the theistic argument.

7. *An infinite regress is logically possible.* There is no contradiction in the
concept of an infinite regress of causes. Indeed the principle of sufficient
reason demands it. For it says that everything must have a reason. If this is so,
there is no reason to stop asking for a reason when we arrive at any given
cause in the series. In fact, reason demands that we keep on asking for a
reason, ad infinitum. (Of course, reason also demands that we find a first
reason that grounds all the other reasons. But this is precisely the contradiction one gets into when he applies reason beyond the senses to reality.) So far
as logical possibility is concerned, an infinite regress is possible.

There are other objections to cosmological arguments. Some apply to some forms and some to other forms. The objections that are applicable to the final form suggested in the next chapters will be taken up at that time.

Taylor's Restatement of the Cosmological Argument

Richard Taylor occasioned renewed interest in the cosmological argument by a restatement that evades many of the traditional objections leveled at the argument. In summary form, Taylor's restatement takes this shape:[20]

1. The universe as a whole does not explain its own existence.
   a. No observable part explains its own existence.
   b. Nor does the whole explain its existence (its nonexistence is conceivable).
   c. Answering *where, how long, what,* or *how large* does not answer *why* the whole world exists when it need not exist (e.g., a large ball found in the forest needs an explanation as to *why* it exists; expanding the ball to the size of the whole universe does not eliminate the need for an explanation).
2. Whatever does not explain its own existence calls for an explanation beyond itself.
   a. It is logically possible that the principle of sufficient reason is not true (it is not analytically true; it can be denied without contradiction).
   b. But it is implausible and unreasonable to deny its truth as applied to the world, because
      1) the nonexistence of the world is conceivable (whether it includes only one grain of sand or all the stars) and
      2) we assume the principle of sufficient reason in all our thought.
3. An infinite regress of reasons is impossible (for it is failure to give a sufficient reason; it just indefinitely avoids giving the reason that is demanded by the world's existence).
4. Therefore, there must be a first self-sufficient (independent) cause of the whole universe.

Taylor adds that it is no less meaningful to speak of God as an independent or necessary Being than it is to speak of square circles as not existing. If it is meaningful to speak of beings that are impossible, then it is also meaningful to speak of a Being that is necessary. A concept of a Being that cannot *not* exist is just as meaningful as a concept of one that *can not* exist (i.e., one that can be nonexistent).

20. See Richard Taylor, "Metaphysics and God," in *The Cosmological Argument*, pp. 279–95.

A few comments are in order on the state of the cosmological argument in the light of Taylor's revision. First, it does not provide a rationally inescapable conclusion. Taylor admits that it is logically possible that the principle of sufficient reason is not true. Second, Taylor's argument does appear to lend plausibility to a cosmological type of argument, since it shows how it is meaningful to ask for a cause of the whole world; it shows how the concept of a necessary Being is meaningful; it argues forcefully against an infinite regress; the argument is grounded in the need for an existence-explanation for the world, not in some alleged conceptual or logical necessity arising out of thought (as in the ontological argument). Third, despite these positive factors for theism, Taylor's argument is subject to the criticisms of the rationalistic Leibniz-Wolffian tradition of placing the success of the cosmological argument in the hands of the principle of sufficient reason, rather than basing it squarely on the principle of existential causality. The hope of evading the most significant criticisms of the cosmological argument is best found in the fact that the world demands a real cause and not merely an explanation or reason. This cannot be accomplished by confusing and/or equating a ground for the actual here-and-now "be-ing" of the world with an explanation of the inconceivability of its nonexistence. Conceptual problems call for only conceptual solutions. Real dependent beings call for an independent Being on which they are depending for their present existence.

Hackett's Arguments Based on Explanation

Stuart C. Hackett has offered two cosmological arguments that we may place in the tradition of Leibniz and Wolff. He considers the first one a conceptual argument and the second one a causal argument.[21] The first one can be summarized as follows:[22]

1. The world order is possible only on the basis of several necessary conditions.
   a. There need to be objective a priori principles of knowledge.
   b. There need to be objective essences that define the properties of the things in the world.
   c. There needs to be a reason or explanation why of all possible worlds this is the one that exists.
2. These realities show all of the properties that are associated with the structuring activity of a mind.

21. Stuart C. Hackett, *The Reconstruction of the Christian Revelation Claim: A Philosophical and Critical Apologetic* (Grand Rapids: Baker, 1984), pp. 90–103.
22. Ibid., p. 96.

3. Therefore, these realities can be understood as the workings of an absolute Mind.

4. Therefore, there exists an absolute Mind as necessary condition to the logical possibility of this world. "God is actually a reasonable explanation of the possibility of the world order."

Hackett summarizes his second argument with three short statements.[23]

1. If anything exists, an absolutely necessary and transcendent Being exists.

2. Something exists (I at least, as a thinker).

3. Therefore, an absolutely necessary and transcendent Being exists (i.e., God, as partly defined by theism).

Of course the first premise needs a tremendous amount of support lest it simply beg the question. The answer lies in Hackett's understanding of a causal explanation. If anything exists, it must have an explanation for its existence (the principle of sufficient reason). But such an explanation must be ultimate in order to be adequate. Hackett asserts that "we have not really given any adequate causal explanation of an entity or a state of things if we merely explain the ground of its existence by referring it to other entities and states which require the same explanation themselves without logical limit."[24] Thus such an explanation must invoke a necessary and transcendent Being.

But at this point the problem inherent in this kind of argument based on sufficient reason becomes clear. For it is not at all compulsory to accept that an explanation is only a true and full explanation if it itself requires no further explanation. As John Hospers has shown, an explanation is always a somewhat subjective thing; there certainly is no objective criterion of when an explanation has become truly adequate. One person is satisfied with an explanation on a lower level than another. But no law says that an explanation is not a true or acceptable explanation if someone else wants to question it more deeply.[25]

Thus both of Hackett's arguments suffer from the same defect. They are both premised on the idea that a phenomenon of the world, whether it be conceptual or causal, can be explained adequately only in terms of something ultimate—absolute mind or necessary and transcendent being. But such an assumption is unwarranted. It is not that these phenomena could not be explained on such an ultimate basis, but there is no inherent compulsion to

23. Ibid., p. 98.
24. Ibid.
25. John Hospers, "What Is Explanation?" in *Reason and Responsibility,* ed. Joel Feinberg (Belmont, Calif.: Dickenson, 1965), pp. 181–91.

have to resort to such a high order of explanatory magnitude. A finite explanation may suffice for finite phenomena.

Ross's Argument Based on Explanation

Perhaps the epitome of a contemporary argument based on explanation is expounded by James F. Ross.[26] He has provided two versions of this argument. We shall illustrate his method by summarizing his first argument.

1. If something is not the case, there must be an explanation for it not being the case. This explanation must be either
   a. a self-explanation that says the proposed state of affairs is logically absurd, or
   b. a hetero-explanation according to which the proposed state of affairs is prevented by some outside agent from being the case.
2. Considering the state of affairs, "God does not exist" cannot be the case because
   a. there is no self-explanation (no inherent absurdity in the idea of God not existing), and
   b. there is no hetero-explanation (no outside agent that could prevent God from existing).
3. Therefore, since "God does not exist" cannot be the case, "God exists" must be the case. Thus God exists.

This interesting argument seems to partake of the ontological argument almost as much as of the cosmological, for an important factor in it is an analysis of the concept of God. But it still is cosmological because it is predicated on the idea that something exists and that existing states of affairs, as well as those not obtaining, need explanations. In terms of the logic of this argument, it clearly emphasizes the strengths and weakness of the argument based on sufficient reason. Given the basic premise of the Leibniz-Wolffian approach of the need for universal causal explanations, this argument works remarkably well. But in light of the reservations with that approach, this argument also falls short of the cogency it wants.

Craig's Kalām Argument

William Lane Craig has produced an argument based on the need to posit an original cause for the universe. His three basic premises are:[27]

26. James F. Ross, *Philosophical Theology* (Indianapolis: Bobbs-Merrill, 1969), p. 173.
27. William Lane Craig, *Apologetics: An Introduction* (Chicago: Moody, 1984), pp. 73–95.

1. Whatever begins to exist has a cause.
2. The universe began to exist.
3. Therefore, the universe has a cause.

The strength of this argument is evident. It is apparently simple without involving the need to posit a lot of preliminary considerations. It is logically tight, partaking of the form of the modus ponens, one of the most elementary forms of argument.

The weakness of the argument lies in the questionableness of the premises. Premise 1 seems intuitively certain, but is admittedly difficult to prove demonstrably. Indeed, it has been questioned by many. However, one can allow Craig's point that to question this notion is surely sophistical and done out of a purely defensive motive. But premise 2 is of course questionable. Craig attempts to give both conceptual and scientific support for it.

Philosophically, Craig argues that if the universe did not have a beginning in time, then it would have to be eternal. But since an actually infinite number of moments is impossible and since it is not possible to obtain an actually infinite collection of things by adding one member after another, then it is impossible for the universe to be infinite in duration.

A serious objection can be leveled against this reasoning. It assumes that there is a real finite world—an assumption that a pantheist would not grant. Hence, at best the argument does not prove theism, since it does not eliminate pantheism.

The scientific support for the premise that the universe had a beginning in time rests on the big bang model for the origin of the cosmos and on the second law of thermodynamics, which states that any closed system will tend toward random molecular motion and loss of energy. Thereby Craig hopes to demonstrate that the universe had a temporal beginning and that it is now on an irreversible course toward an end in time. At this point all one can say is that as long as the scientific consensus runs in sympathy with this conclusion, the argument is convincing. But who is to say what scientists will conclude tomorrow? Although the present scientific evidence indicates a temporal universe, this only makes the conclusion plausible from a scientific perspective,[28] not demonstrable from a philosophical standpoint.

The teleological and moral arguments depend on the principle of sufficient reason and/or causality. If everything is not absurd—if there is a reason and/or cause—then it would seem to follow that some kind of intelligent and moral Mind is behind the world. The conclusion of the ontological argument is that it is not rationally inescapable to think that there is a necessary Being.

28. See Norman L. Geisler and J. Kerby Anderson, *Origin Science: A Proposal for the Creation-Evolution Controversy* (Grand Rapids: Baker, 1987), chaps. 6, 7.

God's nonexistence is conceivable, for it is always possible that nothing ever existed, including God.

However, while total nonexistence is conceivable it is not affirmable, since it implies that someone exists to affirm it. Hence, the only hope for validating the ontological argument is to begin with something that exists. Now on the surface it seems that this is precisely what the cosmological argument (in the tradition of Leibniz, Wolff, and Taylor) does. It begins with the existence of the individual in the world and argues that there must be a sufficient reason for it. However, at this point the cosmological argument runs into several problems. First, it is not a rationally inescapable argument unless the principle of sufficient reason is rationally inescapable. But the principle seems not to be analytic or self-evidently true. It can be denied without contradiction. One can say, "Some things do not have sufficient reasons" without contradiction. And it might be that the existence of the world is one of these things. Further, the very attempt by this type of cosmological argumentation, at two important points, to import conceptual premises leaves it unprotected from the Kantian criticism that in order to prove its case the argument always makes an illicit move into the purely conceptual realm. For example, the defense of the world as contingent or dependent is based on the fact that its nonexistence is conceivable. Just because it is logically possible for the world not to exist does not prove that it is ontologically necessary to conclude that it is contingent. It is logically possible, as Jean-Paul Sartre held,[29] that the world is just "there," that is a gratuitous "given" with no ontological explanation, even though its nonexistence is possible. Unless there is some appeal made to the real conditions of its existence beyond the mere logical possibility that it might not have existed, the theistic conclusion is not necessitated. Likewise, the God of the conclusion of Leibniz's type of cosmological argument is usually wrongly defined in logical terms as one whose nonexistence is inconceivable. God is characterized as one who, granting that something exists (which is a necessary improvement on the ontological argument), logically cannot *not* exist. Nevertheless, a necessary Being is then (fallaciously) defined as one whose nonexistence is logically impossible, rather than one whose nonexistence is actually impossible because it is the necessary ground for what undeniably exists. We conclude, then, that at several crucial points these cosmological arguments leave the actual for the conceptual and are open to Kant's criticisms by confusing (if not replacing) the principle of existential causality with the law of sufficient reason, by importing logical possibility to defend actual contingency, and by forsaking real necessity for conceptual necessity in the nature of a necessary Being. Even in the kalām form of the

---

29. Jean-Paul Sartre, *Being and Nothingness* (New York: Washington Square, 1966), p. 758.

cosmological argument, where the principle of causality is used, there is no philosophical proof offered that there are any real finite, temporal beings. Hence, at best this form of the argument does not prove a theistic God but one that could be pantheistic. But unless these pitfalls can be avoided, there is no hope of defending the cosmological argument, which argument is, as we have already concluded, the only apparent hope for saving theistic argumentation.

9 ✳

The Cosmological Argument Reevaluated

Most attempts to defend the cosmological argument in a non-Leibnizian way emanate from Thomas Aquinas.[1] This is understandable in view of the fact that Thomas did not base his argument on the principle of sufficient reason but on the principle of existential causality. The former calls only for an explanation in the realm of reason; the latter demands a ground in reality. The Leibnizian type of argument is built on logical necessity, whereas Aquinas's argument is based on existential undeniability. These and other differences will become apparent as the argument is elaborated. In this chapter we shall restate the cosmological argument, defend its premises and conclusions, and respond to various criticisms.

The Cosmological Argument Restated

The following is a summary of the cosmological argument, which we will attempt to elaborate and defend in the rest of the chapter.

1. Some limited, changing being(s) exist.
2. The present existence of every limited, changing being is caused by another.
3. There cannot be an infinite regress of causes of being.
4. Therefore, there is a first Cause of the present existence of these beings.
5. The first Cause must be infinite, necessary, eternal, simple, unchangeable, and one.
6. This first uncaused Cause is identical with the God of the Judeo-Christian tradition.

Within the framework of six formal steps, this argument intends to achieve two different objectives: to demonstrate the existence of a first Cause and then to show that the first Cause is the God of the Judeo-Christian tradition. The first Cause is identified as being a necessary Being.

Now an interesting pattern can be observed in the course of examining

---

1. See Thomas Aquinas, *On Being annd Essence*, chap. 7; *Summa Theologica* 1.2.3; 1.3.4; 1.44.1; *Summa contra Gentiles* 1.13.

critiques of the argument, and it is helpful to look for this pattern from the beginning. Critics are concerned with showing that the argument has not demonstrated the existence of the Judeo-Christian God. In order to make that point, however, they need to stop the progression of the argument somewhere. This stoppage involves showing that something must be uncaused (i.e., needs no exterior cause for its existence). But this is to say that it is a necessary Being, in which case the argument has accomplished its first objective regardless, and it can be shown from there that the God of Christian theism is still the most consistent understanding of necessary Being. We shall observe this pattern at several stages in the argument to follow.

1. *Some limited, changing being(s) exist.* The truth of this premise is an undeniable fact of experience. While it is logically possible that nothing ever existed, it is actually undeniable that something exists. For example, I am and the world is. Likewise, the fact that I am limited in a spatiotemporal continuum is an unquestionable datum of my experience. And that the world of which I am a part is limited and changing is also an evident fact of experience. Stated more formally, the argument takes this shape: It is actually undeniable that something exists (e.g., I exist). Any attempt to deny one's own existence is self-defeating, for one always (implicitly) affirms his own existence in the very attempt to deny it. One must exist in order to make the denial, and if he exists, the denial is not true. Hence, all attempts to deny the existence of everything self-destruct. Universal negative statements about existence are self-stultifying. It is necessary to affirm that something exists.

The necessity of this affirmation is not logical but existential. That is, the nonexistence of everything is not inconceivable. It is logically possible that nothing ever existed, including myself. This is logically possible but it is false. And it is false because it is actually undeniable that something exists, not because it is logically inconceivable that nothing exists. The importance of this distinction marks the difference between the forms of the cosmological argument, which operate in the realm of pure logical possibility and necessity, and the form of the argument here espoused, which is not based in mere logical necessity but in existential undeniability.

Mere logic demonstrates no more than the mere possibility of the existence of something. We must consult experience to discover what actually exists. One reason this point is often missed is that the person is assuming his own existence, which is indeed undeniable. But one's own existence is not logically necessary. And once we leave the ground of logical possibility and necessity for what actually and undeniably exists, then we have a radically different basis for the cosmological argument. It is a beginning in the realm of reality and not in the realm of pure reason.

Assertions within the context of a Buddhist metaphysics cannot repudiate this point. It is true that a Buddhist might deny that he exists. The doctrine of *anatta* (*anatman*) is that there is no substantial self. Furthermore, according to the teachings of Theravadin Buddhism, nothing exists. The entire world is construed as *maya*, or pure illusion. Thus a Buddhist who espouses this view could conceivably say that nothing exists, including himself.

But we can respond to such assertions on three levels. First, one can attempt to adjudicate between different metaphysical systems and see whether these (to us) outrageous claims are in fact plausible. Second, one can point out that these metaphysical assertions are not incompatible with our first premise. Something exists, if only maya. After all, maya is only illusion, it still exists as an illusion. Thus the illusion exists. The Buddhist will reply that maya exists only in a flimsy and nonultimate sense. All the better, one can respond; the cosmological argument also indicates that the world's existence is nonultimate.

Third, one has to say that not everything that can be said can be consistently affirmed (said and meant as true). Just because a Buddhist might say that he does not exist does not mean that he can consistently affirm it. Surely the overwhelming burden of proof for such a stupendous statement lies with the person making it. The more plausible view is that even the Buddhist stultifies himself by saying that he does not exist. If he does not exist, there is no one to make his statement.

It may be further argued that if I undeniably exist, then so does something else that I call the world. For I understand myself as a distinguishable entity only because I can make some meaningful differentiation between myself and the otherness that surrounds me. Without the "other" I could never know "myself." But I do know myself and so there must be some otherness in distinction from which I can identify myself. Furthermore, this otherness must really exist, since I can be deceived about part of the world but not about the whole of it. Total illusion is impossible, for illusion presupposes a backdrop of reality by which in contrast particular things can be seen to be not real. One cannot know that he was dreaming unless there is a state of wakefulness with which he can compare it. The fact of illusion in the world demonstrates that we have no total illusion of the world. We conclude, therefore, that it is undeniable that we exist and that the world must exist also.

Again, it is experientially demonstrable that changing things exist. I am a changing thing and I experience other changing things in the world. Indeed, the whole world of my experience is a space-time continuum of change. It seems unnecessary to argue this point but since some do, we will examine their contention.

First, the argument that all change is illusory is indefensible for the simple reason that total illusion about ourselves and the world is impossible. And if only some change is real, on the possibility that we may be deceived about most of the rest of our experience, then it follows that there is at least some real change in real things.

Secondly, the very denial of all change is self-defeating. The person who comes to believe and affirm a proposition is different after that experience from what he was before it. He has undergone a change in both knowledge and position. Likewise, the groom who affirms the proposition "I do" is a changed man. He has changed from an unmarried mode of existence to a married one. That is a real change! Furthermore, our affirmations themselves are only limited perspectives on reality. The only way to deny this would be to claim the obviously false (to have an unlimited understanding of reality). This is clearly false because it is contrary to both the content and character of our consciousness. The content of our consciousness is limited because we know about things perspectively and successively. We do not know completely and simultaneously. In fact, the very character of our knowing is always a consciousness of some truth. There is always the limitation of the knower (the subject) and the known (the object). We are conscious *of* truth but we are not conscious truth itself. We conclude, then, that change and limitation cannot be accounted for as a total illusion. At least some changing limited thing exists.

Neither can change be accounted for as continuous annihilation and recreation. At least if it can, it is of no help in avoiding a theistic conclusion. For if what appears to us to change is really going out of existence and coming back into existence an instant later as a new thing, there must be a God to account for the new creation from nothing at every instant in the process of every "changing" thing. Something does not come from nothing spontaneously; being does not arise from nonbeing without a cause. So if "change" is really annihilation and recreation, then the theistic conclusion is already reached, namely, there is a Cause of the existence of everything that comes into existence. Since this explanation is both unhelpful to the nontheist and contrary to the continuity of our experience of ourselves and of other changing things, we will proceed to argue that there is real change in finite things.

No matter which view of change is taken, it is necessary to conclude that whatever changes is a finite and contingent being. For whatever changes in its being is obviously limited. Only an unchangeable being could be unlimited in its existence, since it would not be subject to any limiting process as change is. Further, whatever undergoes a change of its being must be a contingent being, for a necessary Being cannot come into or go out of existence. If there is a necessary Being it must have being necessarily. Any being that undergoes a change of its being (i.e., either gains or loses it) cannot be a necessary Being. It must be a contingent being. And since, on either view of change, the beings of our experience are not unlimited or necessary, it follows that they must be limited and/or contingent in their existence.

In brief, either experienced change is totally illusory or it is real. Since total illusion is impossible, it must be real. And if change is real, it is either a real change of being (by annihilation and recreation) or else a change in the very being of the thing changing. But the first alternative immediately demands a God to bring the new being into existence once the other one passes out of being. And the latter alternative admits that there are real changes in the very being of the beings we do experience. It is from this last premise that we may continue the cosmological argument.

Perhaps the strongest indication that all persons do indeed experience the reality of their own finite mode of existence is that whether they are theist, pantheist, or atheist they are engaged in a lifelong struggle to overcome the limitations of their finite existence. If finitude is illusory, then even the pantheist must admit that it is the most universal, persistent, difficult, and seemingly real obstacle in life to overcome. Likewise, the atheist admits that all human beings desire to transcend their finite conditions. Jean-Paul Sartre said the person's very project is to become God. Stated less radically, the human has the basic desire to transcend himself. There are many ways to transcend (see chap. 3), but the fact that all people seek to transcend in one way or another, adequate or inadequate, is ample proof that they recognize the reality of their own finitude. Friedrich Schleiermacher said that all people have a "feeling of absolute dependence." Even Sigmund Freud admitted that this was true. Augustine said all persons need God. Even Sartre admitted that this is indeed the case. Martin Heidegger described the human as *Dasein*, the being-there or thrust-one. An honest evaluation of the human mode of being by both theist and nontheist reveals an unmistakable sense of finitude. It is with this finite mode of existence that the cosmological argument begins.

The adamant monist will insist that nothing finite exists, including himself. This means he must affirm, "I am infinite." But this too is self-defeating. For if he were infinite in knowledge, then he always knew it. But the fact that he came to know he was infinite (and tries to help others come to know that they are too) reveals that he did not always know that he was infinite. Hence, the very process of change by which one allegedly comes to realize that he is God proves that he is not. He is really a finite creature after all.

2. *The present existence of every limited, changing being is caused by another.* Whatever changes in its very being must be composed of both a potentiality for that change and an actuality that actualizes or effects the change, since the resultant being is an actually changed being. But no being can actualize its own potential for existence. The sheer possibility of existence does not account for the actual existence of something. Many possible beings are not actual (Pegasus or a centaur). Therefore, every changing (or, change-able) being must be caused to exist by another being. Let us spell out the argument more completely.

A. Whatever changes in its existence must be composed of both an actuality and a potentiality. This flows from the following argument:

1) An uncomposed existence (of pure actuality) would be an unlimited existence, since there is no limit placed upon it by virtue of its having certain kinds of potentialities or limitations.
   a) The only way something can be limited is by its possibilities for actualization.
   b) But pure actuality has no possibilities for actualization; it is pure actuality, full and complete actuality in and of itself.
   c) Hence, an uncomposed existence of pure actuality is unlimited in its existence.

In support of the first premise it may be argued that

(1) Pure actuality is not limited by itself; it is what it is and that is not a limitation on what it is.
(2) Neither can it be limited by nothing, for nonexistence is absolutely nothing and absolutely nothing limits absolutely nothing.
(3) Nor could it be limited by another pure actuality, since it is impossible to have another pure actuality as such. Only one thing could be actuality as such; everything else must be actually as limited in this or that way.
(4) And no limited existence could limit existence as such, for what is limited in a given order places no limits on that order as such (limited good does not limit goodness as such; a dim light does not limit light as such).
(5) Finally, no potential for existence can limit pure existence, since it is already pure actuality and hence has no potentiality to limit what it can be.
(6) Therefore, since there are no other ways something could be limited in its existence, it follows that pure actuality as such is unlimited.

2) But changing things are not uncomposed beings; they are composed beings. Things that change and/or are changeable must have within them both a potentiality for that change and an actuality that shows that the change has been actualized in them. Without the potentiality or possibility for change, change would be impossible. And without the actualization of that potential, the being would remain unchanged. The fact that change occurs indicates that there is both an actuality and a potentiality within changing beings. Formally stated,
   a) Nonexistence is not a limitation on existence (nothing limits nothing).
   b) Existence does not limit itself (the fact that a thing is does not limit its "is-ness").
   c) Only a thing's potential for existence can limit its existence (i.e., only what it can be limits what it is).

d) Therefore, every changing being has within it both an actuality (existence) and a potentiality (essence). Its existence accounts for the fact that it is, and its essence explains why it is what it is, namely, a certain limited kind of existence.

B. Further, no potentiality can actualize itself. A potential is the mere capacity to have a certain kind of existence. And no potential can actualize itself any more than the potential for steel to be a skyscraper is in itself sufficient to make it into a skyscraper. An empty bucket does not fill itself, even though its emptiness is the real potential to be filled (in contrast to a desk top, which does not have this potential). The argument may be stated thus:

1) Essence as such is merely the potential for existence.

2) But no potentiality for existence can actualize itself (the potential is not the cause of the actual; what something can be does not in itself account for what it is).

3) Therefore, a thing's potentiality for existence (essence) cannot explain its actual existence.

It could be argued that when a person develops a capacity, he is actualizing his own potential. For example, if I learn to play the guitar, I actualize my potential to be a guitar player. However, this situation is not a case of a potential actualizing itself. The actuality that is already present in myself actualizes a potentiality. There is no such thing as a purely potential guitar player.

C. Therefore, there must be some actuality outside of composed beings to explain why they actually do exist. Since changing beings are composed of an actuality and a potentiality and since no potentiality can actualize itself, it follows that there must be some actuality outside of changing beings to explain why they actually exist rather than just possibly exist. This conclusion follows in this way:

1) The potential cannot cause the existence of the actual (as was just shown).[2]

2) Only the actual can cause the existence of the actual (actuality follows only from actuality; nothing cannot be the cause of something; nonexistence cannot produce existence).[3]

---

2. It should be stressed that even though potentialities are real aspects of finite beings, nonetheless they are not real things in themselves. That is, potentialities do not exist independently, apart from the actuality which can and does actualize them. Both potentiality and actuality with regard to finite beings are concreated. There is no existing realm of essences (like Platonic Forms) waiting for actualization in the world.

3. The Cause of existence must exist in order to cause existence. What does not exist has no causal power. In fact, it has nothing, for it is nothing. Hence, what is being caused arises only

3) So it follows that some actual existence is the cause of every composed being which exists.

To summarize the whole second premise in the overall cosmological argument: Every limited changing being is composed of both an actuality (its existence) and a potentiality (its essence). But no potentiality can actualize itself. Therefore, there must be some actuality outside of every composed being to account for the fact that it actually exists, as opposed to its not existing but merely having the potential for existence. In brief, the question as to why there is something rather than nothing at all must be answered thus: because there is something beyond it that is causing it to exist. Why is it that what can exist but need not exist actually does exist? It is because its potential for existence was actualized or caused by some existence beyond it.

3. *There cannot be an infinite regress of causes of being.* The next step in the cosmological argument is to show that an infinite regress of existent-dependent causes is impossible. But first we must carefully define what is meant by the terms with which we are working.

By "cause" is meant an efficient or producing cause, as opposed to a final or purposing cause. An efficient cause is a necessary and sufficient condition to account for the actualization of a potential.

By "existence" we mean the present, here-and-now "*be*-ing" or existing in the world. Existence is that which is opposed to that which is not. It is the "isness" of a thing as opposed to its "was-ness" or "will-be-ness." Existence does not denote the origination of a being but its continuation in being. Hence, when we speak about a cause of existence, reference is not made to what caused things to come into being, but rather to what causes things to continue to be. That is, we are asking about the conservation, and not the origination, of things in being. Existential causality, then, refers as such to the cause of the being of things and not the cause of their becoming.[4]

By an "infinite" regress" is meant a series that has no first or beginning cause. It is a series where every cause is being caused by another cause and hence a series in which there is no originating cause of all other causes. No cause in an infinite series is uncaused, for if it were, the series would stop there. That cause would be a first, uncaused Cause of the rest. It is such a first Cause that the infinite series would evade.

With these distinctions in mind the question before us is whether there can

---

from a causal Being. Nothing cannot be the cause of something. Nonbeing cannot be the cause of being.

4. The failure to appreciate this difference between the cause of being and the cause of becoming has led even some theists to fail to see the full force of the cosmological argument. See Keith Yandell, *Basic Issues in the Philosophy of Religion* (Boston: Allyn and Bacon, 1971), pp. 81–105. Also see the answer to objection 14 for more on the cause of here-and-now be-ing.

be an infinite series of existent-dependent causes of the here-and-now "being" of the limited, changing, composed beings that have already been shown to be in need of a cause of their being. Careful examination shows that a definitively negative answer is called for. The argument against the infinite regress arises from the very nature of an existent-dependent cause. In an infinite series of this kind:

a. *There must be causality within the series* to cause the present existence of things.
b. *Every* cause in the series demands a cause for its present existence.
c. Hence, the existential *causality in the series is simultaneous;* that is, every cause is having its existence caused at the very same instant the way an image in the mirror is being caused by the person looking in the mirror.
d. But there cannot be causality within the series unless *at least one cause is doing some causing* of the existence of another (causality comes only from causes).
e. It follows that at least this one cause must be causing its own existence, since it accounts for *all* the causality in the series. For, it must be remembered, *every* cause in an infinite series of this kind is having its own existence caused. (Where there is one cause not being caused, it would be an uncaused Cause of the other causes, which is what the infinite series hopes to evade.)
f. But a self-caused existence is impossible, since to cause oneself one would have to be existentially prior to himself. Formally stated,
   1) A self-caused being is one that *does not have existence,* for if it had existence, it would not need a cause to give it the existence it already has.
   2) But a self-caused being is one that *has existence,* since it must exist in order to cause existence (nothinng cannot cause something).
   3) But to have and not to have existence simultaneously is impossible.
   4) Therefore, self-caused beings are impossible.
   5) But a simultaneously existent-dependent infinite regress necessarily contains at least one self-caused being.
   6) Therefore, such an infinite regress is necessarily impossible.

One way out of this dilemma for the nontheist is to affirm that the series is circular and mutually dependent. In a circle of fallen dominoes each domino might be leaning on another and, in that sense, each in turn is causing another to be where it is. But a circle of existent-dependent simultaneous causes is even more obviously impossible than the alleged infinite regress. It is clearly obvious in such a circle that the reasoning is circular. The same argument applies here. At least one of these causes must be causing existence at the same time its existence is being caused (by itself), which is an impossible self-caused existence. The illustration of the dominoes is deceptive because the dominoes are not really holding each other in place. Take away the table, the laws of friction and gravity, and the dominoes would fall apart. Likewise, take away a cause from beyond the infinite series (or circle) and the whole series crumbles.

This points up the real dilemma the nontheist is in. Either the infinite series has a cause within it to account for the causality in it or else the nontheist must posit a cause beyond it to give causality to the whole series (or circle). But it has already been shown that any cause in the series would have to be a self-caused existence, and this is impossible. And to posit a cause beyond the series to account for the causality in the series is precisely what the theist argues: in any supposed series where *every* cause is existent-dependent there must be beyond that series a cause that is not existent-dependent but which is giving the existential causality to the whole series.

Another ill-fated move by proponents of infinite regress would be to deny outright or by implication that there is causality in an infinite series; hence, nothing is causing anything. This move is doomed, since the very purpose of the series was to explain the caused beings of this world. It was established in premise 2 that there must be a cause beyond every limited changing being, since they are being caused to exist by something beyond themselves. This directly entails the necessity of at least one cause of existence in (or beyond) the supposed infinite series to account for the beings that are being caused. Therefore, to say that there is no causality in the infinite series is to forget that it has already been established that there must be some causality either in or beyond the series. In short, this attempted move by nontheists would be an elimination of the needed existence-explanation or ground for limited beings. Finite beings call for an explanation as to why they now exist when they need not exist. And to posit an infinite regress, which does not really provide any causality to cause finite existence, is no more than an attempt to explain away the need for a real explanation or ground.

There is one more argument against an infinite regress of causes, namely, that no composed being can be the cause of existence. All composed beings are caused beings by nature and not causing beings. Their own existence is caused or received and hence they have no existence to give to anything else. If a being is not able to hold itself in existence, it surely cannot ground the existence of another. A man falling off a cliff certainly cannot catch another man and keep him from falling. In like manner, a being that needs a ground for its own existence cannot be the ground for the existence of another being.

Everything that has its existence from another depends immediately on what is existence in itself. What has only a possible existence (i.e., what by nature may or may not be) must depend for its existence on a necessary existence (i.e., what by nature must be). One contingent being cannot ground another contingent being. What has being contingently has it from what is Being necessarily. If, then, no caused, composed, or contingent being can cause the existence of another being, it follows that the very first cause outside of a caused being must be an uncaused Being. The very first being outside of a contingent being must be a necessary Being. There can be no chain of intermediaries between a received existence and the giver of existence. And it goes without saying that if there can be no links at all between caused existence and the cause of existence, there certainly cannot be an infinite regress of causal links. Everything that has actuality must be grounded in actuality, for nothing else can actualize anything. Potentialities cannot actualize themselves and other actualized potentialities cannot actualize pure potentials, since they needed something to actualize their own potential. Therefore, no composed being can be an intermediary in a chain of existential causality. The first "link" is the first Cause of all composed being. If this is so, then a regress of existent causes cannot even get started, let alone be infinite in extensison.

The proponent of the cosmological argument is at this point frequently accused of reasoning in a circle, that is, begging the question and arguing against the infinite regress after already having legislated against the infinite regress and in favor of a first Cause. But surely the preceding argumentation should alleviate such allegations.

The logical method here is essentially transcendental. We are searching for the necessary conditions that make any sequence of causes possible. We discover that there can be no regression of mutually dependent existential causes apart from an existent external cause. This method is no more circular than positing mind as the necessary condition of thought.

4. *Therefore, there is a first Cause of the present existence of these beings.* This conclusion follows logically from the first three premises. If some limited, changing beings exist, if their present existence is caused by another being, and if an infinite regress of causes of being is impossible, then it follows necessarily that there must be a first Cause of the existence of these changing beings. Indeed, if the last argument against an infinite regress is correct, then this first Cause must be the very first Cause beyond the changing beings, with no intermediary causes in between. But be that as it may, even if there is a series of existent-dependent causes, it is clearly impossible for such a series to go on into infinity. And if the series cannot be without beginning, there must be at its head a first Cause of all the existential causality in the series.

No matter which way it is approached, there is a first Cause of the existence of every finite thing that exists. If there is no series at all, then the first Cause is the immediate cause of finite existence. If there is a series with all but one cause being caused, then that cause must stand first in the series. For if it is not causing the rest of the series, there must be an impossible self-caused cause somewhere in the middle of the series. And if there is a Cause beyond the series, giving causality to the series, then it is still first in the sense that there can be no cause (or series) beyond it. It must give existence to the series without receiving its existence from another (as was demonstrated in premise 3). So in this manner the Cause beyond the series would be first because there is no cause of its existence.

5. *This first Cause must be infinite, necessary, eternal, simple, unchangeable, and one.* Now that we have concluded a first Cause of every limited thing that exists, it remains to be asked what kind of a cause it is. The first question is this: Is this first Cause of existence self-caused, caused by another, or uncaused? The answer is already implied in what has gone before.

To be self-caused is as impossible for a first cause as it is for any other cause. Even the Cause of all finite existence cannot cause its own existence. Self-caused beings are impossible because causality of existence demands existential priority (though not necessarily temporal priority) and it is impossible for a being to be prior to itself.[5] It cannot give existence to itself, for that implies both that it has existence to give and that it did not have existence so that it needed to give it to itself. And a being, first Cause or not, simply cannot both have and not have existence simultaneously.

Neither can a first Cause be caused by another. For a first Cause is by its very function as first in the series not caused by another. The reason the series stopped at this Cause is that there were no causes beyond it. This first Cause gives the causality to the whole series. And as head of the series it has no cause. If it did have a cause, then we must go beyond it to find another to explain the causality in the series (as was shown in premise 3). But since the whole series and existence of limited beings is dependent on this Cause (per premise 4), then it is necessarily that beyond which no other cause is actually effecting the series. Hence, it is the first efficient Cause in the series. And because it is first, it is not receiving its causality from another.

5. Sartre was correct in arguing that a self-caused being is impossible. See *Being and Nothingness* (New York.: Washington Square, 1966), pp. 758, 762. Theists themselves are to blame for the confusion (following Descartes and Leibniz) by designating God a "self-caused" Being rather than an "uncaused" Being. Schopenhauer correctly saw that the problem rested in the principle of sufficient reason (see Alvin Plantinga, ed., *The Ontological Argument: From Anselm to Contemporary Philosophers* [Garden City, N.Y.: Doubleday, Anchor Books, 1965], pp. 65–66). For if, according to that principle, "*everything* needs a reason," then so does God. That is, God must be his own reason or cause. But if God causes himself, then God is really self-caused, which, as Sartre correctly saw, is impossible. On the other hand, if in accord with the principle of existential causality, "*only finite things* need causes," then the first Cause (God) does not need a cause. And hence God does not need to cause himself; indeed, he is himself uncaused.

This leaves only the alternative that this first Cause must itself be an *un*caused Cause. For if it is neither self-caused nor caused by another, then it must be uncaused in its existence. This is an important conclusion for the cosmological argument and the one that not all theists see clearly, especially those who operate with a principle of sufficient reason as opposed to a principle of existential causality. Some nontheists object to theism on the supposed basis that God is an impossible self-caused Being. It seems that this is a legitimate objection, but it does not apply to the God of the preceding argument. A *self*-caused being is logically impossible, but an *un*caused Being is no more incoherent than is an uncaused universe. If nothing cannot produce something, then something must be eternal and uncaused.

Further, it is as an uncaused Cause that the essential metaphysical attributes of this Cause can be shown to identify it with the God of the Judeo-Christian tradition. Let us move directly to reveal what is implied in an uncaused Cause of the existence of finite, limited, changing beings. (Traditional Christian theology would recognize in these properties of the first Cause the so-called incommunicable attributes of God, namely, those attributes that he alone possesses and that he cannot confer on creation because they are the denials of limitations placed on the world.) This is evident from the fact that it is pure actuality with no limiting potential. Only caused beings are limited. So this uncaused being is unlimited.

First of all, an uncaused Cause must be an *unlimited being*. Very simply put, if all caused things are limited beings, then it follows that this uncaused Being is an unlimited Being. It is the unlimited limiter of every limited being. That is, it places the causal limits on all other beings by virtue of the fact that it not only causes them to be but because it causes them to be the specific kinds of beings they are. But since an unlimited Being means a being that is not limited in its existence and since "not limited" is what is meant by infinite (i.e., not finite), then it follows that the first Cause of all finite being must itself be an infinite Being.

Secondly, this one uncaused, unlimited Being must also be a *necessary Being*. This also follows from the fact that all finite beings are contingent beings. For if all limited beings depend for their existence on an unlimited Being and if this unlimited Being does not depend on anything for its existence, then it is an independent Being. Or, to say it another way, if all limited or caused beings are contingent or possible beings (i.e., beings that may not be), then the unlimited or uncaused Being must be a noncontingent or necessary Being (i.e., one that must be). That is, all beings whose essence is not to exist depend on one whose essence is to exist.

It is important to note that the "necessity" here is not logical but ontological. God is not a logically necessary Being. It is logically possible that nothing ever existed, including God. But it is actually false that nothing ever existed. In fact, it is undeniably true that something exists that need not exist (e.g., myself). Therefore, since something exists, it is ontologically necessary that something exists as a ground for all contingent existence. The existence of contingent beings demands a necessary Being on which they can be contingent. For if the contingent beings are caused beings, then the uncaused Cause of these beings must be a noncontingent Being, that is, a necessary Being.

Thirdly, this uncaused Being must be an *eternal Being*. Since nonexistence cannot give rise to existence and since this uncaused Existence is the cause of all existence, then its existence must be eternal. For if there were ever a time that the Cause of all existence did not exist, then it would follow that nothing would ever have existed. The only way the move can be made from nonexistence to existence is by an existing Cause. And since that Cause cannot cause its own existence, then it must have always existed. For if the Cause of all existence was ever itself nonexistent, then nothing would ever have existed. But something does exist. Hence, it is necessary that this uncaused Cause has always existed, eternally.

Fourthly, the uncaused Cause must be a *simple, undivided Being*. Since this uncaused Cause is pure actuality with no potentiality, it has no composition. And what is not composed is not divisible; it is pure indivisible existence. Pure existence is existence purely and simply. And what is existence purely and simply, is pure and simple (i.e., undivided) in its existence.

Only potentialities make things divisible because they can divide things according to various limitations or kinds of existence they receive. But pure actuality has no potentiality or limitations. Hence, uncaused existence is undivided existence; it is simple existence as such. Another way to state the argument is this: what is divisible is composed existence. But composed existence is composed of actuality and potentiality. And what is composed is not pure actuality as such. And since an uncaused Cause is pure actuality, it follows that it cannot be divisible. Uncaused Being is simple Being.

Fifthly, the uncaused Cause of existence must be an *unchangeable Being*. For anything that changes in its existence must possess both an actuality (since it exists) and a potentiality for change. Now change is a passing from a potentiality to actuality; from what it could be to what it actually becomes. But an unlimited existence has no potentiality; it is pure existence as such. It follows, then, that there can be no change in what is existence as such. It must be what it is and it cannot be otherwise. Were it to change, it would demonstrate that it was not really pure actuality. For change is the actualization of some potentiality, and pure actuality has no unactualized potentialities. Hence, a pure and unlimited existence as such cannot change.

Whatever changes must change either accidentally or substantially. But a necessary Being has no accidents, for whatever it is, it is necessarily and not accidentally. There are no characteristics that it may or may not have; whatever it may have, it must have. Otherwise it would not be a necessary Being. But neither can a necessary Being change substantially. For a substantial change in one's being would mean it would either have to come into or go out of being. Both are impossible for a necessary Being. For if a necessary Being exists at all, it must exist necessarily; this is the only way a necessary Being can exist. And since it has already been shown that a necessary Being exists, it follows that it must exist necessarily.

In other words, a substantial change in being means that there is a passage from nonbeing to being or vice versa. But since nothing does not cause something, it follows that the only possible way a substantial change could occur is if there were some ground of being beneath the change, making it possible for something to appear where before there was nothing. Hence, whatever undergoes a substantial change demands a necessary Being as its ground which does not change but which is the unchanging ground of all that changes.

Finally, an uncaused Being must be *one Being* (i.e., there cannot be many). That there can be only one uncaused Being can be seen in several ways. First, from the fact that an uncaused Being is pure actuality it follows that there cannot be two such beings. For pure actuality is being as such and there can only be one Being that is existence as such. Every other existence has to be existence as limited or distinguished in some way from existence as such. Many things may have existence, but only one thing can be existence.

Further, pure actuality cannot be divided or multiplied in any way because it has no potentiality. Only what has some potentiality can be differentiated from another by virtue of the fact that they have differing potentialities or essences. But pure actuality has no potentialities whatsoever. Therefore, what is pure actuality (the uncaused existence) must be one, since there is no way to make it many without adding to it what it by nature cannot have, namely, some potentiality.

Also, pure actuality possesses all the perfections or characteristics of being in the highest and most eminent way possible (infinitely). Whatever perfections actually exist were actualized by this pure actuality. And since in communicating actuality to things it is sharing of its own actuality, we must conclude that perfections produced in the effect are perfections possessed by the Cause according to its own mode of being. This would mean that the uncaused Cause as the source of all perfections must be the most perfect of all beings. Now it follows that there cannot be two most perfect beings. Only one Being can be perfection; all other beings must only share in that perfection in varying ways. But every other being must be less than perfect.

A similar argument may be constructed from the fact that an infinite Cause has infinite causal power. But two such beings could cancel the causal power of each other. And causal power that can be cancelled is not really infinite. If, for instance, one infinite power desired to destroy what the other wanted to preserve, then one power must prevail over the other. In this case the other would not be infinite in power. It is highly problematic to argue that there would or even could be a complete cooperation between them, since (per the previous argument) one is "less perfect" than the other. Furthermore, whatever agreement could be worked out between them would have to be based ultimately on the one that is absolutely perfect, since for him to assent to what is less than perfect would be an evil contrary to his nature.[6] In view of the fact that the one would have to yield to the standard of the other, it is difficult to see in what sense the one yielding could be considered infinite in power. At least on the practical level of operation, as well as on the level of absolute perfection, there would be only one all-powerful Being. So by nature and power the one all-powerful and absolutely perfect Being could never allow anything to occur contrary to his will.

Another argument for there being only one uncaused Cause can be derived from its absolute perfection. For to be really different, one would have to really differ from the other in its very being, since to differ by nonbeing is to differ by nothing. And to differ by absolutely nothing is to have absolutely no difference whatsoever. But neither can they differ in being, for in being they are absolutely the same. Both are infinite, necessary, all-powerful. So when there is absolutely no difference in being between two beings, then they must be really identical. Two infinite beings must be identical, since they are both of the very same kind.

A finite and an infinite being may be conceived of nonunivocally (because they differ in being) but two infinite beings, which are said to be the same in every respect, cannot be so conceived. Whatever univocally conceived beings have no real difference must be really identical. And two infinite beings with all perfections are surely not to be conceived of equivocally, for then they would be totally different. And if the one had being, then the other would be nonbeing, since that is what is totally different from being. Nor will an analogous conception be permitted (where they are only similar), for it has already been agreed that they are identical in attributes of being. If they are not identical, then it follows easily that there cannot be two infinitely perfect beings. For if they are not identical, one has what the other does not have. And if the one is absolutely perfect with that characteristic and the other lacks it, then the one lacking it is not absolutely perfect. Thus we would be left

---

6. See chapter 16 for further discussion on why it would be evil for a perfect Being to do less than its best.

7. Note three differences here between this argument and another one based on the principle of "the identity of indiscernibles." First, we are speaking here of actual identity of what is in

with only one absolutely perfect Being, which is what we set out to show.[7]

6. *This first uncaused Cause is identical with the God of the Judeo-Christian tradition.* In order to compare properly the God whose existence is supported by the preceding cosmological argument, we must briefly inquire into the characteristics of the God of the Hebrew-Christian Scriptures. According to the Bible, God is both the creator (Gen. 1:1; Heb. 11:3) and sustainer of all things (Ps. 36:6; Col. 1:17). He is both one and supreme (Deut. 6:4; Exod. 20:3), as well as infinite and eternal (Ps. 147:5; 41:13). He is changeless in nature (Ps. 102:27; Mal. 3:6; James 1:17) and absolutely perfect and loving (Matt. 5:48; 1 John 4:16).

The God of Scripture has many other compatible attributes, but the preceding list will suffice to show that he is identical with the God of the cosmological argument. For in both he is an absolutely infinite and perfect Being and, as was demonstrated in premise 5, there cannot be two such beings. In order to really differ, two infinitely perfect beings would have to have some real difference. But if there were a real difference, then one would lack some perfection the other had and hence one would not be the absolutely perfect being of both the cosmological argument and the Bible.

Since the God of both the Bible and theism has changeless, eternal existence, which causes the very present existence of everything that exists, it follows in like manner that there cannot be two of them. For, as was argued, there cannot be two beings that are pure existence as such. Pure actuality cannot be differentiated from pure actuality. Only potentiality makes limitation and differentiation possible, and pure actuality has no potentiality in its being. Hence, the God of revelation and the God of cosmological theism are identical. There are not different Gods but only two different approaches to one and the same God: divine declaration and philosophical inference. It should not seem strange to those who believe (via divine revelation) in God's manifestation in his creation (Rom. 1:19–20; Ps. 19:1) that it is possible to arrive at a knowledge of God by inference through these manifestations.

The Cosmological Argument Reconsidered

Many objections to the cosmological argument do not apply to the type just given. Let us note the major objections and how they would be answered in

---

fact indistinguishable and not merely logical identity of what is in thought indiscernible. Secondly, the argument is applied here only to an infinite or absolutely perfect Being, leaving open the question of whether indistinguishable finite beings are identical. Thirdly, the argument applies only to beings that have being in a univocal sense. Beings analogous in their being are not identical, such as a finite being and an infinite being. This is so even if they possess all the same characteristics.

view of the foregoing restatement of the cosmological argument. Of the criticisms offered by David Hume, Immanuel Kant, and others, the following are noteworthy:[8]

1. *Only a finite cause need be inferred from finite effects.* This objection fails in view of premise 5. For a finite being or effect is limited, and *every* limited being is presently caused by some Being. Ultimately (because of the impossibility of an infinite regress) this brings us to a Cause that is not limited but that is the unlimited limiter of every limited thing that exists. The first Cause cannot be finite or limited because if it were limited (i.e., caused), then it would need a cause beyond it to ground its limited existence. For *every* limited being is caused. But existence as such is unlimited, and if there is a limited existence, then something must be limiting it. And ultimately, the something that provides the limits for everything else that exists must itself be unlimited in its existence. The first Cause must be uncaused, and an uncaused cause cannot be a limited cause. It must be the unlimited or infinite cause of everything else.

2. *The words* necessary Being *have no consistent meaning.* The same criticism would be alleged about the words *uncaused Cause* that we have used. The answer is basically this: The meaning of these terms is derived from their relationship to what is dependent upon them. And this meaning is twofold: first, terms like "uncaused" and "independent" are *negative*. God is *not* limited, *not* dependent, *not* temporal, *not* caused, and *not* composed. We know what these limitations mean from experience and so, by contrast, we know that God does not have any of these limitations. However, a negative term does not denote a negative attribute. It is not the affirmation of nothing; rather, it is the negation of all limitation in the first Cause.

Second, there is a *positive* meaning to the word *cause* in the description *uncaused Cause*. A cause is a necessary and sufficient condition for something else. An existential cause is the necessary and sufficient ground of the very existence of something else. And an existential cause of present existence is the here-and-now reality condition for all dependent existence. This provides the positive content to the existing cause from which the negations remove all limitations. The fact that the first Cause is "*un*-caused" (negative aspect) defines it as an unlimited kind of cause. And the fact that it is a "cause" designates it the creative condition for all finite beings (positive meaning of first Cause). So we know that it has the power to bring and maintain things in existence (from the fact that it is an "uncaused" kind of cause). Thus the term *uncaused Cause* has distinct meaning in relation to the effects it produces, both positively and negatively. The same applies to all the other qualities that are implied in "uncaused," such as eternal, necessary, infinite, and simple.

---

8. See chapter 8 for the full statement of Hume's and Kant's objections.

3. *There is no way to establish the principle of causality.* Granting Hume's epistemological atomism—that all empirical impressions are "entirely loose and separate"—there is no empirical way to establish a necessary causal connection for sensible experience. But the preceding cosmological argument is based not on empirical observation but on metaphysical necessity. Hume himself never denied that things have a cause for their existence: "I never asserted so absurd a proposition as that anything might arise without a cause."[9] Indeed, it would be ontologically absurd to suppose that something could arise from nothing. The principle of existential causality is that "every limited being has a cause for its existence." This principle is not based in any mere conceptional or definitional necessity but in the fundamental reality that nonexistence cannot cause existence.

Our knowledge of the need for existential causality arises out of an analysis of finite being (premise 2). The analysis may be summarized thus: Existence as such is unlimited; all limited existence is being limited by something distinct from existence itself (this limiting factor will be called essence); whatever is being limited is being caused (for to be limited in being is to be caused to be in a certain finite way; a limited existence is a caused existence); therefore, all limited beings are caused beings.

We might also note that all limited beings are composed beings; they are composed of existence and essence—an essence that limits the kind of existence they can have. Likewise, an unlimited Being is an uncomposed Being (i.e., a simple Being). Such a Being has no limiting essence as such. Its essence is identical with its unlimited existence. The need for causality, then, is derived from an analysis of what finite being is. Upon examination, finite being is seen to be caused being, and caused being must have a cause of its being.

4. *Theistic arguments convince few, usually only those who like abstract reasoning.* It is not abstract reasoning that is involved in the preceding theistic argument. It is not a purely rational process but an ontological insight, analysis, and inference based on the concrete realities of the experience of limited or finite being. There is no dependence in the argument on purely abstract principles such as the principle of sufficient reason. There are no conceptual necessities such as a Being who logically cannot not exist. Everything flows from the nature of experienced and undeniable (not inconceivable) reality. Something exists (this is undeniable, though not inconceivable); and since this something is experienced as limited existence, it must be limited or caused by some existence that is unlimited. This is not an abstract reasoning process. It is a search for the real ground of real beings.

Whether anyone is convinced by this argument will depend on several

9. David Hume, *The letters of David Hume,* ed. J. Y. T. Greig, 2 vols. (Oxford: Clarendon, 1932), 1:187.

factors. First, granting the argument's validity, it will depend in part on one's understanding of this argument as to whether he will be convinced or not. Second, once the mind understands the argument, it will depend on whether one wills to assent to it. One is never forced to believe what his mind understands as true. There may be other personal factors beyond the analysis here that lead a man to remain unconvinced (i.e., uncommitted to the truth of the argument). Theistic arguments do not automatically convert. On the other hand, persons of good will who understand the argument ought to accept it as true. And an increasing number of thinkers do accept the validity of theistic arguments.[10]

5. *An infinite series is possible.* An infinite series of simultaneous and existentially dependent causes is *not* possible, as was demonstrated (premise 3). There must be a here-and-now ground for a simultaneous series of causes, none of which would otherwise have a ground for its existence. An ungrounded infinite regress is tantamount to affirming that the existence in the series arises from nonexistence, since no cause in the series has a real ground for its existence. Or, if one cause in the series grounds the existence of the others, then it must be a first Cause (and hence the series is not infinite). Otherwise it turns out to be a cause that causes its own existence (which is impossible), while it is causing the existence of everything else in the series.

Confusion sometimes arises because mathematical (abstract) infinites are mistaken for metaphysical (actual) infinite series. An actual infinite series of real finite beings is impossible. For in such a series it is always possible to add one more. But since one more than infinite is impossible, it follows that such a series must always be finite.

6. *The cosmological argument depends on the invalid ontological argument.* This is not true of the argument given here. It begins with existence, not thought (e.g., it begins with "Something exists," not with "that than which nothing greater can be conceived"). It proceeds with ontologically grounded principles and not with mere rationally undeniable thought (i.e., it proceeds with "Nothing cannot cause something" rather than "Everything must have a sufficient reason").

Our restated cosmological argument concludes with a real Ground of all

---

10. There are two other reasons many philosophers never arrive at this theistic conclusion. One is that they never ask metaphysical questions about the nature of reality or being as such. Perhaps they are methodologically preoccupied with procedural questions (How?) or with descriptive questions (What?) or with the existential question (So what?) and never ask the metaphysical question (Why?). Secondly, those who, like Heidegger, do ask basic metaphysical questions do not give any metaphysical answers. Heidegger asked the basic metaphysical question: Why is there something rather than nothing at all? But he did not give a satisfactory answer. *Dasein* (man) is simply the being-there, the thrust one who is gratuitously hanging without any grounding. He is dependent but not dependent on anything. He is thrust there but no one thrust him there. His existence is given but not given by anyone.

finite being as opposed to a logically necessary Being (i.e., with "unlimited Cause of existence for all limited existence," as opposed to "a Being which logically cannot not be"). The restated cosmological argument does not begin with the a priori and at no point does it borrow from the purely conceptual to complete its task. It is not based on the invalid ontological argument.

7. *Existential statements are not logically necessary.* This objection is really self-destroying. For either the statement "No existential statements are necessary" is itself a statement about existence, or else it is not. If it is a statement about existence, it is self-defeating, for it claims to be both necessary and about reality, while it is saying no necessary statements can be made about reality. On the other hand, if it is merely a metastatement, or statement about statements (and not really a statement about reality), then it is uninformative about what kind of statements may or may not be made about reality. In brief, the only way to deny existentially necessary statements as possible is to make (or imply) one in the very denial, which is self-falsifying.

Theists have attempted to offer examples of existentially necessary statements. "Square circles do not exist," "There are an infinite number of prime numbers," and "I exist" are samples of allegedly existentially necessary statements that theists give. The problem with the first one is that it is negative and does not assert that anything does exist. The problem with the second one is that numbers do not exist in the same sense in which material objects or persons exist (and hence cannot be used as a premise in a cosmological argument).

Only the third example is theistically usable, and it is not a logically necessary statement. The basis for the truth of "I exist" is not logic but fact. For my nonexistence is not logically inconceivable. It is not logically impossible that I do not exist. I am not a logically necessary being. True, the statement "I exist" is undeniable (though not logically inconceivable). But it is undeniable only because, as a matter of fact, I do indeed exist. If I did not exist (which is logically conceivable), then a true statement could not be made of me (e.g., "He does not exist"). Hence, the actual basis for the truth of the statement "I exist" or "Something exists," used as a premise in the cosmological argument, is not logical but ontological. I do exist and therefore I cannot consistently deny that I do exist.

Granted that I do exist, it is "logically necessary"[11] for me not to deny that I do exist. But this "logical necessity" is based on the actuality of my existence

11. Logic is not the basis for reality; reality is the basis for logic. The impossibility of square circles existing is not because mere formal logic dictates this is impossible. Formally incompatible concepts of squareness and circleness do not make the actuality of square circles impossible. Rather, what makes square circles actually incompatible is that no state of affairs can be actualized in which one and the same thing is simultaneously square and round in the same way.

and not on the inconceivability of my nonexistence. That is, this "logical necessity" is dictated only by reality; reality is not dictated by logical necessity.[12] Logic flows from reality and not reality from logic.[13] In summation, the reason that the statement "I exist" is true is not the logical impossibility of its opposite ("I do not exist") but the actual undeniability of its truth. I do exist and therefore it is undeniable that "I do exist" (though not logically impossible that I do not exist). The pure rationalist confuses actual undeniability with logical inconceivability. The statements in the cosmological argument (such as "Something exists" and "God exists") are, we suggest, actually undeniable but their opposite is not logically inconceivable. This leads to the next objection.

8. *What is rationally necessary is not ontologically necessary.* We argued earlier that what is rationally inescapable to affirm of reality is undeniably true (chap. 5). Simply put, the argument is this: What is inescapably true, is true of reality. If a given statement is the only affirmable statement about reality, then it must be true. For instance, it is undeniable that the law of noncontradiction is applicable to reality, since it is derived from reality. Every denial that noncontradiction does apply to reality turns out to be either false or self-defeating, such as "It is a noncontradictory affirmation about reality to say that reality is not noncontradictory" or "It is logically possible with regard to reality that logical possibility does not apply to reality." Neither of these statements can maintain itself. Assuming there is some reality (which cannot be denied), then the only affirmably true statement is that what is undeniably so, is true of reality. That is, the only statements that can be successfully made about reality are actually descriptive of reality. What is actually necessary to affirm about reality is undeniably true of reality.

Cosmological theism, such as defended here, is not interested in rational inescapability as such. It is interested in existential undeniability. If something exists, and it is undeniably true that something does exist, then there must be a necessary and sufficient ground for that existence. The necessity that primarily interests us is real necessity, not mere rational necessity.

It is true that logical necessity follows from ontological necessity, and the theist ought to put his argument in logically valid form. But the fact of God's

12. The rational principle of noncontradiction, for example, grows out of the ontological fact that being is not nonbeing. For it is ontologically so that being is and that nonbeing is not. Hence, it follows that being is not nonbeing, which is the ontological basis of the principle of noncontradiction.

13. Some theists are willing to grant that the cosmological argument cannot be put in a logically airtight form (see Eric L. Mascall, *He Who Is* [London: Longmans, Green and Co., 1943], p. 80). Rather than a logical argument it is a metaphysical insight into the cosmological relationship of contingent and necessary being that is beneath the cosmological argument, they contend. Nevertheless, the lack of logical necessity notwithstanding, it is ontologically necessary to have a ground for the existence of all finite beings.

existence does not rest on the *logical* validity of theistic arguments. Of course, the theistic argument ought, if possible, to be put in logically valid form, but if it is not, the theist need not despair. Ontological necessity does not rest on formal logic, and the theistic case is still built on an ontologically necessary inference. One thing, however, must be maintained by cosmological theism: that the theistic argument is derived from and based on actual existence. It begins with the fact that something finite exists and proceeds by means of existential causality to conclude that there exists an infinite Being as the Ground of finite being.

9. *The cosmological argument leads to metaphysical contradictions.* Kant offered several alleged contradictions that he thought resulted from applying cosmological argumentation to reality. Three of these antinomies apply to our cosmological argument.

The first antinomy concerns *time.* If we assume that time applies to reality, then the contradiction results that the world is *both* temporal and eternal. *Thesis:* The world must have begun in time or else an infinity of moments have elapsed before it began, and this is impossible (since an infinity of moments can never be completed). *Antithesis:* The world could not have begun in time, for that implies that there was a time before time began, and this is contradictory.

The answer to Kant's first antinomy is that his view of time is incorrect. Time is not a continuum of successive moments that exist without beginning or end. Creation did not begin in time that was already there; creation is the beginning of time. The only thing "prior" to time is eternity, and eternity is prior in a causal but not a temporal way. Also, Kant's objection overlooks the possibility of an eternal creation, which possibility some theists accept (a la Aquinas).[14] In any event, Kant's objection does not affect the argument based on a here-and-now existential causality. For this type of cosmological argument is not dependent on a specific view about the origin of creation but only its present conservation in existence. The finite world demands a cause right now, regardless of whether it began in time or is eternal.

Another antinomy is about *causality.* It argues that it must be true that the world both has a first Cause and does not have a first Cause. *Thesis:* Not every cause has a cause or else a series of causes would not begin to cause as they in fact do. *Antithesis:* A series of causes cannot have a beginning, since everything demands a cause. Hence, the series must go on infinitely.

This antinomy has already been answered. The antithesis is wrong: not every cause needs a cause; only finite things need causes. Thus there can be a beginning of the series, providing we arrive at a Cause of it that is not finite.

---

14. Aquinas rejects eternal creation, not because it is philosophically impossible but because it is doctrinally incorrect (see Gen. 1:1; Heb. 11:3; Col. 1:16–17).

Only finite causes need a cause; the first uncaused Cause needs no cause, because it is not finite.

The last antinomy concerns *contingency*. Kant insists that everything must be both contingent and not be contingent, if we assume that these concepts apply to reality. *Thesis:* Not everything is contingent or else there would be no condition for contingency (i.e., the dependent must be depending on something that is not dependent). *Antithesis:* Everything must be contingent, for necessity applies only to concepts and not to things.

Theists reject Kant's antithesis. There is no way to deny that necessity can apply to reality without making a necessary statement about reality. Only an ontological disproof could possibly establish Kant's point. And it has already been shown (in chap. 7) that attempted ontological disproofs are self-defeating. Further, the cosmological argument has already concluded that something necessarily exists. The validity of this argument is the refutation of Kant's contention that necessity does not apply to existence.

10. *The conclusion of the argument does not prove a theistic God.* How can the conclusion of the cosmological argument be identified with a theistic God any more than with polytheistic gods, a panentheistic God, a pantheistic God, or even the atheist's material universe? Any of these could be the "uncaused Cause" of the cosmological argument. The answer to this question will relate to each of these other alternatives in turn.

First, the uncaused Cause is not many polytheistic gods, as was shown earlier (in premise 5). There cannot be more than one unlimited existence as such; more than the Most is not possible. Further, in order to differ, one being would have to lack some characteristic that the other one had. But any being that lacked some characteristic of existence would not be an unlimitedly perfect existence. In other words, two infinite beings cannot differ in their potentiality, since they have no potentiality; they are pure actuality. And they cannot differ in their actuality, since actuality as such does not differ from actuality as such. Hence, they must be identical. There is only one unlimited Cause of all limited existence.

Secondly, the uncaused Cause is not identical with the material universe. The ordinary conception of the material universe is of a spatiotemporal limited system. Now it has already been shown (in premise 5) that an uncaused Cause is unlimited. Further, since space and time imply limitations to a here-and-now kind of existence, it follows that God cannot be a being whose existence is limited by space and time. God's existence is unlimited in any way, for he is unlimited existence. Hence, God's existence is not identical with the spatiotemporal existence of the material universe. God is in the temporal world as its very ground of continuing existence, but he is not of the world in that it is limited and he is not.

The claim that the whole of the material universe is not temporal and limited, as are the parts, only proves what theism claims, namely, that there is beyond the contingent world of the limited spatiotemporality a "whole" reality that is eternal, unlimited, and necessary. That is, it is an admission to theism that there is a God beyond the limited, changing world of experience. It is a surrogate of God which admits that there is a "whole" reality that is "more" than the experienced part of reality and that has all the attributes of the theistic God.

Thirdly, the uncaused Cause is not identical with the God of panentheism. Dipolar theism or process theology affirms that God has two poles: an actual pole (which is identified with the changing temporal world) and a potential pole (which is eternal and unchanging). Such a conception of God must be rejected for the following reasons. The conclusion of the cosmological argument demonstrates the need for a God of pure actuality with no potentiality (pole) at all. Further, God cannot be subject to limitations, composition, or spatiotemporality (as was shown in premise 5). Moreover, God cannot have poles or aspects, since he is absolutely simple (i.e., uncomposed) with no duality at all (premise 5). He is a simple and unlimited Existence as such, with no limited pole. A partly limited unlimited existence is a contradiction. Further, God cannot be subject to change. For anything that changes must be composed of actuality and potentiality for change. Change is a passing from potentiality to actuality; from what can be to what actually becomes. But since existence as such has no potentiality, it follows that it cannot change. If something changes, it proves thereby that it was not pure actuality but possessed some potentiality for the change it underwent. A pure and unlimited actuality cannot change. In addition, the God of panentheism or process theology is a confusion of the world process with the God who grounds that process. God is in the process as the unchanging basis for change, but God is not of the process. God is the cause of all finite, changing existence, but he is beyond all finitude and change. God changes relationally (by entering changing relationships with the world), but he does not change essentially. When the person moves from one side of the pillar to the other, there is a real change in relationship, but there is no change in the pillar.

Fourthly, the uncaused Cause is not the God of pantheism. Pantheism affirms that an unlimited and necessary Being exists but denies the reality of limited and finite beings. Everything other than God is illusory; there is really only one Being in the universe. This position must be rejected for several reasons. Pantheism is contrary to our experience of ourselves as real but finite persons. It is contrary to our experience of other persons as real but different centers of consciousness. It is contrary to the experienced reality of interpersonal relationship with other selves, since if there are not two really different selves, then they cannot really fellowship with or love each other. It is contrary to our experience of God. Indeed, it makes religious experience impossible. All I-Thou experience reduces to an I-I dialogue within God himself. For there is only one Being in a pantheistic universe; all other beings turn out to be totally illusory at worst or merely modal or emanational at best. But in any event, in pantheism beings are not really different from God. Also, pantheism is contrary to our experience of evil, suffering, and death. It has no satisfactory explanation for the origin, persistence, and apparent reality of evil. Poetically put, why is it that when I sit on a pin and it punctures my skin, I dislike what I fancy I feel? Pantheism is contrary to our experience of change in the world. It affirms that all change, including that in our own minds and consciousness, is unreal. No river moves, no tree grows, and no man ages. If there is any real change, there must really be changing beings distinct from God, for God is an unchanging Being. The existence of finite, limited, changing beings is not rationally inescapable, but it is existentially undeniable. We do experience finite existence. To deny this is to affirm the obvious absurdity that we are God. That is, pantheism, if true, reduces to self-deification. Also, pantheism is self-defeating. It assumes there are finite beings in order to deny that there are finite beings. The pantheist who is affirming the position of pantheism acknowledges that he speaks from a finite perspective, and yet he is unwilling to deny the validity of his affirmation. But how can there be real finite perspectives without real finite perspectors? Affirmations come only from affirmers and thoughts from thinkers. Hence, the pantheist assumes the reality of what he attempts to deny, namely, that there are finite beings. Finally, the pantheist's denial that he is finite and unchanging is self-defeating. He did not always believe this way; he *came to believe* this way (by some process of enlightenment). But if he went through some changing process, then he is not an unchanging being after all.

11. *There is an equivocation on the word* cause *in the argument.* It is sometimes objected that the word *cause* in the premise means finite cause but in the conclusion it means infinite cause and that this is an equivocation. Hence, the argument commits a four-term fallacy. In answering this charge, it should be pointed out that the word *cause* as such means neither finite cause nor infinite cause. It means a necessary and sufficient condition for the existence of something else, a ground of being, that could be either finite or infinite. Now it turns out by way of conclusion that the ground of being is itself ungrounded by anything else; that the cause is not caused by another; that the limiter is unlimited (i.e., not finite or infinite). Hence, the qualification of the cause of being as an *un*-caused kind of cause specifies that it is not a *non*-finite kind of cause. It is an unconditioned conditioner, an ungrounded Ground of all being. This is not an equivocation but a necessary implication of the negation *not* or *un-*; it is a not-caused kind of cause. And a not-caused or not-limited kind of cause is an in-finite kind of cause.

What was an open possibility in the premise (that it could be either finite or infinite) became definitely determined by way of negation in the conclusion. The first Cause of all that exists is not caused by another and hence it must be a not-limited kind of cause. The first Cause is not caused, because it is *first* (no infinite regress being possible). And an uncaused Cause is unlimited (see premise 5). Hence, it follows that the first Cause is an unlimited kind of limiter or cause. The Ground of all limited existence is itself unlimited. No equivocation is involved. Rather, the infinite Cause is a necessary inference from the premises of the argument that demands that there be an uncaused Cause of all dependent being.

12. *The universe as a whole does not need a cause; only the parts do.* The cosmological argument holds that the universe as a whole is contingent or dependent because the parts are contingent or dependent. But this is usually called a fallacy of composition. The whole world is not small because the parts of the world are all small. The All-Star team is not better than the first-place team because each player on it is the best in his position in the league. This is clearly fallacious reasoning. It is formally invalid. However, what is formally invalid is sometimes actually true. For instance, the whole desk is wooden because each part is made of wood. This whole mosaic is extended because each part is extended. Since it is sometimes clearly true that the whole has what the parts have, precisely *because* the parts have it, then we must ask: What are the necessary conditions under which what is formally invalid is actually true? The answer is this: Whenever the very nature of the parts is such that the whole must possess this characteristic too, then it is true (even if formally invalid) that the whole must have what the parts have.[15] For example, it is of the very nature of extended parts that any combination of them necessitates that the total of these parts be extended. Likewise, pieces of blue tile combined *cause* the whole floor to be blue. This can be known only by an analysis of the properties involved. On the other hand, combining triangles does not necessarily form a triangular whole (two triangles can make a square). A collection of round objects does not cause the whole group to be round. But the very nature of the geometric figures, such as triangles, necessitates that a whole combination of connected geometric figures must itself be a geometric figure. Here again, only an analysis of the properties involved will determine the characteristic of the whole. The nature of a circle is such that many circles obviously do not make a circle. However, the nature of solid parts combined is that they make a solid whole.

Now the nature of dependent beings is such that many dependent beings added together do not make an independent being. The sum total of all grounded beings does not equal a ground for their being. Indeed, if an infinite

15. See Bruce R. Reichenbach, *The Cosmological Argument: A Reassessment* (Springfield, Ill.: Charles C. Thomas, 1972), pp. 97–102.

regress of dependent beings does not make these dependent beings any less dependent on a Cause beyond the series, then certainly no finite number constituting the material universe can do so. No matter how great the number of things that do not explain their own existence, they do not provide an explanation (or ground) of their existence. An endless number of nonexplanations added together do not equal an explanation; they merely equal one monumental nonexplanation. Thus an infinite regress does not provide an explanation; it simply puts off—forever—giving the needed explanation, that is, cause. The apparent plausibility in the-world-as-a-whole-explains-itself argument is derived from the fact that the whole is greater than the sum of its parts. Wholeness is something more than parts, as is readily apparent from the difference between all of the parts of one's car scattered on the garage floor and the whole car that he drives. Three sides ($/\backslash$) do not necessarily make a triangle ($\triangle$). Wholeness is something more than all the parts. A musical composition is more than mere notes, and an artistic composition is more than pigments on a canvas.

The nontheist's argument gains plausibility in the light of the preceding distinction. For what applies to the parts does not necessarily apply to the whole, which is something more. However, even with this distinction, the nontheist's view is not forwarded. For, as is suggested from all these illustrations, the whole needs a cause to account for it. Notes do not put themselves together into songs, nor do pigments transform themselves into paintings. Every composition needs a composer; every painting, an artist. And on a more fundamental metaphysical level, if the universe is finite or limited in its being, then it is composed of essence (potentiality) and existence (actuality). But no potentiality as such can actualize itself. Hence, there must be some pure actuality (God) to actualize it. If, on the other hand, one wishes to argue that the material universe is unlimited or infinite, then we have moved back to pantheism and the objections to pantheism must be repeated. Or else, if the "whole" is not a limited and dependent group of beings, then it is merely a covert way of admitting the theist's position that there is a "moreness" to reality which is itself infinite and unchanging (God).

13. *The universe is mutually dependent and does not need a cause beyond it.* Another objection similar to the former is that the universe is a mutually dependent whole. It needs no cause beyond it, because one part causes another in a mutually dependent whole. But this is clearly an impossibility; if *every* part is dependent on a cause for its present existence, then at least one of the causes must be existence. Otherwise nothing would be caused to exist (which is contrary to the granted fact that everything is depending for its existence on another). But if everything is being caused to exist at the very instant at least one thing is causing existence, then this one thing must be causing its own existence, and this is impossible. Mutually dependent beings

are a vicious circle of beings, since they have at least one impossible self-caused being somewhere among them.

If an attempt is made to deny that at least one being is causing the rest in the group, it must be acknowledged that either the dependent or caused beings are not really being caused (and this is contradictory) or else there is beyond the circle of dependence a Being that is causing their being. This is what the theist contends. In brief, either mutually dependent beings have no cause for their being, have within their midst at least one self-caused being, or appeal to a Cause beyond them to explain why they are existing rather than not existing. The first two alternatives are impossible and the last demands a first Cause beyond the mutually dependent circle to ground it. The first alternative says a self-caused being is possible; the second says uncaused finite being is possible; and the third admits that the circle is not really mutually dependent but is dependent on something outside it for the present existence in the world.

14. *There is no need for a here-and-now cause of existence.* There are two aspects to objections of this kind. Some contend that it is not meaningful to speak of simultaneous cause-effect relations; effects always follow causes temporally, or at least they may. Others simply say that there is no need to insist that the world needs a conserving cause; an originating cause, if anything, would be sufficient.

First of all, simultaneous causality does make sense. There is no contradiction in saying that an effect is being effected at the very instant it is being caused. This is clearly the case with the relation between the premises (cause) and the conclusion (effect) of a syllogism. Cause and effect are simultaneous, for the instant one takes away the premise(s), at that very instant the conclusion does not follow.

Likewise, the causal relation between one's face and the image in the mirror is simultaneous. What clouds the understanding of the simultaneity of causality is the confusion of an effect with an aftereffect. For example, when I throw the ball, it continues to move after I am no longer throwing it. The clock continues to run after I wind it, and so on. However, in each of these and like examples the aftereffect is being directly and simultaneously effected by some cause, after I take my hand off them. The force of inertia keeps the ball moving; the laws of tension and reaction keep the spring moving the clock. If any of these laws would go out of existence, at that very instant the aftereffect would stop dead. If inertia ceased the very instant after the ball left my hand, the ball would instantly stop in midair. Likewise, the clock would stop ticking the instant the physical laws effecting it were nonoperative. Every so-called aftereffect is only an effect of some simultaneous causes. In like manner, there are no existential aftereffects. Whatever is causing something to exist right now must be causing it right now.

It is clearly the case with finite beings that they need present here-and-now causes of their being. A basic distinction will help us see this point. The artist is not the cause of the being of a painting; he is only the cause of the becoming (or coming to be) of the painting. The painting continues to be after the artist takes his hands off it. In like manner, the father does not cause the being of the son but only his becoming, for when the father dies the son continues to live.

Now it is clearly necessary that finite beings have a cause not only of their becoming but also of their here-and-now being. For at every moment of their existence they are dependent for their existence on another. They never cease to be limited, finite, contingent beings. And as such they demand a cause for their existence. For every finite being is caused. Hence it does not matter whether we are referring to John Doe at moment^1 of his existence or m^2 or m^3. He is still existing, he still has a received existence, and therefore he is still receiving his existence from something beyond him. Changing the moment of his dependent existence does not make him a nondependent existent. Perhaps some of the problem would be removed if we did not talk of exist*ence* (as though it were a whole package received at once) but of exist*ing* (which is a moment-by-moment process). Maybe the word *being* is even more misleading in this regard. No one receives his whole being at once, nor even the next instant of it. Each creature has a present "*be*-ing." Existence comes only a moment at a time. But at each moment of a dependent be-ing there must be some independent Be-ing on which he is depending for that moment of his be-ing. In this respect, the distinction between the Latin *esse* (to be) and *ens* (being, thing) is helpful. God is pure *Esse* and our present *esse* is dependent on him. Pure Existence must existentialize our potentiality for existence; otherwise we would not exist. God as pure Actuality is actualizing everything that is actual and not merely potential. Hence, it is the present actuality of all that is actual that demands a causal ground.

15. *The act-potency or contingent-necessity models are arbitrarily imposed on experience.*^{16} This objection states that it is only because we have modeled reality as "contingent" or "dependent" that we are forced to conclude that there is a "necessary" or "independent" being. The reality of our experience is capable of being modeled in other ways that do not demand this conclusion. The world of experience does not carry with it its own models. Models come from elsewhere (the Christian model from the Bible) and they are imposed on experience. The facts of experience are not self-interpreting; there are no self-interpreting facts. We bring interpretative models to the data of experience from elsewhere.

A detailed answer to this question would be a whole treatise on epis-

---

16. See Milton R. Munitz, *The Mystery of Existence* (New York: Appleton-Century-Crofts, 1965) and Thomas McPherson, "Finite and Infinite," *Mind* 66 (1957): 379–84.

temology. It will suffice here to note several things. First, the whole epistemology we have used has been defended premise by premise in the cosmological argument.

Secondly, the model of dependency is not derived from isolated facts but from undeniable experience. We do not merely feel dependent; we are dependent beings. It would be existentially absurd and contrary to our experience of reality to claim that we are not dependent beings. This would mean that we are independent or necessary beings. Even nontheists (e.g., Heidegger) have shown that our whole phenomenology of being in this world evidences a thrustness or contingency that must be formulated into the basic metaphysical question: "Why is there something rather than nothing at all?"[17] The existentially undeniable experience of contingency is not an arbitrary model superimposed on experience. It is an essential model that arises necessarily out of an analysis of the modality of our be-ing in the world.

Thirdly, regardless of where the contingency model comes from, it fits. Whatever its origin, it fits the world and our experience. It is comprehensive, consistent, empirically adequate, and existentially relevant.[18]

Finally, unless one denies the reality of change, the dependency model is necessitated by an analysis of the very nature of changing beings (as was shown in premise 2). In brief, the contingency model is no more arbitrary than the laws of thought (which must also apply to reality, as was argued earlier). For what I experience, including myself, is either contingent or else it is necessary. If it is necessary, then we have already arrived at the necessary Being. If it is contingent, then it must be grounded in a necessary Being. In either case, we have the conclusion of the cosmological argument.

What is at stake is not whether there is a necessary and unlimited Being but whether there are really any contingent and limited beings. As absurd as it may seem to our experience of be-ing in this world, the only successful way to challenge the theistic model is to deny there is any such thing as a limited, dependent, or contingent being. This has already been answered in premise 1 and in answer to objection 10. It will suffice to repeat here only that it is logically possible that there are no contingent beings, but it is experientially and existentially undeniable. So the metaphysical model used in the cosmological argument is based in our undeniably limited existence in this world. Other contrary models are logically possible, but they are neither

17. See Martin Heidegger, *An Introduction to Metaphysics* (New York: Doubleday, Anchor Books, 1961), chap. 1.

18. By "consistent" we mean there are no internal contradictions in theism. By "comprehensive" is meant that the theistic model is applicable to all of reality. "Empirical fit" indicates that the model adequately accounts for all of our experiences in the world. And existential relevance means that this model has real significance for, and applicability to, life.

based on experience nor do they fit the facts of the world. Only the theistic model accurately describes reality.

16. *The cosmological argument commits some modal fallacies.* Modal logic is based on the distinction between what is possible and what is necessary. This form of reasoning has developed its own list of fallacies. For example, it is a fallacy to infer from the mode of a statement to the mode of the content of the statement and vice versa. Thus it does not follow from the statement, "It is possible that the moon is made of cheese," that the moon is made of possible cheese. Similarly, from the fact that it is necessary for the New York Yankees to have a manager in order to win the pennant, one cannot infer that the Yankees have a necessary manager (in fact, in modal logic the term has no meaning).

Now it has been suggested that in various ways the cosmological argument is guilty of fallacious modal reasoning. It might not follow from the fact that universally all things possibly do not exist that the universe possibly does not exist.

In response it can be noted that this objection is only a variety of objection 14. It is true that one statement does not follow from the other on the basis of pure logical possibility, but they are both true. On that same basis it is not legitimate to infer from the fact that each component of my car will possibly fail that the entire car will possibly fail, but both statements are true. What is at stake is not logical possibility, but actual cause of composition.

Alvin Plantinga would argue that it does not follow from the fact that it is possible for all the parts of my car to break down at one time or another that it is necessary that at one time all the parts will break down.[19] Thus, though all contingent beings possibly do not-exist, they do not necessarily not-exist at one time and thus need no universal cause of existence. Of course he is correct in this assertion and thereby he throws some formulations of the argument from contingency into a dubious light. But the argument based on existential causality avoids that problem; it is not concerned with showing that all things that could not-exist needed a single cause to produce their existence, but that all things that do exist (though possibly could not-exist) need a cause for their present existence, both individually and in toto.

A second possible charge of committing a modal fallacy would be to say that it is illegitimate to infer from the fact that the world necessarily needs a being as first Cause that the world needs a necessary being as first Cause. Again, as it is stated, that charge would be correct, but our cosmological argument does not make that inference. God is not considered necessary Being because the argument necessarily demonstrates his being. He is called

19. Alvin Plantinga, *God, Freedom, and Evil* (New York: Harper Torchbooks, 1974), p. 80.

necessary Being because ontologically he cannot not-be. We learn of his necessary being not from the rigor of our premises, but because existentially a first Cause must be a necessary Being. That this is a meaningful assertion has already been shown in conjunction with the refutation of objection 8.

The mistake of many theists, expecially since Leibniz, is to cast the cosmological argument in a context of logical necessity based on the principle of sufficient reason. This ultimately leads to contradictions and an invalidating of the argument. In contrast to this procedure, we have tried to restate the argument beginning with limited existence and by use of the principle of existential causality to proceed finally to an unlimited Cause of all existence.[20] In this way the conclusion is not rationally inescapable. But it is, we have argued, existentially undeniable. In brief, if any finite being exists, then an infinite Being exists as an actual and necessary ground for finite being.

One final word of perspective. The existence of God does not result from the cosmological argument. What results from the argument is a truth (i.e., a statement about God's existence that corresponds to reality). Theistic arguments are not the ground for God's existence; God's existence needs no ground (he is the ungrounded Ground of all other existence). At best the cosmological argument is a logical schema, based on reality, which rationally explains why limited being must be caused by an unlimited Being.

20. The cosmological argument in existential form is not new. Anselm (in *Monologium*) Aquinas, and Scotus all had strong forms of it (see chap. 8). Due to the influence of rationalism, modern philosophy has obscured the full force of this form of the cosmological argument by importing the principle of sufficient reason. See John E. Gurr, *The Principle of Sufficient Reason in Some Scholastic Systems, 1750–1900* (Milwaukee: Marquette University Press, 1959), p. 130.

PART 3 �֍

GOD AND LANGUAGE

GUIDING QUESTIONS

1. To what extent is the controversy on religious language generated internally to the religious community; to what extent is it an issue toward the outside?
2. What are the advantages and weaknesses of negative religious language?
3. Why is positive religious language essential; why must it be analogical?
4. What are the strengths of the theory of analogy based on intrinsic causality?
5. How do modern theories of religious language exemplify the necessity of analogy in order to avoid equivocation?

RECOMMENDED COLLATERAL READING

A. J. Ayer, *Language, Truth, and Logic.* New York: Dover, 1964.

Frederick Ferré, *Language, Logic and God.* New York: Harper Torchbooks, 1969.

Jerry H. Gill, *On Knowing God: New Directions for the Future of Theology.* Philadelphia: Westminster, 1981.

Battista Mondin, *The Principle of Analogy in Protestant and Catholic Theology.* The Hague: Nijhoff, 1963.

10 ❉

The Problem of Religious Language

Means of Expressing God

People have expressed their religious experience in different ways. Among these the most common are ritual, symbol, myth, and dogma.[1] It goes without saying that linguistic expressions are of special importance among literate peoples. But before the nature and problem of religious language are explored, a brief treatment of the major nonlinguistic expressions of religious experience will be helpful background for understanding the linguistic expressions that follow from them. Then we will explore the various ways of construing religious language, beginning with a look at language in general and then outlining the negative, positive, analogical, and model alternatives. These options will constitute the subject matter of the subsequent three chapters.

Some Nonlinguistic Means of Expressing Religious Transcendence

Some have argued that ritual is the earliest formal religious expression, even before myth, because ritualism can be observed in animals, which are destitute of a mythology.[2] Others argue that ritual comes before mythology, since it is more likely that preliterates danced out their religious values before they thought them out.[3] On the other hand, it seems more likely that the "revelation" came before the reenactment of it in ritual.[4] At any rate, it is certainly reasonable to conclude that somewhere behind the plethora of religious expressions there were experiences that gave rise to these mythological and ritualistic religious expressions.[5]

1. Other religious expressions may be found in art, image, conduct, and institution, but they are not directly related to our study here. Wilfred C. Smith has a good comparison of many of these in *The Meaning and End of Religion* (New York: New American Library of World Literature, 1964), pp. 156ff.

2. See Alfred North Whitehead, *Religion in the Making* (New York: World, 1960), p. 25. However, he acknowledges that in specific cases a myth may precede the ritual.

3. Winston L. King, *Introduction to Religion* (New York: Harper and Row, 1954), pp. 141, 142.

4. Mircea Eliade, *Myth and Reality*, trans. Willard R. Trask (New York: Harper and Row, 1963), p. 8.

5. Which comes first will probably depend on whether a myth or a ritual was used to evoke

RELIGIOUS EXPRESSION IN RITUAL

Ritual may be defined as that formalized symbolic way in which a social group periodically expresses and strengthens its beliefs and values.[6] Alfred North Whitehead described it as "the habitual performance of definite actions which have no direct relevance to the preservation of the physical organisms of the actor."[7] The present concern is not with specific rituals or their significance.[8] What is important is that religion invariably engenders ritualistic expressions.[9] Religion will be expressed in whatever way is most appropriate to the believer having the experience.

RELIGIOUS EXPRESSION IN SYMBOL

"Symbol," a broad term for religious expression, includes both myth and ritual.[10] Without pausing here to pass judgment on the validity of the distinction Paul Tillich drew between a "sign" (which, he said, does not participate in the reality to which it points) and a "symbol" (which does),[11] it is sufficient to note that "symbols have one characteristic in common with signs: they point beyond themselves to something else."[12] Symbols, to summarize Winston L. King, are nonliteral figures that point beyond themselves.[13] And religious symbols are directional but not contentful pointers toward the Transcendent. Michael Novak likens religious symbols to arrows shot in the direction of God but which fall back to earth before they touch him.[14] In other words, since religious symbols point beyond themselves, they are a fitting way of getting at the Transcendent, which goes beyond the human. And because religious experience involves something that transcends this empirical world, there is a need for some sort of symbolical or nonliteral

---

the religious experience. If the religious experience came via a myth, the ritualistic expression of that experience would be subsequent, and vice versa. If, however, the religious experience came some other way, the first means of expression would depend on whether the individual had greater propensity to act or to talk.

6. King, *Introduction to Religion*, p. 141.

7. Whitehead, *Religion in the Making*, p. 20.

8. For a treatment of this kind the works of Eliade are suggested: *Myth and Reality; The Myth of the Eternal Return*, trans. Willard R. Trask (New York: Pantheon, 1954); *The Sacred and the Profane*, trans. Willard R. Trask (New York: Harcourt, Brace and World, 1959).

9. See Henri Bergson, *The Two Sources of Morality and Religion*, trans. R. A. Audra and C. Brereton (New York: Doubleday, 1935), p. 20.

10. Paul Tillich, *The Dynamics of Faith* (New York: Harper Torchbooks, 1957), p. 117. Tillich called these latter two the intuitive and the active forms of symbol expression respectively.

11. See the discussion of Tillich's special use of "symbol" later in this chapter.

12. Tillich, *Dynamics of Faith*, p. 41.

13. King, *Introduction to Religion*, pp. 134–36.

14. Michael Novak, *Belief and Unbelief* (New York: Macmillan, 1965), p. 110.

means of expressing it.[15] This is why Tillich once wrote, "Nothing less than symbols and myths can express our ultimate concern."[16] That is, religious symbols are an attempt to express the Object of one's ultimate concern, and no words in their ordinary meaning express this extraordinary Object. Religious symbols are an attempt to express what cannot be literally and empirically stated. They point to something beyond the ordinary experience, to something transcendent. Sometimes symbols take on a linguistic expression (Tillich himself saw religious language as symbolic), but often a symbol can be pictorial (e.g., a crucifix or a mandala) or a sound (e.g., a gong or a mantra).

RELIGIOUS EXPRESSION IN MYTH

Religious experience also engenders myths.[17] That is, to quote Tillich, "the symbols of faith do not appear in isolation. They are united in 'stories of the gods,' which is the meaning of the Greek word 'mythos'—myth. . . . Myths are symbols of faith combined in stories about divine-human encounters."[18] The religious person is a myth-maker, for he has the irrepressible tendency to express what he experiences, and myths are a verbal expression of his religious experience(s).

Perhaps the most important thing that can be said about myth to the modern reader is that for the religious person a myth is a true story.[19] The myth is regarded by the primitive as a true story because it always deals with what he considers to be realities.[20]

Since we are not concerned here with the origin of myths,[21] it will suffice to

15. "It [demythologization] is an attempt which never can be successful, because symbol and myth are forms of the human consciousness which are always present. One can replace one myth by another, but one cannot remove the myth from man's spiritual life. For the myth is the combination of symbols of our ultimate concern" (Tillich, *Dynamics of Faith*, p. 50). With this Jaspers agreed when he wrote, "The real task, therefore, is not to demythologize, but to recover mythical thought in its original purity. . . ." Karl Jaspers and Rudolf Bultmann, *Myth and Christianity* (New York: Noonday, 1958), p. 17.

16. Paul Tillich, *Ultimate Concern*, ed. D. MacKenzie Brown (London: SCM, 1965), pp. 96, 53.

17. See William James, *The Varieties of Religious Experience* (New York: Mentor, New American Library, 1958) p. 423.

18. See Tillich, *Dynamics of Faith*, pp. 48, 49.

19. "What is important is the fact that 'primitives' are always aware of the difference between myths ('true stories') and tales or legends ('false stories')" (Eliade, *Myth and Reality*, p. 11n). Eliade points out that it has been only in the twentieth century that Western scholars have rediscovered myth as a "true" story as opposed to "fable" or "fiction." Ibid., p. 1.

20. See Eliade, *Myth and Reality*, p. 6. From the time of Xenophanes (c. 565–470) on, the Greeks came to reject more and more the mythological expressions found in Homer and Hesiod until the word *myth* was eventually emptied of any metaphysical value. Ibid., p. 1; cf. pp. 152, 153.

21. On the origin of myths see F. M. Cornford, *From Religion to Philosophy* (New York:

say that the myth-making ability seems to be coterminous with rational humanity.[22] What is important, however, is to note that myths are the symbolic forms by which the religious person expresses his awareness of transcendence.[23] A myth, according to Karl Jaspers, is a "cipher" of the Transcendent, a "code" pointing to God.[24] "If a myth is understood literally," wrote Tillich, "philosophy must reject it as absurd."[25] On the other hand, the myth understood symbolically "is the fundamental creation of every religious community."[26] It is because a myth is not to be understood literally that it cannot be empirically verified. "For the reality of the myth," said Jaspers, "is not empirical, [that is], it cannot be investigated in the world."[27]

Mircea Eliade lists five characteristics of myths,[28] but some of them are limited in applicability to myths of origin within primitive religions, and are therefore too narrow to cover religion in general. Jaspers's characterization of myths is more widely applicable: "(1) The myth tells a story and expresses intuitive insights, rather than universal concepts. . . . (2) The myth deals with sacred stories and visions, with stories about gods rather than with empirical realities. (3) The myth is a carrier of meanings which can be expressed only in the language of myth."[29] Briefly put, a myth is a story or series of images

---

Harper and Row, 1912), pp. 139ff.; Eliade, *Myth and Reality,* pp. 145ff., and Bergson, *Two Sources,* pp. 119ff.

22. Bergson writes, "Let us take, then, in the vaguely and doubtless artificially defined realm of imagination, the natural 'cut' which we have called myth-making and see to what use it is naturally put. To this faculty are due the novel, the drama, mythology together with all that preceded it. But then, there have not always been novelists and dramatists, whereas humanity has never subsisted without religion." *Two Sources,* p. 108.

23. Myths have other functions too: they are means by which religious people became aware of the Transcendent (Jaspers, *Myth and Christianity,* p. 3); they supply models for human behavior (Eliade, *Myth and Reality,* p. 8.).

24. Jaspers, *Myth and Christianity,* pp. 85, 87.

25. Tillich, *Dynamics of Faith,* p. 121.

26. Ibid. See also Jaspers, *Myth and Christianity,* pp. 16, 17.

27. Jaspers, *Myth and Christianity,* p. 85.

28. Eliade said, "In general it can be said that myth, as experienced by archaic societies, (1) constitutes the History of the acts of the Supernaturals; (2) that this History is considered to be absolutely *true* (because it is concerned with realities) and *sacred* (because it is the work of the Supernaturals); (3) that myth is always related to a 'creation,' it tells how something came into existence, or how a pattern of behavior, an institution, a manner of working were established; this is why myths constitute the paradigms for all significant human acts; (4) that by knowing the myth one knows the 'origin' of things and hence can control and manipulate them at will; this is not an 'external,' 'abstract' knowledge but a knowledge that one 'experiences' ritually, either by ceremonially recounting the myth or by performing the ritual for which it is the justification; (5) that in one way or another one 'lives' the myth, in the sense that one is seized by the sacred, exalting power of the events recollected or re-enacted." *Myth and Reality,* pp. 18, 19.

29. Jaspers, *Myth and Christianity,* pp. 15, 16. The untranslatability of a myth we take to

through which the transcendent world is symbolized.[30] It is a symbolic way of expressing one's religious ultimate; it is an empirical way of expressing the nonempirical Transcendent.

Linguistic Means of Expressing the Transcendent

The primary means of religious linguistic expression are in written revelation, creed, and dogma. As Ninian Smart observed, it is often not easy to draw a clear line of distinction between the mythological and the linguistic or doctrinal dimensions of religion, but the former is typically more colorful, symbolic, picturesque, and storylike. "Doctrines," he said, "are an attempt to give system, clarity, and intellectual power to what is revealed through the mythological and symbolic language of religious faith. . . ."[31]

THE ORIGIN OF GOD-TALK

F. M. Cornford argued that doctrinal representations of one's faith are an attempt to give a *logos* for the *mythos*. "To the mysticism of all ages," he wrote, "the visible world is a myth, a tale half true and half false, embodying a *logos,* the truth which is one."[32] That is, dogma grows out of a more sophisticated attempt to generalize and universalize the earlier mythological expressions of a religion. Whitehead agreed: "A dogma is the precise enunciation of a general truth, divested so far as possible from particular exemplification."[33]

Granting the close connection between mythos and logos, one can see why many philosophical concepts have mythological ancestors and that most mythological symbols have conceptual elements.[34] And because literate cultures tend to prize intellectual knowledge, the historical religions generally have a more developed doctrinal dimension than there is in tribal and prelit-

mean untranslatable into nonmythical (i.e., nonsymbolic), language. Myths are translatable from one language (e.g., Greek) into another (e.g., English).

30. See Ninian Smart, *The Religious Experience of Mankind* (New York: Charles Scribner's Sons, 1969), p. 8.

31. Ibid., pp. 15, 8.

32. Cornford, *From Religion to Philosophy*, pp. 141, 187; Cornford's discussion is helpful on this point. But we need not agree with him when he adds that "it then becomes an 'explanation' *(aition)*, professing to account for the existence and practice of the ritual, just as the [Platonic] Idea is erected into an explanation or account *(logos)* of the things that partake of it. . . ." Ibid., p. 259. There seems to be no reason why a logos cannot be an expression of a mythos without being an explanation or justification of it. See the discussion following.

33. Whitehead, *Religion in the Making*, p. 122.

34. Cornford lists several examples of concepts borrowed by Greek philosophers from their religious predecessors. *From Religion to Philosophy*, chaps. 1–4.

erate religions.[35] This has proven to be both a great advantage and a grave danger for religion.

THE ADVANTAGES OF LINGUISTIC EXPRESSIONS OF GOD

The great advantage of conceptualizing and rationalizing about one's religious experience is that by so doing he can understand, propagate, and preserve his faith. As Whitehead said, precise expression is in the long run a condition for the vivid realization, for effectiveness, for apprehension, and for survival. Conceptual progress—whether the truth of science or the truth of religion—is mainly a progress in the framing of concepts, in discarding artificial abstractions or partial metaphors, and in evolving notions which strike more deeply into the root of reality.[36] Also, as Rudolf Otto correctly observed, the process of conceptualization of religious transcendence guards a religion from sinking into fanaticism and pure mysticality and qualifies it as a religion for all of civilized humanity.[37] In fact, Otto goes so far as to say that this process of rationalization and moralizing of the numinous is the most important part of the history of religion.[38]

Further, it may be argued that conceptualization of religious experience is not only helpful but is in some sense necessary. Humanity has a propensity to give symbolic and linguistic expression to its deepest feelings about reality. Conceptualization, it would appear, is a mental "grasping together" of experience.[39] And even though experience is foundational to expressions about it, nevertheless experience is not meaningful unless it is conceptualized. Experience without expression is meaningless, and expressions without experience are empty.

THE DANGERS OF RELIGIOUS LANGUAGE

Wilfred C. Smith insists that any attempt to completely conceptualize a religion is a contradition in terms, for there is always more in principle in the Transcendent than a person can see and even more than he himself can say.[40] Nonetheless, he admits that we must somehow conceptualize and intellectualize "in such a way as to do justice to the diversity of the phenomena and at the same time not to do violence to a conviction of those involved that through it all there is a common element of transcendence."[41]

35. See Smart, *Religious Experience*, p. 27.
36. Whitehead, *Religion in the Making*, pp. 139, 127.
37. Rudolf Otto, *The Idea of the Holy*, trans. J. W. Harvey (New York: Oxford University Press, 1967), p. 146.
38. Ibid., p. 115.
39. See Georg W. F. Hegel, *Science of Logic*, trans. W. H. Johnston and L. G. Struthers, 2 vols. (New York: Macmillan, 1931), 3.
40. Smith, *Meaning and End of Religion*, p. 128.
41. Ibid., p. 151.

The real dangers in doctrine and dogma, in creed and conceptualization, are overextension and disassociation from experience. Overextension involves the distortion and stretching of dogma beyond its own sphere of applicability.[42] Disassociation involves the attempt to understand the Transcendent or God apart from any experiential basis for the term. If we have no concrete understanding of the meaning of "God," then, as Josiah Royce observed, "we forget the experience from which the words have been abstracted. To these experiences we must return when we want really to comprehend the world."[43] As Whitehead put it, "The importance of rational religion in the history of modern culture is that it stands or falls with its fundamental position, that we know more than can be formulated in one finite systematized scheme of abstractions. . . ."[44] In brief, if one is not careful, he may be guilty of clinging to words and neglecting the reality they represent.

William James was too severe in saying that when a genuine experience becomes orthodoxy, its day of inwardness is over.[45] And Walter Kaufmann was also extreme when he wrote, "The original sin of religion is to objectify the divine and to accept as final some dogma, sacrament, or ritual."[46] But Tillich was more to the point in saying that creeds are not ultimate; rather, their function is to point to the Ultimate.[47] However, the danger of verbal idolatry is present wherever there are conceptualizations of the Ultimate. "It has led," said Erich Fromm, "to a new form of idolatry. An image of God, not in wood and stone but in words, is erected so that people worship at this shrine."[48] That is, to consider an image of the Ultimate as ultimate is idolatry

42. Whitehead wrote, "Accordingly though dogmas have their measure of truth, which is unalterable, in their precise forms they are narrow, limitative, and alterable: in effect untrue, when carried over beyond the proper scope of their utility." *Religion in the Making,* p. 140.

43. Josiah Royce, "The Problem of Job" in *Philosophy of Religion: Some Contemporary Perspectives,* ed. Jerry H. Gill (Minneapolis: Burgess, 1968), p. 442.

44. Whitehead, *Religion in the Making,* p. 137. But Whitehead was overreacting when he wrote, "You cannot claim absolute finality for a dogma without claiming a commensurate finality for the sphere of thought within which it arose." Ibid., p. 126. This is not true if by "dogma" one means the truth being expressed and not the expression of the truth. For surely the finality of the truth that is being expressed does not necessitate the finality of the way in which it is being expressed. Furthermore, even a given expression of truth can be "final" within a given linguistico-cultural milieu, in the sense of being the very best way possible to express that truth in those terms. Then too, one should be careful not to confuse "finality" and "authority," for a given expression of truth (dogma) may be authoritative within a given linguistico-cultural milieu without being final in the sense that no other or no future expression of it could be better.

45. James, *Varieties of Religious Experience,* p. 330.

46. Walter Kaufmann, *Critique of Religion and Philosophy* (New York: Doubleday, 1961), p. 429.

47. Tillich, *Dynamics of Faith,* p. 29.

48. Erich Fromm, *Psychoanalysis and Religion* (New Haven: Yale University Press, 1959),

whether the image is mental or metal.[49] Perhaps this is why the God of the Old Testament jealously guarded his own name, saying to Moses who enquired about its meaning: "I AM WHO I AM" (Exod. 3:14).[50] It seems unwarranted to conclude that all doctrinal expressions are insufficient. On the contrary, language can be adequate without being final. Its adequacy will depend on how well it expresses and communicates the meaning of God.[51] As Whitehead correctly noted, "The dogma, therefore, is not something merely lamentable or evil. It was the necessary form by which the church kept its very identity." For "the Dogmas of religion are the attempts to formulate in precise terms the truths disclosed in the religious experience of mankind."[52] It is his attempt to render the credible intelligible, to find a logos for the mythos of his faith.

Religious Language and Its Concomitant Problems

Religious language has two basic hazards. It must avoid verbal idolatry on the one hand and experiential emptiness on the other hand. If it is overly transcendent, it departs from an experiential basis for meaning. If it is completely immanentistic, it commits semantical atheism. The shape of the problem has caused some to despair of any answer between these alternatives. Before we examine specific alternatives, perhaps a brief discussion of the nature and adequacy of language in general will clear some of the ground.[53]

The Adequacy of Language as a Means of Expressing God

The adequacy of a theistic language will be measured by its ability to avoid these two extremes. For, since the God of theism is infinite, only the language that cannot avoid applying limiting concepts to God will be sufficiently

---

p. 117.

49. John A. T. Robinson, *Honest to God* (Philadelphia: Westminster, 1963), p. 127.

50. On this point Ian T. Ramsey suggests, "Only God could know his own name. . . . The inevitable elusiveness of the divine name is the logical safeguard against universal idolatry." *Religious Language* (New York: Macmillan, 1963), p. 129.

51. On this matter Tillich wrote, "'Adequacy' of expression means the power of expressing an ultimate concern in such a way that it creates reply, action, communication. Symbols which are able to do this are alive." *Dynamics of Faith*, p. 96.

52. Whitehead, *Religion in the Making*, pp. 138, 57.

53. For an analysis of the adequacy of language with regard to divine revelation, see J. I. Packer, "The Adequacy of Human Language," in *Inerrancy*, ed. Norman L. Geisler (Grand Rapids: Zondervan, 1980), pp. 197–226. Also see Vern S. Poythress, "Adequacy of Language and Accommodation," in *Hermeneutics, Inerrancy, and the Bible*, ed. Earl D. Radmacher and Robert D. Preus (Grand Rapids: Zondervan, 1984), pp. 349–76. Also see the responses by Paul Feinberg and Kurt E. Marquart, ibid., pp. 377–405.

descriptive of God. On the other hand, any God-talk so transcendent as to have no anchorage in human experience will be devoid of any human meaning. Hence, in order to be adequate, theistic God-talk must be both based in finite experience and applicable to the infinite nature of God.

DOES LANGUAGE NECESSARILY IMPLY LIMITATIONS?

If it could be demonstrated in advance that language cannot avoid placing conceptual limits on God, then the quest for an adequate descriptive God-talk is futile. Fortunately for theism, there appears to be no way to disprove that language can express the Transcendent without implying that one does have some understanding of the Transcendent. How can one affirm that understanding of X is impossible unless he already has some understanding of X? The earlier attempts by A. J. Ayer and others to demonstrate that all God-talk is empirically unverifiable turned out to be self-defeating. Not every nonanalytical statement can be empirically verifiable, as Ayer learned; his very principle of empirical verifiability was neither purely definitional nor empirically verifiable.[54] And once the door was reopened for other kinds of meaningful statements, there was nothing in principle to eliminate the meaningfulness of statements about God. The advice of Ludwig Wittgenstein seems best in this regard: meaning should be listened to, not legislated.[55] There is no way to eliminate a priori the possibility of meaningful God-talk. One must look at the various kinds of God-talk to see if they do indeed make sense.

WHAT IS LANGUAGE?

An analysis of language supports the contention that speaking does not necessarily involve a conceptual limitation of the object of one's statements. Language is used to speak of the nonobjective, of universals,[56] and of what is not essentially limited.

Martin Heidegger speaks of a nonobjectifying language. He admits that language often involves objectification but not necessarily so. In the scientific sense, "thinking and speaking are objectifying, [that is], considering something as an object of our study." But "outside of this field thinking and speaking are by no means objectifying."[57] Ian T. Ramsey agreed, saying that the language of pure objectivity is empirically limited, but the language of subjectivity is not, for the former tries to picture but the latter points. Objec-

54. See A. J. Ayer, *Language, Truth and Logic* (New York: Dover, 1946), chap. 1.

55. Ludwig Wittgenstein, *Philosophical Investigations*, trans. G. E. M. Anscombe, 3d ed. (Oxford: Blackwell, 1967), sec. 654.

56. See J. P. Moreland, *Universals, Qualities, and Quality-Instances: A Defense of Realism* (Lanham, Md.: University Press of America, 1985).

57. Martin Heidegger, "The Problem of Non-Objectifying Thinking and Speaking in Contemporary Theology," in *Philosophy and Religion: Some Contemporary Perspectives*, ed. Jerry H. Gill (Minneapolis: Burgess, 1968), p. 64.

tive language is "scale-model" language, but subjective language is "disclosure-model" language. And if language is capable of pointing beyond the purely empirical and objective, then it is not essentially limited.[58]

Novak developed the notion of a nonobjectifying language in what he called a language of intelligent subjectivity. His view is based on two interpretative principles: "Our first assertion is that the experience on which religious language is best grounded is the experience a man has of himself as a subject." And "our second assertion is that of all the experiences of intelligent subjectivity, the one most suitable as a guide to our thinking about God seems to be that of intelligent consciousness, including insight and critical reflection."

In developing this language, Novak offers two guiding principles: "Thus, first, we will not use any predicate about God that does not *at least* apply to ourselves as subjects. Secondly, we will heed the warning that language borrowed from the object world can mislead us into thinking that awareness is like sense perception, or that the 'world' of subjects is an imitation of the world of objects." Therefore, for a person to state fully what he means by "God" he would have to "1) narrate many of his experiences (at prayer, in worship, even in secular action), 2) describe the contexts in which he believes he uses the word 'God' well, and, above all, 3) enunciate his understanding of human understanding. For what we mean by 'understanding' determines what we mean by 'man,' and what we mean by 'man' guides what we mean by 'God.'"

However, Novak admits that by the language of "intelligent subjectivity," "we cannot answer directly what God's mode of life is like; at best, we can single out which things in the world he is not like, and which things he may be more like. The chief virtue in taking intelligent consciousness as a model for conceiving of God is that it does not require a corporeal body for its referent." For example, "in moments of intellectual concentration, or again in moments of artistic contemplation or communion, we find ourselves 'rapt,' forgetful of the demands of our bodies, of the passage of time, of fatigue, or the need to eat." Such experiences as these, he continues, "furnish us the direction in which total, unlimited, unconditioned consciousness is the upper limit."[59]

Plato's philosophy is credited with the conclusion that language is essentially an objectifying procedure. As Cornford noted, the Greeks transformed the original expressions of the symbolic mythos into a scientific logos. And when it was decided that the logos was an objective expression of the *ontos*, language was viewed as the objectifying essence of reality. Wittgenstein is

58. Ian T. Ramsey, *Models and Mystery* (London: Oxford University Press, 1964), pp. 19–20.

59. Novak, *Belief and Unbelief*, pp. 98–103, 68–70.

credited with emphasizing that language does not have an essence.[60] If we take this to mean that language is not an objectification of reality, the theist need not object. If, however, it is taken to mean that language is not truly expressive of reality, then theists must object. For how could one possibly know that language is not expressive of reality unless he knows what reality is like? And how can one know (i.e., have a cognitive understanding of) reality apart from mental or verbal language which is the means of cognitive expression? The point at which the Greek ontologizing of language misled subsequent thought was in the Platonic identification of Forms (essences) and verbal expressions (logos). Platonic essences are entities, and if language is viewed as having an essence in this sense, then of course thought has been thereby ontologized.

But language need not be thought of as essentializing Forms. It can express objective reality without thus essentializing the reality it expresses. In one sense language is a logos; it is a word about reality. But in this sense of the word logos language does not define reality but declares it. Language can convey reality without conceptualizing it; it can point without picturing. Language can reveal without reifying. It can express God without attempting to explain his essence. Religious language can reveal God without rationalizing him. In order to avoid the misleading objectifying connotations of the word *logos* some prefer to think of language as a "macromyth" or "supermyth."[61] This designation is not entirely inappropriate. Like a myth, language points beyond itself to a transcendent reality. And if a myth is a kind of cipher of transcendent reality, one can expect to arrive at reality by "deciphering" revelatory language. The problem with designating language as a macromyth is the misleading implication that language is not rooted in human history and experience, but is nonhistorically based. For, as has already been noted, unless language has meaning rooted in human experience, it has no meaning for humans.

In this sense Ramsey's empirically grounded models are a better designation for religious language. Language is a kind of "master disclosure model." That is, language is a way of modeling reality as one sees it. It is a "fitting" of linguistic terms into one's experiences. The reservation here is Ramsey's distinction between picturing and pointing models. For if religious language is not descriptive of reality but merely points to it, then one does not know the

60. Wittgenstein, *Philosophical Investigations*, p. 91.

61. The Christian paradigm for the meaning of Logos in the incarnate Christ (John 1:1, 14) is especially revelatory of this meaning of logos. Christ is a declaration of God. He "fleshes out" the meaning of the infinite reality of God in a personal, concrete, human manifestation. As the Logos of God, Christ by no means objectifies God, but he does reveal the objective existence of the divine subject who claimed to be the "I AM" (Exod. 3:14). Marshall McLuhan uses the former and King uses the latter term. See King, *Introduction to Religion*, pp. 138–39.

object to which language is pointing. How would one know there was even an object there at which the disclosure model was pointing or what it was unless he had some descriptive understanding of it? If, on the other hand, language in general is viewed as a master disclosure model that discloses something, then this would seem to be an apt designation of the function of language. Religious language in particular must disclose something meaningful about God or else the theist will be a semantical atheist. Paul M. van Buren would have been right: the term *God* and all of its equivalents are dead.[62] Whatever models are used to disclose God cannot be so qualified as to eliminate all of their cognitive meaning or else the theist is left with cognitive meaninglessness. Hence, if religious language is a macro-disclosure model, then it must affirm something meaningful of God. Otherwise, religious language is cognitively inadequate.

Some Attempts at Building an Adequate Religious Language

A brief survey of several attempts at establishing a meaningful religious language will serve several purposes here. First, it will serve as an introduction to the various alternatives taken within the field of religious language. Second, it will lay the groundwork for mapping out a general typology of possible solutions to the problem and a synthesis of them in the succeeding chapters.

NEGATIVE LANGUAGE OF GOD

The improbability of gaining any positive content knowledge of an infinitely transcending Being seems so slim to some that they have almost despaired of speaking meaningfully of God in anything more than negative terms. It is for this reason that G. W. F. Hegel identified religion with a philosophical process, insofar as both must negate the given. "For religion equally with philosophy refuses to recognize in finitude a veritable being, or something ultimate and absolute, or non-posted, uncreated and eternal."[63] Even Immanuel Kant admitted that "the concept of a *noumenon* is thus a merely *limiting* concept . . . and it is therefore only of negative employment."[64] Tillich likewise admitted the need of negations to express the Ultimate, saying that it "cannot be defined beyond these negative terms."[65] Benedict Spinoza's famous dictum "All determination is by negation"[66] is

---

62. Paul M. van Buren, *The Secular Meaning of the Gospel* (New York: Macmillan, 1963), pp. 100, 83–84.

63. Hegel, *Science of Logic*, vol. 1, bk. 1, chap. 3.

64. Immanuel Kant, *The Critique of Pure Reason*, trans. Lewis W. Beck (New York: Bobbs-Merrill, 1956), p. 272.

65. Tillich, *Ultimate Concern*, p. 43.

66. Benedict Spinoza, *Epistola 50 (Opera)*, 4, p. 240.

typical of a philosophy of definition by negation that is traceable as far back as Plato's "nonbeing"[67] and can be seen in Whitehead's "negative prehensions."[68]

However, the classic example of negative theology in the West is that of Plotinus. The transcendent source of all things (which he often called the One) is so far beyond all sensible and even intellectual awareness that he says the One is even beyond all being. Agreeing with Plato, Plotinus wrote, "It can neither be spoken nor written of." When he did, nevertheless, speak of the One in any terms other than absolute simplicity or oneness, he readily admitted that these "assertions can be no more than negations." In fact, "if we are led to think positively of the One there would be more truth in silence." Although Plotinus said many apparently positive things about the transcendent One, such as calling it Good, Supreme, or Beauty, nevertheless he carefully qualified all these with warnings like the following: "When therefore you seek to state or to conceive Him, put all else aside; abstracting all . . . ; see that you add nothing; be sure that there is not something which you have failed to abstract from Him in your thought."[69]

The merit of negative religious assertions cannot be denied, for they avoid the ever-present danger of verbal idolatry. Idolatry is idolatry whether the images are mental or metal. Finite concepts cannot be literally applied to an infinite God. But this is avoided by negative assertions, for it is precisely all limitations and finitude that are being negated so that the negative words may express the unlimited and transcendent. However, there is a serious difficulty with purely negative religious assertions. Plotinus himself touched on it when he admitted, "It is impossible to say 'not that' if one is utterly without experience or conception of the 'that.'"[70] That is, all negative predications presuppose some positive understanding of that about which the predications are being made. As Tillich recognized, "There would be no negation if there were no preceding affirmation to be negated. . . ."[71] Ludwig Feuerbach's remark is instructive in this regard: "The truly religious man can't worship a purely negative being. . . . Only when a man loses his taste for religion does the existence of God become one without qualities, an unknowable God."[72] Every negative presupposes a positive. Without some

---

67. Plato wrote, "What is not, in some respects has being, and conversely that what is, in a way is not." *Sophist* 241d, in *The Collected Dialogues*, ed. Edith Hamilton and H. Cairns Huntington (New York: Pantheon, 1941), p. 985.

68. Alfred North Whitehead, *Process and Reality* (New York: Harper and Row, 1929), pp. 7, 35, 39, 66, 72, 346, 366.

69. See Plotinus, *Six Enneads* (Chicago: Encyclopedia Britannica Press, 1952), 5.2.1; 5.3.11; 6.9.4; 6.8.11; 5.5.6; 2.9.1.

70. Ibid., 6.7.29.

71. Paul Tillich, *The Courage to Be* (New Haven: Yale University Press, 1952), p. 40.

72. Ludwig Feuerbach, *The Essence of Christianity*, trans. George Eliot (New York: Harper and Row, 1957), p. 15.

positive knowledge of God, how can negative assertions be made?

UNIVOCAL LANGUAGE OF GOD

Within the Scotistic stream of scholastic philosophy there has been an insistence that the only alternative to skepticism is a positive and univocal understanding of terms appropriate to God. John Duns Scotus's basic argument is this: Either a characteristic has a common meaning as applied to God and creatures or it does not.[73] If it does not, it is either because its meaning does not apply formally to God (which is skepticism) or else it has meaning that is proper to God and not to creatures. The latter alternative is contrary to fact; creatures do have some of the same characteristics attributed to God (e.g., will, intellect, being). Consequently, every characteristic found in creatures and in God is predicated univocally about both. If notions derived from creatures may not be applied to God univocally, then the disconcerting consequence ensues that from the proper notions of characteristics found in creatures nothing whatsoever can be inferred about God. God is wholly other than our concepts.[74]

The central point of the Scotistic contention is that unless there is univocity in our concepts about God, then there can be no certainty in our knowledge of God. For "one and the same concept cannot be both certain and dubious. Therefore, either there is another concept [which is certain], or there is no concept at all, and consequently no certitude about any concept." Lest univocal concepts be misunderstood, Scotus explained that they mean that which has sufficient unity to be used as the middle term in a syllogism, and that which if affirmed and denied of the same thing would be a contradiction. Univocal cannot be either equivocal or analogical, for were it totally different, there would be no common meaning. And were it partly different, there must be some univocal concept by which one distinguishes which part is the same and which is different. An infinite regress of ambiguous nonunivocal concepts will never extricate one from skepticism. There must be a univocal notion at the base of all meaningful predication of God.

ANALOGOUS LANGUAGE ABOUT GOD

The problem with univocal God-talk was pinpointed by Thomas Aquinas and his followers. No finite concepts are adequate for expressing the infinite essence of God. Indeed, claimed Thomas, far from being univocal, our language about God is "almost equivocal." "It is impossible for anything to be predicated univocally of God and a creature: this is made plain as follows. Every effect of an univocal agent is adequate to the agent's power: and no

73. John Duns Scotus, *Philosophical Writings*, trans. Allan B. Wolter (Indianapolis: Liberal Arts, Bobbs-Merrill, 1962), pp. 27–28.
74. Ibid., pp. 22, 23.

creature being finite, can be adequate to the power of the first agent which is infinite."[75] How can a created concept univocally express the infinitude of the Creator? Univocal prediction of creature and God would lead to an equation of the two. Either the Creator must be thought of via finite conceptualizations (i.e., purely anthropomorphically) or else the creature will be viewed via infinite concepts. The former is skepticism and the latter is conceptual deification.

But how can one maintain any positive knowledge of God without univocal predication? Aquinas's answer is in analogy. Analogy for Thomists is the only alternative to total skepticism or complete dogmatics.[76] For if language has a totally different meaning (i.e., equivocal) as applied to creatures and God, then we have no true knowledge of God. If, on the other hand, our concepts have totally identical meaning (i.e., univocal), then our knowledge of the infinite must be infinite. But since no concepts from the finite world adequately express the infinite essence of God, it follows that we do not comprehend God's essence via univocal concepts.

Since all our concepts have a limited basis, none is adequate to express an infinite essence. Hence, only those concepts that can be removed from their finite conditions and applied to God in an unlimited way may be predicated of God properly. This predication is possible only because of a similarity between Creator and creatures based on the causal relation between them. That is, God, in causing the very existence of the creature, communicates to it prefections that he possesses more eminently in himself. God is not merely said to be like goodness because he causes goodness in creation; God actually is goodness. This is called an analogy of intrinsic attribution because both cause and effect possess the same perfection, only the cause in this case has the perfection infinitely.[77] This is in contrast to an analogy of extrinsic relation where the attribute would merely be attributed to a cause, not because the

75. Thomas Aquinas, *On the Power of God*, trans. The English Dominican Fathers, 3 bks. in 1 (Westminster, Md.: Newman, 1952), Q. 7, A. 7.

76. The first systematic treatment was made by Thomas Cardinal Cajetan (1469–1554), *The Analogy of Names and the Concept of Being* (Pittsburgh: Duquesne University Press, 1953). The most comprehensive textual study is a recent one by George P. Klubertanz, *St. Thomas Aquinas on Analogy* (Chicago: Loyola University Press, 1960). Another significant contribution has come recently from Ralph McInerny, *The Logic of Analogy* (The Hague: Nijhoff, 1961). Until recently Eric L. Mascall's *Existence and Analogy* (New York: Longmans, Green and Co., 1949) perhaps has been more well known than the others, but is superseded now by the work of Battista Mondin, *The Principle of Analogy in Protestant and Catholic Theology* (The Hague: Nijhoff, 1963).

77. Saint Thomas Aquinas, *Summa contra Gentiles*, trans. The English Dominican Fathers, vols. 1, 2 (London: Burns, Oates and Washbourne, 1923, 1924), 1.29–30; *Summa Theologica*, trans. the English Dominican Fathers (Chicago: Benzinger Brothers, 1947, 1984), 1.4.3.

cause really has that attribute, but because it causes something else to have it. For example, food is called healthy because it causes health in the body, even though, properly speaking, only the organism (the body) is healthy. God's relation to creation is not simply by way of extrinsic attribution. God produces in creation perfections that he possesses himself, albeit more eminently. Of course, some characteristics of creation (e.g., finitude, contingency, change) God does not possess. But others (e.g., justice, goodness, truth) flow from the very nature of God by way of intrinsic attribution.

MODEL LANGUAGE ABOUT GOD

Thomistic analogy of intrinsic attribution has not enjoyed a wide acceptance outside of Thomistic circles. Frederick Ferré's criticisms of it are typical. Ferré offers six objections that apply to the Thomistic analogy of divine attributions.[78] First, a wholly extrinsic analogy says nothing about the intrinsic or proper attributes of God. "We are left with no more idea of God's own characteristics than that he is responsible for the various characteristics of creation. . . ." Second, if there is an extrinsic causal relation between God and the world, why are not all qualities drawn from the world applied to God? Why select some and reject others, if God is the cause of all of them? Knowledge of which attributes are appropriate presupposes some univocal knowledge of God. Third, when words are disengaged from their finite mode of signification and applied to an infinite Being, they become entirely vacuous and without meaning. Fourth, analogy of intrinsic attribution rests on the (challengeable) assumption that the causal relation between God and the world provides a basis for their similarity (i.e., that the effects resemble their cause). Fifth, even if analogy could be based on some (Platonic) ontological similarity between cause and effect, properties drawn from finite (conditioned) creatures could not be attributed to an infinite (unconditioned) first Cause in any univocal sense. And to attribute them to the first Cause in a nonunivocal sense would embark one on an infinite regress of equivocation on the meaning of the word *cause*. Sixth, even assuming the (challengeable) metaphysical assumption that there is an ontological structural similarity among all beings, this ontology is not univocally expressible. But if it is not univocally expressible, we embark again on an infinite regress of equivocation. And if there is a univocal understanding of this ontology, there is no need for analogy.

What is offered in place of analogy? Ferré and others offer model language as the most adequate form of religious language. Ramsey develops a similar

---

78. Frederick Ferré, "Analogy in Theology," in *Encyclopedia of Philosophy*, ed. Paul Edwards, 4 vols. (New York: Free Press, 1973), 1:94–97.

approach to the question in what he calls qualified disclosure models. We will examine Ramsey's presentation.

According to Ramsey, God is revealed via disclosure models. In contrast to "picturing models" or "scale models," a "disclosure model" does not attempt to describe anything; rather, it becomes currency for a moment of insight. "The great value of a model," said Ramsey, "is that it enables us to be articulate when before we were tongue-tied." Disclosure models are the means by which the universe reveals itself to man. They are to be judged primarily on their ability to point to mystery, not on their ability to picture it. Indeed, part of the purpose of a model and its qualifiers is to leave a mystery intact (e.g., God may be modeled as "love" and qualified by the word *infinite*). The intention is to produce, from a single model, and by means of some qualifier, an endless series of variants, . . . in this way witnessing to the fact that the heart of the theology is permanent mystery."[79]

Language about God is not primarily declarative; it is evocative. Ramsey holds that by the use of nondescriptive, evocative language one can avoid being literalistic or purely anthropomorphic about God, for no one model has a single, all-exclusive track to mystery any more than one metaphor can do full justice to a sunset or to human love and affection. That is to say, disclosure models "are not descriptive miniatures, they are not picture enlargements; in each case they point to mystery, to the need for us to live as best we can with theological and scientific uncertainties."[80]

Ramsey's models do seem to answer Wittgenstein's challenge to keep silent unless one can speak meaningfully. Even if disclosure models do not allow one to speak descriptively about God, nevertheless they do permit one to speak. Indeed, by virtue of the fact that Ramsey's disclosure models are indefinitely qualifiable, one can not only speak about God but also speak endlessly. And in so speaking, Ramsey contends, one's language does not suffer "death by a thousand qualifications" but rather gives "life by a thousand enrichments."[81]

The question, says Ramsey, is not whether we can speak descriptively about the divine nature; "the real question is: How can one be reliably articulate?" Models help one to be reliably articulate in theology when two conditions hold: "In all cases the models must chime in with the phenomena; they must arise in a moment of insight or disclosure," and "A model in theology does not stand or fall with . . . the possibility of verifiable deductions. It is rather judged by its stability over the widest possible range of phenomena, by its ability to incorporate the most diverse phenomena not

79. Ramsey, *Models and Mystery*, pp. 7, 12–13, 19–20, 60–71.
80. Ibid., p. 20.
81. Ibid., pp. 12–17.

inconsistently." This is what Ramsey calls the method of "empirical fit" which has no scientific deductions emerging to confirm or falsify the stated theories. "The theological model," he wrote, "works more like the fitting of a boot or a shoe. . . ." In brief, religious language is empirically anchored (in disclosure situations)[82] and pragmatically tested by the way it enables a person to piece together the empirical data.

Further, even though disclosure models are not ontologically descriptive,[83] nevertheless they do help to build "family resemblances." "Let us always be cautious," Ramsey warns, "of talking about God in straightforward language. Let us never talk as if we had privileged access to the diaries of God's private life. . . ." When we speak of God as "supreme love," for example, "we are not making an assertion in descriptive psychology. . . . Rather, we are using a qualified model ("love" is qualified by "supreme") whose logical structure can be understood only in terms of the disclosure-commitment situation in which it arose.[84] "Qualifiers" are "words which multiply models without end and with subtle changes." They create what Wittgenstein called family resemblances or a family of models. By means of qualification of one model or metaphor, many of them can be related in an overall meeting place between contexts. And it is in this meeting place or connection where the mystery resides. That is, by mapping out the similarities engendered by the meeting of the many metaphors, one may gain increased insight into the mystery. The master model for theism is found in the term *God*.[85] God-talk, then, is the result of family resemblances built out of qualified disclosure models integrated into the term *God*.

Autonomous Language About God

The philosophical movement to think of religious language in terms of models spawned an increasing commitment to the autonomy of religious language. Exponents of this latter position are resisting all pressure to justify the legitimacy of religious language in terms of other language. Why should scientific language be the paradigm for meaningfulness on which religious language then has to build?

The guiding light in this understanding is Wittgenstein with his *Philosophical Investigations*.[86] Wittgenstein argued that particular linguistic systems, "language games," arise out of particular "forms of life." These language

82. Ibid., pp. 13, 15–17.
83. Ibid., p. 20.
84. Ramsey, *Religious Language*, pp. 104, 99.
85. Ramsey, *Models and Mystery*, pp. 48, 51, 60–61, and Ian T. Ramsey, *Prospects for Metaphysics* (London: George Allen and Unwin, 1961), pp. 153–64.
86. Wittgenstein, *Philosophical Investigations*, p. 5.

games are meaningful to the persons in the form of life under consideration, and external criteria are neither possible nor useful. Thus, for example, a person who is not religious cannot pass judgment on the meaningfulness of the religious language game. C. Steven Evans comments that after Wittgenstein the insider's perspective is the only acceptable starting point for an analysis of religious language.[87]

One exposition of this approach is found in the writings of D. Z. Phillips.[88] Phillips argues that the believer does not owe the unbeliever an account for his beliefs, but the believer also cannot simply impeach the unbeliever's position on rational grounds. More is involved in religious belief than a simple cognitive account. Only the person immersed in the religion can truly see its inherent rationality and justification. In short, the criteria for meaningfulness are internal to the language game, not external. There is only internal coherence but no correspondence to some external reality.

Jerry H. Gill also propounds this position.[89] In addition to making extensive reference to Wittgenstein, Gill expands on the work of Ramsey by bringing the contributions of Michael Polanyi into the picture.[90] At the heart of his effort lies the attempt to make more room for the tacit aspect of knowledge which carries over into language.

Gill asks us to see the human being as a whole person, and to pay special attention to our physical, embodied side. We are not merely mental beings; we are multifaceted. Our concept of knowledge needs to reflect this "incarnational" or "mediational" dimension. To be sure, there is such a thing as explicit knowledge, which is focal and verbal. But there is also tacit knowledge, which Gill calls nonverbal and subsidiary. Tacit knowledge is logically prior to explicit knowledge.[91]

Religious knowledge, in particular, partakes of a high degree of this tacit character. Consequently, religious language also is rooted in the nonconceptual and unconscious side of the human being. Gill follows Ramsey by understanding religious language as primarily metaphorical and evocative. But he does so not only for reasons of an empirical approach, as was true of Ramsey, but more importantly to be faithful to the mediational nature of all knowledge.

Religious language is not primarily descriptive. Its setting is in the practical life of the believer, and much of it is performative in function. Most impor-

87. C. Steven Evans, *Philosophy of Religion: Thinking About Faith*, Contours of Christian Philosophy series (Downers Grove: Inter-Varsity, 1985), p. 152.

88. D. Z. Phillips, *Religion Without Explanation* (Oxford: Blackwell, 1976).

89. Jerry H. Gill, *On Knowing God: New Directions for the Future of Theology* (Philadelphia: Westminster, 1981).

90. Michael Polanyi, *The Tacit Dimension* (Garden City, N.Y.: Doubleday, 1966).

91. Gill, *On Knowing God*, p. 95.

tantly, it is the language of the believer, not just someone's language about believers. Thus Gill states, "Given the contextual and functional character of linguistic meaning in general and religious discourse in particular, it would seem imperative that a consideration of the latter needs to begin with and always be grounded in the concrete expressions actually used by those who speak religiously and theologically."[92]

Gill has provided a broad and provocative theory that merits consideration on many points.[93] Let us for now concentrate on his specific agenda on religious language. His is one of the most sophisticated implementations of the Wittgensteinian language-game program.

Believers and unbelievers alike are dissatisfied with the total isolation of the religious language game from other language games. John S. Feinberg argues that "Wittgenstein's implicit definition of the language-game of religion is to be rejected in favor of one that includes the concept that at least many of its propositions are empirically testable."[94] Else the result would be that religious language is not cognitive at all.

Kai E. Nielsen refers to the position under consideration as "Wittgensteinian fideism."[95] He opposes what he sees as the attempt to arbitrarily insulate religious language from all common rational critiques. Nielsen argues that if concepts are incoherent, they are incoherent, regardless of the language game in which they are at home. Special pleading is not allowed. And the concept of God is incoherent on many fronts. Just to mention one, the concept of personal action always requires a body in which the action is carried out. But God is said to be incorporeal; thus to speak of God's actions is to say something contradictory.[96] Locating an incoherence into a special language game does not make it any less incoherent. Thus for him religious language remains incoherent, and he rejects belief in God as not only meaningless, but also false.

To seek to establish religious language as purely autonomous is thus a two-edged sword. On the one hand, it bears all of the marks of allowing for a wholly univocal character in which all doubts about meaning can be ruled out a priori. But, on the other hand, because the religious language game is

92. Ibid., p. 31.
93. E.g., see Winfried Corduan's review of On Knowing God in Trinity Journal 3 (1982): 119–22.
94. John S. Feinberg, "Noncognitivism: Wittgenstein," in Biblical Errancy: An Analysis of Its Philosophical Roots, ed. Norman L. Geisler (Grand Rapids: Zondervan, 1981), p. 201.
95. Kai E. Nielsen, Scepticism (New York: St. Martin, 1973); idem, An Introduction to the Philosophy of Religion, New Studies in the Philosophy of Religion series (New York: St. Martin, 1982); idem, Contemporary Critiques of Religion (New York: Herder and Herder, 1971).
96. Nielsen, "In Defense of Atheism," in Philosophy of Religion: Contemporary Perspectives, ed. Norbert O. Schedler (New York: Macmillan, 1974).

then totally isolated, it is actually also equivocal. One can then use terms with any meaning with the mere excuse of playing that language game. Surely there must be some way of cross-referencing language to assure meaning. And then the religious language game still needs to use analogy or models.

The basic problem in theistic language is how one can speak meaningfully about the Infinite in language drawn from the finite world. Mystics have answered by the *via negativa:* No positive affirmations of God are possible. Others, like Scotus, have insisted that unless there is a positive and univocal conceptualization of God, we are left in skepticism. Thomists, on the other hand, deny that any terms drawn from the finite world could possibly have any more than an analogous application to God. Many contemporary analysts, however, fail to see how analogy can be saved from equivocation without univocity. Instead of a descriptive language about God built on questionable metaphysical assumptions, they offer a nondescriptive but evocative language of religious disclosure. By using qualified models rooted in the empirical world, but evocative of religious insight, they hope to evade both the older metaphysical assumptions as well as the additional inadequacies of the other alternatives.

But there is an obvious problem with model language about God. It can be revealed by considering the logical alternatives for descriptive God-talk. Either it is equivocal (totally different), univocal (totally the same), or else analogical (similar). Ramsey's and Gill's qualified models seem confessedly not univocal. Ferré also disavows Thomistic analogy. It would seem, then, that model language is equivocal. It does not really provide us with any descriptive knowledge of God. It can evoke an experience of a we-know-not-What. One seems to be left with a religious a-*cog*nosticism; that is, he has no cognitive knowledge of God.

What is the way out of the dilemma posed by the alternatives of religious language? A thorough reexamination of all the positions seems to be called for. Only then will we be able to draw the insights of each into a meaningful whole that makes religious language what it is.

11 ❋

Negative Religious Language

From earliest times in Western philosophy there has been a felt need for using negation in thinking about reality. Faced with the metaphysical dilemma bequeathed by Parmenides, Plato in his later works struggled with how one being could differ from another if each being was absolutely simple. His answer was a form of negation via nonbeing. Plato's view became determinative of much later thought on the subject. Thus we will use Plato's philosophical conception as a springboard for a look at negative religious language. We shall see this view epitomized in the works of Plotinus, elaborated by Moses Maimonides, and echoed in mysticism. Finally, we shall observe how the best aspects of this view are incorporated into the ideas of Thomas Aquinas.

Plato: Determination by Nonbeing

Parmenides posed the problem with which Western philosophy has wrestled since. It is the basic logic of monism to which all pluralisms must respond.

The Parmenidean Problem

According to Parmenides, there can be only one Being in the universe. To affirm two or more beings is impossible. His logic ran like this:[1] If there are more beings than one, they must differ. They must differ by either something (i.e., by being) or by nothing (i.e., by nonbeing). They cannot differ by nothing, for to differ by nonbeing or nothing is not to differ at all. Nor can they differ by being, for that is the only respect in which all things are identical. And they cannot differ in the very respect in which they are identical. Hence, there cannot be more beings than one. Of course, Plato believed that there were many beings. Each Form in his world of Ideas had being, and yet each was irreducibly and qualitatively different from the other.[2] The

1. Parmenides, in *The Presocratic Philosophers,* ed. G. S. Kirk and J. E. Raven (Cambridge: Cambridge University Press, 1964), pp. 269–78.
2. Cf. *Phaedo* 100d, 102d, 103e; *Republic* 7.526a–b.

Form of horse was not that of a chair; the Form of tallness was not the Form of shortness. This being true, it would seem that Plato was faced squarely with the Parmenidean dilemma. Do these many different forms of being differ by something or by nothing?

Plato's Answer to Parmenides' Problem

Plato chose the nonbeing horn of the dilemma. One being differs from another by nonbeing—not by absolute nonbeing, to be sure, but by relative nonbeing. In Plato's own words, "We shall find it necessary in self-defense to put to the question that pronouncement of father Parmenides, and establish by main force that what is not, in some respect has being, and conversely that what is, in a way is not."[3] That is, things differ from each other by negation. A horse is not a chair; a tall thing is not a short thing. This does not imply that a horse is not anything nor that something else cannot be what the horse is not. It is only to say that relative to a chair, tree, or anything else in the world, a horse is not any of them. What then is a horse? A horse is not anything else in the universe but itself. All determination of what something actually is in itself is by negation of all other things. One thing differs from another in that it is not that other thing nor is it any other thing. An illustration will serve Plato's point. How does the sculptor determine the form of a statue out of the rock before him? By negating (chiseling off) pieces until all that is left is what he did not negate from the rock. In like manner, Plato wished to hold that the only way to distinguish one being from another is by relative nonbeing. Any particular being, relative to another being, is not that other being nor any other being. All actual differentiation is by ontological negation.

There is an obvious problem with Plato's solution.[4] Unless the sculptor already has some positive understanding of the form he wishes to emerge from the stone, he will not know what pieces to negate from it. Likewise, unless one knows the characteristics of one being, he cannot confidently affirm that this being is not like all other beings. There might be some similarity between them that he is disavowing because he does not know anything positive about the being that he is trying to determine by negating all else from it. This leads to a second problem with Plato's way of negation. If the only way to determine what something is involves negating everything else from it, then all determination must await an indefinite number of negations. For there is an endless number of other qualities that might be possible for a given being. All of these other possibilities must be negated before one can truly know what this given being is like. The first difficulty with Plato's

3. Plato, *Sophist* 241d.
4. Plato gives the argument against this proposed solution himself. See his *Parmenides* 130b–d.

negation by relative nonbeing is now more clearly in view. All negations imply some positive understanding. How would one know which of the endless variety of things to negate unless he had some positive understanding of the thing from which they were being eliminated? Every negative presupposes a positive. It cannot be said of a being that it is not this or that, unless one already has a positive understanding of what this or that is.

Furthermore, the relative nonbeing does not answer Parmenides' monistic dilemma. For to differ by nothing is not to differ at all. Unless there is some difference in the very being of one being as opposed to another being, they differ by nothing at all. If there is no difference in their constitutive reality, then there is no real difference. Whatever has no distinction from another in its actuality has no actual difference from that other. When one places, as Plato did, all differentiation in the realm of nonbeing, then the realm of being is left without any distinctions at all, that is, wholly identical. Monism follows necessarily.

The problems of Parmenides' and Plato's inadequate answers were bequeathed to the Platonic tradition which culminated in Plotinus in the early third century A.D. Plotinus offered a different solution by way of negation.

Plotinus: Negation by Intuition of the Beyond-Being

Plotinus felt that he was not trapped by the Parmenidean dilemma. Parmenides had wrongly assumed that being was pure and simple, that it never came in degrees or kinds. This was not so for Plotinus. There is a complete hierarchy of Being that ascends all the way from the least nearly perfect to the most nearly perfect being and even to God who goes beyond all being. Hence, in answer to Parmenides, Plotinus affirmed that beings differ in the degree of unity they possess. Not all things have the same amount of being. Beings are graded by the degree of unity they have. If true, this would avoid absolute monism, but how does it solve the problem of knowledge of God who goes beyond all being?

A Brief Sketch of the Plotinian System

The way things differ is by the degree of unity they have. The more unity something has, the higher degree of being it possesses. Hence, the basic movement in Plotinian thought is from unity to multiplicity and then back to unity. It all begins with absolute unity (God).

FROM UNITY TO MULTIPLICITY

Since all multiplicity presupposes some prior unity, there must be ultimately some absolute simplicity at the source of all multiplicity in being. This absolute simplicity (God) does not have being, for being involves multiplicity and God has no multiplicity whatsoever. Hence, God is the absolute

Unity (the One) beyond all being. Absolute Unity is without knowledge of itself, since all knowing involves at least the self-duality of knower and known. Therefore, when out of the necessity of its nature this absolute simplicity unfolded and reflected back upon its own absolute unity it became a Mind *(Nous)* or knowing being. When this Mind reflects inward upon itself, it produces other minds, and when reflecting outward, it gives rise to Life (World Soul) and through Soul it gives rise to all other souls (living things). Since the entire process is a necessary unfolding of unity to greater and greater multiplicity, it must end at last in the most multiple of all—matter. It is here that the whole process peters out. For matter is the brink of oblivion; it is the place at which the multiplicity has reached the point that if it went further it would become absolutely nothing. And since Being is good, it follows that matter is evil (since it is the most multiple of all). Matter has no residue of good in it but is the mere vacuous capacity for good (5.4.1; 5.6.6; 6.7.37; 4.2.2; 2.4.11).[5]

There is, then, a complete hierarchy of being (and goodness) from the First to the last; from Good to evil; from Beyond Being to nonbeing; from Beyond Mind to matter; from absolute Unity to absolute multiplicity. And the latter follows from the former with the same emanational necessity that rays radiate from the sun or that a flower unfolds from a seed. However, there is also an inherent necessity in that the latter (and lower) cannot destroy the former (and higher). Absolute multiplicity cannot destroy absolute Unity. Darkness cannot annihilate Light, and nonbeing cannot abolish Being. There is, in fact, a kind of boomerang of Being. When the last emanation from God overlooks the brink of utter oblivion, it recoils back toward Being. The last remnant of good is repelled in the face of utter evil. The move upward from total multiplicity and evil is thus necessitated by the nature of unity and goodness. For it is evil that is necessitated by the Good and not the reverse. It is multiplicity that is contained within Unity and not the opposite. As Unity necessarily unfolds into diversity, so diversity must ultimately be enfolded again in Unity. Emanational necessity is a two-way ticket; the return trip is guaranteed because the Source of all is superior to all and must ultimately subsume all.

FROM MULTIPLICITY TO UNITY

The return trip is focused in human beings. They alone partake of all levels of unity. Their bodies are composed of matter, the most multiple and evil of all. The soul has a lower aspect in touch with the body but a higher dimension in contact with the realm of Mind. In order to begin the trip toward Unity, the person must turn from the outward material multiplicity to the inner unity of the soul (i.e., asceticism). And on the inward side, man must turn upward to

5. All references from Plotinus are from his *Enneads,* translated and edited by Stephen Mac-Kenna.

the higher mental realm of the soul (i.e., meditation) by which one is in touch with Mind itself. In brief, one must move from the sensible to the intellectual.

In further quest of the absolute Unity from whence he came, a human must become one with the Nous, the Mind which is the source of all minds. To know Mind one must become identical with it, since knowing is an identification of Knower and known. However, even when the human mind becomes one with universal Mind, it has not yet returned home to absolute Unity. For Mind itself has a simple duality of knower and known. Since one cannot transcend the realm of Mind by an act of mind, only a transmental act of intuition will suffice. One must move, then, from the sensible to the intellectual and from the intellectual to the intuitional to complete the trip to absolute Unity. In order to reach the One it is necessary to merge with it; a person must become one with the One. This cannot be achieved in any cognitive state but only by mystical intuition, which ascends out of the sensible through the intellectual to the intuitional. By turning away from multiplicity and mounting toward greater unity one will come at last to the greatest Unity, when he has become one with the One (4.8.4; 1.6.7; 3.8.10; 6.9.4,10).

The Need for Negative Language of the One (God)

Plotinus is very careful to insist that no positive descriptions of this absolute Unity (God) are possible. He agrees with Plato about the One that "it can neither be spoken of nor written of" (6.9.4).[6] Even when God is called One, "this name, The One," contains really no more than the negation of plurality. This is why the Pythagoreans used the symbol *Apollo*, meaning literally "not-many." "Plotinus noted that if we are led to think positively of The One, name and thing, there would be more truth in silence." For the designation *the One* is "a mere aid to inquiry, [and] was never intended for more than a preliminary affirmation of absolute simplicity to be followed by the rejection of even that statement" (5.5.6).

Everything Plotinus affirms of God in one place he denies in another. The name *One* means only "not-many." It does not have being but is beyond all being (3.8.9). "The One, therefore, is beyond all things that are 'Thus': standing before the indefinable, you may name any of these sequents but you must say, 'This is none of them'" (6.8.9). The One has no knowledge. "There is, we repeat, duality in any thinking being; and the First is wholly above the dual" (5.6.6). Further, the One cannot even have power. "The Source of all this cannot be an Intellect; nor can it be an abundant power: it must have been before Intellect and abundance were" (3.8.11). Even the term *First* does not really apply to it. For "in calling it The First we mean no more than to

6. See Plato, *Parmenides* 142a.

express that it is the most absolutely simplex . . . only in the sense that it is not of that compound nature which would make it dependent on any constituents" (2.9.1). The term *One* is not to be taken as the first in a series of numbers. "It refuses to take a number because it is measure and not the measured" (5.5.4).

Although Plotinus often refers to God as Good and Beauty, both qualities of goodness and beauty are denied of God. For "shape and idea and measure will always be beautiful, but the Authentic Beauty, or rather the Beyond-Beauty, cannot be under measure and therefore cannot have admitted shape or be Idea" (6.7.33). In brief, the One cannot be anything that is derived from it—and everything comes from it—because it "bestows what itself does not possess" (6.7.15). For "in order that Being may be brought about, the source must be no Being but Being's generator" (5.2.1). According to Plotinus "He had no need of Being, who brought Being to be" (6.8.19).

The need for negations is now evident. The Source of all multiplicity must be absolutely simple. But all names taken from the world of multiplicity and even from the intellectual world (which involves a duality of knower and known) cannot be applied to an absolutely simple Being without negating the multiple implications from the terms. Since the One is the qualityless source of all qualities, no quality may be affirmed of it without qualification by negation. Put another way, the reason that there can be no positive names of the One is that it is the Ultimate and there is nothing more ultimate in terms of which it can be described. It would be to "ask for a principle beyond, but the principle of all has no principle" (6.8.11). The One is nothing but itself and cannot be named in terms of anything else. "Thus the One is in truth beyond all statement; any affirmation of a thing . . . ; we can but try to indicate, in our own feeble way, something concerning it" (5.3.13). "We must be patient with language; we are forced for reasons of exposition to apply to the Supreme terms which strictly are ruled out; everywhere we must read 'So to speak'" (6.8.13). But in what way can we learn how "so to speak" of God? He never calls God Matter, Evil, or Non-Being. How does one learn "so to speak" appropriately of God? Plotinus has two aspects to his answer: First, we name God indirectly from his effects or emanants. Second, we know God by direct mystical intuition, which transcends all cognitive knowing and which serves as a positive basis for all cognitive negations of God.

Naming God from His Emanational Effects

The positive names given to God by Plotinus are many. God is called Good, Beauty, Being, Actuality, First, Supreme, Energy. All of these names are improperly applied to God; that is, the characteristic belongs properly to the created effects of God. Plotinus wrote, "The One is all things and no one of them: the source of all things is not all things: and yet it is all things in a transcendental sense" (5.2.1). The One "eludes our knowledge, so that the nearer approach to it is through its offspring" (6.9.5). In brief, although we cannot speak It, we are able to speak of it in terms of what has come from the One (5.3.14).

Several observations about this causal naming of God are called for at this point. First, God is thus named only from his sequents in a transcendent sense. God is not really like the goodness, beauty, and being he causes. They are at best only a visible and multiple "copy" of the invisible One that caused them (5.5.5). The created world is merely a "vestige" or "image" of the God who completely transcends it (6.8.18; 6.7.38). According to Plotinus we know that the One is "a nobler principle than anything we know as Being; fuller and greater; above reason, mind, and feeling; conferring powers, not to be confounded with them." But how does it confer these things, "as itself possessing them or not? How can it convey what it does not possess, and yet if it does possess how is it simplex?" Plotinus continues, "The explanation is, that what comes from the Supreme cannot be identical with it and assuredly cannot be better than it—what could be better than The One or could exceed it in any sense? The emanation then must be less good . . ." (5.3.14–15). All that comes from God is nothing more than a trace of the transcendent One from which they emanate. God is in no way actually like his multiple effects.

Second, God is named from his emanations by way of extrinsic attribution. That is, God is called Good because he causes goodness, not because he actually possesses such goodness. Plotinus clearly affirmed that the One "bestows that itself does not possess" (6.7.15). God gave rise to all being but does not have being himself. The reason for this is that unity is the basis for being and not being the basis for unity. Plotinus is clear on this point: "It is, therefore, an existent Unity, not an existent that develops Unity. . . . In the pure Unity there is no Being save in so far as Unity attends to producing it" (6.6.13). Unity (God) is beyond being and the only sense in which he is called Being is by extrinsic attribution because he is the Cause of being. Properly speaking, God is not Being but he is the Unity that is the cause of the varying unity that beings have.

The Intuitional Basis for All Naming of God

One problem remains: giving God positive names from his extrinsically related created effects does not provide any proper knowledge of God. God is really not Being, Good, Beauty. God is the transcendent Unity beyond all these. All of these must be affirmed of God only to be negated of him. God is described in these terms really inappropriate to him only to stimulate human search in his direction. These terms are used for "conveying a conviction, at the cost of verbal accuracy" (6.8.13).

Plotinus insisted that the One can neither be spoken of nor written of. "If we nevertheless speak and write about it, we do so only to give direction, to stimulate toward that vision beyond discourse . . ." (6.9.4). Rational and cognitive thought and language can do no more than point in the direction of the ineffable God who can be known only by mystical intuition. "Our knowledge of the One comes to us neither by pure thought . . . but by a presence which is superior to science . . . , for science implies discursive reason and discursive reason implies manifoldness" (6.9.4; Katz's translation).

In this superior mystical intuition "no longer is there thing seen and light to show it . . . ; this is the very radiance that brought both Intellect and Intellectual object into being . . ." (6.7.36). In fact, "only by a leap [from the intellectual] can we reach to this One which is to be pure of all else . . ." (5.5.4). The person who experiences this mystical union is "no longer himself nor self-belonging; he is merged with the Supreme, sunken into it, one with it: center coincides with center . . ." (6.9.10). If a person does not attain this temporary meditative union, it is because he has not completely purified himself of all multiplicity. According to Plotinus, "There is no vision, no union, for those handling or acting by anything other: the soul must see before it neither evil nor good nor anything else, that alone it may receive the Alone" (6.7.34).

There is an important function for this noncognitive intuition of God in relation to the negative religious language used to describe God. Plotinus recognized that every negative presupposed a positive. He realized that it would be impossible to negate multiplicity of God unless there was some prior awareness of his unity. He wrote, "It is impossible to say 'Not that' if one is utterly without experience or conception of the 'That'; there will generally have been, even, some inkling of the good beyond Intellection" (6.7.29). In Plotinus's case it is this nonrational experience of the One that enables him to make rational negations such as that it is not-many. For example, his positive intuition of the Beyond-Being is the basis for him to make the negations that it is not Being. Without positive awareness of what God is, it would of course be impossible to affirm what he is not. And since even the emanations of God do not properly describe him, the appropriateness of applying to God certain things that flow from him is dependent, too, on a prior awareness of the God to whom they are appropriately (albeit not positively) attributed. Negative language about the Transcendent is utterly dependent for its meaning on prior positive intuition of God gained via mystical union with the One.

The neo-Platonist Proclus (410–485) systematized Plotinus's philosophy in his *Book on Causes*. Through the unorthodox Syrian monk Pseudo-

Dionysius (c. 500), this neo-Platonic thought was passed on to the Christians of the Middle Ages. In his book *On the Divine Names*, Dionysius affirmed the incomprehensibility of God. God, he said, cannot be known directly but only indirectly in a threefold way. First we may *affirm* of God what the Bible says of him. This is called positive theology. Next, we must *deny* that these qualities apply to God in the same sense in which they apply to creatures. This is negative theology. Finally, these terms must be applied to God in a *higher way*. Thus one ends with a negation of a negation. In true Plotinian style, God remains above all affirmations.

Moses Maimonides: Negative Attributes of God

Moses Maimonides was a highly respected Jewish philosopher of the later medieval period. He too had a very strong negative theology. Maimonides considered a literal interpretation of the Scriptures to be the root of all evil in theology. Assuming that figurative and anthropomorphic language is actually descriptive of God leads to polytheistic error or a defective monotheism. If one wishes to leave the realm of empirical metaphor and "rise to a higher state, [namely], that of reflection, and truly to hold the conviction that God is One," then he "must understand that God has no essential attribute in any form or in any sense whatever. . . . Those who believe that God is One, and that He has many attributes, declare the unity of God with their lips, and assume plurality in their thoughts."[7]

The Way to Positively Attribute Something to God

Maimonides outlined five possible ways an attribute could be positively affirmed of God. He denied the applicability of the first four to the monotheistic God of Judaism and opted for the last one. "First, an object is described by its *definition*, as, [for example], man is described as a being that lives and has reason; such a description, containing the true essence of the object, is . . . nothing else but the explanation of a name." Of this kind of attribution Maimonides said, "All agree that this kind of description cannot be given of God; for there are no previous causes to His existence, by which He could be defined."[8] That is, there is nothing more ultimate than God in terms of which he can be defined.

"Secondly, an object is described by *part of its definition*, as when . . . man is described as a living being or as a rational being." But, added Maimonides,

---

7. Moses Maimonides, *The Guide for the Perplexed*, trans. M. Friedlander (New York: Dover, 1904), p. 67.
8. Ibid., pp. 69–70.

"all agree that this kind of description is inappropriate in reference to God; for if we were to speak of a portion of His essence, we should consider His essence to be compound."⁹ That is, God is simple and has no parts. Hence, one cannot speak of part of God's essence.

"Thirdly, an object is described by something different from its true essence, by something that does not complement or establish the essence of the object" [i.e., by a quality]. This kind of attribution does not befit God. For "quality in the most general sense, is an accident. If God could be described in this way, He would be a substratum of accidents."¹⁰ This would mean that God possesses these qualities only accidentally and not essentially, in which case they would not be truly descriptive of his essence. Furthermore, all qualities imply composition. "Hence, it follows that no attribute coming under the head of quality in the widest sense, can be predicated of God."¹¹

"Fourthly, a thing is described by its relation to another thing, [for example], to time, . . . or to a different individual; thus we say, Zaid, the father of A, . . . who dwells at a certain place, or who lived at a stated time." Now "this kind of attribute does not necessarily imply plurality or change in the essence of the object described." But, on the other hand, "such relations are not the essence of a thing, nor are they so intimately connected with it as qualities." Now, at first thought, commented Maimonides, "it would seem that they may be employed in reference to God, but after a careful and thorough consideration we are convinced of their inadmissibility. It is quite clear that there is no relation between God and time or space." God cannot be related to time, "for time is an accident connected with motion, which includes befores and afters in a numbered series (1, 2, 3, etc.). And clearly God cannot be related to any temporal numerical series. Further, "since motion is one of the conditions to which material bodies are subject, and God is immaterial, there can be no relation between Him and time. Similarly, there is no relation between Him and space."¹²

"But what we do have to investigate and to examine is this," wrote Maimonides, "whether some real relation exists between God and any of the substances created by Him, by which He could be described." The answer to this is also negative. "That there is no correlation between Him and any creatures can easily be seen; for the characteristic of two objects correlative to each other is the equality of their reciprocal relation. Now, as God has absolute existence, while all other beings have only possible existence. . . , there consequently cannot be any correlation" [between God and his creatures]. It is impossible to imagine a relation between intellect and sight.

9. Ibid., p. 70.
10. Ibid.
11. Ibid., p. 71.
12. Ibid.

"How, then, could a relation be imagined between any creature and God, who has nothing in common with any other being; for even the term existence is applied to Him and other things, according to our opinion, according to pure homonymity [the sound being the same but the meaning different]." Consequently, Maimonides concluded, "there is no relation whatever between Him and any other being." The reason for this radical disjunction is brought out in Maimonides' next comment: "For whenever we speak of a relation between two things, these belong to the same kind; but when two things belong to different kinds though of the same class, there is no relation between them." How, then, "could there be any relation between God and His creatures, considering the important difference between them in respect to true existence, the greatest of all differences."[13] Therefore, even though relational attributes do not necessarily imply plurality or chance, one is wrong in applying them to God in any positive sense.

"Fifthly, a thing is described by its *actions;* I do not mean by 'its actions' the inherent capacity for a certain work [as the ability of a carpenter to build] . . . but I mean the action the latter has performed" [i.e., of the act of building]. Only this kind of predication can be made of God. For "this kind of attributes is separate from the essences of the thing described, and, therefore, appropriate to be employed in describing the Creator, especially since we know that these different actions do not imply that different elements be contained in the substance of the agent, by which the actions are produced. . . ."[14] For all actions flow from the essence of God and not from any alleged accidents superadded to his essence. In brief, the only things appropriately attributed to God are actions that flow from his essence but are not in any positive way descriptive of his essence.

Having eliminated philosophically any positive descriptive attributes of God, Maimonides is faced with the innumerable biblical passages that predicate many things of God in a positive way. His answer is summed up in this principle: "The Torah speaketh in the language of man." Biblical language is anthropomorphic. "Many of the attributes express different acts of God, but that difference does not necessitate any difference as regards Him from whom the acts proceed." For instance, a fire can bleach, blacken, boil, burn, harden, melt, and consume. Surely these actions of fire do not relate at all to the nature of fire. Thus, the many actions of God, a free Cause, give us no information of his essence.

The so-called relations between God and creatures "exist only in the thoughts of men." When Moses asked to know the essence of God, "God promised that He would let him know all His attributes, and that these were

13. Ibid., pp. 71–72.
14. Ibid., p. 72.

nothing but His actions. . . . Consequently the knowledge of the works of God is the knowledge of His attributes, by which He can be known." But none of these works provide any knowledge positively descriptive of God. In short, "nothing can be predicated of God that implies any of the following four things: corporeality, emotion or change, nonexistence, . . . and similarity with any of His creatures." And, "those who believe in the presence of essential attributes in God, [namely], Existence, Life, Power, Wisdom, and Will, should know that these attributes, when applied to God, have not the same meaning as when applied to us. . . . When they ascribe to God essential attributes, these so-called essential attributes should not have similarity to the attributes of other things . . . just as there is no similarity between the essence of God and that of other beings." Hence, "the terms Wisdom, Power, Will, and Life are applied to God and to other beings by way of perfect homonymity, admitting of no comparison whatever." [15]

Maimonides provided the key to his elimination of all positive attributes to God in the following passage: "It is known that existence is an accident appertaining to all [caused] things, and therefore an element superadded to their essence. . . . But as regards a being whose existence is not due to any cause . . . existence and essence are perfectly identical; He is not a substance to which existence is joined as an accident, as an additional element." Consequently, "God exists without possessing the attribute of existence. Similarly, He lives without possessing the attribute of life; knows without possessing the attribute of knowledge . . ." and so on. Likewise, "God's unity is not an element superadded, but He is One without possessing the attribute of unity." In brief, God does not have any attribute appropriately applied to him. For example, God does not have existence in any way similar to that of a creature; God's existence is absolute and unique. In like manner, God does not have wisdom as a creature does; God's wisdom is infinitely different. How can this be known, since there is no positive knowledge of the essence of God? The answer is found only in negative theology.

The Use of Negative Attributes to Describe God

According to Maimonides, "the negative attributes of God are the true attributes . . . while the positive attributes imply polytheism. . . ." For "we cannot describe the Creator by any means except by negative attributes." The only thing negative attributes have in common with positive ones is that both circumscribe their object by excluding what would otherwise have not been excluded. But unlike positive attributes, negative ones do not provide us with any direct information about the essence of the object being described. From

15. Ibid., pp. 73–75, 78–80.

this it is clear to Maimonides that God has no positive attributes what-soever.[16]

What, then, is the function of negative attributes? They "are necessary to direct the mind to the truths that we must believe concerning God, for, on the one hand, they do not imply any plurality, and, on the other hand, they convey to man the highest possible knowledge of God." For when we say that God's nonexistence is impossible, we learn that he is totally different from all other kinds of beings. Likewise, when we say that God is not many (i.e., he is One) we learn that there is no other unity like his. And by way of these negative attributes "all we understand is the fact that He exists, that He is a Being to whom none of His creatures is similar, who has nothing in common with them, who does not include plurality, who is never too feeble to produce other beings, and whose relation to the universe is that of a steersman to a boat; and even this is not a real relation. . . ." And one advances in his knowledge of God by the addition of more negative attributes. For by "each additional negative attribute you advance toward the knowledge of God, and you are nearer to it than he who does not negative, in reference to God, those qualities which you are convinced by proof must be negatived."[17]

Attributing positively to God the perfections found in creatures would imply imperfections in God. For "though [characteristics would be] perfections as regards ourselves . . . in reference to Him they would be defects. . . ." Silence is better than predicating positive characteristics of God. For "the glorification of God does not consist in *uttering* that which is not to be uttered, but in *reflecting* on that which man should reflect." And the only appropriate reflections on God are that he is totally removed from any similarity with his creatures. He is not like any perfection found in creation.[18]

Maimonides shows by illustration just how one goes about negating certain characteristics of God. One may know that a ship exists without knowing what it is. For if it can be determined that it is not a mineral, a body, or a plant, that it is not flat or round or solid, then soon one can arrive at the notion (by negation) of what it is. "In the same manner you will come nearer to the knowledge and comprehension of God by the negative attributes." But you "arrive at some negation, without obtaining a true conception of an essential attribute." And "those who do not recognize, in reference to God, the negation of things, which others negative by clear proof, are deficient in the knowledge of God, and are remote from comprehending Him." In fact, "the smaller the number of things which a person can negative in relation to God, the less he knows of Him . . . but the man who affirms an attribute of

16. Ibid., pp. 81–82.
17. Ibid., pp. 83–84.
18. Ibid., pp. 85–87.

God, knows nothing but the same; for the object to which, in his imagination, he applies that name, does not exist."[19]

Only the Tetragrammaton (YHWH, Yahweh) indicates God's true essence, and its meaning cannot be known. It denotes "absolute existence" but this can be known only negatively as that which cannot not be. In brief, God can be understood only in terms of his own essence and no human being can know the essence of God. God's name is peculiar to himself. The best that people can do is safeguard its transcendent unity by negating all plurality from it. Thus negative theology is the only protection of monotheism.[20] Despite the fact that Maimonides refers to God as Wisdom and Absolute Existence, he has no positive conception of what these mean. God has no intrinsic causal relation to his creatures and hence cannot be named from perfections found in them. What God is essentially must remain unknowable, except negatively.

Mysticism: Ineffability

Up to this point, the discussion has been concerned with negative language about God on the basis of some cognitive considerations. But a second way of constructing a negative theology, which was probably also highly determinative in each of the aforementioned thinkers, is possible. The view that language about God can be only negative is often found in mysticism, as was the case with Plotinus. In that case there is added to the cognitive assumptions an experience that also defies words. Let us look at this phenomenon in greater detail.

A Definition of Mysticism

Much has been written on the question of a supposed common core of mysticism, with a present trend toward denying that such a core exists.[21] Let us set aside this difficult question and simply assume the unquestionable vantage point that there is significant similarity among mystical systems regardless of whether they share a univocal core. Much of what can be said of one mystical system can mutatis mutandis be said of almost all other mystical systems.

F. C. Happold has outlined the nature of mysticism in four points:[22]

19. Ibid., pp. 88–89.
20. Ibid., pp. 90–91.
21. See Steven T. Katz, ed., *Mysticism and Philosophical Analysis* (New York: Oxford University Press, 1978). Katz and his associates specifically deny an "essence" of mysticism.
22. F. C. Happold, *Mysticism: A Study and an Anthology* (Baltimore: Penguin, 1963), p. 20.

1. The phenomenal world is a manifestation of an Absolute, a "Divine Ground," and as such this world is not true reality. Only the Absolute is truly real.
2. Human beings can know the Absolute by a direct intuition. In this intuition a union of the person with the Absolute takes place.
3. This intuition is the unique function of the true human self, which is usually obscured by the phenomenal self. Thus identification with the Absolute is synonymous with identification with one's true self.
4. This possibility is the main goal of human existence and is the door to the experience of ultimate reality.

These basic points are fleshed out in many different ways. And though the differences may be crucial, the pattern remains. According to the teachings of some Upanishads, the human being must leave the world (maya) and his own phenomenal existence (jiva) to discover his true self (atman) and so become one with the Absolute (Brahman). In Taoism the phenomenality of the "ten thousand things" in the multiplicity of yin and yang must be overcome in the nonduality of the unspoken Tao, the ground of all. In the Christian mysticism of Meister Eckhart, deep in the soul there is a divine spark that is potentially unified with the Godhead. Many more examples could be cited.

The intuition of union with the Absolute is usually part of an overwhelming experience. William James ascribed to it four main characteristics:[23]

1. Ineffability—The experience cannot be contained in words.
2. Noetic quality—The impression of having received absolute truth is part of the experience.
3. Transiency—The experience will not last very long (at most a few hours).
4. Passivity—The experience appears to be received by or given to the person. He does not create it.

It is the first point, the ineffability, that is of most interest to us.

One thing appears clear from the outset: whereas before we concentrated on the fact that God is beyond language, now the experience of God is said to be ineffable. But whereas it is usual practice to distinguish between an experience and the object of experience, in mysticism that distinction breaks down. James likens the experience to having a sensation, for example, a feeling of pain. Let us say that someone is experiencing a headache. It is nonsensical to distinguish between the headache and the experience of the headache as the object and the experience respectively. Similarly the mystic does not allow for a divorce between the Absolute and the experience of the Absolute. (The

23. William James, *The Varieties of Religious Experience* (New York: Collier, 1961), pp. 299–301.

reader who may not be able to conceptualize this claim is undergoing his first lesson in nondual ineffability.)

It is due to that absolute identity that the mystic feels utter irrefragability with regard to his experience. If he believes that he has experienced union with Brahman, Tao, or God, then nothing can shake his conviction. Alan Watts, for instance, emphasizes the immediacy and thus the absolute certainty of the realization of the Ultimate that he advocates.[24] To return to our prior example, one cannot doubt that one is having a headache, and in the same way one cannot doubt one's mystical awareness.

But, as James pointed out,[25] the mystic's personal indubitable experience carries no authority whatever for the outsider who has not shared that experience. Furthermore, no cognitive persuasiveness can arise out of the mystic's experience either. For, as soon as the mystic attempts to relate his experience to others, he must put it into words. But this means to speak of the ineffable. And that seems to be a contradiction in terms.

Stace's Theories of Ineffability

The problem with the ineffability of mystical experience, as we have seen, is twofold. First we have the phenomenon that all true mystical experience is supposed to be ineffable. Certainly that seems to be at least the claim of the mystic. Second is the phenomenon that the mystic characteristically does not let that supposed ineffability stand in his way of using language to the best of his ability to describe the experience. Furthermore, not all of the language used is in fact negative language; much positive language appears, though usually with the qualification that it does not strictly apply. But this is to give with the right hand and take away with the left.

W. T. Stace has provided us with an interesting summary of the issues involved in mystic ineffability and various theories to account for it.[26] He dismisses four theories as inadequate. The first two are classified together as common-sense theories. What they have in common is that they try to reduce mystical experience to a naturalistic denominator. These two theories are

1. The emotion theory. According to this theory, mystical experience is ineffable because it essentially consists of emotions that are too deep for words. Stace counters by pointing out that at bottom mystical experiences and emotional experiences are very different.
2. The spiritual blindness theory. This theory says that mystical experience is ineffable because those who have not had it cannot understand

24. Alan Watts, *The Supreme Identity: An Essay on Oriental Metaphysic and the Christian Religion* (New York: Random, 1972), pp. 46–73.
25. James, *Varieties of Religious Experience,* p. 335.
26. W. T. Stace, *Mysticism and Philosophy* (Philadelphia: Lippincott, 1960), pp. 277–306.

it. Stace repudiates this view on two counts: first, because mystical experience is not simply an empirical perception that must be had to be understood, and second, because mystics themselves admit that they cannot express their experience; they do not blame their audience.

Stace accords the other two theories more respect, even though he rejects them also. He feels that at least they try to do justice to the actual claims of the mystics. These two theories both reckon with the language of the mystic as symbolic, that is, not expressing a literal meaning. But these two theories differ insofar as they account for the nonliteral meaning in different ways.

3. The Dionysian theory. This idea, which Stace finds to be grounded in the thought of Dionysius, holds that positive language does not apply literally. But God can be said to hold various qualities because he causes these qualities in his creation. For example, God is described as "love" because he causes love. Stace is puzzled by the notion of labeling the cause of a property with the name of that property, and he judges that it is not legitimate to use such a term of God. (Even though Stace does not state so explicitly at this point, Dionysius would of course agree with him.)

4. The metaphor theory. Under this theory the positive language used by the mystic is only metaphorical. But Stace raises a point commonly made when someone claims to speak metaphorically. Paul Edwards has distinguished between reducible and irreducible metaphors.[27] In order for a metaphor to have any communicable meaning, it must somehow be at least partially reducible to a literal concept. If no literal common denominator whatever can be discovered, then the metaphor is technically meaningless. Stace makes this point of the mystic's language. In Edward's phraseology, he argues that the mystic either uses reducible metaphors, in which case his language is not ineffable, or he uses irreducible metaphors, in which case he communicates nothing at all. In either case, the problem is unsolved.

Having rejected these four theories, Stace suggests one of his own. He begins by distinguishing what happens to the mystic during his experience and after his experience. Of the former he states that is it truly ineffable. While the mystic is having an experience, words are certainly beyond him: "Mystical experience, during the experience, is wholly unconceptualizable and therefore wholly unspeakable. This must be so. You cannot have a concept of anything within the undifferentiated unity because there are no separate items to be conceptualized."[28]

27. Paul Edwards, "Professor Tillich's Confusions," *Mind* 74 (1965): 197–206.
28. Stace, *Mysticism and Philosophy*, p. 297.

But after the experience the mystic is once again in the realm of differentiated concepts, and thus can speak of his experience. As he now remembers his experience, he can apply words to it. But he still may have difficulty doing so and occassionally take flight into ineffability. Why should this be so?

Stace blames the logical paradoxicality that is typical of mystical experiences. He argues that it is not a problem of whether the mystic can apply concepts to his experience. He can and often does so very well. The problem is that as he applies concepts, he finds himself contradicting himself, and thus he blames the inadequacy of language. But it is not really the language's fault. "The result is that it is possible to use concepts correctly and yet to disobey the laws of logic. This is what the mystic does. . . . The language which he finds himself compelled to use is, when at its best, the literal truth about his experience, but it is contradictory."[29]

Now the question is where the logical paradoxicality comes from. Stace asserts that it arises out of the experience itself. "The language is only paradoxical because the experience is paradoxical."[30] Thus Stace sees himself as having given a psychological explanation of mystical ineffability.

But if the experience itself is too paradoxical for words, it is hard to see why the problem is not still conceptual and epistemological. It seems as though the mystic is still confronted with a datum beyond his conceptualization. If the problems with language are due to a problem with (the application of) logic, the problems with logic are due to the nature of the experience itself and the object the experience self-encompasses.

Thus, without further help, the problem of mysticism is not really different from the more general problem of the application of language to a God who is beyond our concepts. We still need to either consign ourselves to negative language alone or find some way of allowing the language used to be an admixture of negative and positive language (to find ways of reducing the metaphors or to delineate common meaning in the terms used). This task could of course be done through either analogy or model language. Mysticism appears to be only a special case of religious language in general.

Thomas Aquinas: *Via Negativa*

Scholastic philosophers held Maimonides in high regard. Thomas Aquinas agreed with Maimonides that no person could in this life grasp the essence of God in a positive way. For "the divine substance surpasses every form that our intellect reaches. Thus we are unable to apprehend it by knowing *what* it is. . . . For this reason, we must derive the distinction of God from other

29. Ibid., pp. 304–5.
30. Ibid., p. 305.

beings by means of negative differences."[31] This Aquinas calls knowledge of God by way of remotion. In this regard also it is improper to say that God is like any of his creatures. "For although it may be admitted that creatures are in some way like God, it can in no way be admitted that God is like creatures; because, as Dionysius says: 'A mutual likeness may be found between things of the same order, but not between a cause and that which is caused.'"[32] Elsewhere Aquinas adds, "What is comprehended is perfectly known. . . . But no created intellect can attain to that perfect mode of the knowledge. . . ." For "God, whose being is infinite is infinitely knowable. Now no created intellect can know God infinitely. . . . Hence, it is impossible that it should comprehend God."[33] Further, God is simple and "reason cannot reach a simple form, so as to know *what* it is; but it can know *whether* it is."[34] As far as the essence of God is concerned, "we cannot grasp what God is, but only what He is not. . . ."[35]

But unlike Maimonides, Dionysius, and Plotinus, Aquinas was convinced that positive affirmations of God were possible. There is an intrinsic causal relation between God and creation. For if God caused goodness, he must be Goodness; if he caused existence, he must be Existence, and so on. Therefore, even though it is not possible to know the essence of God as such, it is possible to make some positive affirmations about God's essence by virtue of what comes from God.[36] God cannot produce what he does not himself "possess"; he cannot give what he does not have. In Aquinas's own words, "Since every perfection of creatures is to be found in God, albeit in another and more eminent way, whatever terms denote perfections absolutely and without any defect whatever, are predicated of God and other things."[37] The basis, then, for positive affirmations about God is the intrinsic causal similarity between Creator and his creatures.

There are three important differences between the Thomistic via negativa and the method of the neo-Platonic and mystical philosophers before him.[38] First, the via negativa is not the negation of all positive attributes of God but the denial of any imperfections in him. "Negative theology does not assert

31. Saint Thomas Aquinas, *Summa contra Gentiles,* trans. the English Dominican Fathers, vols. 1, 2 (London: Burns, Oates and Washbourne, 1923, 1924), 1.14.

32. Saint Thomas Aquinas, *Summa Theologica,* trans. the English Dominican Fathers (Chicago: Benzinger Brothers, 1947, 1948), 1.4.3 ad 4.

33. Ibid., 1.12.7.

34. Ibid., 1.12.12.

35. Aquinas, *Summa contra Gentiles* 1.30.

36. Aquinas, *Summa Theologica* 1.12.12.

37. Aquinas, *Summa contra Gentiles* 1.30.

38. Nicholas of Cusa (fifteenth century) carried on the strict negative tradition among Christian mystics after Aquinas. See Cusa's *On Learned Ignorance,* trans. G. Heron, O.F.M. (New Haven: Yale University Press, 1949), chaps. 24–26.

negations of God; it denies limitations of Him."[39] Second, "the idea of negation is always based on an affirmation; as is evidenced by the fact that every negative proposition is proved by an affirmative: wherefore unless the human mind knew something positive about God, it would be unable to deny anything about Him."[40] Third, the positive affirmations are made possible only by the intrinsic causal relation between Creator and creatures. God must "possess" the perfections he produces. Or, more properly, if God causes goodness and being, then he must be Goodness and Being.

Two factors emerge from our discussion of negative God-language. First, a totally negative God-talk is meaningless. Unless there is some positive prior knowledge of God, there is no meaningful way to know what to negate of God. Every negation implies a prior affirmation. Complete negation without any affirmation is total skepticism about God. Second, without some kind of negation there is no way to preserve the transcendence of the theistic God. Unless all plurality, change, and finitude are eliminated from God, the theist falls into pure anthropomorphism or semantical idolatry. Finite, limited concepts cannot be applied descriptively to an infinite God without qualification. Hence, some form of qualification or negation is absolutely essential to meaningful attributions of the transcendent God of theism. But negations alone will not suffice. For unless there is also some affirmative knowledge of God, the theist, like the mystic, is also left in skepticism.

39. Austin M. Farrer, *Finite and Infinite,* 2d ed. (Naperville, Ill.: Allenson, 1959), p. 60.
40. Saint Thomas Aquinas, *On the Power of God,* trans. the English Dominican Fathers, 3 bks. in 1 (Westminster, Md.: Newman, 1952), 7.5 body.

12 ✻

Positive Language About God

There are two basic attempts to develop a positive God-talk. One is by way of univocal language and the other by way of analogical language. The former was expounded by Scotus and the latter by Aquinas. Each makes an essential contribution to theistic language. Although the positions seem to be mutually exclusive, their complementarity provides a crucial insight into the nature of religious language.

Thus this chapter will proceed in three parts. First there will be detailed historical expositions of the viewpoints of Scotus and of Aquinas. Our own position will emerge out of this discussion. It will be a form of analogy based on intrinsic causality. Finally, objections from the contemporary discussion on analogy will be answered.

The Scotistic Insistence on Univocal Concepts

John Duns Scotus made one point unmistakably clear: there can be no meaningful positive talk about God unless it involves at the basis of it univocal concepts. Equivocal or analogical concepts leave one in skepticism. Scotus's argument may be summarized in two parts: first, the impossibility of analogous concepts; second, the necessity of univocal concepts.

The Impossibility of Analogous Concepts

Henry of Ghent, a contemporary of Scotus, defended what he called an "analogous concept of being." According to Henry, God is known in a "universal" concept that is only analogically common to himself and to creatures. This concept is conceived of as though it were one notion because of the close resemblance of the concepts it contains, but in reality the concepts are diverse. As creatures actually exist, they are determinate forms of being. But the mind prescinds from all these determinations and forms a simple concept of being that is undetermined but determinable. As applied to God, this concept of being is unqualified and undetermined in any sense, because his being is incapable of any restrictions. Being in this sense is both undetermined and indeterminable. Now determinable being (creatures) and indeterminable being (God) have nothing positive in common; they agree only in what is denied, namely, determination. Therefore, the concept of being common to God and creatures is really not one concept but two. But because of the similarity of these two concepts the mind fails to distinguish between them, as two distant objects tend to fuse before the eye. This dual concept is what Henry calls an analogous concept.[1]

Scotus strongly objects to Henry's analogous concept. First of all, Scotus reminds Henry that if God and creatures are distinguished only by a negation, then there is no distinction at all. For "there is no need to make the distinction that we cannot know what God is; we can only know what He is not. For every denial is intelligible only in terms of some affirmation." Second, Scotus notes that an analogous concept is really two different concepts. Hence it is really equivocal. For either there is at the base of these two concepts one univocal concept from which they draw their common meaning or else they are two entirely different concepts. If the former, there must be a univocal concept at the basis of the so-called analogous concept. If the latter, there is no common meaning in the so-called analogous concept. And whatever is predicated of God and creatures by way of such an equivocal concept must mean something entirely different. Therefore, if concepts of God were analogous, they would be equivocal.[2]

The Necessity of Univocal Concepts of God

But language about God is not equivocal or analogical for Scotus; it is univocal and hence it evades the alternatives of skepticism and meaninglessness. By univocal Scotus means that "which possesses sufficient unity in itself, so that to affirm and deny it of one and the same thing would be a contradiction. It also has sufficient unity to serve as the middle terms of a syllogism." Scotus then gives four arguments to support his contention that concepts must be univocally understood of both God and man.[3]

First, "every intellect that is certain about one concept, but dubious about others has . . . another concept of which it is certain." Scotus offered proof of this premise as follows: "One and the same concept cannot be both certain and dubious, or [else] there is no concept at all, and consequently no certitude about any concept." The other premise is this: "Every philosopher was certain that what he postulated as a first principle was a being. . . . Yet he was not certain whether it was created or an uncreated being, whether it was first

---

1. John Duns Scotus, *Philosophical Writings*, trans. Allan B. Wolter (Indianapolis: Liberal Arts, Bobbs-Merrill, 1962), (from Ghent's *Summa* 24.6), pp. 20–21, 180–81.

2. Ibid., pp. 18, 22–23.

3. Ibid., p. 23.

or not first." The reason for this is as follows: "Someone perceiving the disagreement among philosophers can still be certain that any of the things that they have acclaimed as the first principle has being [e.g., fire, water]."

Scotus dismissed the possibility that the different philosophers had different concepts of being. He said, "By such an evasion all possibility of proving the unity of any concept would be destroyed. The fact of great similarity plus the irreducible simplicity of all the concepts argue that ultimately they are one. Further, if there were two different formal concepts, one would have to conclude that there were two formally opposed first principles of being."[4]

In summation, if the intellect can be certain about the concept of being without knowing it refers to created or uncreated being, and if it is necessary to have a univocal concept in order to be certain about anything, then we must have a univocal concept of God's being. Otherwise, we would have no knowledge at all of God, which is contrary to both faith and philosophy.

Secondly, the concepts used of God must be univocally understood because "no object will produce a simple and proper concept of itself and a simple and proper concept of another object, unless it contains this second object essentially or virtually. No created object, however, contains the Uncreated essentially or virtually. . . . Therefore, it produces no simple and proper concept of the 'uncreated' at all." But "no concept could arise in virtue of the active intellect and the sense image [which are the way all created objects are understood in this life] that is not univocal but only analogous with, or wholly other than, what is revealed in the sense image." Hence, it would be impossible to have any natural knowledge of God unless it is known via univocal concepts. But we do have natural knowledge of God. Therefore, this knowledge must come by way of univocal concepts.[5]

Third, our concept of God must be univocal, since "the proper concept of any subject provides sufficient ground for concluding to everything conceivable which necessarily inheres in that subject." But "we have no concept of God . . . that enables us to know every necessary attribute which we conceive of Him, as is evident from the fact of the Trinity, and other necessary attributes that we know by faith." Therefore, we have no proper concept of God. But this is patently false, as revelation teaches us much about God. Hence, we must have at least some concept that is properly (i.e., univocally) applicable to him.[6]

Fourth, "either some pure perfection has a common meaning as applied to God and creatures or not. If not, it is either because its meaning does not

4. Ibid., pp. 23–25.
5. Ibid., pp. 25–26.
6. Ibid., p. 26.

apply formally to God at all (which is inadmissible), or else it has a meaning that is wholly proper to God [and not to creatures]. . . ." But this latter alternative is contrary to the truth affirmed by Anselm that "we first know something to be a pure perfection and secondly we attribute this perfection to God."

Furthermore, if pure perfections were found only in God, there would be no such perfections among creatures. The proper metaphysical approach is to begin with a concept (such as will or intellect) and finding that it contains no imperfection, "attribute [it] to God—but in a most perfect degree." Finally, "if you maintain that this is not true, but that the formal concept of what pertains to God is another notion, a disconcerting consequence ensues; namely that from the proper notion of anything found in creatures nothing at all can be inferred about God, for the notion of what is in each is wholly different."[7]

Beneath these four arguments for univocity is one fundamental contention. If there is no univocity in our concepts about God, then there is no certainty in our knowledge about God. For "one and the same concept cannot be both certain and dubious. Therefore, either there is another concept [which is certain], or there is no concept at all, and consequently no certitude about any concept." In other words, if there is no univocal basis for meaning, then one is forced to an infinite regress of nonunivocal concepts in search for the one elusive univocal concept by which the nonunivocal ambiguity can be resolved. "For every intellect that is certain about one concept, but dubious about others has, in addition to the concept about which it is in doubt, another concept about which it is certain." Hence, Scotus concluded, "I say that God is conceived . . . in some concept univocal to Himself and to a creature."[8]

In summation, there are only three alternatives in our concepts about God. Either they are understood equivocally (i.e., in a totally different sense), in which case we know nothing about God; or they are understood analogically (i.e., with partly the same but partly different meaning), in which case we must have some univocal concept of God enabling us to know which part of the analogous concept applies to God and which does not apply to him; or else the concepts of God must be univocal (i.e., having totally the same meaning) in the first place. Therefore, either there are univocal concepts about God or else we know nothing about God. There must be either univocity or skepticism.

It would appear that Scotus made his point. Equivocal God-talk says nothing about God. And analogical God-talk seems to work only if there is in

7. Ibid., pp. 27–28.
8. Ibid., p. 23.

the analogy an identifiable univocal element. If there is no such identifiable univocal element, the concept is at best ambiguous and at worst equivocal. If it is ambiguous, it can be clarified only in terms of a nonambiguous univocal concept. But if there is an identifiable univocal element in the analogy, then analogy is actually a form of univocal understanding of God. For it involves an identifiable univocal concept that can be applied to God without change, along with the other elements of the combined analogous statement that cannot be applied to God. In brief, analogy either has a univocal element in it or it does not. If it does not, it is ultimately equivocal talk, which leaves us in skepticism about God. On the other hand, if analogy does have a univocal element in it, then it really contains a univocal concept after all, which proves some true knowledge about God.[9]

Thomistic Contention for Analogous Predication

Thomas Aquinas was familiar with and flatly rejected the insistence on univocal God-language. He wrote, "It is impossible for anything to be predicated univocally of God and a creature."[10]

Aquinas's Rejection of Univocal Predication

In the *Summa contra Gentiles* Aquinas offered six arguments against univocal predication of God and creatures. They are as follows:[11]

First, only those effects that receive from their cause the specific form of that cause can receive a univocal predication of that form of them and of God. But "the forms of the things God has made do not measure up to a specific likeness of the divine power." All creatures are "in a divided and particular way that which in Him is found in a simple and universal way." So, "it is evident that nothing can be said univocally of God and other things."

Secondly, even if "an effect should measure up to the species [kind] of its cause, it will not receive the univocal predication of the name [attribute] unless it receives the same specific form according to the same mode of being." But no creature has the same mode of being that God has, for "there is nothing in God that is not the divine being itself, which is not the case with other things. Nothing, therefore, can be predicated of God and other things

9. This same argument for the necessity of a univocal concept has been repeated by many others. See W. G. T. Shedd, *Dogmatic Theology* (New York: Charles Scribner and Sons, 1868–94), 1:89ff.; Stuart Hackett, *The Resurrection of Theism* (Chicago: Moody, 1957), pp. 127–30.

10. Saint Thomas Aquinas, *On the Power of God*, trans. the English Dominican Fathers, 3 bks. in 1 (Westminster, Md.: Newman, 1952), 7.7 body.

11. Saint Thomas Aquinas, *Summa contra Gentiles*, trans. the English Domican Fathers, vols. 1, 2 (London: Burns, Oates and Washbourne, 1923, 1924), 1.32.

univocally." That is, God's mode of being is infinite and necessary, but the creature's is finite and contingent. Hence, no univocal predication according to the mode of being is possible between God and creatures.

Thirdly, "whatever is predicated of many things univocally is either a genus, a species, a difference, an accident, or a property." But God's essence cannot be defined in any way; nor are there any accidents in God; he is what he is essentially. He is unique in kind and does not share in class or kind with any other being. "It remains, then, that nothing is predicated univocally of God and other things."

Fourthly, "what is predicated of many things univocally is simpler than both of them, at least in concept. Now there can be nothing simpler than God either in reality or in concept. Nothing, therefore, is predicated univocally of God and other things." Since the one thing in common is always simpler than the many things having it in common, any univocal predication of God and others would have to be more simple than God, which is impossible.

Fifthly, "everything that is predicated univocally of many things belongs through participation to each of the things of which it is predicated. . . . But nothing is said of God by participation. . . . Nothing, therefore, can be predicated univocally of God and other things." In short, God does not participate in anything; rather, all things participate in him. If there were a common univocal predication in which God participated, then this something would be more ultimate than God.

Sixthly, "nothing is predicated of God and creatures as though they were in the same order, but rather, according to priority and posteriority." For God is Being essentially and all other things have being only by participation in God. But "what is predicated of some things according to priority and posteriority is certainly not predicated univocally." For the prior possesses the characteristic essentially and the posterior possesses it only by participation in the prior. "It is impossible, therefore, that anything be predicated univocally of God and other things."

In the *Summa Theologica* (1.13.5) Aquinas rests his case against univocal predication on the first argument from *Summa contra Gentiles.* "All perfections existing in creatures dividedly and multiply pre-exist in God unitedly." Hence any perfection applied to a creature signifies something distinct from its essence. But when applied to God, this perfection signifies God's very essence. For example, creatures have wisdom but God is wisdom. "Hence it is evident that the term wise is not applied in the same way to God and to man. The same applies to other terms. Hence, no name is predicated univocally of God and other creatures."

Implied in Aquinas's objection to univocal predication is another argument. He implied an argument with which he did agree:[12] "God is more

12. What Aquinas would disagree with is the conclusion: "Therefore, whatever is said of

distant from creatures than any creatures are from each other. But the difference of some creatures [from each other] makes any univocal predication of them impossible, as in the case of those things which are not in the same genus. Therefore, much less can anything be predicated univocally of God and creatures."

In essence, then, the argument for analogous God-talk is this: between an infinitely perfect being and finitely perfect beings there is an infinite difference in perfection (certainly an infinite differs from a finite in more than a finite way). And where there is an infinite difference in perfection there cannot be a univocal predication. A given perfection cannot mean totally the same thing as applied to God and creatures, for God and creatures are separated by an infinite degree of perfection. As Thomas put it elsewhere, "Every effect of an univocal agent is adequate to the agent's power: and no creature being finite, can be adequate to the power of the first agent which is infinite."[13] And what is true of power is also true of any other perfection. An infinitely perfect Cause produced finitely perfect effects. And the perfections found in these effects cannot be predicated in exactly the same manner (i.e., univocally) of God.

The Need for the Via Negativa

At this point the need for the via negativa (way of negation) becomes apparent. As Plotinus correctly observed, God cannot possess perfections the way created things possess them. In this sense God does "produce what He does not possess."[14] because God does not really possess anything he produces. God does not have wisdom and being; God is wisdom and being. Whatever perfections creatures possess must be completely negated of God, for the sense in which he "possesses" those perfections is completely different from the way they are possessed by creatures. Properly speaking, God does not really possess them at all; rather, these perfections are of the essence of God.

Univocal predication destroys the distance between God and creatures necessitated by the different kinds of beings that they are. God is an infinitely perfect Being and all other beings are only finitely perfect. If any attribute were predicated in the same way (i.e., univocally) of both God and creatures, then it would either imply the finitude of God or else the infinitude of creatures. As long as God is viewed as infinitely perfect, nothing that is finitely

God and of creatures is predicated equivocally." He clearly defends analogical predication, which is his view.

13. Aquinas, *On the Power of God* 7.7 body.

14. See chapter 11 (cf. Plotinus, *Six Enneads* [Chicago: Encyclopaedia Britannica Press, 1952], 5.3.14–15).

perfect can be applied to God without qualifications. The proponents of negative theology appreciated the necessity for these qualifications in order to preserve God's transcendence. When a perfection taken from the finite world is applied to God, it must be applied to God infinitely, since he is an infinite Being. Unless the finite conditions of a perfection can be negated, there is no way it can be appropriately applied to an infinite Being.

Aquinas's Rejection of Equivocal Predication

However, as it was also shown in chapter 11, the via negativa alone will not suffice. For if all meaning is negated when one removes the finite connotations of a term, he is speaking mere equivocations. Unless there is some common meaning that applies to both God and creatures, the meaning it has as applied to creatures is totally different from the meaning it has as applied to God. And a totally different meaning is an equivocation that leaves us in skepticism about God. Aquinas agrees with Scotus that equivocal language leaves one with no knowledge of God. Although Aquinas refers to God as an "equivocal Cause" (i.e., of a different order than finite causes), he offers several arguments against equivocal predication of that Cause.[15]

First, in equivocals "it is entirely accidental that one name is applied to diverse things: the application of the name to one of them does not signify that it has an order to the other." But "this is not the situation with names said of God and creatures, since we note in the community of such names the order of cause and effect. . . . It is not, therefore, in the manner of pure equivocation that something is predicated of God and other things." That is, terms with the same spelling but different meaning [as "bark" of a tree or a dog] are equivocals by chance. But where one thing is the cause of the other, there is no mere chance connection between the terms expressing these things, but there is an order of reference that signifies that one is related to the other.

Secondly, "where there is pure equivocation, there is no likeness in things themselves; there is only a unity of a name. But . . . there is a certain mode of likeness of things to God. It remains, then, that names are not said of God in a purely equivocal way." The minor premise was supported by a preceding article (1.29) where Aquinas argued that "some likeness must be found between them [cause and effect], since it belongs to the nature of action that an agent produce its like, since each thing acts according as it is in act." The similarity of Creator and creature is supported, too, by Holy Scripture, which says that God made man in his image and likeness (Gen. 1:26).

Thirdly, "when one name is predicated of several things in a purely equivocal way, we cannot from one of them be led to the knowledge of an-

15. Aquinas, *Summa contra Gentiles* 1.33.

other. . . ." But "from what we find in other things, we do arrive at a knowledge of divine things, as is evident from what we have said." Therefore, "such names are not said of God and other things in a purely equivocal way." That is to say, unless there is some likeness between creatures and God, we could never rise, as we do, from a knowledge of created things to a knowledge of God.

Fourthly, "equivocation in a name impedes the progress of reasoning." And "if nothing was said of God and creatures except in a purely equivocal way, no reasoning proceeding from creatures to God would take place. But the contrary is evident from all those who have spoken about God." That is to say, not only would equivocation make knowledge of God impossible (as the third argument contends) but it would impede any reasoning about God built on knowledge gained from the world in which reasoning all theologians engage.

Fifthly, "it is also a fact that a name is predicated of some being uselessly unless through that name we understand something of the being. But if names are said of God and creatures in a purely equivocal way, we understand nothing of God through those names." For "the meanings of those names are known to us solely to the extent that they are said of creatures. In vain, therefore, would it be said or proved of God that He is a being, good, or the like."

Sixthly, even if nonequivocal names tell us only what God is not, at least they agree in what they deny of God. A totally equivocal denial of God would be the same as affirming the same thing that is being denied of God. Hence, even negations of God cannot be equivocal.

In a later work Aquinas rests the case against equivocal predication on one central argument: Equivocal predication is impossible "because if that were so, it follows that from creatures nothing at all could be known or demonstrated about God."[16] But it is patently false that we know nothing about God. Hence there must be some nonequivocal predications about God.

Analogical Predication: The Only Alternative

If terms can be applied to God neither univocally nor equivocally, then they must be predicated of him analogically. In Thomas's own words, "This name God. . . is taken neither univocally nor equivocally, but analogically. This is apparent from this reason—Univocal names have absolutely the same meaning, while equivocal names have absolutely diverse meanings; whereas analogicals, a name taken in one signification must be placed in the definition of the same name taken in other significations."[17] Therefore, terms denoting per-

16. Aquinas, *Summa Theologica* 1.13.5.
17. Ibid., 1.13.10.

fections taken from creatures can be applied to God only in an analogous way. "For we can name God only from creatures. Hence, whatever is said of God and creatures is said according as there is some relation of the creature to God as to its principal cause, wherein all the perfections pre-exist excellently." Further, comments Aquinas, "this mode of communion [i.e., analogy] is a mean between pure equivocation and simple univocation. For in analogies the idea is not, as in univocals, one and the same [in its application]; yet it is not totally diverse as in equivocals; but the name which is used in a multiple sense signifies various proportions to some one thing."[18] For example, God is named Good because he is the Cause of goodness. The Cause is Good and hence when it causes goodness in something else it communicates of what it is to what its creature has by created participation. The causal connection between Creator and creatures is the basis for the similarity in the analogous predication. Creation cannot be totally unlike its Creator, since every perfection it possesses it has acquired from him.

There is another fundamental argument for analogy that takes us back to Parmenides' dilemma.[19] According to the monist Parmenides, if there is more than one being in the universe, these beings must differ by either being or nonbeing. But they cannot differ by nonbeing for that is nothing, and to differ by nothing is not to differ at all. Neither can things differ by being, for that is the very respect in which they are identical, and they cannot differ in the very respect in which they are identical. Hence, there cannot be more than one being in the universe. Thus there is only one being—that is, monism. Now there are only two horns to this dilemma.[20] Either one's principle of differentiation is inside of being or it is outside of being. If outside, then things do not differ in being; they are identical in being and monism is true. The only way to maintain a pluralism essential to theism is to insist that things differ in their very being. But how can they differ by the only thing they have in common? The answer is that they cannot, if being is univocal. For if being means exactly the same thing wherever it is found, it follows that there can be only one being.

There are only three alternatives. Being is either equivocal, univocal, or analogical. If being is univocal, indicating exactly the same thing, wherever it is found, then there can be only one being in the universe. For whatever one points to as being here is identical with whatever one points to as being there or anywhere else. Unless there is a real difference between this or that being,

18. Ibid., 1.13.5.

19. See chapter 11.

20. For an excellent article on the pluralistic alternatives to monism see Leonard J. Eslick, "The Real Distinction: Reply to Professor Reese," *The Modern Schoolman* 38, no. 2. (January 1961): 149–61.

they are really the same. If there are no differences in being, then being cannot have differences; it must be all the same.

On the other hand, if being is equivocal, there cannot be more than one being in the universe. For if *this* is a being, *that* cannot be a being. In equivocation the meaning is entirely different and the only way to be entirely different from being is to be nonbeing. Hence, if this is a being, then that is nonbeing. Once one being is identified, it is the only being possible, if being is understood in an equivocal sense. For the opposite from something is nothing. And if this being exists, then every other "being" (taken in an equivocal or totally different sense) does not exist. Hence, if being is understood in an equivocal sense, there can be only one being in the universe. This philosophy is called monism.

There is only one way out of this monistic dilemma for the theist—the analogy of being. That is, being does not mean exactly the same thing wherever it is found. Being is not univocal; beings differ in their very being. There is an infinite Being and there are finite beings. And there are different kinds of finite beings. God is uncomposed Being and all creatures are beings composed of essence (what they are) and existence (that they are).[21] In God, essence and existence are identical, but they are not identical in finite things. The difference in the very being of things makes it possible for there to be many different kinds of beings. Of course, beings are not totally different in their being. They all exist, but their kinds of existence differ. God exists necessarily; all other things exist contingently. God is Existence; all other things have existence. God and creatures differ in their kind of being (essence) but they are alike in the *be*-ing. God exists and man exists; herein is the similarity in fact. The difference is in the mode of existence each possesses. God exists independently and man exists dependently, but both exist. This similarity and difference comprises the analogy of being and the only alternative to a monism of being.

Since being is used analogously between God and creatures, being can be predicated of God and creatures only in an analogous way. Were it to be predicated any other way, it would not be truly descriptive of the different ways in which God and creatures have being. Since there is a similarity in being between God and creation, being cannot be predicated either equivocally (differently) or univocally (identically) of them. And since the being of God is necessary and essential, anything that is predicated of him must be predicated of his essence; that is, he must have it essentially. It follows, then, that not only being but goodness, truth, power, and whatever may properly be said of God must be predicated in an analogous way. For God does not

21. See Thomas Aquinas, *On Being and Essence*, trans. Armand Maurer, 2d rev. ed. (Toronto: Pontifical Institute of Medieval Studies, 1968).

have these in the same way creatures do. In fact, God does not have them at all; God is the perfections that his creatures only have by causal participation. The Cause is most eminently the same perfections which his created effects have only finitely.

In summary, analogy of being (and predication) is the only salvation from monism and from skepticism. It is the only alternative to monism, since if beings cannot differ, there can be only one being. It is the salvation from skepticism because, unless there is a similarity in being, there can be no knowledge of infinite Being derived from finite beings.

Univocal Concepts but Analogical Predication

One apparent contradiction has not yet been resolved. Scotus demonstrated that analogous concepts would not save one from skepticism. Only univocal concepts can guarantee knowledge. But if Thomas rejects univocal predication, how then can he avoid skepticism? The answer and reconciliation between Scotism and Thomism lies in the distinction between a concept and a predication. Scotus was right that the concept that is applied to both God and man must be univocally understood; but Aquinas was correct in arguing that this concept must be analogically affirmed of God and creatures. That is, the definition of the attribute applicable to both God and creatures must be the same, but the application of it differs. For in one case (God's) it is applied without limits; in the case of man it is predicated with limitations. God, for instance, is good infinitely; man is good only finitely. Good may be defined in the same univocal way for both, for example, as "that which is desired for its own sake." But God is to be desired for his own sake absolutely, whereas creatures are to be desired for their own sake only relatively. Likewise, being may be defined univocally as "that which is," but this univocal concept is predicated of God and creatures in an analogous way. God is "that which is" infinitely; a creature is "that which is" only finitely. Or, more properly, God is Existence and creatures merely have existence.

This distinction has not always been fully appreciated by Thomists, but in recent works on analogy Thomists have come to recognize its validity. Armand A. Maurer states the distinction clearly: "It is not generally realized that St. Thomas' doctrine of analogy is above all a doctrine of the *judgment* of analogy, and not of the analogy of concept. . . ."[22] For generic concepts are univocal when abstracted but analogical when asserted of different things, as man and dog are equally animal but are not equal animals. That is, "animal" is defined the same way (say, as "a sentient being"), but animality is predicated differently of Fido and of Socrates. Socrates possesses animality in a

---

22. Armand A. Maurer, "St. Thomas and the Analogy of Genus," *New Scholasticism* 29 (April 1955): 143.

higher sense than Fido does. Likewise, both the flower and God are said to be beautiful, but God is beautiful in an infinitely higher sense than flowers are. For if beauty means "that which, being seen, pleases," then the pleasure of the beatific vision of God is infinitely greater than the pleasure of viewing a flower. In brief, Scotus was correct in insisting that our concepts must be univocally understood and defined. But Aquinas was right in insisting that any concept drawn from the finite world must be predicated of God in an analogous way.

Finite Concepts and Finite Predications

Aquinas recognized that all concepts are finite; they are limited by the very finite circumstances in which they arise.[23] People never derive infinite concepts from sensory experience. "Since God infinitely exceeds the power of our intellect, any form we conceive cannot completely represent the divine essence, but merely has in some small measure an imitation of it. . . ."[24] This is why Aquinas said God "is one in reality and many things logically."[25] For the simple essence of God is not known simply by any concept of it but only by way of many predications about it. There is no concept taken from creation that is adequate to express the divine essence, yet many things can be affirmed of the essence of God. We cannot know the substance of God, but we can predicate many things about God substantively.[26]

But how can univocally understood finite concepts be predicated analogously of God without losing their meaning? Does not a limited concept lose all of its meaning when it is applied without limits to an infinite Being? Aquinas answered this question by making a distinction between the (unlimited) thing signified and the limited mode of signification. The mode in which concepts are conceived is always finite for human beings, but what these concepts signify is not necessarily finite. In fact, "since every perfection of creatures is to be found in God, albeit in another and more eminent way, whatever terms denote perfections absolutely and without any defect whatever, are predicated of God and other things; for instance, goodness, wisdom, and so forth." On the other hand, "any term that denotes such like perfections together with a mode proper to creatures, cannot be said of God except by similitude and metaphor. . . ."[27]

Some terms by their very denotation cannot be applied to an unlimited being. Other terms, however, do not necessarily denote what is limited, even

---

23. See Aquinas, *Summa Theologica* 1.84.1–8.
24. Thomas Aquinas, *On Truth* (Chicago: H. Regnery, 1952–54). 2.1 body.
25. Aquinas, *On the Power of God* 7.6 body.
26. Aquinas, *Summa Theologica* 1.12.4; 1.13.2.
27. Aquinas, *Summa contra Gentiles* 1.29.

though they are conceived in finite concepts. For instance, there is nothing essentially limited about being ("that which is") or goodness ("that which is desired for its own sake") or beauty ("that which, being seen, pleases"). Hence, these terms may be predicated of God metaphysically (i.e., actually) and not merely metaphorically (i.e., symbolically). Such terms do not lose their content, because they retain the same univocal definition; neither do these terms carry with them the necessary implications of finitude, because they are not applied to God univocally (i.e., in the same way they are applied to creatures). They are predicated analogically, meaning not identically nor in a totally different way.

How is it known that God must be (in an infinitely perfect way) what these terms denote? Because God is the cause of these perfections and causes communicate according to their own perfections in a mode appropriate to the effects they cause. An infinitely perfect God communicated perfections to his creatures in a finitely perfect manner. Hence, even though there is an infinite difference in perfection between God and creatures, there is nevertheless not a total lack of similarity. The created sequents are similar to their creative Source, because the creature must bear some similarity to its creator.

It could be argued that a metaphysics, let alone a natural theology, is impossible apart from having first established the analogical nature of religious language. For, after all, such terms as "first cause" or "creator of the universe" must be analogical. But then it would appear that we are caught in a vicious circle since, as we shall see, analogy is dependent on the reality of the metaphysical relationship between God and the world. Thus natural theology works because of analogy, and analogy works because of natural theology. Each grounds the other, which means that neither is grounded.

But, even though both sides are dependent on each other, the dependencies are of two different kinds. There is no circularity. In natural theology we establish certain conclusions by using religious language, which then turns out to be analogical. But we would never have to know that analogy was at work. The language was analogical, whether we were ever cognizant of that fact or not. When we are dealing with analogy, we are in a sense merely discovering what has been true of the nature of our language all along. It is only in explaining how this language works that we need to make reference to metaphysical truths. Niels C. Nielsen, Jr., has elaborated the ontological requisites for analogy, particularly in theological contexts.[28]

The Causal Basis for Analogy Between God and Creatures

Aquinas rested the case for a similarity between God and creatures in the causal relation. Each of the first four ways of proving God's existence is

---

28. Niels C. Nielsen, Jr., "Analogy and the Knowledge of God: An Ecumenical Appraisal," *Rice University Studies* 60 (1974): 21–102.

clearly based on causality and it is implied in the fifth way. Even the very Platonic appearance of the fourth way imports causality to complete the argument.[29] And once it is shown by causality that God is, then Aquinas can demonstrate what God is from the analogy implied in this causal relation. Just how often Aquinas makes explicit reference to causality as the basis for analogy will become apparent in the following quotations. The important question here is what kind of causality is the basis for the similarity between God and creatures. The most helpful work on Thomas's doctrine at this point is the classic by Battista Mondin, *The Principle of Analogy in Protestant and Catholic Theology*.[30] The analysis here follows that of Mondin.

1. *Analogy is based in intrinsic causality.* Unlike Maimonides and the neo-Platonists, Aquinas held to an intrinsic causal relationship between God and creation. An extrinsic causal relation is such that only one thing possesses the characteristic properly and the other thing improperly by virtue of a causal relation to it. To illustrate, food is called healthy only because it causes health in a body, but, properly speaking, only organisms are healthy. And God is called good only because he causes goodness, not because he is good. Not so with the causal relation between God and the world; it is an intrinsic relation where both God and creatures possess the perfections properly, only each according to its own mode of being. God must be good because he causes goodness; he must be Existence because he causes things to exist, and so on. There is an intrinsic causal connection and, therefore, analogy between the Cause and its effects.[31]

2. *Analogy is based on efficient causality.* God is the producing cause of all that exists, not merely the purposing (final) Cause of neo-Platonic philosophy. For Aquinas, God brought the world into being from nothing. The world did not come about by any imitation of the divine being but by a creation flowing from it. The theistic God is the cause of the world's being, not merely of its form. God created the world; he did not simply make it out of stuff that was already there. In brief, creation is *ex nihilo*, not *ex materia*. God is the efficient cause of the very *be*-ing of the world. For, wrote Aquinas, "everything that, in any way whatever *is*, must needs be from that to which nothing else is the cause of being. . . . Therefore, from Him is everything that in any way whatever *is*."[32]

Elsewhere he wrote, "It belongs to a thing to have an efficient cause according as it has being." And "the reason why an efficient cause is required

---

29. Aquinas, *Summa Theologica* 1.2.3.
30. (The Hague: Nijhoff, 1963).
31. See Aquinas, *Summa Theologica* 1.13.5; *Summa contra Gentiles* 1.29–30.
32. Aquinas, *Summa Theologica* 2.15.2.

is not merely because the effect can not-be, but because the effect would not be if the cause were not."[33]

3. *Analogy is based on essential causality.* It is clear from the foregoing that God is the essential *(per se)* Cause of creation and not merely an accidental *(per accidens)* cause of it. That is, God causes the very being of the world and not merely its becoming. Further, essential causes generate their own kind. For instance, musicians give birth to nonmusicians (per accidens), but humans generate only humans (per se). Hence, when beings are created, it is by virtue of an essential causal relationship. Only Being gives rise to being. Thomas wrote, "Some likeness must be found between them [i.e., between effects and their cause], since it belongs to the nature of action that an agent produces its like, since each thing acts according as it is in act. The form of the effect, therefore, is certainly found in some measure in a transcending cause, but according to another mode and in another way."[34] Only that which exists can communicate existence to another. Nothing cannot cause something. And since all caused existence is communicated to it by its cause, there must be some essential similarity in existence between this existing effect and its cause.

4. *Analogy is not based on material causality.* God, as efficient Cause, is the cause of the existence and all of the perfections of everything that exists, but it does not follow from this that everything resulting from his causality resembles him. The material upon which efficient causality operates causes some characteristics that do not flow from the nature of the cause itself. For example, when the sun causes heat in clay this is efficient causality, for the sun is communicating heat of itself to another. But when in the process of doing so the sun also hardens the clay this is by way of material causality in the clay. That is, the hardness does not flow from the nature of the sun (for the same rays soften other things, such as wax) but from the condition of the clay upon which the sun is exercising its efficient causality. Also, boiling water causes an egg to be hot by efficient causality, but it causes the egg to harden only because of the material condition of the egg (i.e., by material causality). Likewise, God is the cause of the existence of matter, but he is not material; he is the cause of all perfections but not of the imperfection resulting from the limiting conditions of a material world. An effect resembles its efficient cause only insofar as the effect flows from the nature of the cause but not insofar as that causality is conditioned by the finite world on which it operates.

5. *Analogy is based on principal, not instrumental, causality.* Effects resemble their primary causes but not necessarily their instrumental causes. To illustrate, the pen is the instrumental cause of the exam, and the student is the

33. Ibid., 1.44.1 ad 2 and 3.
34. Aquinas, *Summa contra Gentiles* 1.29.2.

principal cause of it. Only the student's mind resembles the exam; the pen does not. The exam does reflect the thoughts of the student, even though it is not like the pen. In like manner, the perfections of the world resemble their principal Cause (God) but not necessarily their instrumental causes.

In summation, the analogy between creature and Creator based on causality is secured only because God is the principal, intrinsic, essential, efficient cause of the being and perfections of the world. In any other kind of causal relationship an analogical similarity would not necessarily follow. But in an analogy of being similarity must follow. For Being communicates only being, and perfections or kinds of being do not arise from an imperfect being. Existence produces only after its kind, namely, other existences.

Objections and Responses

In chapter 10 we presented Frederick Ferré's objections to analogy. Now that we have expounded analogy more completely we can respond to those objections that are relevant here. In addition, it will be helpful to refer to the comprehensive work of David Burrell, who has raised some objections, not all of which he found answerable from the standpoint of a traditional understanding of analogy.[35]

1. *Why select some but not all qualities drawn from the world and apply only these to God?* Because only some things flow from God's efficient, essential, principal, and intrinsic causality. Only these are the perfections found in finite creation which do not necessarily denote what is finite. Hence, since only these concepts do not necessitate a limited application of their meaning, they alone may be appropriately applied to an unlimited Being.

Burrell gives a more fluid answer to this question. He defers to the theologian and states that only in the process of theologizing can it be actually observed which perfections should be applied to God. This is a correct observation, but it is also an empty one. For surely the theologian does not work without criteria. And even though he can and does use different methods for his understanding of God, the philosophical one previously indicated is not thereby invalidated. Simultaneously it does exonerate analogy from the charge of being indeterminate and vacuous as to its subject matter.

2. *Words divorced from their finite mode or conditions are vacuous or devoid of meaning.* This critique ignores the distinction between a concept and its predication. The univocal concept of the words remains the same; only the way in which they are predicated changes. And even in the predication there is a similarity based on the efficient causal relation to God. The

35. David Burrell, *Analogy and Philosophical Language* (New Haven: Yale University Press, 1973). Of the six criticisms mentioned by Ferré in chapter 10, two are directed against extrinsic causality and thus do not apply here.

meaning of the words *goodness, being,* and *beauty* is not emptied when applied to God; the words are merely extended without limits. That is, the perfection indicated by an analogous predication is not negated; rather, it is released from any limiting mode of signification and applied essentially to God. Since the perfection denoted by some terms does not necessarily imply any limitations, there is no reason why perfection cannot be predicated of an unlimited Being. Simply because all terms are limited in derivation does not mean that they must be limited in application.

3. *Analogy rests on the assumption that causality provides a similarity.* This assumption is justifiable in terms of intrinsic, essential, principal, efficient causality but not in terms of just any kind of causality. Mondin, whose work was not mentioned in Ferré's criticism of analogy, successfully defends analogy against this charge. Being communicates only being. The Cause of existence cannot produce perfections that it does not "possess." If God causes goodness, then he must be good. If he causes existence, then he must exist. Otherwise the absurd consequence ensues that God gives what he does not have to give.

4. *Any analogous predication of God as a "first Cause" involves an infinite regress of meaning to identify the univocal element.* This objection holds true for nonunivocal concepts, but it is not true of univocal concepts that have analogical predications. It is true that one must have a univocal understanding of what is being predicated of the first Cause, but it does not follow from this that how it is predicated of different kinds of beings must be identical (i.e., univocal). Indeed, if it is known that one Being is infinite and another being is finite, then how a quality is predicated must differ from what is being predicated. For to predicate a perfection in the same way of an infinite Being as it is predicated of a finite being (viz., finitely) is really to predicate it equivocally, since an infinite Being does not have qualities in a finite way. The only way to avoid equivocation when predicating the same perfection of both finite beings and infinite Being is to predicate it differently (i.e., analogously) according to the mode of being that each is.

5. *Even assuming the challengeable metaphysical assumption that there is a similarity among beings, that ontology is not univocally expressible.* First of all, this is not a mere assumption for a theist; it is the only alternative to monism. If there are many beings, there must be an analogical similarity among beings. Were this not so, there could be only one being in the universe. For if being means entirely the same thing wherever it is found (univocity), there can be only one being. And if being means something entirely different (equivocity), then once one being is identified everything else must be totally different which is nonbeing. Only if beings are similar, but neither totally identical nor totally different, can there be more than one being in the universe. But God is and I am (and you are). We are all different beings. Hence,

there must be an analogy of being that permits all of us to exist (the similarity) and yet allows each to exist differently; each of us has being (existence) but each is a different kind of being (essence). In God existence and essence are identical. Hence, creatures, like God, exist, but the existence of creatures is only analogous to that of God. For God exists essentially and all else exists dependently.

Secondly, being is univocally conceived but it is analogically predicated of God and finite beings. The concept is understood to mean the same thing, namely, being is "that which is or exists." God exists and a man exists; this they have in common. But God exists infinitely and independently, whereas a man exists only finitely and dependently; this they have in difference. In short, that they both exist is univocally conceived; how they each exist is analogically predicated. For God exists necessarily and creatures exist only contingently; there is a distinct difference in the mode of existence, even though the fact of their existence is the same (i.e., they both exist).

6. *Since Ludwig Wittgenstein the distinction between univocal and equivocal is obsolete and consequently the notion of analogy is obsolete.* To understand this objection we need to remind ourselves of Wittgenstein's proposal for understanding language. Expressions receive their meaning from their use in the context of language games. Each language game is autonomous insofar as there are no universal criteria for meaning. Words that carry over from game to game or words with similar meanings bear family resemblances, but we can never isolate a core meaning they must share. Thus the rigid designations of language being univocal or equivocal breaks down before this dynamic understanding based on usage.

Burrell responds to this idea by insisting on an equivalence between language in ordinary use and univocal language. There may not be any obligatory standard for univocal language, but that fact is irrelevant because all we mean by "univocal meaning" is language in its ordinary context of meaning. He says, "We can, then, speak of an ordinary or univocal usage so long as we neither insist on its fixity nor count on it as our final norm."[36] Burrell observes that in this sense even terms such as "disc jockey" or "girl Friday" may take on a univocal role. Thus the distinction between univocal and equivocal still holds, and analogy is still called for.

7. *A general theory of analogy does not work.* Even though Burrell defends a theory of analogy (which will be summarized in the next chapter), he is wary of making it too rigid. In particular, he objects to the theory of analogy of proper proportionality as expounded by Cardinal Cajetan. Burrell contends that it simply does not work, no matter how hard we try to fill in all of our parameters. Any formula we try to set up will still leave us with

36. Ibid., p. 221.

ambiguity and equivocation.[37] The same problem applies to other theories of analogy as well.

In response to Burrell, we need first to note that the present account does not provide a specific formula for univocal language meaning. Critics of analogy, including Ferré, usually bring their criticisms down to the conclusion that models of analogy do not ultimately yield only univocal meaning for language as applied to God. Burrell recognizes the nonsense of this, for then there would be no need for analogy at all. Still he faults traditional understandings of analogy for getting involved in complicated systems that do not resolve equivocation.

Second, we can point out that the present account gives no formula for meaning at all. We have stayed away from picking one or more of Cajetan's categories and locking ourselves into it. One could conceivably argue that what we have in our understanding of Aquinas is the analogy of intrinsic attribution combined with proper proportionality. But these are not Thomas's categories, and it is well not to be tied to one formal understanding of language mechanisms. Instead, we have presented a primarily metaphysical scheme into which language fits. And this scheme is rooted in reality. As long as analogy is tied to the metaphysics of intrinsic causality it must work, even if a theoretical language formula does not do the trick. This response should not be far from Burrell's intentions either.

The objections to analogous God-talk based on existential causality appear insufficient. Analogy seems to be the only adequate answer to the problem of religious language.

All negative God-talk implies some positive knowledge of God. But positive affirmations of God are possible only if there are some univocally understood concepts that can be applied to both creatures and Creator (as Scotus argued). On the other hand, since God is infinitely perfect and creatures are only finitely perfect, no perfection found in the finite world can be applied univocally to both God and creatures (as Aquinas argued). But to apply them equivocally would leave us in skepticism. Hence, whatever perfections are found in creation and can be applied to God without limits are predicated analogically. The perfection is understood univocally (in the same manner), but it is predicated analogously (in a similar manner), because to affirm it univocally in a finite way of an infinite Being would not truly be descriptive of the way he is. And to affirm it equivocally in an infinite way would not be descriptive of him at all. Hence, a univocal concept drawn from the finite world can be predicated of God only analogically.

37. Ibid., pp. 9–20.

13 ✳

Model Religious Language

Much of contemporary religious language is concerned with the adequacy of experientially grounded language models that are appropriate to religious discourse. The background of this interest is traceable to David Hume, the Vienna Circle of philosophers in the early 1900s, and the views of Ludwig Wittgenstein. The primary interest in contemporary philosophy of religious language is with the possibility of meaningful religious discourse.

This chapter will have four components. First we will lay the foundation for contemporary concerns on religious language. Then two representatives of modern understanding will be discussed: Ian T. Ramsey and Frederick Ferré. Finally, we will look at some recent trends to incorporate the later work of Wittgenstein.

The Background of the Contemporary Language Problem

The contemporary problem of religious language springs out of British empiricism from Hume. Early logical positivists, such as A. J. Ayer, popularized the cause that culminated in the semantical atheism of men like Paul M. van Buren. Let us trace the development of the problem.

Hume: Two Kinds of Propositions

In the last lines of his famous *Enquiry Concerning Human Understanding,* Hume sounded the battle cry:

> If we take into our hands any volume; of divinity or school metaphysics, for instance; let us ask, *Does it contain any abstract reasoning concerning quantity or number?* No. *Does it contain any experimental reason concerning matter of fact and existence?* No. Commit it then to the flames: for it contains nothing but sophistry and illusion.[1]

That is, according to Hume, there are only two kinds of meaningful statements: statements expressing relation of ideas, which are true by definition

---

1. David Hume, *Enquiry Concerning Human Understanding* (Indianapolis: Bobbs-Merrill, 1955), sect. 12, pt. 3.

but are not informative about the real world, and statements about matters of fact, which are informative about the world but which are derived only from empirical experience. The first kind are certain, being true a priori (e.g., mathematical statements); the second are known to be true with varying degrees of probability from experience (a posteriori) and are subject to change by future experience. Immanuel Kant later called Hume's first kind of statement analytic (i.e., explicative), because the predicate adds nothing to the concept of the subject; the latter he called synthetic (i.e., ampliative), because the predicate does add something not found in a mere analysis of the subject. For Hume there were only these two kinds of meaningful statements; everything else was to be consigned to the flames as meaningless. "When we entertain any suspicion," he said, "that a philosophical term is employed without any meaning or idea (as is but too frequent), we need but inquire, *from what [sense] impression is that supposed idea derived?* And if it be impossible to assign any, this will serve to confirm our suspicion." Anything, therefore, that is not purely definitional or tautological must be derived from sensory impressions, or else it is meaningless. Granted this twofold categorization of meaningful statements, one could prognosticate the future of theology without too much difficulty. It, too, is destined for the flames.

Wittgenstein: Linguistic Silence

The father of linguistic analysis, Ludwig Wittgenstein, was not as radical as Hume, although he operated in the same general framework. Wittgenstein ended his famous *Tractatus* with these words: "What we cannot speak about we must consign to silence." Silence, it is true, seems less severe than flames, but the implications for religious language are grave nonetheless. What Rudolf Otto called the experience of the Numinous and Friedrich Schleiermacher a feeling of absolute dependence Wittgenstein referred to as "the feeling of the world as a limited whole . . . the mystical feeling." Wittgenstein was not attempting to eliminate the religious experience; his concern was with whether or not it could be expressed in words. He wrote, "There are indeed, things that cannot be put into words. . . . They are what is mystical." Again he wrote, "It is not how things are in the world that is mystical, but that it exists," for "*how* things are in the world is a matter of complete indifference for what is higher. God does not reveal himself *in* the world."[2] In essence, Wittgenstein suggested that if God is truly inexpressible, then we are not able to express him. And what cannot be put into words we must be speechless about. If true, this would not eliminate religious experience but it would eliminate religious language.

2. Ludwig Wittgenstein, *Tractatus Logico-Philosophicus*, trans. D. F. Pears and B. F. McGuinness (London: Routledge and Kegan Paul, 1961), 6:45; 6:522; 6:44; 6:432.

Ayer: Religious Language and Verification

One of the more vocal members of the early Vienna Circle was A. J. Ayer, who in his popular *Language, Truth and Logic* attempted to eliminate all metaphysics and theology.[3] Carrying through the implications of Hume's two kinds of meaningful statements, Ayer laid down a verificational principle for meaning: no statement can be meaningful unless it is either purely definitional (tautological) or empirically verifiable. The former are certain but the latter can never be certain.[4] A statement can be empirically verifiable for a person, "if, and only if, he knows how to verify the proposition which it purports to express—that is, if he knows what observations would lead him, under certain conditions to accept the proposition as being true, or reject it as being false."[5] Anything neither purely definitional nor verifiable by sense experience is literally nonsensical.

Ayer felt that an application of the verification principle to religious language would eliminate any meaningful God-talk. The only propositions that are informative are empirical, and empirical statements do not tell us anything about God, who is transempirical.

The first chapter of Ayer's book is entitled "The Elimination of Metaphysics." Since no metaphysical statement is empirically verifiable, "all metaphysical assertions are nonsensical." And as for "the possibility of religious knowledge," wrote Ayer, "we shall see that this possibility has already been ruled out by our treatment of metaphysics."[6]

The problem with Ayer's strict view of meaning became apparent: his principle of verifiability was neither purely tautological nor empirically verifiable. It, too, was meaningless on his own grounds. In later revisions Ayer expanded the sphere of meaningful statements. "I do not wish to deny," he wrote, "that in some of these senses [of meaning] a statement may properly be said to be meaningful even though it is neither analytic nor empirically verifiable." But even in this revised form he quickly added, "I confess that it is unlikely that any metaphysician would yield to a claim of this kind." In other words, he still intended to rule out metaphysics and theology, even though he realized "that for an effective elimination of metaphysics it needs to be supported by detailed analyses of particular metaphysical arguments."[7] There is no way to eliminate the whole of metaphysics in advance, but there is still the hope that, piece by piece, every statement about God will be shown to be

---

3. A. J. Ayer, *Language, Truth and Logic* (New York: Dover, 1946), chap. 1.

4. Ayer later modified this view to include some empirically certain statements such as those that refer to the content of a single sensory experience. See ibid., p. 10.

5. Ibid., p. 35. This principle, too, was later modified by Ayer. See ibid., p. 10.

6. Ibid., pp. 41, 114.

7. Ibid., p. 16.

meaningless. For, according to Ayer, there is no apparent way that noncognitive reality can be put into cognitive language. Statements about God are literally "non-sense" statements.[8]

The logical positivism of Ayer must be distinguished from atheism. He clearly denied atheism or agnosticism. "Our view that utterances about the nature of God are nonsensical . . . is actually incompatible with them. For if the assertion that there is a god is nonsensical, then the atheist's assertion that there is no god is equally nonsensical. . . ." As for the agnostic, "he does not deny that the question whether a transcendent god exists is a genuine question. . . . But we have seen that the sentences in question do not express propositions at all. And this means that agnosticism also is ruled out."[9] What, then, is Ayer's position if it is neither theism, atheism, nor agnosticism? It might be called a-*cog*nosticism, that is, it is noncognitivism. No cognitively meaningful statements can be made about any supposed transcendent reality. We are again consigned to the Wittgensteinian silence about God.

Van Buren: Semantical Atheism

Contrary to Ayer's expectations, some theologians did accept his kind of verification. And predictably it led to a semantical atheism. Paul M. van Buren, admitting his linkage to Hume, wrote, "The empiricist in us finds the heart of the difficulty not in what is said about God, but in the very talking about God at all." For "we do not know 'what' God is, and we cannot understand how the word 'God' is being used." Hence, "simple literal theism is wrong and qualified literal theism is meaningless." In brief, "today, we cannot even understand the Nietzschian cry that 'God is dead!' for if it were so, how could we know? No, the problem now is that the *word* 'God' is dead." The word *God* and all of its transcendent equivalents have no meaning. There appears to be no way empirically to ground language that attempts to express that which is transempirical. We are left, not with no God, but with a God that we cannot talk about, that is, with semantical atheism.[10]

It is out of this context that contemporary religious philosophers of language have struggled to develop meaningful God-talk. Two representative examples are Ian T. Ramsey and Frederick Ferré. Let us begin with Ramsey.

8. Ayer has modified his view even more, so that he too has rejected his earlier position on empirical verification. See A. J. Ayer, *Metaphysics and Common Sense* (San Francisco: Freeman, Cooper, 1970).

9. Ibid., p. 115.

10. Paul M. van Buren, *The Secular Meaning of the Gospel* (New York: Macmillan, 1963), pp. 100, 83–84. Van Buren too has discarded his earlier view. See *The Edges of Language: An Essay in the Logic of Religion* (New York: Macmillan, 1972).

Ramsey: Qualified Disclosure Models

Ramsey built his religious language out of an empirical setting and tests it by its empirical adequacy. He begins with what he calls disclosure situations and proceeds to elaborate a religious language by way of qualified models.

Disclosure-Commitment Situations

There are two aspects to the kind of experiences that may be called religious: an empirical situation that evokes discernment and also elicits a total commitment to what is discerned. The unusual empirical situations that evoke discernment Ramsey takes as the experiential anchorage for the meaning of religious language.

DISCERNMENT SITUATIONS

Sometimes ordinary empirical situations "come alive." In routine, everyday occurrences, suddenly the "ice breaks" and the "light dawns." For example, when a judge recognizes the accused as his long-lost love, then "eye meets eye." Or, the twelve lines on a paper suddenly take on the "depth" of a cube. Or, a formal dinner party instantly takes on a "new dimension" when someone splits his jacket. In each of these ordinary empirical settings there is a disclosure; something more is revealed than the purely empirical. The situations take on a depth of dimension beyond the sensory; they are disclosure situations that provide a discernment that goes "beyond" the mere empirical facts of the situation.[11]

According to Ramsey, metaphors and verbally odd words have the same disclosure power. He even goes so far as to say that "what is not verbally odd is void of disclosure power."[12] Nicknames (e.g., "sweetheart") evoke personal response better than given names. Ramsey also finds tautologies such as "I am I," "duty for duty's sake," or "love for love's sake" to be revelatory of more than they say linguistically. In fact, he takes "I-language" to be a key to God-talk in two ways: both are verbally odd; both are straightforward but strained, and both gain their meaning in use.[13] But their literary and logical oddity do not make them nonsensical. On the contrary, odd words and metaphors by their very similarity-with-a-difference can generate significant insight, just as two slightly different pictures can create a depth perspective when they are seen in a 3-D viewer.[14]

11. Ian T. Ramsey, *Religious Language* (New York: Macmillan, 1963), pp. 20–30.

12. Ian T. Ramsey, *Models and Mystery* (London: Oxford University Press, 1964), p. 69.

13. Michael Novak develops "I-language" in *Belief and Unbelief* (New York: Macmillan, 1965), pp. 74ff.

14. Ramsey, *Religious Language*, pp. 42–50.

What Ramsey wishes to illustrate by both his empirical and his verbal examples is that there is disclosure value in both ordinary empirical and ordinary verbal expressions. The oddity available in both these ordinary areas has disclosure value. There is more in empirical language and situations than "meets the eye." Ordinary language, with its verbal oddities, and ordinary empirical experience, with its "ice-breaking" ability, amply demonstrate that both experience and language are capable of conveying what goes beyond the immediate data given in either.

COMMITMENT SITUATIONS

Of course, not every disclosure situation provides a religious disclosure. Beholding one's lost lover does not thereby bring God into focus. And ripping one's jacket does not reveal Divinity, and so on. A religious disclosure has another dimension; it is a disclosure that evokes a commitment, a total commitment.

First of all, Ramsey clarifies what is meant by a total commitment. It is like the patriot's "my country, right or wrong" or the moralist's "duty for duty's sake." Further, religious commitment can be understood by distinction from two other kinds of commitments. In a hobby, one is totally committed to only part of the universe (e.g., to coins or stamps). Commitment is total because it is all-absorbing but it is partial because there are other areas of life besides these. Conversely, in doing mathematics one is partly committed to the whole universe. That is, one is loosely committed to a given set of axioms (say, Euclid's), knowing that others are possible, but he is committed to applying them everywhere. The Pythagorean theorum will be just as true in Moscow and Peking as in New York. But in a religious commitment, one is totally committed to the whole universe. To borrow terms reminiscent of Plotinus and Schleiermacher, it is a commitment of one's all to the All. The religious commitment is total because of the extent of its loyalty; it is universal, since "it is a commitment suited to the whole job of living—not one just suited to building a house, studying. . . ."[15]

Combining these two dimensions of discernment and commitment, Ramsey defines a religious experience as one in which one responds to a discernment situation by making a total commitment. The empirical situation provides the meaningful grounding for the "more" or "beyond" it reveals, and other total commitment situations (to duty or one's country) offer meaning for one's response to the disclosure. Together, the discernment-commitment situations express what is meant by a religious experience.

15. Ibid., pp. 36–37, 40, 55. Ramsey is getting at the same thing Paul Tillich called an ultimate commitment.

Religious Language: Qualified Models

Since the religious experience itself is "odd" or unusual, it is only natural that no straightforward empirical language will be adequate to express it. It is necessary, then, in developing an adequate religious language to qualify models and metaphors from human experience in order that their disclosure power can be evocative of what goes beyond the ordinary empirical situations, namely, to the Transcendent.

THE MEANING AND USE OF MODELS

Ramsey seeks to elaborate a meaningful language about transcendence by what he calls disclosure models. Unlike "picturing models" or "scale models," a "disclosure model" does not attempt to describe anything; rather, it becomes currency for a moment of insight. "The great value of a model," said Ramsey, "is that it enables us to be articulate when before we were tongue-tied." Disclosure models are the means by which the universe reveals itself to humanity, and they are to be judged primarily on their ability to point to mystery, not on their ability to picture it. Indeed, part of the purpose of a religious model is to leave a mystery intact. "The intention is to produce, from a single model, and by means of some qualifier, an endless series of variants, . . . in this way witnessing to the fact that the heart of theology is permanent mystery."[16]

Ramsey gave examples of words that have evocative power, such as indefinite pronouns or nicknames. A nickname is a "word which has intrinsically the fewest possible empirical connections, but is very much filled out 'in use.'" That is, language about God is not declarative; it is evocative. Ramsey holds that by the use of nondescriptive, evocative language one can avoid being literalistic or purely anthropomorphic about God, for he has learned that no one model has a single, all-exclusive track to mystery any more than one metaphor can do full justice to a sunset or to human love and affection. That is to say, disclosure models "are not descriptive miniatures, they are not picture enlargements; in each case they point to mystery, to the need for us to live as best we can with theological and scientific uncertainties."[17]

If Ramsey's models are not descriptive of God, at least they do answer Wittgenstein's challenge to keep silent unless one can speak meaningfully.[18]

16. Ramsey, *Models and Mystery*, pp. 7, 19–20, 12–13, 71, 60–61, 65, 21.

17. Ramsey, *Religious Language*, pp. 162, 56. Ramsey said, "The intention is to produce, by a single model, and by means of some qualifier, an endless series of variants . . . in this way witnessing to the fact that the heart of theology is permanent mystery." *Models and Mystery*, p. 20.

18. "It is interesting to notice, first, that the possibility of articulation is still, as it always was, the basis of a model's usefulness. The great virtue of a model is that it enables us to be articulate when before we were tongue-tied. But it is evident that articulation now is much more tentative

That is to say, even if individual disclosure models do not speak descriptively about God, nevertheless they do permit one to speak.[19] Indeed, even though each of Ramsey's models is not cognitively descriptive nor empirically verifiable, yet by virtue of the fact that they are indefinitely qualifiable, not only can one speak about God but also one can speak endlessly. And in so speaking, Ramsey contends, one's language does not suffer "death by a thousand qualifications" but rather gives "life by a thousand enrichments."[20]

THE QUALIFICATION OF MODELS

Even though individual disclosure models are not ontologically descriptive, nevertheless they do help to build "family resemblances." But, Ramsey warned, "let us always be cautious of talking about God in straightforward language. Let us never talk as if we had privileged access to the diaries of God's private life. . . ." When we speak of God as "supreme love," for example, "we are not making an assertion in descriptive psychology. . . ." Rather, we are using a qualified model ("love" is qualified by "supreme") whose logical structure can be understood only in terms of the disclosure-commitment experience in which it arose.[21]

What Ramsey calls qualifiers are "words which multiply models without end and with subtle changes." They create what Wittgenstein called family resemblances or a family of models. By means of qualification of one model or metaphor, many of them can be related in an overall meeting place between contexts. And it is at this juncture that the mystery resides.[22] That is, by mapping out the similarities engendered by the meeting of the many metaphors, one may gain increased insight into the mystery. As Max Black put it, "A memorable metaphor has the power to bring two separate domains into cognitive and emotional relation by using language directly appropriate to the one as a lens for seeing the other. . . ."[23] In this way metaphors help us to visualize the similarity in various situations and thus to begin to form a

---

than it was before, that is when it was developed on the basis of a scale model. . . . In fact on the new view, the crucial question is: *How* can we be reliably articulate?" Ramsey, *Models and Mystery*, pp. 12–13.

19. In a doctoral dissertation on Ramsey, Jerry H. Gill concludes that "Ian Ramsey's interpretation adequately meets the challenge of Logical Empiricism concerning the cognitivity of Christian language." "Ian Ramsey's Interpretation of Christian Language" (Duke University, 1966), p. v.

20. Ramsey wrote, "We must emphasize that models in science . . . enable us to generate verifiable deductions, and models in theology . . . make possible empirical fit." *Models and Mystery*, p. 19.

21. Ibid., p. 20, and *Religious Language*, pp. 104, 99.

22. Ramsey, *Models and Mystery*, pp. 60–61, 48, 51.

23. Max Black, *Models and Metaphors* (Ithaca, N.Y.: Cornell University Press, 1962), p. 54.

master map of family resemblances. "Metaphors then are not just link devices between different contexts. They are necessarily grounded in inspiration. Generalizing, we may say that metaphorical expressions occur when two situations strike us in such a way as to reveal what includes them but is no mere combination of them both."[24]

Ramsey develops three groups of qualified models. First are the negative attributes of God, which do not describe everyday experience but hold together all aspects of everyday experience in a unity. "God is immutable" is an example. Here the model is drawn from changing experience and is qualified by the "im" or "not," which points to a transcendent dimension beyond the experience. A second group of models is one-word positive attributes of God, such as "perfection" and "simplicity." Here one begins by assessing various imperfections in everyday experience in a decreasing order until the "light dawns" and there is a disclosure of what "perfection" means. The third class of qualified models is composed of two-word positive attributes of God, such as "first Cause" or "infinitely good." The nouns are the models drawn from experience and the adjectives are the qualifiers pointing to a dimension beyond experience.[25] Here the two purposes of qualified models can be seen: to point to a dimension beyond the empirical and to indicate the logical limits to the model itself by virtue of its qualification.

It is important at this point to indicate the function of the term *God*. According to Ramsey, "God" is an integrative term, bringing together the separate discernment-commitment disclosures into a unifold whole. It is a master map that combines all of the perspectives gained from the individual models. "God" is "the integrator word which provides the most simple, far-reaching and coherent metaphysical map." The term *God* functions like the term *I* in ordinary language—the term that brings together the whole language-logic of self-awareness.[26] The term *God* is the linguistic integrator of religious awareness (arising out of discernment-commitment situations) the way the term *I* linguistically summarizes one's self-awareness.

THE ADEQUACY OF MODELS: EMPIRICAL FIT

The question, according to Ramsey, is not whether one can speak in literal descriptions about the divine nature; the real question is: How can one be reliably articulate? Models help us to articulate theology reliably when two conditions hold: "In all cases the models must chime in with the phenomena; they must arise in a moment of insight or disclosure," and "A model in theology does not stand or fall with . . . the possibility of verifiable deduc-

24. Ramsey, *Models and Mystery*, p. 53.
25. Ramsey, *Religious Language*, pp. 56–57.
26. Ian T. Ramsey, *Prospects for Metaphysics* (London: George Allen and Unwin, 1961), pp. 153–64, 174.

tions. It is rather judged by its stability over the widest possible range of phenomena, by its ability to incorporate the most diverse phenomena not inconsistently." This is what Ramsey calls the method of "empirical fit," which has no scientific deductions emerging from it to confirm or falsify the stated theories. "The theological model," he said, "works more like the fitting of a boot or a shoe than the 'yes' or 'no' of a roll call." In brief, religious language is empirically anchored (in disclosure situations) and pragmatically tested by the way it enables one to piece together the empirical data. That is, there must be something in man's experience of the universe that matches to a degree the model under consideration. "There must be something about the universe and man's experience in it which, for example, matches the behavior of a loving father (portrayed, for instance, in Luke's parable of the two sons)."[27]

According to Ramsey there is no strict verification for these models, but there is confirmation based on the way the model "fits" the range of phenomena it consistently incorporates. The wider the range of experience that is consistently incorporated (i.e., the better the "fit"), the more adequate is the master model. Each additional disclosure incorporated makes the fit more nearly perfect, in a manner similar to the way a polygon with ever-increasing sides approaches closer to a circle.[28] So the many qualified models that constitute one's master model, "God," also constitute the empirical basis for meaning for all talk about this "God." And the adequacy of the macro-model ("God") is judged by its empirical "fit" over the entire range of human experience.

Evaluation of Ramsey's View

Ramsey disclaimed that individual models are descriptive of God. However, when the models are appropriately qualified and combined into a master map (which is integrated by the word *God*) and confirmed by their empirical fit, it would seem that Ramsey has the equivalent of a description of God. It is not a literal description, to be sure. Every model must be qualified; no metaphor or term from finite experience can be applied to God without being qualified. But when the overall map is made which incorporated all of the insights gained from the various disclosure situations (a map that fits with increasing adequacy the total range of human experience), then it would seem that we have an adequate description of God. Whether evocative or descriptive or both, the master model is discourse about God. It does answer the problem of an empirically grounded God-talk.

27. Ramsey, *Models and Mystery*, p. 16.
28. Ian T. Ramsey, "Talking about God: Models, Ancient and Modern" in *Myth and Symbol*, ed. F. W. Dillistone (London: SPCK, 1966), p. 91.

The remaining question is this: Which of the categories of religious language—univocal, equivocal, or analogical—do Ramsey's qualified models fall into? At least one serious student of Ramsey, Jerry H. Gill, contends that Ramsey's view falls into the broad tradition of Thomistic analogy. Gill speaks of "the similarity between Ramsey's view and that of Thomas Aquinas. Little, if any, distortion results from roughly classifying Ramsey's position within the tradition which maintains the analogical nature of talk about God."[29] Ramsey himself wrote, "To talk of God as 'heavenly father' or 'divine creator' is to speak analogically. . . . That is, one is endeavoring to suggest a qualified similarity between a concrete aspect of past and present experience, and future experiences."[30]

If this interpretation is correct, the model must serve as the univocal concept and the qualifier as the via negativa by which the model is applied without limits to an infinite Being. The many models correspond to the many predications of one absolutely simple Being. And the master model expressed by the term God is a contemporary attempt to indicate that there is only one God, about whom, nevertheless, it is necessary to say many things. If this is in fact what Ramsey is doing, then his whole project will fall into equivocation, unless he, along with Thomas, establishes a metaphysical causal link or similarity between God and the world. Without this, there is no basis in reality for the similarity between God-talk and the God about whom one is talking. Disclosure situations, because of their subjective nature, cannot accomplish that. At best, all of his God-talk will be nothing more than authorized parables that are not really descriptive of God.[31] Or, at worst, it will be a linguistically possible and empirically adequate way of engaging in religiously evocative language that is not cognitively descriptive of the way God really is.[32] In short, without an analogy built squarely on the ontological similarity of Creator and creature, God-talk is purely equivocal. Only metaphysical analogy can save qualified models from equivocation.

Ferré: Metaphysical Models

Ferré clearly intends that his religious model language have cognitive truth value. He confessedly builds a metaphysical synthesis based on the religious model, which is subject to truth tests.

29. Gill, "Ian Ramsey's Interpretation of Christian Language," p. 42.

30. Jerry H. Gill, "The Meaning of Religious Language," *Christianity Today* 9, no. 8 (January 15, 1965): 19.

31. See I. M. Crombie, "Theology and Falsification," in *Essays in Philosophical Theology*, ed. Antony Flew and Alasdair MacIntyre (London: SCM, 1963), pp. 122–29.

32. Ramsey does speak elsewhere about establishing the reality of God in other ways, e.g., via a historical argument of miracles. See his "History and the Gospels: Some Philosophical Reflections," *Studia Evangelica*, vol. 3 (Berlin: Akademie Verlag, 1964).

The Nature and Function of Models

Ferré defines a model as that "which provides epistemological vividness or immediacy to a theory by offering as an interpretation of the abstract or unfamiliar theory-structure something that both fits the logical form of the theory and is well-known. . . ."[33] Models have two traits in common with metaphors: their language is literally false and yet they are not without "point." Religious models are no exception.[34] Like other models, religious models benefit theories by giving them "ideational definiteness" that is not directly observable; that is, by providing "conceptual unity" that suggests otherwise unseen areas that could be incorporated into the proposed theory, and by suggesting fruitful lines of future inquiry.[35]

Ferré classes models along three lines: type, scope, and status. By type he means the degree of concreteness that the model has (i.e., its ability to be "built" or "pictured"). Scope shows the degree of inclusiveness the model has (i.e., how much reality it purports to represent). And status reveals how much importance is attached to each model, such as its dispensability or indispensability. A model of sufficient scope can link otherwise divergent areas of experience into a coherent world view.[36]

In Ferré's thinking there are at least three functions for models. First, models suggest a point-by-point resemblance. Next, they serve a heuristic value of pointing the investigator toward new discoveries. Finally, models fulfill the holistic desire in man to have an "explanatory model" that approximates in a limited way the general coherence he would like to find in the world as he experiences it.[37]

Models in Religious Language

Religious models have some differences from scientific models, as well as similarities. One significant difference is that a scientific model can largely achieve separation between reality and the observer, whereas in theological model theory, the observer's views of himself and of the world are both involved in the ultimate models themselves. A second important difference is that scientific models are judged only as more or less helpful but not as true or false. In theology, truth questions are relevant to models and the models are

---

33. Frederick Ferré, "Mapping the Logic of Models in Science and Theology," *The Christian Scholar* 46 (Spring 1963): 24.

34. Frederick Ferré, "Metaphors, Models and Religion," *Soundings* 51 (Fall 1968): 332.

35. Frederick Ferré, *Basic Modern Philosophy of Religion* (New York: Charles Scribner's Sons, 1967), pp. 373ff.

36. Ferré, "Mapping the Logic of Models in Science and Theology," pp. 13ff.

37. See Ferré, "Metaphors, Models and Religion," for this analysis.

incomprehensible apart from the theories they illuminate.[38] Further, theological models draw upon a different set of facts than do scientific models. In theism the facts are composed of spiritual characteristics—will, purpose, wisdom, love. And for Christianity in particular the facts center in the "creative, self-giving, personal love of Jesus Christ. . . ."[39] Finally, there is a difference in scope: in science, theories change only rarely and reluctantly, while models change more rapidly. But in theology, theories (which tie models with other cognitive areas) change occasionally, while high-level models are quite resistant to change.[40]

Ferré finds his core of religious imagery in the Scriptures, the creeds, and the traditions of the believing community. When this imagery is used to represent the "ultimate character" of the universe, it serves as a "metaphysical model."[41] This spiritual imagery serves as a focusing model which in turn gives more concrete interpretation to the relatively more abstract conceptual scheme which attempts to put one's beliefs into propositional form. The key concept, of course, is "God."[42] The theistic model built of religious imagery serves to shape the attitudes and values of those in the believing community, but it also has truth value. This is not to say that religious language is to be taken literally. On the contrary, God-language is richly anthropomorphic; God is beyond all our inadequate pictures and concepts. Hence truth is ascribed "*not to the individual expressions which together form the dominant model for the biblical understanding of reality but to the model itself.*"[43] The believing community justifies this ascription by building an all-inclusive conceptual synthesis around this theological model drawn from the imagery of Scripture. All data from other areas of knowledge, as sense perceptions, history, and science, are incorporated into the total synthesis provided by this organizing theistic model.

Testing Religious Models

Religious models serve many noncognitive functions,[44] but Ferré is

38. Ferré, *Basic Modern Philosophy of Religion*, p. 381.

39. Frederick Ferré, *Language, Logic and God* (1961; New York: Harper Torchbooks, 1969), p. 164.

40. Ferré, "Mapping the Logic of Models in Science and Theology," p. 36.

41. Frederick Ferré, "The Logic of Our Current Opportunity," *The Philosophy Forum* 8 (June 1970): 61–87.

42. Frederick Ferré, "Science and the Death of God," in *Science and Religion: New Perspective on the Dialogue*, ed. I. Barbour (New York: Harper and Row, 1968), p. 148.

43. Frederick Ferré and Kent Bendall, *Exploring the Logic of Faith: A Dialogue on the Relation of Modern Philosophy to Christian Faith* (New York: Association, 1962), p. 56.

44. Ferré lists at least nine noncognitive functions of religious models as "ceremonial," "self-committal," "liturgical," "reassuring," "judging," "challenging," "ethical," "existential,"

strongly against reducing religious language to purely noncognitive functions. What he calls noncognitive autonomy is unnecessary, since attitudes and actions are just as subject to critical demands as are matters of fact; irresponsible, for commitments have consequences that demand critical examination; and dangerous, because one's own life policies seriously affect the lives of others. "To throw critical reflection to the winds in just the most important aspects of life would be the ultimate example of penny-wisdom and pound-foolishness. . . . I cannot conceive a more perfect definition of the unexamined life."[45]

No world view (metaphysical model) should ever be adopted arbitrarily; one should always have reasons for adopting a given master model. Technically speaking, however, one cannot directly test a theistic model; the tests are applied directly only to the synthesis that results from applying the organizing theistic model to the whole range of human experiences. There are really three strata in one's total account of things. The first level is a preverbal metaphysical model of symbol (taken from the imagery of Scripture). Next comes the set of propositions that attempt to express this in a cognitive way. Finally, there is the whole range of functions, cognitive and noncognitive, verbal and nonverbal, that make up the religious language game. Now the last cannot be evaluated directly, and the first is precognitive. Thus, truth tests must be applied to the second level only. These propositions on the second level do two things: first, they explicate the primary model, and second, they give structure to the totality of the third level. So the truth tests are applied not to the metaphysical model (first level) but to the metaphysical synthesis (second level).[46]

Ferré offers five truth tests for the truth of the total synthesis built on religious models:[47]

1. *Consistency.* The synthesis must be free of contradiction both among and within the key statements involved.
2. *Coherence.* Consistency must also be external, extending in a unified way to all bodies of knowledge.
3. *Applicability.* It must be relatable to individual experience.
4. *Adequacy.* It must be applicable not just to some experiences but to all domains of feeling and perception.

---

and "convictional" (*Exploring the Logic of Faith*, chap. 4). He also lists some quasicognitive functions of religious language as "bliks," "parables," "imagery," "heuristic," and "attentional" (*Language, Logic and God*, pp. 129ff., and elsewhere). The noncognitive functions of religious language Ferré summarizes under "conative" and "emotive" (*Basic Modern Philosophy of Religion*, pp. 350ff.).

45. Ferré, "Science and the Death of God," pp. 150–51.
46. Ferré, *Exploring the Logic of Faith*, pp. 165–66.
47. Ibid., pp. 166ff.

5. *Effectiveness.* The synthesis must be a usable instrument for coping with the total environment of human experience.

Subsequently Ferré summarized these under three headings: consistency, coherence, and adequacy.[48] In brief, a metaphysical synthesis is adequate only if it is able "to put all experience into a pattern that is *whole*, that is *pervasive*, and that is *adequate*."[49]

How would one know whether his religious language, which serves as an organizing model to the overall metaphysical synthesis, is adequate? The answer is, in short, by applying the five tests. This is not an afternoon's activity. In fact, as Ferré notes, "the true falsification of a metaphysical position is more like an erosion than an explosion—a gradual process in which the inadequate metaphysical view is not disproved but rather, is quietly abandoned."[50]

Just how does the theistic model fare on Ferré's tests? This question is not answered in detail by Ferré, but he does suggest the direction the answer might take.[51]

1. Christianity has been *effective* in the past, but there is doubt about its effectiveness in the present and in the future.
2. Few would dispute the *applicability* of love and reverence, but this is only a minimal test.
3. *Adequacy* is a complex test involving many levels that Christianity appears to meet fairly well.
4. No clear *contradictions* have been demonstrated in Christianity but never have the proposed solutions gained universal acceptance.
5. Christianity has a striking internal *coherence* but the external coherence with other bodies of knowledge is not as obvious. There are almost certainly some empirical statements in Scripture that are false (as the sun standing still for Joshua).

Our conclusion, says Ferré, can only be tentative. But commitment is integral to any life worth living, so we must make our leap of faith based on what seems to be the most adequate metaphysical system arising out of one's religious models.[52]

Ferré is by no means irrevocably committed to the position that the Christian theistic model is the most adequate in terms of these truth tests. Other

---

48. Ferré, *Basic Modern Philosophy of Religion*, chap. 1.
49. Ferré, "Science and the Death of God," p. 147.
50. Ferré, "Mapping the Logic of Models in Science and Theology," p. 36.
51. Ferré, *Exploring the Logic of Faith*, pp. 172ff.
52. Ibid., pp. 178–79. See also "Science and the Death of God," p. 153.

theistic models and even nontheistic models may be of equal or even greater weight than Christian theism.[53]

Evaluation of Ferré's Metaphysical Model

There is no question that Ferré has an interest in truth. He takes religious language as the metaphysical model by which one can make propositional statements that are subject to truth tests. But are these statements descriptive of reality? Ferré disavows any literal descriptions of God. The Bible, which provides the imagery for the theistic model, is anthropomorphic. Religious language, he tells us, is not to be taken literally of God. Hence, it seems clear that Ferré is not in the univocal camp. Our models, when applied to God, do not give us positive knowledge as they do when applied to finite things in this world.

There are only two alternatives left for Ferré: equivocity and analogy. We may assume that Ferré wishes to avoid equivocation in God-talk; otherwise, the whole stress on the cognitive and the test for truth would be redundant. Presumably he wishes not merely to speak truth linguistically but to speak truth about reality. If so, his metaphysical synthesis built on religious model language is to be taken as the most nearly adequate expression of truth he can come up with about reality. If this is not what Ferré has in mind, his propositional "truths" are not really true about anything; they are at best merely the most nearly complete and adequate way of conceptualizing one's experience of the we-know-not-what that is otherwise called reality. On the presumption, then, that truth statements are statements about something (i.e., about reality), Ferré's keen interest in truth would rule out the possibility that he intends religious language to be understood equivocally.

The only remaining alternative is that Ferré intends his metaphysical synthesis (built on religious model language) to be taken analogously. There are indications both in Ferré's own writings and in those he highly respects that Ferré's view is a kind of analogy. Ferré's thinking was highly influenced by that of Dorothy Emmet: "Metaphysics starts from the articulations of relationships, which are judged to be constitutive of an experience or experiences in a significant way. . . . A conceptual expression of such a relationship is then extended *analogously* as a coordinating idea, in terms of which further ranges of experience may be interpreted."[54] However, Ferré severely criticized analogy based on intrinsic causality, as was discussed earlier.[55] But what does this leave Ferré? He also objected to analogy based on an extrinsic

53. Ibid., pp. 153ff.
54. Dorothy Emmet, *The Nature of Metaphysical Thinking* (London: Macmillan, 1946), p. v, emphasis added.
55. See the end of chapter 12.

connection: "A wholly extrinsic attribution of qualities to God says nothing at all about the intrinsic or proper attributes of God." In an extrinsic analogy, he continued, "we are left with no more idea of God's own characteristics than that he is responsible for the various characteristics of creation. . . ."[56] Now it would seem that Ferré has hedged himself in and must choose a way out. Is his implied kind of analogy really a kind of extrinsic analogy?[57] If so, then according to Ferré it really tells us nothing about God. But, on the other hand, God-talk is clearly not univocal for Ferré. Ferré must choose, then, between equivocation and the analogy of intrinsic attribution (which he rejected).[58] In view of the conclusion of the preceding chapter, one could only hope that Ferré would reexamine the intrinsic analogy built on the causal connection between Creator and creatures. There seems to be no other way to establish a meaningfully descriptive God-talk.

Recent Trends: Retreating from Models

As we have seen, much of contemporary discussion on religious language has been motivated by the extreme empiricism of Hume, the logical positivists, and the early work of Wittgenstein. And many writers have attempted to meet the empirical attack on its own ground. Thus we saw, for example, Ramsey begin with the notion of a disclosure situation, which provided the empirical basis for his analysis.

But of late, there has been greater conviction that the battle has been fought too much on ground and with weapons chosen by the enemy. The demand for the empirical justification of religious language may be quite unfair in the light of the nature and meaning of religious language.

At the forefront of this movement has been the later work of Wittgenstein with his program of autonomous language games. No longer is language required to conform to any standard other than what is inherent in the use of a specific language game in a specific form of life. This new program does not rule out use of models and metaphors, but it does not legislate that the models and metaphors must be legitimated outside of the context of religion itself.

Gill: Mediation and Metaphor

As we mentioned earlier (chap. 10), a representative thinker who relies extensively on the later Wittgenstein is Jerry H. Gill. He attempts to build on

56. Frederick Ferré, "Analogy in Theology," in *Encyclopedia of Philosophy*, ed. Paul Edwards, 4 vols. (New York: Free Press, 1973), 1:95–96.

57. Battista Mondin calls Emmet's analogy (which Ferré seems to follow) an "analogy of representation." *The Principle of Analogy in Protestant and Catholic Theology* (The Hague: Nijhoff, 1963), p. 76.

58. Since Ferré did not interact with Mondin's classic work on analogy, perhaps a better understanding of analogy based on intrinsic causality of being would help to move him in the direction of Aquinas.

a wholistic understanding of human beings and human knowledge, instead of a purely cognitive or empirical basis. These are the conclusions Gill reached:[59]

1. Religious language is linguistically constituted. This means that one cannot know religious reality apart from its being conveyed to us somehow in words and concepts.
2. Religious language is social activity in which many uses (e.g., persuasion, confession, exhortation) are more important than description.
3. Religious language, like any language, is meaningful with significant, not absolute, precision.
4. It makes no sense to consider religious language outside of the circle of those who are using it in the contexts of their lives.
5. Religious language is primarily metaphorical. Gill follows Ramsey quite closely in his description of the nature and function of metaphors. Because they begin with a this-worldly figure, which is then qualified, they mediate religious disclosure to us.

Gill's understanding typifies the recent concern for the autonomy of religious language. Even though his understanding of metaphor is not unlike that of his mentor, Ramsey, his motives are different. The one element that is different is that Gill is not concerned with the public empirical grounding that motivates Ramsey. As we saw before, Gill is committed to the tacit dimension that makes religious experience and language uniquely the property of the believer.

Gill's Proposal Evaluated

Gill has provided us with a helpful understanding of the function of religious language within the life of the religious person. His proposal underscores that people do not normally raise questions of the meaningfulness of their language prior to its utilization; they go ahead and use it—meaningfully. But such an assertion, even if accompanied by a solid description of how the use takes place, may just substitute one kind of philosophical imperialism for another. Valid philosophical concerns must still be responded to.

Again it is fairly easy to think of mediation through metaphor as a kind of analogy. However, the same critiques that we raised with regard to Ramsey and Ferré are true a fortiori here. Analogy must be grounded in a metaphysical reality, and Gill will not provide us with such an ontological link. In fact, Gill's flight into the tacit realm of knowledge rules out the possibility of

59. Jerry H. Gill, *On Knowing God: New Directions for the Future of Theology* (Philadelphia: Westminster, 1981), pp. 129–40.

such a justification of language. Whereas in Ramsey the disclosure situation served as a bridge between realms, albeit a rather flimsy one, even that bit of help is removed further from us. In short, Gill has made a strong analysis of the functional, and thereby meaningful, role played by religious language in the religious community, but in the process has forfeited all buffers against the problem of equivocation.

Burrell: Combining Aquinas and Wittgenstein

In chapter 12 we promised a summary of David Burrell's proposal for a "soft" form of analogy that seeks to be true to Aquinas, but is also sensitive to modern insights into the nature of language. Here are Burrell's reflections:[60]

1. Univocal language may be understood as ordinary usage language in a Wittgensteinian setting. Wittgenstein's concept of family resemblance, if nothing else, bears a strong resemblance to analogy.
2. Transcendental terms, such as "is," are transcategorical. This means that they are found in all language games, but they have no meaning of their own apart from their role in a specific language game. Their crossover capacity without being carriers of designated meaning demonstrates their analogical use.
3. Appraisal terms, such as "good," actually function similarly to transcendentals. Burrell contends that they also have no meaning apart from a particular linguistic framework with its life setting. But they are an integral part of any such scheme.
4. These terms now become crucial for language about God. "On the account I am proposing, transcendentals and appraisal terms form a set open to use in characterizing a God who must remain uncharacterizable."[61] This occurs ontologically and semantically.
   a. Ontologically, God is the cause of the world, and thus there is analogy between talk of God and talk of the world.
   b. Semantically, the transcendentals and appraisal terms are applied to God without their usual form of predication. Thus we say, "God is being," and "God is goodness."
5. The final justification for use of analogic language lies in a decision. This is to say that the analogic use, no matter where it occurs, is not forced, but originates out of the community of the speaker or listener.

Burrell's proposal is innovative and, one hopes, trendsetting for future discussion of religious language. Not only has he given us a scheme that fills

60. David Burrell, *Analogy and Philosophical Language* (New Haven: Yale University Press, 1973), pp. 215–51.
61. Ibid., 230–31.

the bill for true analogy, but also he is true to Aquinas by giving analogy its deserved ontological setting. At the same time, he has shown how this can be accomplished while engaging the modern insights of Wittgenstein and others.

But what happened to the need for a univocal concept? It is gone, lost in the crack between language games. According to Burrell, appraisal terms have no specifiable meanings that remain true from scheme to scheme. He states that this is so because appraisal terms originate specifically out of human subjective experience. But are there no generalizable human subjective experiences? We argued in the first four chapters that there are. These must be more universal than accidental family resemblances, and they must be specifiable in language. One can hold to such a view without immediately subscribing to Platonic forms or Augustinian illumination. By being too restrictive about carry-over of linguistic signs without fixed meaning, Burrell is not entirely protected against equivocation. We still need to be assured that when we say that God is goodness, his goodness is not entirely dissimilar from our goodness. And the only way that this can happen is if there remains a univocal concept underneath all analogy.

Contemporary religious language vacillates between equivocation and analogy. At times it seems to be a restatement of Thomistic analogy in the contemporary context of qualified models.[62] On other occasions it appears to be reducible to equivocal God-talk. At best, models can be used as univocally conceived expressions that must be appropriately qualified of their limiting connotations before they are attributed to an infinite God. But even here the problem remains as to how one could know that the characteristics expressed in his model were really descriptive (in an analogous way) of God. Unless an ontological causal connection and similarity between God and creation is established (such as we attempted in chapters 9 and 12), then the hope for a meaningfully descriptive God-talk is nil. All that remains is "discourse" and "disclosure" about a we-know-not-what. But this is only discourse and disclosure without description. Only an analogy based in the similarity of creature and Creator can support meaningfully descriptive religious language.

---

62. For a restatement of analogy in analytic terms by a neo-Thomist see James F. Ross, "Analogy as a Rule of Meaning for Religious Language," *International Philosophical Quarterly* 1, no. 3 (September 1961).

PART 4 ✳

GOD AND EVIL

GUIDING QUESTIONS

1. What is the nature of the problem of evil; what is the basic plan of a theodicy?
2. What are the dimensions of the problem of evil, and why is it important to respect their distinctions?
3. What is meant by the idea that metaphysically evil is a privation? What is not meant by it?
4. What is meant by the "best way" theodicy? How does human freedom contribute to it? How can Calvinism be reconciled with the "best way" theodicy?
5. Why does physical evil not count decisively against theism?

RECOMMENDED COLLATERAL READING

Augustine, *Confessions and Enchiridion.* Edited and translated by A. C. Outler. Philadelphia: Westminster, 1955.

John S. Feinberg, *Theologies and Evil.* Washington, D.C.: University Press of America, 1979.

Alvin Plantinga, *God, Freedom, and Evil.* New York: Harper Torchbooks, 1974.

14 ✳

The Nature of the Problem of Evil

A traditional topic in philosophy of religion is the problem of evil. This is so partly because almost any religion attempts to deal with the reality and causes of evil in the world. But this issue becomes especially acute in the context of Judeo-Christian theism. For, if there is an all-powerful, all-knowing, all-loving God who has endowed his creation with qualities derived from his nature, how could there possibly be evil in this world?

There are many different ways of construing this problem. In this treatment we set up a slightly different paradox than is often found, namely, the conflict between God's obligation to create the best world and the apparent reality that this world is not the best he could have created. We shall also distinguish between different dimensions to the problem of evil—metaphysical, moral, physical.

The problem of evil arises out of the nature of theism. If there is no commitment to the existence of a God, at least heuristically, there is no conflict between God and evil. Michael Peterson asserts that the theist begs the crucial question in the argument by assuming God's existence.[1] But this claim is surely overstated. For if there is no God, there is no problem of inconsistency between God and evil. The theist would be guilty of begging the question if he did not allow for an apparent problem, given the unquestionable existence of God. But such is not the case.

Significant light can be shed on the nature of the problem of evil by making a classical distinction between the problem of inconsistency and the problem of theodicy.

First let us look at the nature of an inconsistency. Inconsistencies are different from contradictions. In a contradiction there are two statements, one of which must be true and one of which must be false. For example, the two statements

1. All politicians are honest.

and

---

1. Michael Peterson, *Evil and the Christian God* (Grand Rapids: Baker, 1982), p. 16.

2. Some politicians are not honest.

are irreconcilable. They cannot both be true, but neither can both be false. Assuming there are politicians, then either 1 is true and 2 is false, or 2 is true and 1 is false. There is no other alternative.

By contrast, in an inconsistency, all that is required is that two statements cannot both be true. Both could be false. For instance,

3. Jones is a pauper.

and

4. Jones has a million dollars.

are inconsistent with each other. One or the other could be false or both could be false. But on the surface it appears that they cannot both be true.

Looked at from the point of view of inconsistency, the problem of evil would take the following shape:

5. God is an omnipotent and omnibenevolent being who, in accord with his nature, would abolish all evil.
6. Evil exists.

Logically, one or the other of statements 5 and 6 could be false. In fact, both could be false. But they cannot both be true.

In general terms, the obvious strategy of dealing with an inconsistency is to show it to be a paradox, something that can be resolved by adding to one's understanding in such a way that the inconsistency vanishes. We can add to statements 3 and 4 another statement:

7. Jones's million dollars are worthless Monopoly money.

In this case one can see how Jones can both have a million dollars and be a pauper. The inconsistency is gone. A similar strategy is applied to the problem of evil. A popular attempt to resolve the inconsistency is to link statements 5 and 6 with another statement:

8. God expressed his omnipotent and omnibenevolent nature by creating free beings who are solely responsible for evil.

Again, assuming that the logical form is tight and tidy, the inconsistency might disappear.

But how does Jones, our pauper, come to have a million dollars in Monopoly money? Surely there is a mystery that should be cleared up before we are satisfied with the solution to the inconsistency. In the same way, simply showing a possible way of reconciling the inconsistency between God and evil may leave one wanting to know more. Not all possibilities are truths. For example, statement 8 may not be the actual truth about how God and evil can coexist. And even if it is true, someone may still want to know why God chose to create such beings and tolerate the resulting evil when he could have done otherwise. This latter way of dealing with the problem of evil is the problem of theodicy, literally the "justification of God." It wants to know not only if there is a way of reconciling God and evil, but also if this way is plausible and itself consistent with the nature of God.

In our treatment of the problem of evil we shall not only address the question of consistency, but also proceed from there to the need for theodicy. In the process, we will allow for the two different ways in which theism is usually formulated. Most of the discussion will concern itself with the understanding of God in which his sovereignty is compatible with the creation of free creatures. But, where necessary, we will also include reference to a strong Calvinistic position, according to which there are no truly free creatures.[2] On the whole, the considerations applying to the two points of view are probably more similar than different.

Nontheistic Solutions to the Problem of Evil

Several solutions to the problem of evil are not open to traditional theism that we have defended (in chap. 9). Each of these views is representative, in fact, of a nontheistic view.

Illusionism's Answer to Evil

The theist does not deny the reality of evil. He cannot say, as many pantheists do, "Nothing is really evil; it only appears to be so." Evil is taken as an undeniable fact of human experience. Evil (broadly defined) is anything that frustrates human aspirations and expectations. Evil is pain, sickness, disease, hate, murder, and cruelty. Who can consistently deny the reality of these things?

Persons influenced by an Eastern world view may deny the reality of evil. They may declare that evil is no more than an illusion that vanishes in the context of the Ultimate where all distinctions are irrelevant, including the one between good and evil. For example, Frederic Spiegelberg praises the insights of an Indian sage, Aurobindo. After presenting a supposedly inadequate Christian theodicy, Spiegelberg finally launches into an exposition of Aurobindo's contribution with the words, "He begins by minimizing the power of pain . . . ."[3] The upshot of the defense is that "pain is less a fact than a matter

---

2. See John S. Feinberg, "And the Atheist Shall Lie Down with the Calvinist: Atheism, Calvinism, and the Free Will Defense," *Trinity Journal* 1 (1980): 142–52.

3. Frederic Spiegelberg, *Living Religions of the World* (Englewood Cliffs, N.J.: Prentice-Hall, 1956), p. 212.

of perspective."[4] In short, if one comes to know the truth, there is no longer a problem with evil because there is no evil.

Alan Watts also adopts an Eastern perspective on the nature and problem of evil.[5] He charges Western humanity with not being willing to reckon with one's finitude and thus looking for a solution to the problem of evil in the acts of free individuals. But, he argues, down that road lies an irreconcilable dualism. The only acceptable alternative is to see good and evil as only relative distinctions that do not obtain with ultimate reality. Inside the finite world there is a harmony of apparent good and evil, but both of those qualities are swallowed up in the greater reality of the infinite.

The theist takes as inadequate the illusionist's contention that evil has no reality, for several reasons. First, illusionism does not account for the origin of the illusion. Whence has come this strong and all-pervading myth that evil does exist? Further, it does not explain the apparent reality of the illusion. Why is it that if I sit on a pin and it punctures my skin, I dislike what I fancy I feel? Also, denying the reality of evil does not eliminate the presence of evil. Even illusionists experience pain and death. They, too, are subject to harm and hate from others, and, like all nonillusionists, they finally die. In brief, there is little if any advantage gained by denying the reality of evil; the illusionist, like the rest of us, still experiences evil. Finally, illusionism is no more than a beautiful theory that is ruined by a brutal gang of facts. To paraphrase Sigmund Freud: "It would be nice if it were true that no evil existed, but the very fact that men wish it to be so makes this belief highly suspect."

In short, illusionism is itself an illusion. There is no distinct advantage gained by denying the reality of evil, and it does stretch one's credulity to believe that something so apparently real, so totally pervasive, and so persistently present in life is a lie. Accepting the illusionist's position demands that one admit that all of life as he experiences it is deceiving him. Whereas this is logically possible, it is practically unhelpful and existentially distasteful, to say nothing of being philosophically improbable. It is more likely that the illusionist is being deceived about evil than that all persons are being deceived by evil.

Sadism's Answer to Evil

Few people have troubled themselves with believing that God is a cosmic sadist who deliberately created the world and inflicted evil on it because he enjoyed observing things suffer.

---

4. Ibid., p. 213.
5. Alan Watts, *The Supreme Identity: An Essay on Oriental Metaphysic and the Christian Religion* (New York: Random, 1972), pp. 99–130.

Such a possibility is, however, raised by a few writers, such as Elie Wiesel, in light of the Holocaust. Wiesel in his numerous writings is willing neither to exonerate God from all responsibility nor to justify God's ways in that horror. Still, his suggestions certainly represent a minority view. Harold S. Kushner raises the same possibility in his best-selling book, *When Bad Things Happen to Good People,* when he says that we need "to forgive the world for not being perfect, to forgive God for not making a better world, to reach out to the people around us, and to go on living despite it all."[6] But Kushner's view as a whole is probably best classified with finitism.

Besides the fact that this view is eliminated for a theist by his commitment to God as all-good, there are several nontheistic reasons for rejecting it. First, the term *God* seems eminently inappropriate for such a being with such malicious intent. Second, how can the universe be ultimately evil? Does not evil presuppose good? By what standard, if there is no ultimate Good (or, God), could one declare the activity of this demonic creator to be *not*-good? And if there is a good God more ultimate than this evil demon, then it is not he who is the cosmic sadist but lower demonic forms. The problem, then, takes on the shape of traditional theism, which will be discussed subsequently. Third, as Charles Hartshorne remarked,[7] it does seem incongruous to say there is a demonic God who is both responsible for and at the same time adverse to all that exists; who is both intimately united with and savagely opposed to all he made; who loves the world enough to create and sustain it only because he wants to hate it. In short, a cosmic sadist would not be a being worthy of the name *God;* it presupposes an ultimate Good in the universe, and its very functions as preserver and destroyer are incompatible.

Finitism's Answer to Evil

A far more popular view since David Hume is to concede that God is finite in either power or love (or both). For if God is willing to prevent evil but not able, then he is impotent. And if he is able but not willing, then he is malevolent. But since there is evil, God cannot be both all-good and all-powerful. Finitism seems to be the only alternative.

Finitism is represented most prominently today among process thinkers. Hartshorne writes, "No worse falsehood was ever perpetrated than the traditional concept of omnipotence. It is a piece of unconscious blasphemy condemning God to a dead world, probably not distinguishable from no world at

6. Harold S. Kushner, *When Bad Things Happen to Good People* (New York: Schocken, 1981), p. 147.

7. Charles Hartshorne, "The Necessary Existent," in *The Ontological Argument: From Anslem to Contemporary Philosophers,* ed. Alvin Plantinga (Garden City, N.Y. Doubleday, Anchor Books, 1965), p. 127.

all."[8] Thus Hartshorne denies the infinity of God for the sake of elevating the significance of the world, and any evil is the world's problem, not God's. Among writers with more traditional roots it is also becoming fashionable to adopt similiar views of God. Some would say that God is not essentially limited; he merely limited himself. For example, Bruce R. Reichenbach asserts, "God is sovereign in authority and power. Yet at the same time he willingly limited himself. . . ."[9] It may be questioned whether a self-limited God is a coherent concept, but regardless, God's relationship to the world becomes identical to that postulated by Hartshorne.

The theist rejects the finitist's solution for several reasons. First, a finite god, like all finite beings, is a dependent and caused being and therefore needs a cause to explain its existence (as was shown in chap. 9). Only an infinite Cause explains the existence of finite things. Further, a finite god is not a religiously worthy object of worship. Anything less than an ultimate is not worthy of an ultimate commitment. A less than perfect being should not be the object of religious devotion.[10] Finally, a finite god cannot guarantee the outcome in the struggle against evil. The cause of good may lose. Hence, moral initiative is diminished and discouraged where there is no assurance that the cause of right will prevail. In essence, a finite god is metaphysically impossible, religiously unworthy, and ethically demoralizing for people in their struggle against evil.

Theism must reject finitism's solution to the problem of evil. The only hope that evil can and will be destroyed and/or ultimately justified is that there is an all-loving and all-powerful God who can accomplish this formidable task.[11] There is every indication that nothing less than infinite wisdom could devise a plan to destroy evil; that nothing short of infinite love would desire to completely eliminate evil; and that nothing but infinite power could possibly bring these plans and desires to fruition. If there is no infinite God, there appears to be no final solution to the problem of evil.

Determinism's Answer to Evil

There is another way out of the problem of evil for those who believe in God: perhaps God was not free *not* to create the kind of world that inevitably

8. Charles Hartshorne, *Omnipotence and Other Theological Mistakes* (Albany: State University of New York Press, 1983), p. 18.

9. Bruce R. Reichenbach, "God Limits His Power," in *Predestination and Free Will*, ed. David Basinger and Randall Basinger (Downers Grove: Inter-Varsity, 1985), p. 118.

10. J. N. Findlay, an atheist, makes a strong case for this same point, arguing that anything less than an absolutely perfect Being would be unworthy of religious devotion. See "Can the Existence of God be Disproved?" in *New Essays in Philosophical Theology*, ed. Antony Flew and Alasdair MacIntyre (London: SCM, 1963), pp. 47–53.

11. Two other atheists, Edward H. Madden and P. H. Hare, make this same observation. See *Evil and the Concept of God* (Springfield, Ill.: Charles C. Thomas, 1968), pp. 110–11.

engendered evil (i.e., the world we have). That is, maybe God was forced to create the kind of world we have. This is commonly a pantheistic view but it is open to certain forms of theism that hold that creation does not flow freely from God's will but follows necessarily. If God is a necessary Being, then creation must unfold from him as necessarily as a flower develops from a seed.[12] As Benedict Spinoza said, "Things could not have been brought into being by God in any manner or in any order different from that which has in fact obtained."[13] Since God is the "most perfect" Being possible, it follows that he must produce every degree of perfection possible. And every degree of perfection from highest to lowest necessarily includes within it every possible imperfection as well. Hence, the world as we have it is the necessary and "most perfect" product possible of the necessary and "most perfect" Being possible.

Theism has traditionally and consistently denied this possibility for various reasons. First, biblical theists have concluded from revelation that creation was a free act of God (Rev. 4:11; Eph. 1:11). Creation flows from God's will freely and not necessarily. God was free not to create. Second, God has no need to create. An absolutely perfect Being lacks nothing, but is completely self-sufficient. The theistic infinite God is not a seed that needed to unfold in order to realize itself; he is eternal reality who needs no further realization of his Being. The pantheistic God is imperfect because it is not complete without creation; it must produce in order to perfect itself. Not so with the theistic God who is absolutely perfect eternally. Also, the nature of an absolutely perfect Being does not necessitate that it do anything but merely that it be the absolute Good that it is. The determinist's view of creation is built on the highly questionble application of the Platonic principle that "the Good is diffusive of itself." This is taken by Platonists to mean that Good must overflow itself to others; that absolute Good must flow outward and generate more "goods." The theist contends that if there were a need within Good to reproduce, then God would not be absolutely good. Any being that must produce in order to perfect itself is not perfectly good to begin with. An absolutely perfect Being has no need to share its goodness by creating anything else; he creates only because he wills to do so. Furthermore, even granting a necessary creation (which the determinists hold), it is not at all obvious why an absolutely perfect Being had to make an imperfect world. A perfect world would follow from a perfect Being, but why is an imperfect world necessitated from the nature of a perfect Being? Finitude does not necessitate evil; it only makes evil possible. It is not obviously contradictory to have a finitely perfect world. Why, then, did not the perfect nature of such a

---

12. See Plotinus, *Six Enneads* (Chicago: Encyclopaedia Britannica Press, 1952), 6.8.6.

13. See Benedict Spinoza, *Ethics*, trans. Andrew Boyle (New York: Dutton, 1963), proposition 23.

God necessitate the creation of a finitely perfect world? Surely the world as it now is—with cancer, cruelty, and war—is not perfect. It does not take infinite intelligence to see that just a little less sin, sickness, and sorrow would make this world better. And if the world could be improved, then it obviously is not a perfect world.

Impossibilism's Answer to Evil

There is another possible evasion of the problem of evil that a theist may take and yet believe in a free and infinite God. It may be that it is impossible for even a God infinite in knowledge to foreknow future free events. God may have knowingly created free beings without the ability to foresee what they would do with their freedom, namely, bring all this evil into the world. God, let us grant, could control by his almighty power everything that is not free. But God cannot control what free beings will do with their freedom without violating their freedom. Even an infinite God cannot do what is contradictory. He cannot make square circles; he cannot not be God, and he cannot know what is impossible to know. This position deserves more attention.

Two arguments indicate that even an all-knowing God cannot foresee future free acts and their results. The first argument is as follows:[14]

1. God can foresee events only if there is a necessary order of causes over which he has control.
2. But a necessary order of causes under divine control is contrary to human freedom.
3. Hence, either God cannot foresee free acts or else there are no free acts.
4. But there are free acts.
5. Therefore, God cannot know free acts and their results.

The second argument has been recently stated this way:[15]

1. Whatever is foreknown by God is known to be true in advance (God cannot know an error to be true).
2. Whatever is known to be true in advance by God cannot be changed (an all-knowing God cannot change his mind about what is true).
3. But whatever cannot be changed eliminates freedom (for freedom implies the ability to do otherwise).
4. Hence, whatever is foreknown by God eliminates freedom; and con-

---

14. See Nelson Pike, *God and Timelessness*, Studies in Ethics and the Philosophy of Religion series (New York: Schocken, 1970), for a discussion of this argument deriving from Cicero (cf. Augustine, *City of God* 5.9.2).

15. This is Arthur N. Prior's way of putting it. "The Formalities of Omniscience," *Philosophy* 37 (1962): 114–29.

versely, dreedom eliminates the ability of God to foreknown what it will do.

Several responses are open to the theist. A strong Calvinist might want to agree hypothetically with the flow of the argument, but then draw a different conclusion. The impossibilist accepts as a given premise that free creatures act freely and concludes that therefore some things are impossible for God. But this argument can be turned into a reductio ad absurdum on human freedom. If the (hypothetically) given fact of free acts by free creatures limits God, then there must be no such things as true creaturely freedom. Why should an argument that limits God not be used to limit creatures? A theist who wants to sustain the idea of creaturely freedom is not impeded by this argument either, however. He can bring up several objections against the first argument. First, some argue that foreknowledge does not imply foredetermination; God can foresee something will happen without foredetermining that it must happen.[16] Second, the theistic God is timeless and does not foresee anything; he sees everything in one eternal now. Hence, knowledge of what men do with their freedom does not determine what they do; it merely observes what they do. God sees what they are doing (by their own freedom) but not what they must be doing (by any alleged divine necessity). Third, just because an event is determined does not mean it cannot be freely chosen. One may have freely chosen to eat an apple yesterday, even though it is now determined and cannot be changed. Since God knows the future with the same certainty with which we see the past, there is no reason God could not have determined from all eternity what creatures will freely do.[17]

The second argument of impossibilism is also deficient.[18] First, it may make no sense to speak of something as true in advance. It may be better to speak of it as known in advance that it would be true later when it actually happened. Second, a man may have the ability to do otherwise, even though he does not choose to do so. And God could know that this is the case (viz., that the man was free to do otherwise but would not choose to do so). Finally, an eternal God does not foresee; he sees all right now. And if God sees something is true right now, then this eliminates any problem about it being true in advance.

---

16. See Augustine, *On Free Will* 3.

17. See Norman L. Geisler, "God Knows All Things," in *Predestination and Free Will*, ed. David Basinger and Randall Basinger, (Downers Grove: Inter-Varsity, 1985), chap. 2.

18. See Thomas Aquinas, *Summa Theologica*, trans. the English Dominican Fathers (Chicago: Benzinger Brothers, 1947, 1948), 1.10.2–3. The arguments are these: first, God is immutable (changeless); whatever is temporal involves change; hence, God cannot be a temporal being. In other words, God is unlimited and if he were not eternal, then he would be limited in time. But since God is unlimited in his existence in every way, he cannot be limited in his existence in any way (including limitation by time).

The implications of this for impossibilism's answer to the problem of evil are four. First, God can foresee without forcing. Second, in traditional theism God does not foresee at all; he knows what is going on in the whole course of time in one eternal now.[19] Accordingly, God cannot be exonerated of the responsibility for an evil world on the grounds that it was impossible for him to see that evil would occur in the world he created. Third, even granting that God could not foresee future free acts, certainly there is nothing contrary to omniscience in claiming that God knew what could happen if he made free creatures. That is, even if God did not know what would happen if he created free beings, nevertheless he certainly knew what could happen. And it did happen, with God knowing in advance that it might happen. Why did he take the great risk that became a reality? God must still be charged with the responsibility of creating the possibility of all the evil that did actualize. For surely it is not contradictory for an all-knowing mind to be aware in advance of all the possibilities inherent in or available to that which it creates. Finally, centering attention on freedom does not answer why there is apparently much evil in the world not traceable to free acts. Why does not God eliminate natural evil and suffering which, by virtue of his omnipotence, he can control without violating man's free acts?

Solutions to the Problem of Evil Open to Theism

Granted the conclusion that the theistic God is one who freely created the world, knowing the evil that would result, the alternatives for a solution are numbered. There are two sets of alternatives; the hypothetical ones and the actual ones.

The Hypothetical Alternatives for Theism

The theistic God had before him six basic alternatives with respect to creating anything, as they bear on the problem of evil. And in view of the evil that has happened, one can ask: Why did God not choose one of the other alternatives open to him?

1. *God could have decided not to create anything at all.* A God who freely creates was free not to create. And a God who knew that creation would become so corrupt should not have created at all. A nonevil nothing would be better than an evil something. According to theism, this was an actual possibility for God. Gottfried Wilhelm Leibniz attempted to avoid the difficulty by contending that other worlds were logically possible for God but that this

19. God knows everything in the eternal present but he does not know everything as the present moment in time; he knows the past as past and the future as future.

world was morally necessary for him to create.[20] But this solution will not do when it is applied to the choice to create or not create, since it violates God's freedom. Moral necessity comes from the nature of God. And God was not under any compunction of his nature to create anything.

It may be argued properly that the best of all beings must do his best in creating only if he decides to create something. But nothing in the moral nature of God necessitates that he create anything. The only necessity in God's nature as such is that he be God—nothing else. In brief, it was morally possible that God not create anything; it would not have been immoral if he had not created anything. The application of Leibniz's position would be an unnecessary concession to determinism which either, as pantheism, implies a lack in God or else is built on the unjustifiable Platonic principle of plenitude. But in either case, it is ultimately unhelpful to Leibniz's own theism, for God did create a world that could be better. This world is not the best of all possible worlds; it could be improved upon, as any reasonable theist or atheist can readily see, by reducing just some of the evil.

But the fact that it was actually possible for God not to have created this world that he did create causes a discomfort to theism. If God could have avoided making a world that he knew would become this corrupt, then why did he not do so? This actual possibility for God is an actual problem for theism. No theistic solution to the problem of evil will be complete without satisfactorily addressing this possibility that was open to God.

2. *God could have created only beings who are not free.* Another option open to a theistic God is the creation of a world without free beings. Since free creatures, not being under God's direct control, are able to bring about evil, it would have been an effective guarantee against such evil not to create such beings at all. If God was under no necessity of his nature to create any specific kinds of beings, then why did he specifically create the kind he knew would choose evil?

Here again, theists are sometimes tempted to appeal to the Platonic principle of plenitude to justify their cause. René Descartes, for example, argued that "God always wills what is best," which included for him the fact that a person was free to choose wrong even if he knew the right.[21] But if this is taken to mean that whenever God wills to do something, it must be something moral, then there are problems for theism. First, is it really necessary that whatever God does must be a moral activity? Cannot God make an amoral world if he wishes to do so? Second, granted that whatever God does, he must do his best (for less than his best would be an evil for God), does it

---

20. Gottfried Leibniz, *Monadology and Other Philosophical Essays*, trans. Paul Schrecker and Ann Schrecker (Indianapolis: Bobbs-Merrill, 1965), pp. 53–55.

21. René Descartes, *Meditations*, trans. L. J. Lafleur (New York: Liberal Arts, Bobbs-Merrill, 1951), 4.

follow that God cannot make the best possible amoral world? If God is really free to create any kind of world not contradictory to his nature, then why not a perfect amoral world (without free creatures), as well as a perfect moral world (with free creatures)? The nature of God only necessitates, at the most, that whatever God chooses to do, he must do his best.

As has already been shown, God did not have to choose to create anything. And if he chose to create something, there seems to be no reason why it had to be something moral. As long as it was not something immoral, there is no problem in holding that the theistic God could have made an amoral world. But here again theism faces a problem. For if God could have avoided evil by creating a world without any free creatures in it, then why did he not choose to do so? It would have eliminated in advance the sum total of human misery which has ensued because God did not create a world of beings which are not free.

It does not take much thought to see that even the strong Calvinist does not escape from this problem. Certainly he would deny that God has created free creatures who are not under his control. But this idea only exacerbates the problem. For if it is puzzling that God would have created free creatures who chose evil, it is even more puzzling that God would have created unfree creatures who chose evil. If he could have done otherwise in the first case, he certainly could have done otherwise in the second case a fortiori.

3. *God could have created beings who are free to sin but who never do sin.* Another option apparently open to the theistic God was the creation of free beings who never exercise their option to sin. This kind of world would have the advantages of having free creatures without the obvious disadvantages of any evil resulting from the misuse of freedom. In fact, it would seem to be a better alternative among possible moral worlds than the one we have (where there are creatures who do sin). And if God is obligated to do his moral best whenever he decides to do something with moral implications, then it would seem that God has failed to do his best in creating the kind of evil world that we have.

Theists have sometimes tried to evade this dilemma by holding that a world of free creatures who never do sin is impossible.[22] They say it is impossible to be free and yet not be free to sin. If one is not really free to do otherwise, he is not free at all. Freedom without sin is a contradiction, it is argued. But this seems to be an ill-advised tack for theism for a number of reasons. First, there is no obvious logical contradiction involved in affirming that men are able to do otherwise but never actually do otherwise than good. It seems obvious enough that people who get up at 6 A.M. are free to get up at

22. See J. M. E. McTaggart, *Some Dogmas of Religion* (London: E. Arnold, 1930), p. 166.

4 A.M. but do not choose to do so. However, it would be contradictory to affirm that free persons never sin because it is impossible for them to sin. But it is not contradictory to hold that they never sin because they are unwilling to do so. People in fact sometimes choose not to do evil and, hence it is not impossible in theory that humans would always choose to avoid evil. Further, it would seem that the theistic God has infinite persuasive power. With the proper conditioning and motivation supplied by God, the perfect Persuader, these free beings could be divinely enticed to always do what is right. Moreover, God is free but is not free to sin. Proper freedom is the freedom only to do the good, not evil. And if special case is pleaded here in that God's nature will not permit him to sin whereas man's does, then what about Christ's human nature? Is it not impossible for Christ to sin as a human? If not, then the whole temptation would appear to be a farce and his moral example for believers would lose its motivating force. If he had nothing to worry about in facing sin but humans do, then how can his sinless life be of any encouragement to men? Finally, most theists believe in a final state of perfection that the Bible calls heaven. This, it is believed by many theists, will be a state of perfection where there is no more sin or sorrow (Rev. 21–22). Therefore, freedom without sin is not a contradiction in heaven.

The dilemma, then, must be faced. If God will produce in the end a condition for free creatures where there will be no more sinning, why did he not make it this way from the beginning? If heaven will be a place with free beings who do not sin, then why did God not make earth that way too? If God has the power to create the conditions for freedom to exercise itself without abuse ultimately, then surely God should do it immediately if he can. If having free beings who will not sin is possible in heaven, why is it impossible on earth? Or, more specifically, if there is some better way to do it (as is indicated by these alternatives), why did not God do it this way for the rest of humankind? Surely an all-perfect God should do it (even, must do it) the best way possible. And it would seem best to create free creatures who do not sin from the beginning, rather than to permit sin and evil only to produce in the end what could have been done in the beginning without all the waste and suffering. Why beat one's head on the wall because it feels so good when it is over? It feels even better not to have done it in the first place.

Following Antony Flew, some have argued that freedom is not necessarily incompatible with creatures who consistently choose not to sin. For God could have arranged the world in such a way that the creatures are influenced toward good in each of their choices.

This contention rests on a distinction between compatibilist and incompatibilist views of freedom. Compatibilist freedom means freedom to choose in the context of "contingently sufficient non-subsequent conditions of an action."[23] In other words, even though a person chooses freely, his choice is already predetermined by the circumstances within which he freely chooses. An incompatibilist theory of freedom would hold that a choice can be said to be free only if on the basis of all surrounding circumstances it could have been made either way. Accepting a compatibilist view of freedom, one may claim that it is philosophically as viable an option as its counterpart and is theologically preferable. Thus, they argue that God could have arranged things in such a way that (compatibilistically) free beings freely choose not to sin in every instance. This, of course, raises a serious problem for such a theist as to why God did not choose to do it this way for all free creatures and thus avoid all evil.

4. *God could not have created beings who are free but who must sin.* The position that God could have created beings who are free but who cannot avoid sin, we take it, is contradictory. A being would not really be free not to sin if he were under necessity to sin. If a creature cannot avoid evil, he cannot be held responsible for doing what was unavoidable. Responsibility for sin can be laid at the doorstep of only those who have the ability to respond against sin, even if this ability is never exercised. That one ought to do something implies that he can do it.

Some might object that the Christian doctrine of depravity affirms precisely the opposite, namely, that sin is inevitable. The fallen person cannot avoid sinning. He has lost his ability not to sin. Sin is inevitable and unavoidable for human beings. Several observations are pertinent to this objection.[24] First, according to Christian teaching, human beings were not created in a depraved state; they were created with the ability not to sin, and they lost this ability when they sinned. Second, even fallen persons have the ability not to sin, only it is not their own inherent ability; it is the ability made possible by the grace of God. Ought always implies can, but the "can" or ability not to sin may be taken in two ways: either one has the ability not to sin in his own power (which the doctrine of depravity denies), or it may be taken to mean that one has the ability not to sin by means of the grace of God available through redemption (which the doctrine of depravity does not deny). Finally, the doctrine claims that all persons will sin, but not that all persons must sin. Sin is unavoidable, not because it is necessitated by God in violation of human freedom but only because it is known by God who sees the exercise

23. Feinberg, "Atheist." Also idem, *Theologies and Evil* (Washington, D.C.: University Press of America, 1979). Compare Antony Flew, "Divine Omnipotence and Human Freedom," in *New Essays in Philosophical Theology*, ed. Antony Flew and Alasdair MacIntyre (London: SCM, 1963), p. 146.

24. See the treatment of depravity in Norman L. Geisler, *Ethics: Alternatives and Issues* (Grand Rapids: Zondervan, 1971), pp. 100ff.

of human freedom. God knows that all people will sin, but he does not determine by the created conditions of their freedom (or, nonfreedom) that all persons must sin. In brief, God pronounces that sin is inevitable in general but that each sin is avoidable in particular (by the grace of God). Fallen humans have the God-given ability (whether they have received it or not) to resist each particular sin they encounter,[25] even though God knows that all persons will freely choose not to avail themselves of this divine grace. Hence the biblical doctrine of depravity does not entail the acceptance of the contradictory proposition that God created beings who are free but who must sin. If they have the ability not to sin, they cannot also be under the necessity to sin. Their choice is determined from the standpoint of God's knowledge, but it is free from the vantage point of their choice. God simply determined what he knew they would freely do. However, to claim that God forced humans to freely sin is a contradiction. Forced freedom is logically incoherent.

5. *God could have created beings who were free and who would sin.* The preceding alternative showed that it is impossible for God to create beings who both must sin and cannot sin. But this last alternative reveals that it is possible to create beings who need not sin but who will sin. Just as it is possible to have creatures who can sin but never will sin (as Christ or as the blessed in heaven), even so it is possible to have creatures who have the ability not to sin but who nevertheless do sin. It is possible to have an ability that one does not choose to exercise. A man who is a total abstainer from alcoholic drinks has the freedom to drink them, but he chooses never to exercise that freedom. Or, conversely, an alcoholic has the ability not to drink (indicated by the fact that many do quit), even though he may choose not to exercise that ability. Likewise, the fallen person has the ability not to choose evil, even though inevitably he does not choose to exercise that ability to avoid evil.

This latter alternative, according to theism, is that which brought about the kind of world we do live in. It is the alternative that the theistic God did choose. Hence, in view of the fact that the world of theism is one in which an all-loving, all-knowing, all-powerful God chose to create beings who would inevitably bring evil upon themselves and others, all of the other positions (1–4) are purely hypothetical. Even if the theist might wish another one were true, he is committed to defending this last alternative. God did it this way, and the theists who believe this is the case must offer their justification for the way God chose to do it.

Even the strong Calvinist is in no different position, except as a matter of emphasis and degree. There might be differences as to his understanding of

25. If sin were not always avoidable by God's grace, then Christ would have had to sin, too, which the Bible denies. For a critique of the view that sin is unavoidable (but forgivable) see ibid., pp. 110–12.

freedom, but he also needs to account for the fact that God created beings who chose to sin. Thus Cornelius Van Til states, "Man is responsible for sin, and he alone is responsible for sin. . . . On the other hand, it was God's will that sin should come into the world."[26] Thus the puzzle is intact and needs a similar solution.

The Actual Alternatives for Theism

The actual alternatives for theism are dictated by the kind of world we do have, not the kind of world there might have been. The hypothetical alternatives just discussed show only the possible alternatives open to God. But since, according to theism, God chose one of these alternatives, there is only one alternative open to theism, which is to defend the option that God took. There is, in fact, only one actual alternative for theism, namely, to defend the claim that a world where beings can choose and do evil (this world) is at least as good as any other option available to God.

1. *A theist need not prove three things in order to answer the problem of evil.* First, he need not show that this world is literally the best of all possible worlds but only that there could be no better world or nonworld. That is, he needs to demonstrate that this world is at least as good as any other possibility open to God. The theistic God cannot be expected to do better than what is possible, for this is impossible and he cannot do what is actually impossible. On the other hand, it seems eminently fair to show God did the best that is possible for him to do. Anything less than the most nearly perfect possible would be incompatible with an all-perfect Being. Second, the theistic solution to evil need not demonstrate exactly how God can achieve the highest perfection out of a world with evil in it. The ultimate modus operandi of the Infinite may be beyond the grasp of finite beings. Finally, the theistic solution need not definitely prove that this world is the best possible alternative. Definite proof is rare in any philosophical endeavor. It will be taken as sufficient if the theist can offer a plausible but verifiable solution that is not incompatible with the theistic God but is achievable by him. Proving that an evil world is definitely as good as a nonevil world is unnecessary; establishing a probability that it is as good is a necessity for theism.[27]

---

26. Cornelius Van Til, *The Defense of the Faith* (Philadelphia: Presbyterian and Reformed, 1955), p. 160.

27. If theism had no other line of evidence (such as it has in the cosmological argument), then it would be necessary to do more than establish mere plausibility for the justification of evil. For in that case the whole theistic argument would turn on the seemingly most probable solution to the evil question. (The reason for the word *seemingly* will become clear in the answer to the problems of evil in chapter 16.) But the favorable probability (we think even undeniability) of the cosmological argument gives theism an edge as it enters the question of

2. *A theistic solution to evil must meet three conditions.* The theist must show that his solution is at least possible (i.e., it is not contradictory or impossible), offers evidence to indicate that it is achievable, and presents a way to know how it can be verified and/or falsified if it is or is not achieved.

The first of these three conditions needs little comment. The theist cannot reject other positions that are contradictory and accept a contradictory or impossible position of his own. Whatever mystery may be involved in showing how an evil world is reconcilable with a perfect God, there can be no reservations in showing that the two are not necessarily incompatible.

The second condition is an important requirement in view of the nature of the problem. It will be granted that it is not sufficient for theism to establish the mere possibility of an answer to evil; the theistic solution must be plausible. There must be some evidence to indicate that the theist's solution is actually true. The reasons for this requirement are obvious enough. First, evil is prima facie incompatible with a perfect God. Second, evil is used as the main evidence against theism, and one cannot do away with an opponent's main evidence by simply showing that it is possible that it is not true. Third, even believers in God cannot rest content in him if there is any doubt about the achievability of his good intentions with their lives and world.

The third condition stated is a necessary test for truth. No position can be justified as true unless there are some stipulated conditions under which one could know that it is or is not true. An unjustifiable and/or unverifiable faith is not worth believing, if it is believable at all.

The Apparent Dilemma Facing Theism

It might seem to the careful reader by this point that the structure given the problem has already prevented a successful theistic answer, since two seemingly incompatible positions have already been claimed for theism. For it has been stated that God must do his best and that this world that he made is not the best. That would seem to settle the question against theism. On the contrary, this apparent dilemma does not eliminate a theistic alternative but it would, if true, eliminate all theistic alternatives save one. Let us put the apparent dilemma in more complete form.

First, it will be taken here as true that God must do his best. It seems axiomatic that to do less than his best would be an evil for God, as it is for man. We would not praise a man for rescuing only one drowning man if he could have saved two more. Doing good is not enough, if it means that one

---

evil. In short, a theist enters the area of evil armed with the infinitely good and perfect God of the cosmological argument. This kind of God may be his greatest apparent liability (because this kind of God makes the problem of evil more acute), but such a God is also the theist's only hope for a solution to evil.

chooses a lesser good as opposed to a greater good. The man who rescued one man when he could have rescued three has really chosen a greater evil, namely, allowing two men to drown rather than allowing none to drown. There is no reason not to believe that the same applies to God.[28] If God is opposed to a little unjustified suffering, then surely it would be a twisted logic to conclude that he is not opposed to a lot of unjustified suffering. Likewise, if God is under moral obligation to help some innocent sufferers, then surely he is bound to help many, even the most he possibly can. The Christian doctrine that God loves all men and that Christ died for all men would support this from the point of view of biblical theism (see John 3:16; 1 John 2:1).

God must do his best or else it is an evil for him. Hence, if God produced anything less than a world that could be produced by an absolutely perfect Being, then God is not an absolutely perfect Being. But, according to theism, God is an absolutely perfect Being. Hence, the theist must show that what God produces in this world of free but evil beings is the best possible world that could be produced.[29]

Even though we accept as axiomatic the idea that God must do his best, that idea has not been immune from questioning. Peterson expressed this notion as the "principle of meticulous providence (MP)" in this way; "An omnipotent, omniscient, wholly good God would prevent or eliminate the existence of really gratuitous or pointless evils."[30] In other words, according to MP, there is no evil in the world which does not contribute to God's plan for the world but that God would eliminate it. God will eliminate evil wherever possible. But Peterson denies MP. He does so essentially because he sees MP as being in conflict with human experience, human freedom, and the nature of the world. Whether or not Peterson's suggestion is philosophically feasible, it is certainly a theological disaster. This is so not because he draws a conclusion contrary to traditional notions, but because methodologically he apparently develops a view of the nature and acts of God purely in order to pull his philosophical chestnuts out of the fire. We need to have a concept of God that stands on its own feet and is not an ad hoc modification for the sake of handily solving the problem of evil. There is no escape from the fact that God must always do his best in relation to evil.

28. The same ethical principle does not apply to God because it applied to man, as if everything that men ought not do, God ought not do either. For this is not so. For example, God, the Author of life, has the right to take life; men do not. But God's nature also commits him to doing his very best infinitely, as man's nature demands that he do his best finitely.

29. We reject the tradition in ethics stemming from Ockham that contends that God is free to act contrary to his own nature. If this were so, then ethics would be arbitrary, reversible, futile, and unbelievable, and God may decide that hate is normative tomorrow or that unbelievers will go to heaven. If such an ethic were possible, it would be unworthy of God and unbelievable by men.

30. Peterson, *Evil and the Christian God*, p. 81.

The second horn of the theist's dilemma is this: this world is not the best of all possible worlds. Even granting that some of the evil in it is necessary, this world still has too much evil in it. Not only could the world easily get along without so much violence, cruelty, and cancer, but it would seem to be much better off without these altogether. Again, if this were not the case, then all of the theistic talk of a state of immortal perfection (or, heaven) without these is meaningless. If this world, as it is, constitutes the best of all possible worlds, then the nontheist can scarcely be criticized for insisting that the best God can do could be improved. The theist not only can conceive of how to improve the world but hopes for improvement and works for it when calamities strike him. The hope of heaven and immortality are the theist's own arguments against this being the best of all possible worlds.

In view of what seems to be such an obvious point, it is misdirected effort for theism to defend the thesis that this world is the best of all possible worlds. If this is the case,[31] Voltaire was right in satirizing Leibniz's "best of all possible worlds" in *Candide*. For all of the conceivable misfortune that can and does happen to people in this world cannot (other than satirically) be attributed to the best of all possible Beings. Clearly this is not the best possible world a perfect God could create. Just a little less corruption, hatred, and war would easily improve this world.

The dilemma seems most painful for theism. God must do his best and yet this world he made is not the best. Is there any way out? Only one: *this is not the best of all possible worlds, but it is the best of all possible ways (i.e., a necessary way) to achieve the best of all possible worlds.* A sinless heaven is better than an evil earth, but there was no way for God to achieve a sinless heaven unless he created beings who would sin and did sin in order that out of their sin he could produce the best world where beings would not sin. An imperfect moral world is the necessary precondition for achieving the morally perfect world.

The achievement of this final goal is possible only if God is infinite. Certainly nothing less than an infinitely wise and powerful God could guarantee the outcome. And if the outcome cannot be guaranteed, then the present evil world would not be worth it. Another alternative would have been better. Hence, the possibility of this solution depends on the infinity of God. The plausibility of this answer will depend on the evidence that can be gathered to indicate that God exists and is at work performing this task. And the verifiability of this solution will be determined by the criteria a theist can offer to

31. The "aesthetic" illustrations used by both Augustine (see *On Order* 1.1.2; 2.4.12.) and Leibniz (*Theodicy*, trans. E. M. Huggard [Indianapolis: Bobbs-Merrill, 1966], objection 1) lend to the belief that they are defending this present evil world as the best possible. Chapter 16 will offer an explanation for this inadequate solution and place these illustrations in another context.

test his solution. Indeed, if there is an all-good and all-powerful God, then there is automatically a solution to the problem of evil. For such a God can do his best, since he is all-powerful. And he will do his best, because he is all-good. Hence, whatever evidence favors the existence of such a God (see chap. 9) also favors the theistic solution to the problem of evil.

Before we turn to these discussions, we must look more closely at the various dimensions of the problem of evil that the theist must address.

The Dimensions of the Problem of Evil for Theism

There are three aspects to the problem of evil for theism: the metaphysical, the moral, and the physical. The problems will be stated here only briefly. The theistic answers will be indicated here but elaborated on in the next three chapters.

The Metaphysical Aspect of the Problem of Evil

The shape of the metaphysical dimension to the problem of evil is this:

1. God is the author of everything in the world.
2. Evil is something in the world.
3. Therefore, God is the author of evil.

It would seem that the theist would not want to deny either the first or second premise. A denial of the first would capitulate the sovereignty of God to some form of dualism. Theists would not want to admit some kind of given or surd for which God is not responsible and/or over which he has no control. Neither does the denial of the minor premise seem appropriate to theism, for such would appear to be a denial of the existence and reality of evil. Since theism opposes illusionism, it would seem inconsistent to deny that evil really exists in the world.

The theist's reply, in brief, is this: there is an equivocation on the word *something* in the second premise of the antitheistic argument.

1. God is the author of everything.
2. But evil is not a thing (i.e., a substance).
3. Hence, God is not necessarily the author of any evil (substance).

Evil is not a substance or thing. Everything God made was good (Gen. 1:31; 1 Tim. 4:4; Titus 1:15). Further, to deny that evil is not a real entity or substance is not to say that evil is not a reality. On the contrary, evil is real; it is a real privation in things. And this real privation or lack in things does not derive from God but from free creatures who brought about this corruption in the nature of things. And there is nothing evil about freedom as such, but this good thing called freedom is responsible for bringing about the corruption in the world. This answer to the metaphysical aspect of evil leads naturally to the moral problem of evil. Why did God create a free world wherein he knew this corruption would arise?

The Moral Aspect of the Problem of Evil

The entire first part of this chapter has centered on the moral aspect of the problem of evil. There are several ways of summarizing the moral problem, most of which include, by implication at least, what will later be separated as the physical aspect of the problem of evil. The dilemma was shaped by Pierre Bayle in the seventeenth century:[32]

1. Evil exists.
2. An omnipotent God could destroy evil.
3. A benevolent God would destroy evil.
4. Therefore, since evil is not destroyed, then either
    a. God is omnipotent and hence malevolent in some way, or
    b. God is benevolent and hence impotent in some way, or
    c. God is both malevolent and impotent, or
    d. there is no God at all.

In view of what has been said, the theistic answer can be anticipated; premise 4 is denied by theism. According to theism, God is working on the problem in the best way to handle evil, and he will eventually destroy it. This is not the best world, but the theist believes that it is the best way to achieve the best world. It remains to be seen whether the theist can provide the evidence for this view. Prima facie, at least, it is a possibility.

Another way to state the moral problem zeros in more specifically on the matter of human freedom. It can be put in this form:

1. God is responsible for making everything in the world, including human freedom.
2. Human freedom brought about moral evil in the world.
3. Hence, God is responsible for what brought about moral evil in the world.

Theists would not deny this conclusion; they would want to clarify the conclusion and deny the unwarranted deduction the antitheist would want to draw from the ambiguous conclusion. First, the conclusion is not that God is responsible for all the evil in the world; rather it is that God is responsible for creating the freedom through which evil came into the world. That is, God is

---

32. See the end of chapter 6 for the other ways to state the problem and for theistic answers to it.

responsible for creating that which made evil possible (free creatures), but he is not culpable for what they actually do with their freedom any more than automobile manufacturers are responsible for all the accidents resulting from reckless driving.

Second, if God is responsible only for the possibility of evil, not its actuality, then the antitheist cannot validly conclude that God is responsible for all the actual evil in the world. Especially is this so if the theist can support his contention that with the possibility of evil (freedom) also comes the possibility of achieving a greater good. And if this is so, then God who is obligated to do the best he can would be obligated to create a world wherein the greatest good can be achieved. That is, if he was going to create a moral world at all, then he was morally obligated to create the best one he could. If theism can establish the plausibility of this claim, it will have answered the moral aspect of the problem of evil.

The Physical Aspect of the Problem of Evil

There is at least one residual problem: not all evil is clearly a result of human freedom, and even the physical evil that does result from free choice could apparently be thwarted by intervention of the Almighty. But if God allowed these physical evils, then it would seem to be immoral for men to work against the purposes of God in resisting physical evil. Albert Camus's statement of the problem is perhaps best known. Speaking about a plague brought on a city by rats, he argued that

1. Either one must join the doctor and fight the plague or else join the priest and not fight the plague.
2. Not to fight the plague is antihumanitarian.
3. To fight the plague is to fight against God who sent it.
4. Therefore, if humanitarianism is right, theism is wrong.

The most appropriate response of theism is to deny the third premise. The Christian theist believes the plague is universal and that it is the plague of sin resulting from the abuse of freedom. Hence, Christians should work against the plague, not merely against its results but against its cause. It is morally right to do both, but it is most essential that we do more than treat symptoms. The deadly disease itself must be cured. Indeed, this is precisely where the cross of Christ and true love for humanity springing from it are essential to the cure. Hence, the Christian works more vigorously, and certainly more effectively, against the plague by attacking it at its very source in a human free choice to rebel against God and bring the plague of sin on his own head (Gen. 3:16–19; Rom. 5:12).

In brief, the plague is ultimately caused by human self-will and hence to work against it is not to work against God but to work for God and against man's sinful choices. Treating the symptoms is an act of mercy, and works of mercy are the works of God (Luke 10:29–37). Treating the cause of the plague is basic as a work of redemptive love which is also to work for God (1 John 3–4).

Theistic belief eliminates several proposed solutions to the problem of evil. The theist, as opposed to the illusionist, admits that evil is real; and, unlike the dualist, the theist does not hold that evil is an eternal given. The theist, in contrast to the sadist, acknowledges that God is good. Also, the theist denies that God is limited, as the finitist claims; and he denies that God was not free in creation, as the determinist contends. Nor does the traditional theist beg off, as the impossibilist does, on the grounds that God could not foresee that evil would happen. On the contrary, the theist admits that God could have refrained from creating anything; that he could have created a world without free creatures in it; that he could have created a world where creatures are free but do not sin; but that God could not have created a world where humans are free but must sin, for this is a contradiction; finally, that God could have created a world where humans could and would sin. The latter is the kind of world God did create, presenting the problem for theism as to why God did not choose any other alternatives, some of which appear to be better than this evil world.

The problem of evil has three dimensions for theism. Why did God create anything imperfect (metaphysical problem)? Why does God permit the imperfect to exist (moral problem)? Why does unnecessary human suffering and pain exist if there is an absolutely perfect God (physical problem)?

15 ✳

The Metaphysical Problem of Evil

The first dimension of the problem of evil for theism is the metaphysical. If God created everything that exists and since evil exists, is God the author of evil? Theists obviously deny that God created any evil things, but in denying this, theism is open to attack from two sides, dualism and illusionism. Was evil already there coeternally with God? Or is evil unreality and hence that which would not come under the creation of God? Either choice is contrary to traditional theism. In this chapter we will attempt to escape from the dilemma by taking recourse to the time-honored notion of evil as privation of good. We will explore its roots in the writings of Augustine and Thomas Aquinas and assess what it does and does not contribute to our discussion of evil.

The Problem of Metaphysical Evil and Alternatives for Theism

As was indicated in the preceding chapter, the basic metaphysical problem for theism can be put into these propositions:

1. God is the cause of everything that exists.
2. Evil is something that exists.
3. Therefore, God is the cause of evil.

In view of this form of the problem, there are only two alternatives open to the theist: he may deny the first premise and by so doing accept a type of dualism, or he may deny the second premise and be charged with accepting illusionism. But actually the theist cannot retreat to either of these positions, for in so doing he would deny theism.

Illusionism Is a Denial of Theism

If the theist denies the reality of evil, he has capitulated to pantheism. The thesis that all sin, suffering, and death are only illusory has already been rejected by theism.[1] Futhermore, the theist cannot change his mind and reverse course here on the basic reality of what he experiences, for to do this

1. See chapter 9 and the beginning of chapter 14.

318

would be to forsake his whole position for pantheism. If I do not exist and/or if there is no real finite world, then theism is not true, but pantheism. And, on the contrary, if the finite world that people experience is real, then the evil that people experience in this world is real, too. But if evil really exists, how can a theist disclaim that God created it?

Dualism Is a Denial of Theism

Does theism necessitate the position that God created everything that exists? Is it not possible that there is outside of God some surd evil that he did not create but with which he is locked in deadly struggle? The answer to this is yes for some quasitheisms or panentheisms, but no for Judeo-Christian theisms. Plato, for example, held that the Demiurgos only formed the matter that was eternally there; he did not bring the matter into existence. Plato's God was only a Former, not a Creator; he formed the world ex materia (out of matter already present) but did not create it ex nihilo (out of nothing).[2] The Judeo-Christian types of theism have consistently rejected this position and attributed all of creation, including the matter or stuff of which the world is made, to God's causality.[3]

In like manner, Judeo-Christian theisms have rejected the quasitheisms or panentheisms of Charles Hartshorne and Alfred North Whitehead. These thinkers posit a consequential pole to God which relates to the world. But this side of God can only attempt to entice the world or to make suggestions that the world eliminate evil. God cannot directly control the evil world, which of course does not eliminate the problem; in one sense it makes evil a worse problem than it is for traditional theism. At least the theistic God is sovereign over evil and is in no way hamstrung by the process of evil in the finite world. The positing of a bipolar God is a futile attempt to Christianize Platonic dualism. It robs the theistic God of his supremacy, purity, and ability to defeat evil.

The theistic objections to a God whose nature in part plays cheerleader to the finite world process in the struggle with evil can be summarized as follows: such a limited God is not powerful enough to guarantee a greater value in the future than he has achieved in past ages, to realize any maximal value for the universe at any one time (but only serially over eons of time at best), to stop any devaluation process that sets in, to attain aesthetic value (order in the world) without unwarranted pain to creatures, to overcome the lack of unachieved value in himself, or to elicit proper admiration and worship from creatures. Who could worship a God so ghastly as to be helplessly bound to

2. See the discussion on Plato in chapter 8.
3. Biblical support for creation ex nihilo is taken from passages like Genesis 1:1; John 1:1–2; Colossians 1:16; Hebrews 11:3; Revelation 4:11.

the world processes that he cannot even jam the creative process and stop the whole show? Who could make a total commitment to a God so impotent that he is not able to guarantee optimal value in himself, to say nothing of value in the universe or for the individual?[4]

It is an outrageous slur on the nature of God to paint him as more interested in aesthetic order, in a serial accumulation of values, or in self-development than with relieving the pain of his creatures. The best realizable by a finite God in the struggle against evil may be a very bad world. And to console creatures with the fact that much value has been realized and preserved in God over the long run is as unhelpful as saying that a million dollars will be given to a certain family over the next several thousand years.

Only an infinite God could possibly guarantee a better kind of world than the present one. And the dualistic God of panentheism is not infinite in his active struggle with evil. He is in fact tied by his nature to an evil process in which there is no assurance of change for the better.

Theism cannot afford the panentheistic alternative. Imperfection and evil cannot be of the very essence of an absolutely perfect being which the theistic God is held to be. Accepting this kind of dualism (or any other kind) would entail rejecting theism. Therefore, the dilemma remains: evil is real and God is the cause of every reality and hence the cause of evil.

The Theistic Answer to Metaphysical Dualism: Evil Is Not a Real Entity

In terms of the preceding antitheistic argument, the theist denies the second premise and restates the syllogism this way:

1. God is only the efficient Cause of every finite substance (and nothing else).
2. Evil is not a substance (either finite or infinite).
3. Therefore, God is not the efficient cause of evil.

The ambiguity in the argument against theism is in the phrase *everything that exists*. This phrase may be taken in two ways: everything that exists in itself but not in another, or everything that exists in another but not in itself. The first meaning is what traditional theists ascribe to "substance" and the second is what they mean by "evil" in a metaphysical sense. That is, evil has no existence of its own; it exists only in substances that God has created but it has no subsistence of its own.

4. See discussion in chapter 9. The atheists Edward H. Madden and P. H. Hare have some good arguments against these quasitheisms too. See *Evil and the Concept of God* (Springfield, Ill.: Charles C. Thomas, 1968), chap. 6.

Augustine: All Things Are Metaphysically Good

The classic theistic answer to the problem of a metaphysical dualism of good and evil was given by Augustine in reply to Manichaeism. The Bishop of Hippo insisted that substances as such are good; all things are good because God created them. Any corruption of these substances cannot come from the incorruptible God and, furthermore, all corruption can occur only in a good substance that is being corrupted.

1. *Every substance as such is good.* In opposition to the Manichaeans, who held that there were two co-eternal substances, one Good and the other Evil, Augustine argued that every substance as such is good. He offered two reasons for his position. First, positively speaking, "God is the supreme existence, [and] it follows that non-existence is contrary to Him." For "the contrary of existence is non-existence." But God is good and everything he creates is good. "Consequently as from Him is everything that by nature is good. Thus every nature is good, and everything good is from God."[5] More formally stated:

1. God is the Creator of all being.
2. Everything God creates is good like himself.
3. Hence, everything that exists is good.

This is precisely, Augustine reminds us, what the Book of Genesis declared: God viewed everything he had made, and "it was very good" (1:31).

Secondly, a negative argument supports the contention that every substance as such is good. This can be observed by the fact that when evil is removed from a substance, the nature remains in a purer state, but when all good is removed, nothing remains at all. So, "if after the evil is removed, the nature remains in a purer state, and does not remain at all when good is taken away, it must be good which makes the nature of the thing what it is, while the evil is not nature, but contrary to nature." So then, concluded Augustine, "no nature as far as it is a nature is evil; but to each nature there is no evil except to be diminished in respect of good."[6]

In order to dramatize his point, Augustine declared thorns and thistles to be metaphysically good, along with formless matter and even the flames of hell.[7] And to the Manichaean retort that anyone who believes all substances to be good should offer his hand to a scorpion, Augustine replied that poison is not evil; it is good, good in itself and good for the scorpion. "For if the

---

5. Augustine, *Against the Epistle of the Manichaens* 40.46 and *On the Morals of the Manichaeans* 1.1 Augustine's works are collected in English in *A Select Library of Nicene and Post-Nicene Fathers of the Christian Church*, ed. Philip Schaff (Grand Rapids: Eerdmans, 1956), vols. 1–8.

6. Augustine, *On the Nature of the Good* 17.

7. Ibid., 36, 17, 38.

poison were evil in itself, the scorpion itself would suffer the first and most."[8] Even the Manichaean kingdom of evil had in it things like power, memory, life, and intelligence—all of which are good. Augustine concluded, "All these things . . . cannot be called evil: for all such things, as far as they exist, must have their existence from the most high God, for as far as they exist they are good."[9]

2. *The supreme Good is incorruptible.* Not only is every nature as such good, but the supreme Good is incorruptibly good. "For the chief good is that than which there is nothing better, and for such a nature to be hurt is impossible."[10] The supreme Good is the standard of absolute perfection and the standard of all perfection cannot be less than perfect. God is simply perfect, and no simple nature can be destroyed. In order for something to be torn apart it must have parts; in order for it to be decomposable, it must be composed. Since God, the absolute Good, has no parts or composition, he cannot be corrupted in any way. That which is the very standard by which evil is measured cannot itself be evil.

3. *Only created goods are corruptible.* All creatures are corruptible. Anything of God (and there is only one—the Son of God) is incorruptible; all other things are merely from God and are corruptible. In Augustine's words, "For *from* Him are heaven and earth, because He made them; but not *of* Him because they are not of His substance." Hence, all creation is not ex deo (out of God) but ex nihilo (out of nothing).[11] And because created things are not of an incorruptible substance, they are corruptible. So, created being by its very nature contains within it the possibility (but not the necessity) of metaphysical evil. Creation makes evil possible; evil is made actual only by the creature, nor the Creator. For God has no evil and can do no evil.

4. *Evil is not a substance.* "For evil has no positive nature; but the loss of good has received the name 'evil.'" Evil "is not a substance; for if it were a substance, it would be good." Since evil lacks any nature of its own, it is not a substance but a privation of the substance of another. Evil is not a nature; "evil is that which is contrary to nature. . . ."[12] What is called evil, then, is not a sustance or nature of its own but a deficiency in some substance. Evil does not subsist in itself; it lives only in another.

5. *Evil is a corruption of substance.* "It must first be inquired," wrote Augustine, "what is evil, which is nothing else than corruption, either of the measure or the form, or the order, that belongs to nature." Elsewhere he said, "This is a general definition of evil; for corruption implies opposition to

8. Augustine, *Morals of the Manichaeans* 8.11.
9. Ibid., 9.14.
10. Ibid., 3.5 Cf. *Epistle of the Manichaeans* 35.40.
11. Augustine, *Nature of the Good* 27, 30, and *Epistle of the Manichaeans* 25.27.
12. Augustine, *City of God* 11.9; *Confessions* 7.12.18; *Morals of the Manichaeans* 2.2.

nature, and also hurt. But corruption exists not by itself, but in some substance which it corrupts; for corruption itself is not a substance." Evil is like rottenness and rust which do not exist in themselves but only in something else as the corruption of it. There is a sense, however, in which a nature is called evil (viz., when it becomes a corrupted nature). He commented, "Nature therefore which has become corrupted, is called evil, for assuredly when incorrupted it is good; but even when corrupt, so far as it is nature it is good, so far as it is corrupted it is evil."[13] A substance, then, that is privated is called an evil substance. However, despite the privation, what there is of the substance is good.

6. *Evil is not caused by God.* What is the cause in the privation of a substance; why are some created things evil? Augustine was sure of one thing: God, the absolute Good, is not the cause of metaphysical evil. "For how can He who is the cause of the being of things be at the same time the cause of their not being—that is, of their falling off from essence and tending to non-existence?" He frankly confessed that one cannot know an efficient cause of metaphysical evil, for a cause of nothing is nothing and "that which is nothing cannot be known." In short, there is no efficient cause of metaphysical evil. Being as such does not corrupt being. Hence, there is nothing in being as such to explain why beings corrupt. Created beings, insofar as they are beings, do not corrupt either their own beings or those of others. And it is certain that uncreated Being cannot corrupt being. "For as far as they are corruptible, God did not make them: for, corruption cannot come from Him who alone is incorruptible."[14] If no being, finite or infinite, is the efficient cause of the corruption of substances, then how does it come about?

7. *Freedom is the cause of evil.* The ultimate cause of metaphysical evil is moral; the cause of privation is pride. Without the freedom of the creature to exalt itself as the greater good, there is no explanation of the origin of evil. Augustine wrote, "Sin is indeed nowhere but in the will" and "justice holds guilty those sinning by evil will alone. . . ." In fact, sin is so much a voluntary evil that it is not sin at all unless it is voluntary. If one asks what is the cause of evil willing, Augustine replies, "What cause of willing can there be which is prior to willing. . . ? Either will is itself the first cause of sin, or the first cause [a free creature] is without sin."[15] In other words, if freedom is the cause of evil, then it is meaningless to ask what is the cause of freedom; freedom is the first cause of evil and one cannot ask what is the cause of the first cause. Free will is the reason why evil natures exists, and it is not meaningful to ask why of the reason why.

13. Ibid., 5.7; *Epistle of the Manichaeans* 35.39; *Nature of Good* 4.

14. Augustine, *Morals of the Manichaeans* 2.3; *On Free Will* 2.20.54; *Epistle of the Manichaeans* 38.44.

15. Augustine, *Two Souls: Against the Manichaeans* 10; *On Free Will* 1.1.1; 3.17.49.

It is meaningful, however, to ask how evil arose. Evil results when the free creature turns away from the infinite good of the Creator to the lesser goods of creatures. "For it is evil to use amiss that which is good." Freedom itself is a good thing (i.e., it is a perfection belonging to some finite beings), but evil results from a misdirection of this freedom. Evil "is not the striving after evil nature but the desertion of better [nature]." How evil begins in free creatures is illustrated by how it began in Satan: "If the mind, being immediately conscious of itself, takes pleasure in itself to the extent of perversely imitating God, wanting to enjoy its own power, the greater it wants to be the less it becomes. Pride is the beginning of all sin. . . ."[16] In brief, a nature is corrupted when by the abuse of the perfection of freedom it engages in the pride of self-deification (i.e., of considering its own finite good more ultimate than God's infinite good). Pride is the ultimate source of metaphysical privations.[17]

8. *Evil never completely corrupts a good.* God permits evil but never to the point of completely destroying a good. For "the goodness of God does not permit this end, but so orders all things that fall away that they may exist where their existence is most suitable. . . ." The saved are suited by their nature for heaven and the wicked by their nature for hell, but both kinds of beings have an ordered existence that is appropriate to them. So even though God did not originate evil, he does order it for his own good purpose. "In this way, though corruption is an evil, and though it comes not from the author of natures, but from their being made out of nothing, still, in God's government and control over all that He made, even corruption is so ordered that it hurts only the lowest natures, for the punishment of the condemned" but the righteous are enabled to "keep near to the incorruptible God, and remain incorrupt, which is our only good."[18]

But even when creatures misuse the good things God has made, they do not vanquish God's will to preserve the good. For "He knows how to order righteously even the unrighteous; so that if they . . . should misuse good things, He through the righteousness of His power may use their evil deeds, rightly ordaining to punishment those who have perversely ordained themselves to sins."[19] In spite of the tendency of evil willed by creatures to corrupt things, God is able to preserve both existence and order in his universe to produce an overall good.

16. Augustine, *Nature of the Good* 36.34; *On Free Will* 2.19.52; 3.25.76.
17. Augustine taught that Adam's evil choice passed on moral corruption to the whole race so that even infants are born guilty, having been implicated to guilt by Adam's evil will even before they express their own. See *Retractions* 1.9.4. The will of fallen man is affected by sin but it is enabled by God's grace to keep his commands. See *On Grace and Free Will*.
18. Augustine, *Epistle to the Manichaeans* 37.44.
19. Augustine, *Nature of the Good* 37.

9. *Evil is part of a total picture of good.* Because God does control and order evil, evil itself is part of a total picture of good in the universe. Failure to see this ultimate harmony in the universe with evil in it is like charging an artist for lack of harmony in his mosaic by concentrating on only one piece of it. One must step back and view the overall picture in order to get the proper perspective on evil. Even a cock fight, the act of prostitution, and "ugly" members of the body provide by contrast part of the total picture of good.[20] The divine Architect of the universe knows how to bring an ordered harmony out of a world of free but evil creatures. Artists cannot give a total picture without ordered contrasts, and the divine Artist is no exception.

Augustine's position on the metaphysical problem of evil may now be summarized: An absolutely good God created a finitely good universe containing good creatures who freely chose the lesser good of themselves to the higher good of God, thus corrupting creation. God nevertheless is able to use the evil of the parts for the greater good of the whole according to his own good purposes. A summary in Augustine's own words is given in this passage: "There is no way of solving the religious question of good and evil, unless whatever is, as far as it is, is from God; while as far as it falls away from being, it is not of God, and yet is ordered by Divine Providence in agreement with the whole system."[21]

Aquinas: Evil Is a Metaphysical Privation

The theistic answer to the problem of metaphysical evil that Augustine began was further elaborated by Aquinas. According to the latter, evil is a metaphysical privation with no formal cause and only an indirect efficient cause.

1. *Evil is a privation in a good.* Agreeing with Augustine, Thomas wrote, "Evil denotes the lack of good," not a mere absence. Because "not every absence of good is an evil." If mere absence were evil, then nonexistents would be evil. And if every absence were an evil, then a person would be evil for not having the strength of a lion. "But what is evil is *privation;* in this sense blindness means the privation of sight." In short, "a thing is called evil for lacking a perfection it ought to have; to lack sight is evil in man, but not in a stone."[22] This is so because sight is a perfection that is not constitutive of the nature of stones, but is of the nature of a human being.

20. Augustine, *On Order* 2.1.2; 3.8.49; 2.4.12.

21. Augustine, *Morals of the Manichaeans* 7.10.

22. Saint Thomas Aquinas, *Summa Theologica* 1.48.3; *Compendium of Theology* 114, in *St. Thomas Aquinas: Philosophical Texts*, ed. T. Gilby (London: Oxford University Press, 1951), p. 465.

Evil, then, is a privation in a nature, but "a privation is not a nature or real essence, it is a negation in a subject." Hence, "every evil is based on some good, for it is present in a subject which is good. . . . Evil cannot exist but in good; sheer evil is impossible."[23] Evil has no essence of its own; it is a privation of good belonging to another.

Not just any kind of evil, however, can exist in just any kind of good. For "not any kind of good is the subject of evil, but that alone which is potential to a perfection of which it can be deprived."[24] In other words, a being must naturally have the perfection before he can be privated of it. Stones cannot lose their sight; only sighted beings can lose sight.

2. *Evil has no essence of its own.* According to Aquinas, "there is no justification for holding that there are two kingdoms, one of good, the other of evil." The erroneous idea that there are two kingdoms arose by people mistakenly supposing that all contraries are based on first principles. But "there is not one first principle of evil as there is of good. (1) In the first place, the original principle of things is essential good. . . . (2) In the second place, the first principle of good things is supreme and perfect good containing all goodness in itself. . . . (3) In the third place, the very notion of evil is irreconcilable with the notion of a first principle, because evil is caused by good [incidentally]. . . ." In brief, "nothing can be essentially bad. Every being as being is good; evil does not exist except in a good subject." And "there cannot be a supreme evil, for though evil lessens good, it can never totally destroy good. . . ."[25]

3. *Nothing can be totally evil.* It follows that no essence can be completely corrupted. "Were all good entirely destroyed—and this would be required for evil to be complete—evil itself would vanish since its subject, namely good, would no longer be there." When a substance is completely corrupted, it is no longer a substance, because it is completely gone. For "while good remains, nothing can be an entire and unmitigated evil. For this reason . . . a wholly evil thing would be self-destructive."[26] And God, the Cause of all being, will not permit anything to go out of being contrary to his desires.

4. *Evil has no formal cause.* When evil is examined on the typology of Aristotle's four causes it becomes evident that evil has no formal cause and it has only an indirect efficient cause. The *material* cause (subject) of evil is good, since evil has no essence of its own but exists only in the subject of another (viz., in a good). And evil has no *formal* cause because it lacks any form; it is disorder, not order. Evil is a corruptor or privation of form.

---

23. Thomas Aquinas, *Summa contra Gentiles* 3.7 and 11 (Gilby, 467).
24. Aquinas, *Compendium of Theology* 117 (Gilby, 469).
25. Aquinas, *Summa Theologica* 1.49.3 (Gilby, 477).
26. Ibid.

Further, evil has no *final* cause (end or goal) "but is rather a privation of due order to end." But "evil has an *efficient* cause; this, however, is indirect, not direct." That is, since "only what is good can cause," then "evil is a by-product" of the action of good causality. "Hence, it is true to say that evil has naught but an incidental cause; in this sense good is the cause of evil." Evil is caused by good accidentally in several ways:[27] by a defect in the action of either the principal or instrumental cause, by the very energy of the agent producing the action, and/or by the intractibility of the matter receiving the action. For example, the proper objective of fire is to heat. If it burns that which it was intended merely to heat, it does so accidentally by the very energy of its causal power, not because destruction is its proper goal. And if the fire does not heat, it is either because it lacks sufficient energy or because the object of the heat is not suitable to receive heat.

5. *How God caused evil incidentally.* In view of these distinctions, Aquinas refines Augustine's view that God is not the efficient cause of evil. God "as it were indirectly causes the corruption of things," not because this is his proper end but because sometimes there is a defect in the instrumental cause God uses (a genetic deformity passed from parent to child), the very action of causal efficacy causes a defect (God destroys some things in the process of making others), or there is an incapacity or impotence in the object being caused (e.g., physical beings are limited by the very nature of their material composition).[28] Hence, in the very creative process even a perfect principal cause can be the incidental efficient cause of imperfections in creation by virtue of the action, instrumentality, and receptivity of its causal efficacy.

6. *Human nature is neither diminished nor destroyed by evil.* The corrupting influence of evil on a person does not touch his nature as such but only the ability of that nature to function properly. "The very principles, components, and resulting properties of human nature, such as the psychological abilities of the soul and so forth . . . are neither destroyed nor diminished by moral evil." For "sin cannot destroy man's rationality altogether, for then he would no longer be capable of sin."[29] That is, "the ability of the subject to act in the proper fashion" is not destroyed by evil. In the fall, the human did not lose his ability to act as a human, that is, as a rational being.

Furthermore, the diminution because of sin is "the slackening of qualities and forms," not the subtraction of them. For instance, "the more multiplied the acts, the readier the subject becomes to receive the perfection and form of activity. And, conversely, the more weakened the subject becomes by con-

27. Ibid., 1.49.2 (Gilby, 487). The illustrations are ours, not Aquinas's.
28. Ibid., 1.49.2.
29. Ibid., 1.45.1.

trary dispositions induced by repeated and strong contrary acts, the slacker grows the power for right activity. . . . But sin does not strike at the root, since it does not diminish nature itself; what it does is to block the ability from reaching its end; the disability consists in interposition of a barrier." For "the capital of human nature diminished by sin is the natural inclination to virtue instinctive in man as a rational being; to act aright is to act according to reason." Now "the inclination to virtue should be taken as a kind of intermediate between two extreme terms," one rooted in human nature and the other the process of activity toward reaching its end or goal. "Weakening may affect either side. But sin does not strike at the root, since it does not diminish nature itself." Furthermore, the ability of human nature to function as good cannot be destroyed even by an infinite interposition of the barriers of sin that infinitely lessen the ability to act virtuously, for beneath all these layers and rooted within human nature "the instinct for right action always remains radically intact."[30]

In summary, for Aquinas the nature of the human being as a rational and moral being is not directly diminished nor destroyed by evil. But the inclination to do good can be infinitely diminished (though not completely destroyed) by sin. In brief, a fallen human is metaphysically good and only morally weakened. A person can by the habitual practice of sin effectively block his own natural ability to do good (which can be overcome by God's grace), but the metaphysical nature being blocked is still essentially good. The inclination to good can be diminished even infinitely, but the nature of the human as good cannot be destroyed without destroying the human as human. Depravity does not destroy one's humanity. In fact, evil is not centered in human nature as such but in his will. Evil results from free choice, not from any created inclination of human nature to do evil.

Conclusions from the Augustinian-Thomistic Solution

Without entering into the dispute as to whether evil corrupts the actual nature of man or merely human ability to act according to his nature, it would seem that we can draw from these two great theistic thinkers seven points regarding the problem of metaphysical evil.

Metaphysically speaking, evil has no essence or being of its own; it is a privation of the essence or being of another. Evil has no form of its own (i.e., it has no formal cause).

---

30. Ibid., 1.45.2. Thomists who want to depart from Aquinas and speak more directly of the human nature being corrupted itself would certainly not deny the essential humanity of even the corrupt nature. See Winfried Corduan, *Handmaid to Theology: An Essay in Philosophical Prolegomena* (Grand Rapids: Baker, 1981), chap. 10.

God is not the direct efficient cause of evil. Metaphysical imperfection can occur only as a by-product of God's efficient causal activity.

Moral evil, which can and does affect the functioning of human nature (if not the nature itself), is rooted in human freedom. God willed the freedom (which is good) but creatures will the evil.

The nature of human beings cannot be totally corrupted or else they would no longer be human.

Human metaphysical nature is not diminished to the point that a person is no longer rationally and morally responsible for his actions.

The grace of God enables the person to overcome whatever propensities to evil he has so that he is able not to sin.

The fact of finitude makes evil possible but not necessary. Corruption is possible because the human being is a corruptible creature (only God is incorruptible), but evil is actual only because of human freedom. That is to say, all metaphysical evil is either a condition of, or result of, or in some way connected with, free will.

Unnecessary kinds of evil are a redundancy in a theistic universe. Whatever corruptions of substances there are must be either a necessity born out of the creative process or else a necessity for the conditions and functioning of human freedom. In essence then, theism's answer to the problem of metaphysical evil is intertwined with its answer to the problem of moral evil. Free creatures are ultimately responsible for the metaphysical corruption in the world (either directly or indirectly). The answer to metaphysical evil is found in moral evil.

In summation, the theistic solution to the problem of metaphysical evil answers how things (or, substances) can be evil (by way of privation), but it does not answer why they are corrupted. For even the total picture of contrast of good and evil in the present world is not as good as it apparently could be. Why, then, did God allow the possibility of evil to be actualized? The hope for the solution to this problem comes from the theist's answer to the moral problem of evil. In other words, the theistic answer to metaphysical evil raises another question, namely, the problem of moral evil. For, granted that God is perfect and that he can make a world with no metaphysical imperfections in it, the theist must look elsewhere for a solution as to why there are metaphysically imperfect things in the world.

In other words, metaphysical privations explain how evil exists without entailing dualism but do not ipso facto account for why a perfect God permits these imperfections to exist. Before attention is turned to the theist's moral answer to the apparent metaphysical imperfections in the world, there remains one more problem that is created by the answer to the metaphysical aspect of the problem of evil.

The Theistic Answer to Metaphysical Illusionism

The insistence on the fact that evil has no ontological status of its own, that it is a privation of being, opens up another problem for theism. If evil has no existence of its own, then how can theism defend the reality of evil? This problem can be treated much more briefly in view of the foregoing discussion. The answer is this: *Evil is not a real entity but it is a reality.* Evil is not a thing but it is a real lack in things. Affirming that evil is no thing does not mean that evil is nothing at all. To say that evil does not exist in itself (i.e., it is not a substance) is not to say that evil does not exist in anything else. Evil does exist in things, and its existence there is not illusory. For instance, blindness is a reality. It is a real lack to be blind; the blind lack the quality of sight. And the inability to see is a real privation. In like manner, it is real to be crippled, handicapped, or retarded. It is no doubt easier for those who do not have these deprivations to think that they are not real; those who are deprived know the reality of the privation. Metaphysical evil is as real as the metaphysical privations that exist, for evil is a corruption of what is or, better, of what ought to be.

Evil is not nothing; it is the lack of something that should be there. The difference between evil and nothing is like the difference between a zero and nothing at all. There is a real difference, for example, between having a zero after two fives (550) and having no zero there (55); the difference would be almost five hundred dollars if it were on one's paycheck. The zero, like evil, is not nothing at all. It is the capacity or potentiality for something. And in the case of evil, this nothing in itself is the privation of something that should be there. Metaphysical evil indicates something missing that ought to be there. And it is a reality to have something missing that ought to be there, as hundreds of illustrations from everyday life give ample testimony. True, metaphysical evil is no thing (it has no thinghood), but it is the real lack of something (i.e., some characteristic) that belongs to a thing.

The reality of evil is as great as the reality of darkness when one needs light. It is as real as the reality of sickness when one wants to be well and as the reality of death when one desires to live. None of these—darkness, sickness, death—is literally nothing. Darkness is not nothing; it is the absence of light. Likewise, sickness is the absence of health, and death is the absence of life which belongs to a being. All of these are real lacks. Similarly, evil is just as real, although it has no more being of its own than does darkness or sickness.

Total and complete evil would be nothing. But as long as some things exist imperfectly, evil is a reality, a real privation in existing things. And so long as this is the case in a theistic world, some explanation is called for to indicate why a perfect God would allow imperfect things to exist.

Contemporary Rejoinders

According to G. Stanley Kane, in contemporary critical discussions the notion of evil as privation is almost universally ignored or misunderstood.[31] Kane has documented that the critics who attempt to refute the privation theory do so by making elementary mistakes such as

1. confusing privation with illusion,
2. demanding that the theist must posit God as the efficient cause of the privation, or
3. asserting that the privation theory does not comfort the person who is suffering (it was not intended to).

But Kane believes that, even if rightly understood, the privation theory can be shown to be inadequate. Kane's argument can be summarized in the following way:

1. The theory of evil as privation has been advanced as a general theory to account for all evils.
2. Some evils are clearly not privations.
   a. Pain is a positive evil.
   b. Moral evil is a positive evil.
3. Therefore the privation theory does not fulfill its intended purpose.

Kane's argument pivots naturally around his two apparent counterexamples. He contrasts having a pain in one's hand with a paralysis in one's hand. The latter case would constitute a privation, that is, the absence of normal feelings in the hand. But if there is pain, there is not only the absence of normal feelings, but also the added positive evil of bad feelings; it hurts. Kane grants that some moral evils, such as sins of omission, can be plausibly construed as privations of what is right and proper. But in the case of sins of commission, we are not only confronting the absence of good; something evil, the evil act, has been added. In each case, the pain and the immoral act, evil is positive. Thus, since the privation theory is supposed to account for all evils, it is not adequate and is best abandoned.

Bill Anglin and Stewart Goetz have responded to Kane. To do so they have attempted to refute his counterexamples.[32] In short, they argue that pain should be understood as the absence of normal human psychic harmony. Moral evil can be construed as privation of the highest good or, following

31. G. Stanley Kane, "Evil and Privation," *International Journal for Philosophy of Religion* 11 (1980): 43–58.

32. Bill Anglin and Stewart Goetz, "Evil Is Privation," *International Journal for Philosophy of Religion* 13 (1982): 3–12.

M. B. Ahern, as the privation of rights.[33] As long as such constructions are possible, the privation theory cannot be seen as falsified by counterexample.

Our own response to Kane can be somewhat more categorical. We can begin with Kane's assertion that the privation theory is intended to account for all evils. This is true, but it is not intended to account for all dimensions of evil. Neither Augustine nor Aquinas derived this theory inductively as the best understanding of specific occurrences of evil, but in order to deal with the metaphysical question of God as the alleged cause of evil.

Anglin's and Goetz's construction of pain and moral evils as privations is sufficient to salvage the metaphysical dimensions of those problems. But of course Kane is doing us the service of pointing out that there are other dimensions. Moral evils such as sins of commission need to be explained also from the positive aspect of the misdirected will. And even though pain should be understood metaphysically as a privation, the experience of pain comes under the heading of physical evil. In neither case does the privation theory do more than it was intended to do, that is, to explain the problem of the nature of metaphysical evil. Moral evil and physical evil are treated in the next two chapters respectively.

If God is the cause of all that exists, the theist must explain how and why evil exists. Evil exists parasitically as a privation in other things. For evil never exists in itself but exists only in other things as the corruption of them. Just how evil is possible in finite things is explainable in two ways: since all finite things are composed, they are decomposable, and in the process of causality certain evils can occur as the result or by-product of free choice. Why the absolutely perfect God will allow metaphysical evil to actually happen is not accounted for on a metaphysical ground alone; one must look to freedom and the solution to the moral problem of evil for a solution to this problem. In short, privation successfully explains how evil could exist in a nondualistic universe (viz., as a real corruption in other things), but it does not thereby show why a theistically perfect God would permit such privated or imperfect beings to exist. The theistic answer to this must be found in the analysis of moral evil.

33. M. B. Ahern, "The Nature of Evil," Sophia 5 (1966): 40–42.

16 ✳

The Moral Problem of Evil

There are three kinds of evil: moral, metaphysical, and physical. Cruelty is an example of moral evil, blindness is an instance of metaphysical evil, and an earthquake is an example of physical evil. Some physical and metaphysical evils result from human freedom, but it seems obvious that some nonmoral evil is not the result of human free choice. Therefore, there is justification in treating the question of natural evils separately. By natural evil we mean, then, those evils that do not result directly from human choice. And by moral evil we mean those evils, whether spiritual or natural, that do result from human choice. In this chapter we will begin to develop a theodicy based on the notion that even though this is not the best of all possible worlds, this world represents God's way of bringing about the best of all possible worlds.

The Problem of Moral Evil and the Alternatives for Theism

Moral Evil: The Problem and Actual Alternatives

The basic shape of the problem of evil was stated by Pierre Bayle in the seventeenth century.[1]

1. Evil exists.
2. An omnipotent God could destroy evil.
3. A benevolent God would destroy evil.
4. Therefore, since evil is not destroyed, either
    a. God is omnipotent and hence malevolent in some way, or
    b. God is benevolent and hence impotent in some way, or
    c. God is both malevolent and impotent, or
    d. there is no God at all.

But alternatives a, b, or c are not in accord with the infinitely perfect and powerful God of theism. Hence, the conclusion d, "there is no God," would

---

1. *Selections from Bayle's Dictionary*, ed. E. Beller and Lee M. Beller, Jr. (Princeton: Princeton University Press, 1952), pp. 157–83.

333

follow. That is, if the only kind of God that can exist is an infinitely perfect one (according to theism), and an infinitely perfect God cannot exist (in view of the problem of evil), then it would follow that no God exists at all.

Or, if the theist wishes to retreat from his insistence that God must be absolutely powerful and perfect (and hence forsake his theism), then some kind of finite god is the most he can conclude in view of the problem of evil.

The theist objects to the third premise and replies thus: *God is destroying evil and will one day complete the process.* If true, this would qualify as an explanation for evil, but it would leave at least two problems for theism. Why did such a God permit evil to begin with? What is the evidence that evil will finally be destroyed? Before we examine the theistic answer to these questions, let us look at another way to put the problem of moral evil.

1. God is responsible for making everything in the world, including human free choice.
2. Human free choice brought about moral evil in the world.
3. Therefore, God is responsible for what brought about moral evil in the world.

A theist would not deny this conclusion, but he would deny that it is morally incriminating to God. God is responsible only for the possibility of evil resident in human free choice but not for the actuality of evil that results from free choice. The theist's reply could be stated this way:

1. God is morally culpable only for acts he actually performs.
2. God does not actually perform morally evil acts (humans who are free to choose do).
3. Therefore, God is not actually culpable when men perform morally evil acts.

It is unlikely that the antitheist will accept the truth of the first premise, on the grounds that there were better alternatives open to God. At this point, the burden on theism is to show that there were no better ways to produce a moral world (which is what we will attempt to show). Or, to phrase the antitheist's reply differently, he may charge that God is responsible for permitting evil, even though he does not produce it. And this would be morally reprehensible in an absolutely perfect and powerful God who both knew evil would result and yet does nothing to prevent it. The task of theism is to show that evil is permitted by God for morally good purposes.

In brief, no matter how the problem is phrased, the minimal burden on theism is to give the moral justification for why God created the possibility of evil, since he knew that it would be actualized by human free choice and why God is permitting evil to continue when he has the power to stop it. Without an adequate answer to these problems, theism has not met its challenge in the face of the moral problem of evil that exists in the world.

Moral Evil: The Bind of the Hypothetical Alternatives

PLANTINGA AND THE FREE WILL DEFENSE

Some of the most influential work recently done by a theist on the problem of evil comes from the pen of Alvin Plantinga.[2] He has replied to the problem extensively within the context of modal logic. Let us consider one of the several formulations of his argument. We shall avoid some of the detailed technical apparatus he utilizes, not because it is unimportant to the ultimate success of his argument, but because one can understand the flow of his logic without it.

Plantinga's strategy is to concentrate on the apparent inconsistency in these statements:

1. God is omnipotent, omniscient, and wholly good.

and

2. There is evil.

Plantinga believes the way to reconcile such an inconsistency is to find a third proposition that is consistent with 1 and entails 2. And we need to be clear about the truth status of this third proposition. The problem with an inconsistency is that there appears to be no way (in modal terms, no possible world) in which both propositions can be true. All that is necessary is to show that there is a possible world in which both statements can be true, and the inconsistency is resolved. Thus the reconciling proposition also need only to be possibly true in any one possible world. It does not have to be actually true.

Plantinga locates this reconciling proposition in a conjunction of two propositions:

3. Every essence suffers from transworld depravity.

and

4. God actualizes a world containing moral good.

Let us briefly look at these two propositions in reverse order. First of all, 4 is clearly consistent with 1. This is exactly the kind of thing we would expect such a Being to do. But in order for there to be moral good in the world, there

2. The following summary is derived from Alvin Plantinga, *The Nature of Necessity* (Oxford: Clarendon, 1974), pp. 164–95.

must be creatures who do moral good. And, unless those creatures are significantly free, it would not make sense to call their actions morally good.

But freedom has a price tag attached to it. If people are to act freely, then their free actions are not under God's control. One cannot say that someone chose freely if that choice was brought about either directly or indirectly by God. Consequently even God cannot do the impossible and prevent free creatures from choosing to do moral evil. God cannot contradict himself and make free creatures who do not choose freely.

Thus there is no logical reason why creatures might not eventually choose wrongly in each possible world. This is what Plantinga means by "transworld depravity": a creature is significantly free and chooses to act wrongly in every possible world. This possibility is expressed by statement 3. Conjoined to 4 it is still consistent with 1. But in that case, if the free creatures choose wrongly, there is evil, and statement 2 follows. Thus 3 and 4 conjointly are consistent with 1 and entail 2. The apparent inconsistency has been resolved.

Plantinga's formulation has engendered much discussion, both pro and con. For our present purposes, we can grant that there are no logical holes in his case. But one may still be dissatisfied with Plantinga's answer. For ultimately, believer and unbeliever alike will want to know not only if the statements are possibly true within modal logic, but if they are actually true metaphysically.

Plantinga is not concerned with that issue: he very carefully distances his defense from a theodicy. Thus he rightfully claims to have provided us with a successful defense. But, as Keith Yandell, following Nelson Pike, states, one of the first things someone wants to know is whether God did in fact create such significantly free creatures who exhibit transworld depravity.[3] And if so, why would God do such a thing? Thus we move on from a possibly successful defense to a theodicy.

THE QUESTION OF FREEDOM

Plantinga's defense pivots on the notion that human beings have significant freedom. This idea implies that the creature is not influenced in certain choices by God. As Plantinga puts it, "if I am free with respect to an action A, then God does not bring it about or cause it to be the case either that I take or that I refrain from this action."[4] Very simply, if God somehow directly or indirectly makes sure that my action comes out one way rather than another, I did not really act freely. The very concept of freedom seems to entail such a lack of constraint.

---

3. Keith Yandell, "The Problem of Evil" (paper delivered at the Wheaton Philosophy Conference, October 1980).

4. Plantinga, *The Nature of Necessity*, p. 171.

But Antony Flew, J. L. Mackie, and John S. Feinberg, among others, have argued that the notion of freedom does not necessarily entail indeterminacy. Flew and Mackie both take this point of view in order to show that the free will defense fails; God's having created free creatures does not imply that he could not prevent them from choosing wrongly.[5] Feinberg takes that same line in order to preserve his strong Calvinistic theological commitments.[6]

As we mentioned in an earlier chapter, Feinberg distinguishes between a compatibilist and incompatibilist view of freedom. He opts for the former, according to which an action may be said to be free even though it was taken under causal influences and was predictable.[7] For him, then, it is quite consistent to speak in terms of a person's action being free even though God directed him to take such an action, just so long as the person chose to act in such a way without experiencing constraint.

The notion of compatibilist freedom is not entirely implausible. The issue of freedom versus determinism is a long-standing one, and it may sometimes seem that the theist jumps to some quick conclusions on this matter when it comes to construing a theodicy. Perhaps human beings are not so free as that their actions are indeed causally indeterminate. Yet, if Feinberg is right the concept of human freedom is still not meaningless.

Nonetheless, for our present purposes, construing freedom along compatibilist lines does not contribute significantly to a theodicy. That this is so becomes apparent even in Feinberg's work, where the free will defense is replaced by a free desire defense and the causal origin of evil is simply postponed by one stage.[8]

The strong Calvinist holds that God significantly constrains certain human actions, particularly the choice to believe in him. To anyone who would argue that this constraint violates human freedom the compatibilist argument undoubtedly has a hollow ring. Such a freedom must be to him an ersatz that falls far short of the authentic thing. It may be best to simply negatively identify the strong Calvinistic position with the view that human beings do not have significant freedom in Plantinga's sense. Nothing else will sound convincing to the critic anyway.

But such a Calvinist does not (nor need he) deny that human beings have a will, the capability of making choices, or moral responsibility. These are

5. Antony Flew, "Divine Omnipotence and Human Freedom," in *New Essays in Philosophical Theology*, ed. Antony Flew and Alasdair MacIntyre (London: SCM, 1963); J. L. Mackie, "Evil and Omnipotence," in *The Philosophy of Religion*, ed. Basil Mitchell (Oxford: Oxford University Press, 1971), pp. 91–104.

6. John S. Feinberg, *Theologies and Evil* (Washington, D.C.: University Press of America, 1979).

7. Ibid., pp. 57–62.

8. Ibid., pp. 119–33.

notions that are often put into their mouths by their opponents, but not even hyper-Calvinists would say that humans are mere puppets.[9] For them, the ultimate theological authority is Scripture, which affirms a human will, human choices, and human moral responsibility. What they are not willing to do is to draw the rational inference from there to a free will, free choices, and responsibility based on significant freedom. So we can weaken the thesis of compatibilist freedom to speak of humans making significant, though non-free, choices.

These observations will make themselves felt in the subsequent discussion in the following way. The primary argument proceeds on the assumption that human beings are significantly free moral agents. However, most of the ensuing argument is combatible with strong Calvinistic belief, though occasional memoranda of divergence will be in order. In almost all cases where we speak of the free actions of human beings, it suffices for the argument to speak of the significant actions of human beings. A reader who is so inclined may make that mental switch.

This theodicy embraces both Calvinistic and non-Calvinistic views of human choice because its major premise does not depend on a particular view of free will. The major premise is based on the nature of God and the fact that God is carrying out his plan for the world that is the best of all possible ways of bringing about the best of all possible worlds. This premise can be true if God does so with creatures who are significantly free, but it is not excluded if his creatures are not significantly free.

THE STRUCTURE OF THIS THEODICY

What makes the problem of evil so acute is that theists admit by the very kind of God in which they believe that God could have chosen but did not choose to take three other alternatives. Traditional theism admits that God could have elected not to create a world of any kind. God was free not to create. Creation flows from God's will and not from any necessity of his nature. Further, theism acknowledges that God could have created an amoral world where there were no free creatures. Without freedom there would be no moral evil. Finally, we admitted that God could have produced a moral world of free creatures who simply would never choose to sin.[10]

This third alternative provides the most discomfort to theism and bears further examination. Some theists object to the possibility of a perfect world, contending that even if it is logically possible that no one will ever sin, it is

9. See Gordon H. Clark, *Religion, Reason and Revelation* (Nutley, N.J.: Craig, 1961), pp. 194–241.

10. Of course there is another alternative, namely, a world where some (or all) do good (i.e., be saved). However, since this possibility has the same character and will elicit the same response, they will be treated together.

virtually certain that sooner or later some creature will sin. How could God guarantee that free creatures would never sin without eliminating their free choice?

One answer is his supernatural prevention of their evil acts. An omnipotent God would have no problem in turning the murderer's knife into putty, the assassin's bullet into cotton, and the lyncher's noose into a noodle. Every time someone intended evil toward another, God could intercept the results of his act and prevent evil. But the theist could protest two things: first, that this would not really eliminate evil, for people would still be thinking and intending evil; secondly, that in preventing evil from happening in the world, God has also destroyed the possibility of improving the world. The second objection has merit and will be discussed later. The first objection is a possibility but it is not destructive of the view that God could make free creatures who will never sin.

Another possibility is that God could have created only those beings that he foreknew would not do evil. This seems possible because if creatures sometimes do not sin, there seems to be no reason why they could not always freely choose not to sin. But the theist might object that this is both contrary to what we know of human free choice and leaves no guarantee that someday someone might not decide to exercise his option to do evil. Without some factor or force to prevent evil will, surely evil choices will occur.

But there is another way for God to have kept creation from evil without destroying free choice, namely, by his infinite power to persuade humans not even to think evil by unveiling the infinitely appealing good of his own nature to them. Surely the beatific vision is an infallible method of persuasion, and an omnipotent God can assure its completely effective operation.

We would not claim that this is logically impossible but only that it would be morally unworthy of God to do so. It would be like eliciting the desired response from a child by bribing him with candy. In effect, luring people to God before they freely choose to come by irresistible persuasion is a violation of full human free choice. As C. S. Lewis aptly noted:

> the Irresistible and the Indisputable are the two weapons which the very nature of His scheme forbids Him to use. Merely to over-ride a human will (as His felt presence in any but the faintest and most mitigated degree would certainly do) would be for Him useless. He cannot ravish. He can only woo.[11]

One could always wonder what humans would have chosen to do on their own. It bespeaks more of divine dignity to allow free choice to do evil before one is permanently persuaded to do only the good. Hence, a world with evil is a morally necessary prerequisite to the most perfect world possible. A less perfect moral world is possible, but then it would not be the most perfect

---

11. C. S. Lewis, *Screwtape Letters* (New York: Macmillan, 1952), p. 46.

moral world that an infinitely perfect God could achieve. In brief, permitting evil is the best way to produce the best world.

Obviously we have reached a point where the strong Calvinist needs to argue slightly differently. Since he denies human beings implied significant freedom, but attributes to God irresistible persuasion, he cannot take the same approach. Nonetheless, he is not barred from asserting that by permitting evil God is taking the best way to produce the best world.

Cornelius Van Til has summarized this kind of Calvinistic position. "Man is responsible for sin, and he alone is responsible. . . . On the other hand, it was God's will that sin should come into the world. He wished to enhance his glory by means of its punishment and removal."[12] This statement needs elaboration. At the heart of this is the belief that the best possible world is one in which God's glory is maximized. But this goal for God needs to be understood properly. God is not an Oriental potentate who cruelly enslaves his subjects for the sake of his sadistic pleasure. Rather, a maximization of God's glory is also for the ultimate benefit of his creation.

From this Calvinistic point of view it may be said not only that God is bringing about the best world, but also that his very method (not merely the result) of bringing it about is significant. God is in the process of giving a demonstration of his sovereignty over the universe. To that end he allowed the rebellion that began with Satan and then enslaved all of humanity to proceed. God is demonstrating that he is superior to any form that this rebellion may take. He is allowing sin to unfold in all of its manifold varieties and dimensions. But regardless of how intense the opposition to him may be, God is able to show that he is still in control: he can still punish rebellion and, most importantly, his grace can contravene in unconditional love and forgiveness. When the demonstration is over, God not only has confronted all possible rebellion against him, and not only has displayed his sovereignty under all conditions, but also will have brought about the best of all possible worlds. Thus, for the strong Calvinist also, permitting evil is the best way to produce the best world, even though he may hold a diminished view of the nature of human free choice.

But in order to establish the thesis that this evil world is the best way to achieve the best world possible, the theist must show that no world at all, or at least no moral world, would not have been better than an immoral world and that a moral world where humans never sin would not have been better than one where people do sin.[13] In short, why did God choose what appears

12. Cornelius Van Til, *The Defense of the Faith* (Philadelphia: Presbyterian and Reformed, 1955), p. 160.

13. See J. L. Mackie, "Evil and Omnipotence," and Antony Flew, "Divine Omnipotence and Human Freedom," in *New Essays in Philosophical Theology*, ed. Antony Flew and Alasdair MacIntyre (London: SCM, 1963).

to be less than the best alternative (a moral world with evil) when he is allegedly the best possible Being?

Theistic Answers to the Problem of Moral Evil

How can theism establish that this is the best way to obtain the best world? How can all the evil brought about by human free choice be justified, to say nothing of the physical evil that is apparently not the result of human free choice?

In terms of the shape of the problem already given, the theist must support three premises to establish probability for this "best way" (to the best world) position. First, the view that this world is the best way to obtain the best world is possible (i.e., it is not an impossible or contradictory position). Next, no other possible alternative is more probable. Finally, there is sufficient reason to believe that the best possible world is achievable. Let us examine these in more detail.

The Possibility of a Theistic Answer to Evil

If it can be demonstrated that this present world is not the best of all possible ways to achieve the best of all possible moral worlds, then our answer to the problem of evil fails. Let us first acknowledge that we offer nothing like rationally inescapable arguments here. However, we have reason to believe that there is no impossibility involved in this view for the following reasons. First, there is no apparent contradiction in affirming that evil can be the condition for a greater good. We are not arguing that evil is the greater good (this would be contradictory); we are contending only that permitting evil can lead to a greater good.

Further, there is experiential precedent for this kind of solution. It is sometimes the case in our common experience that evils lead to good, and there is no apparent reason why it cannot be true of the universe as a whole. That is to say, there are certain things that we freely choose to permit as means to a greater good which, if they were chosen as ends in themselves, would be considered evil. For instance, the pain of getting a tooth pulled is a case in point. Pain for pain's sake would be an evil, but permitting pain for the sake of a healthier, happier life is not an evil. And this is precisely the point we wish to make about this evil world being the means to a better one. It is not a question of beating one's head on the wall because it feels so good when one stops. Rather, it is more like the strain and pain of training that is a necessary condition for achievement in any area of life.

No theist who believes there is a better possibility would will the evil of this present world as an end in itself. But if this evil can be suffered as the necessary condition to a greater good, there is no reason why one should rule out in advance the possibility of this being an answer to the problem of evil. In brief, the fact that there is no logical contradiction in our view that this evil world is the best way to the best world and the fact that we have experiential examples of evil means being the condition to good ends are sufficient to establish the possibility of this view.

Finally, there is apparently no way to disprove the possibility of the truth of this position. Indeed, as we saw earlier,[14] total disproofs of God from evil are self-defeating, for they assume an ultimate or divine perspective in order to prove there can be no such perspective.

Further, there is nothing logically contradictory about the statement "This evil world is a condition for achieving a better one." And any premise based on how the world was experienced in the past and is experienced in the present cannot logically eliminate the possibility that it may be different in the future. We conclude, therefore, that the position that this world is the best way to achieve the best world is at least a possible position, whatever probability or improbability it may turn out to have.

The Probability of a Theistic Answer to Evil

The probability of the theistic solution to evil, which we will call the "best way" to the best world view (in contrast to the "best world"[15] view) can be established in three ways:

By an inference from the nature of God as the best Being combined with the fact that this present world is not the best world, we can infer that this evil world must be the best way to produce the best world.

By comparing the alternatives available to the theistic God, it can be concluded that the morally best world is better than a morally good world or than no moral world at all.

By examining human history and experience, one can see the evidence of the probability of this best world to come.

The first two arguments are internal to theism. One is based on the actual alternative God chose and the second on the hypothetical alternatives open to him. The third argument is external to theism in that it indicates a way to verify our "best way" view from other than a direct inference from the nature of God.

---

14. See chapter 6 for a theistic defense against a contradiction in the antitheistic argument from evil.

15. Leibniz held the "best world" view. See Gottfried Wilhelm Leibniz, *Theodicy*, trans. E. M. Huggard (Indianapolis: Bobbs-Merrill, 1966).

THE ARGUMENT FROM THE NATURE OF GOD AND THIS WORLD

The basic logic in this first argument for our theodicy is this:

1. God is an absolutely perfect Being.
2. Producing less than the best possible world would be an evil for an absolutely perfect Being.
3. But an absolutely perfect Being cannot produce evil.
4. God produced this world.
5. But this world as is and as has been is not the best possible world.
6. Therefore, there must be a perfect world to come (of which this present world is a necessary prelude to its production).

Two comments are called for on this statement of the argument. Since we have already defended the truth of the five premises of this argument earlier (and even granted them to the nontheist in his argument against theism) there is no reason to withdraw them here.[16] The first premise is verifiable.[17] The agument is not a priori. The cosmological argument is an a posteriori argument from human experience. It is based in our experience of beings as contingent or dependent and proceeds to infer that there must ultimately be an independent Being upon which dependent beings are depending. Anything that would falsify the cosmological argument, therefore, would militate against the conclusion we have just drawn from it. What could that be? Several things would undermine the cosmological argument. If nothing existed (i.e., if everything went out of existence), there would of course be no one (and no need) to verify God's existence (God needs no verification of his own existence). If nothing contingent existed (i.e., if one no longer experienced his own contingency or that of anything else), then the cosmological argument could not get off the ground. That is, if only one being existed, namely, an eternally self-conscious necessary Being, then the cosmological argument would be invalid. One could also falsify the cosmological argument by showing that an infinite regress of existentially dependent causes of present existents is possible. In that case it would not be necessary to conclude a *first* Cause of all that exists. Finally, if it could be shown that being can be caused by nonbeing (i.e., that the principle of existential causality is not true), then the theistic argument could be refuted. But since we have here offered a means of refuting the argument and have given our argument that the theistic God has been verified, then there is no reason why this theistic conclusion cannot be used as a premise in an argument for the "best way" hypothesis on

16. See chapter 9.
17. On the need to show how one's beliefs can be verified or falsified, see "Theology and Falsification" in *New Essays in Philosophical Theology*, ed. Antony Flew and Alasdair MacIntyre (London: SCM, 1963), chap. 6.

evil.[18] In short, theism can be used to support theodicy. For if there are good reasons to believe that the best of all possible Beings exists, then it is reasonable to infer that he will take the best of all possible ways to achieve the best of all possible worlds he chooses to create.

THE ARGUMENT FROM THE ALTERNATIVES OPEN TO GOD

Another argument from within the theistic framework deals directly with the alternatives open to God. It was admitted that God has four possibilities with respect to creating a moral world (i.e., a world with free creatures in it):

God did not have to create any world at all; he was free not to create either a nonmoral or a moral world but to simply create nothing.

He did not have to create a moral world at all; he could have not created free creatures and hence prevented all the evil that free creatures have brought on themselves.

God could have created free beings who would never use their freedom to bring about any evil.

God could have (and evidently did) create free creatures who did exercise their freedom to do evil.

The problem for our theodicy is to show just cause for God's choice of the last option rather than the first three alternatives.

Before our argument is set forth, it should be pointed out again that it is not necessary to demonstrate that the third alternative is best but only that the other alternatives would not have been better. By "best way" we mean there was no better way for God to do it. This fulfills the requirement that the best Being did his best in that there was no better way available to him than the one he chose.

No world versus some world. Would no world have been better than some world, especially this world? Would nothing have been better than something?

There is a basic fallacy in this reasoning: it assumes nothing is better than something when there is no common standard by which nothing and something can be measured. Nonbeing and being have absolutely nothing in common.

In what sense could a nonworld be better than a world? It could not be metaphysically better, since nothing has no metaphysical status; it does not exist. So it is meaningless to speak of no world as metaphysically better than a world. If anything has the metaphysical advantage, it would certainly be something (even if it is imperfect) rather than absolutely nothing. For if it is meaningful to speak this way, then a cracked vase would be metaphysically better than no vase at all.

18. See chapter 9.

Be this as it may, there is another problem with the contention that no world is better than this one. In order for it to be effective as counteralternative to this moral world, it must hold that no world is morally better than this world. But clearly no world is not a moral world at all. Hence, there is no ground for the comparison. For the moral and nonmoral have nothing in common by which to compare them. Thus it is meaningless to contend that no world is morally better than this moral world.[19]

But why did not God create a nonmoral world of creatures who, because they had no free choice, would never do evil? Would not such a world be preferable to this world where free creatures have brought about such evil?

Here again there is no basis for the comparison. For there is no way to compare nonfree creatures and free creatures so that we may say one is morally better than the other. To be free is good and not to be free is not to have that good, but it is not thereby to be evil (stones are not evil because they have no free choice. In fact, stones do not lack free choice; free choice is simply absent in them.) Further, to be free to do evil (which is what a moral world entails) is good, and not to have this freedom is not thereby an evil.

But what about both being free to do evil and doing it? Is this not morally worse than not being free at all? No, the abuse of free choice is wrong, not because no free choice is evil but because free choice to do only the good is better than free choice to do both good and evil. But this is only another way of saying that a morally imperfect world cannot be declared worse in comparison to a nonmoral world but only in comparison to a morally better one. There is no way to affirm meaningfully that a nonmoral world would be better than a moral world (whether it be a good or bad one). The final and decisive battle against theism on moral grounds must be fought on moral grounds, that is, by comparing moral worlds where each has free creatures in it.

---

19. The statement of Jesus that "it would be better" if Judas had never been born does not support the view that no world would have been better than this one. First, we are not talking about a world where all are lost (like Judas) but one where many are saved (where the greater good is achieved). One might rightly question a world where all are lost compared to one in which some or all are saved. Happily, biblical theism knows no such world where all are lost. Second, the statement of Jesus about Judas was meant to be a moral comparison; it was not a comparison of the merits between nonbeing and bad existence. It was probably a hyperbole indicating the severity of Judas's sin. Elsewhere such statements are made to describe the severity of the sin that was in question. In one instance, Jesus simply called Judas's act a "greater sin" than other sinful acts (John 19:11). In parallel thoughts, Jesus used the same type of hyperbole to indicate severe judgment by using the phrases "it would be better . . . if" and "more tolerable . . . for" (Luke 17:2; 10:14). Thus, it is safe to say that this statement was not intended to imply that no world is better than the present world. No world is not better morally than the present world, since a nonworld has no moral status. See Norman L. Geisler, *The Roots of Evil* (Grand Rapids: Zondervan, 1978), p. 56.

A morally good world versus a morally better world.[20] The real rub for theism in establishing the probability of a "best way" theodicy is that it seems both logically possible and morally preferable to have a world where humans are free but do not sin as opposed to a world where humans are free but do sin. Why then, if there is a theistic God, does the latter kind of world exist if the former would have been better? This is a meaningful question because it is comparing like with like (viz., two moral worlds, one of which appears to be morally better than the other). But once the problem is stated in this form it immediately poses problems for the antitheist.

One problem concerns the standard of the comparison. How can one world be judged better than another world unless there is a moral basis beyond the world by which the worlds are compared? And if the antitheist grants an ultimate standard of Good beyond the world, then he is arguing in a vicious circle. For he is claiming that there is no ultimate Good (God), because he has posited something (evil) that is not ultimately good. If the antitheist retreats from his claim that he has found some evil that is really ultimately evil, then he cannot use it to disprove that there is an ultimately good God in the universe.

To state the dilemma in other terms, how can an antitheist use the nature of God as the standard of what is morally better in order to prove that there is no God? For once he grants that there is an ultimate standard for morality beyond the world, he has thereby granted what the theist calls God. And if the antitheist insists that this moral Basis beyond the world is not to be identified with God but with some eternal (Platonic) Good to which even God (if there is one) must be subject, then the theist may reply that the dispute is merely verbal. For the antitheist really believes as does the theist, that there is an eternal and ultimate moral law beyond this world.

But how can there be an ultimate moral law without an ultimate moral Lawgiver? How can there be ultimate prescriptions without an ultimate Prescriber? Indeed, such a morally perfect Source of all morality is exactly what the theist believes God is.

The antitheist may take another tack in view of his dilemma. He may simply wish to press the charge that theism is internally inconsistent (i.e., that this kind of evil world is incompatible with the theist's own conception of God as the morally best Being). The antitheist may insist that, judged on the theistically granted definition of God, this evil world is not as good as a moral

20. Some philosophers have questioned whether such an originally perfect world is possible. See Ninian Smart, "Omnipotence, Evil and Supermen," in *Philosophy of Religion* (New York: Random, 1970), pp. 485–93; Alvin Plantinga, "The Free Will Defense," *God and Other Minds: A Study of the Rational Justification of Belief in God*, Contemporary Philosophy series (Ithaca, N.Y.: Cornell University Press, 1967), chap. 6.

world where sin never happens. What could be better than a world where there is complete free choice without evil?

In outline, the basis for our contention that permitting an evil world is the best way to achieve the morally best world is twofold. First, a world with the greater number of moral virtues is morally better than one with a lesser number of them. And certain virtues like courage, fortitude, mercy, and forgiveness are attainable only in a world where sin occurs.

Secondly, a world with a higher attainment of moral virtues is better than one with lesser attainment of them. And experience shows that many virtues, such as love and kindness, are heightened by the presence of evil. Experience also shows that the appreciation of something is enhanced by the threat of reality of its loss. This being so, the highest degree of moral perfection is possible only if evil is permitted as a precondition for the achievement of this higher good. And theism is forced by its own commitment, as well as by antitheistic criticism, to acknowledge that the best possible Being must employ the best of all possible means to produce the best of all possible ends. We can summarize the argument this way:

1. God must produce the morally best world he can produce (i.e., if he is going to produce a moral world at all).
2. A world where evil serves as a condition for the attainment of higher virtues is better than one where less than the highest virtues are achieved.
3. This world is a world wherein evil serves as a condition of the attainment of the highest virtues possible.
4. Therefore, this world is better than a world where evil never occurred.

The proviso of the argument, of course, is that the best possible world will be achieved by this present evil world. More will be said in a moment about the achievability of the perfect world.

A nonevil world versus an evil world. There are two levels of response to the hypothetical possibility that God could have created a world of free creatures who simply would never choose to sin. First, it is possible that no such world would ever have actually occurred. And, second, even if such a world would have actually materialized, nevertheless it would not be morally better than this one.

First of all, not everything that is logically possible actually happens. My nonexistence is logically possible, but is not actually the case, since I do exist. It is logically possible that the United States could have lost the Revolutionary War since other armies have lost against lesser odds. But they won, and it is futile to speculate what might have been or would have been if they had lost. Likewise it is logically possible that no one would ever sin, but the fact is that men have actually sinned. In short, we contend that in a world of free choice a state where no one ever sins is logically possible, but it is in the nature of free choice that God could not secure such a state. Nothing he could build into a free world would make sinlessness inevitable, as long as someone chooses to sin.

That is, it may not be possible, without tampering with human freedom, to produce a free world where men never choose to sin. If a man decides to sit on the back porch but is chased by hornets to the front porch, did he freely choose to go? Not really. He was coerced by physical threat contrary to his real choice. He acted under duress. And in this sense, it would be less than perfectly loving for God to coerce someone against his real choice. Love is persuasive but not coercive. Forced love is not really love at all.

It may be that God could create a world where all men would always choose the good by programming them (like behavior conditioning) so they would never want to do evil. But it must be noted that such programing would go "beyond freedom and dignity." This itself would be a violation of the free choice of men and cannot be in a moral world. Freedom is an absolute essential to a truly moral universe. Love cannot be programed. Love is personal and subjective, and no amount of programing can automatically and inevitably produce a loving response. Some divorces will occur no matter how loving and desirous of reconciliation one partner is.

Second, a world where evil never occurred is morally inferior because it would never provide occasion for achievement of the highest virtues or the highest degree of other goods. The highest goods are dependent on the preconditioning of evils. Where there is no tribulation, patience cannot be produced. Courage is possible only where fear of evil is a reality. If God created a world where evil never occurred, he could not produce the greatest good.[21]

Now let us summarize the overall argument.

1. God would not produce a world where free beings will always do evil if it were possible to produce one where they will nevermore do evil.
2. This is a world where free beings do evil.
3. Therefore, this world is not God's final production (there will be a better one where free beings will nevermore do evil).

Since the truth of the premises has already been discussed and they are an obvious part of the theistic argument by now, we proceed to combine the two arguments to support the "best way" thesis as follows:

1. It is morally better for God to create the morally best world possible (to do less than his best is evil for God).
2. A world with higher moral virtues is a morally better world.

21. Geisler, *Roots of Evil*, pp. 57, 58.

3. A world where humans are permitted to sin as a precondition to a better world is better than one where they are not.
4. This present world is one where humans are free and do sin.
5. Therefore, this present world is better than a world where humans never sin.

Perhaps the ambiguity that misleads antitheists can be cleared up by this distinction: the free world where humans never sin would be the best world possible, but it cannot be the first world. For unless an imperfect world is permitted (as the condition for achieving the freedom without evil), the perfect world cannot become a reality. There is no way to get to the promised land except by going through the wilderness. The antitheist is right about the final goal, a world where humans are free but will not sin. But he is wrong about the possibility of creating such a world fully achieved and perfected from the beginning. Even an all-powerful God cannot do the impossible, and it is impossible for him to create directly consequences that demand conditions without first permitting the conditions.

1. God cannot do what is impossible.[22]
2. It is impossible to create conditional virtues directly.
3. A world with the highest moral virtues is conditioned on the presence of evil.
4. Therefore, God cannot create directly (without allowing the presence of evil) a world with the highest moral virtues in it.

Since the second premise is the one to which an antitheist is most likely to object, it calls for justification. Is it really impossible for God to create directly a morally finished or perfected world? Why could he not have done so? According to biblical theism, God created Adam fully adult. The first trees in the Garden of Eden could have been created "fully grown." There is no reason why the Grand Canyon could not have been created with all the strata in it. All of these things imply process in the ordinary sense but none of them actually demand a process; an omnipotent God could have created them without a process. If so, why did he not create the world from the beginning with its full moral perfection? Why did not God produce the best from the very first without any evil process leading up to it? Surely it would have been better.

We lay aside the argument that even some physical things cannot be produced by God without a process, and rest our case on the argument that at least optimally free beings cannot be morally perfected without the presence

22. Elton Trueblood has some helpful suggestions on what is impossible to God with regard to evil. See his *Philosophy of Religion* (New York: Harper and Row, 1957), chap. 17.

of evil. First, Adam was not created with morally achieved perfection; only testing could do that.

Second, even Christ the perfect man was said to have been made "perfect through suffering" (Heb. 2:10). That is, the perfection he had became even more perfect through suffering in an evil world. The cross itself, the highest expression of love (John 15:13; Rom. 5:8), would not have been possible without the presence of evil. Christ prayed, "My Father, *if it be possible*, let this cup pass from me"; but, knowing it was not possible, he added, "Nevertheless, not as I will, but as thou wilt" (Matt. 26:39). Surely, if it had been possible to avoid the horrible agony of the cross, then an all-loving and all-powerful God would have spared his son from it; but he did not. Biblical theists can only assume that no other way was possible.

Third, human experience shows that some ends cannot be attained except through certain means. There is no way to become a great pianist without long and hard practice, or a great athlete without strenuous training, and so on. One cannot learn patience except through tribulation. Even God cannot create patience directly in a free life, because patience and the other higher perfections are learned. God can only teach; the person must do the learning. And learning is a process for humans. The human is a being in process (i.e., a spatiotemporal being), and the only way beings in process learn anything is by the process of learning. And without the presence of evil, the greatest lessons in life will never be learned. Jesus was said to have "learned obedience through what he suffered" (Heb. 5:8) and thereby was "made perfect" (Heb. 5:9). As we shall see later, obedience to God is the ultimate lesson to learn. And the very best way to learn it is by testing from God. For if God never permitted actual suffering, how would a human ever learn from experience (and experience is the best way men learn) that obedience is better than disobedience?

Finally, only brief mention needs to be made here that even logically some things cannot be learned apart from certain antecedent conditions. Courage cannot be learned apart from danger; resistance to temptation makes sense only in the presence of the possibility to sin. This leads to our last point.

The best and only truly effective way to teach any lesson to free beings (i.e., to their wills as opposed to their minds) is to persuade by the good, not merely to instruct by the right. If any lesson emerges from human experience it is that morally right conduct does not follow automatically from simply making laws and informing free persons what is right and what is wrong. The law does not automatically elicit obedience. The only way to get free persons to do the right is to persuade them by the good. If a human being sees that it is good (i.e., what is best) for him, then his will is moved to do it. Simply preaching right and wrong to him falls on deaf ears (even Adam in the state of innocence had the same problem) unless his will is moved by the good in it. If this is so, why did not God reveal the infinite good of his nature (i.e., give men the beatific vision) from the very beginning? In this way their will, being persuaded by an infinite good, would never have turned to evil and we would have our perfect world in which sin never arose.

It is because a beatific vision from eternity would not have gained the highest moral perfection of the universe and hence would have been less worthy of God and less worthwhile to humanity. Such a divine infusion of absolute good would short-circuit the very process by which a person learns everything, namely, by the process of experience. And learned perfections are more valuable to free creatures than those that are not learned, just as hard-earned money has more value than money inherited without effort. Of course this does not apply to God. For he does not need to learn anything as God; he already knows all that anyone else can ever learn. The learning process, then, can only be more valuable to free creatures. And that is precisely the point we are trying to make. But a perfect God would by his perfections be obligated to do what is better for his free creatures. For it is the free creatures that he wants to learn the most they can from their experiences in an evil world. God needs to learn nothing about good by contrast with evil, since he is absolutely good. But creatures are only finitely good, and the only way a finite free being can gain the maximum freedom out of his condition is to have it tested under less than ideal circumstances. God is free to do only the good, since he has nothing to learn from evil. But a finite person, on the other hand, has much to learn from evil. The presence of evil is in fact a necessary condition for the maximization of moral perfection for free creatures. If people were shown "the sweet by and by" before they lived in the wretched here and now, they would possibly be persuaded not to do evil but they would never have learned for themselves why doing evil is wrong. And it is a greater good for free creatures that they learn for themselves. An initial infusion of absolute good into everyone's life would mean that God would have forced free choices in a certain way. And it is not morally best to so determine how free creatures will use their freedom. It would be like a teacher telling his students how wise he is, rather than teaching them what he knows and letting them decide for themselves even in the strong Calvinistic understanding, not much is different. Here too, God is teaching his creatures the moral implications of their significant choices. Thus, the same logic applies to both views.

Finally, there is reason to believe that an initial infusion of absolute good into the lives of people would not only be morally less worthy of God (as just argued), but that it would actually be contrary to full finite freedom.[23] For an infinite persuasion is irresistible and what is irresistible allows no room for free choice; it is in fact a coercion of freedom. For instance, if I choose to sit on

---

23. For our discussion of freedom see the end of chapter 17.

my patio on a beautiful summer day and am "persuaded" to leave by some hornets, I am not really free to stay. Only the original choice to sit there was truly free, not the coerced choice to leave. And an infinite good is even more persuasive than hornets. A world of good and evil is a necessary condition for determining who really desires to choose the good and who chooses the evil. A world that finalizes these choices may follow, but it would be a violation of free choice to persuade humans' wills by infinite goodness to do what they would not have done were they really free to do otherwise.

If an infinite good is irresistibly persuasive in its power so that humans would not truly be free were God to expose them to it, then does it not follow that the saints will no longer be free in heaven? Heaven becomes a place of bondage and the loss of true freedom. On the contrary, true freedom is the freedom to do the good, not the free choice to do evil. And this is the lesson persons of good will learn while on earth. In heaven freedom will be emancipated from the bondage of doing evil. Evil is privation or lack, and it is better not to have a moral lack. And even though it is true that in heaven humans are no longer free to sin (a freedom that was highly valued here on earth), nonetheless humans were once free to do so, whereas persons with a beatific vision from the beginning would never have been free to do evil.

Furthermore, the inability to do evil in heaven (i.e., the loss of free choice) is only a permanentizing of what one, by his free choice here on earth, really desired to be achieved. That is, the beatific vision is, by God's irresistibly persuasive power, not a frustration but a fulfillment of what the godly have really chosen. And it is of no small significance to note, too, that without this permanentizing of choices made here on earth there would be no way to guarantee the destruction of sin. That is, the only way to produce a permanently perfect world is by permanentizing the choices made here on earth so that it is no longer possible to change them for the worse. (Whether it will be possible to change them for the better will be discussed subsequently.) People will choose to do only the good because they will to do so. And they will not choose evil, because they no longer have any desire to do so, being perfectly satisfied with an infinite good.

What we are suggesting is not necessarily incompatible with what strong Calvinists mean by "irresistible grace." The Calvinist does not believe that God coerces anyone into his fold apart from the response of faith or apart from a person's will. Rather the Calvinist believes that God works through the human being's faith and repentance.

In order to understand better how the present considerations apply to a Calvinistic framework, we can remind ourselves of the analogy of a parent and his child, which is a frequent picture in the Bible. As a parent teaches a child certain concepts and behaviors, he may put the child into certain planned circumstances where the child will show certain predictable reactions. For example, the parent who wishes to teach his children obedience will not remove all temptations for disobedience from the child's environment—knowing full well that a cookie may be snatched or a vase may be broken. But through the experience of success and failure (obedience and disobedience) the child learns to love and obey the parent with his full will. The point is to teach the human being the moral implications of his moral choices. And in this life, that lesson can be learned either in the context of a significantly free choice or in the context of a merely significant (though not actually free) choice. Still, the choice is made and, almost all versions of theism would agree, is permanentized in heaven.

In summation, it is impossible for God to create directly a world with achieved moral values of the highest nature. He must first allow evil as a precondition of the greatest good. Hence, this world with freedom and evil is the best way to produce the morally best possible world. So far we have offered two arguments for the probability of our "best way" hypothesis, one from the inference that God as the best Being must do what is best; another from the fact that an evil world is a better way of achieving the best world than a world where evil was never permitted. We now turn to our third and final means of verification for this theodicy.

ESCHATOLOGICAL VERIFICATION OF THIS THEODICY

If sometime in the future a perfect world is achieved, our theodicy will have been finally verified. But what if such a world never comes? Will theism have been falsified? No, theism will not have been falsified; at most, only this theistic solution to the problem of evil will be unsuccessful.[24] Theism could still be true and/or another solution to the problem of evil could be the right one.

Further, as John H. Hick showed, there is not a symmetrical relation between verification and falsification. Some things can be verified but not falsified. Hick uses immortality as an example.[25] If people can witness their own funerals and continue consciously in life, their immortality will have been verified. But if no one survives death, there is no one to falsify the hypothesis that humans are immortal. In a similar but somewhat different way, we argue that if the perfect world comes, our thesis will be confirmed. But if at any given time the perfect world has not come, the thesis has not thereby been falsified, for the perfect world may yet come. There is no specified time limit as to when the eschaton will appear. Whenever it comes, there

---

24. Two other possible directions for theism are that this present world is the very best that God can do with fully free beings, and that God is not obligated to produce the best world possible but only a good one. Plantinga defends the former alternative and Aquinas the latter.

25. See John H. Hick, "Theology and Verification," in *The Existence of God*, ed. John H. Hick (New York: Macmillan, 1964), pp. 253–74.

is still an eternity of bliss ahead, which will make the sufferings of time minute by comparison and eminently worthwhile.

The skeptic may wish to level the same criticism against our thesis that is leveled against Hick's eschatological verification: something that can be confirmed only in the future is of no assistance in deciding the truth now. And both theist and nontheist want to know the truth now. It makes a good deal of difference in the way they think and act in this life as to what will be the truth about the supposed next life. At best, eschatological verification saves the theistic position from meaninglessness, but it does nothing to establish any probability of its truth (at least not for the all-important present when truth questions must be decided upon, according to theism).

For two reasons this is a valid criticism of Hick's use of eschatological verification but not of ours. First of all, this is offered by Hick (at least in "Theology and Verification") as the only way to verify theism. We have already established by an independent argument (based on human present experience as contingent, dependent beings) verification for the existence of the theistic God. We do not have all our theistic eggs in the eschatological basket. Eschatology will confirm our case for theism but it is not the only support for it. The cosmological argument is the basic evidence that there is an absolutely perfect Being who operates with absolute perfection. Furthermore, unlike Hick, we do offer verifiable indications from both the present and the past that the final, perfect end will be achieved. It is to this evidence which we now turn.

There are two kinds of presently obtainable evidence for the probability of our thesis that this evil world is the best way to achieve the perfect world: human experience and divine intervention. First, as was indicated earlier, human experience is witness to the fact that free beings achieve higher moral perfection through suffering than without it. Second, divine intervention is an evidence that something has been done to reverse the course of world events for the better.

Let us examine the first line of evidence. Certain virtues are unachievable without the presence of evils. Fortitude cannot be achieved without suffering; courage is not possible without danger, and patience cannot be perfected without tribulation. Other virtues cannot be realized in their highest degree without the precondition of evil. One gains a greater appreciation for food after he has hungered and for water after he has been thirsty. Similarly, the highest appreciation for health is realized only after experiencing illness. And the indications of human experience are that this is in fact what happens to individuals. Evil is the occasion of greater good. The presence of social injustices does activate humans' social consciousness. The cry of the needy does touch the hearts of the philanthropic, and the fact of cancer does occasion determined research to cure it.

But even if one grants that there is progress in the lives of individuals toward a higher moral perfection, is there any reason to believe that the world as a whole is progressing toward this perfection? Is humankind learning the proper use of freedom by the abuse of freedom? It seems safe to say that in the history of humankind virtually every lesson from the experiences of persons with evil will has been learned by some individual somewhere at some time. The problem is that the race as a whole has not been able to profit from these experiences. The lessons have been learned by some individuals in the race but they are not remembered by the race as a whole. And even if they were remembered, some people would still not be motivated to apply them. Perhaps if these lessons were stored in some giant computer as a total fund of human experience that could be appealed to by supreme authority as decisive for all human activity, then the race could profit by what its individuals have collectively learned. History shows that humans are fruitlessly learning the same lessons over and over again. If there were a memory bank available to the united authorities of people which could be appealed to as decisive experience for what is good for free creatures, then there would be grounds in human experience for demonstration to all other free creatures who had not these experiences. It would be a wasted effort if every person had to learn every lesson of evil for himself.

But there is no such giant computer memory bank available to store these lessons and no united authority to apply them to the race. Or is there? The theist says there is. The omniscience of God has stored every lesson learned by every individual; the omnipotence of God can apply it to the whole race, and the love of God can provide the motivation for people to want to learn the lesson of freedom.

So the infinite power and perfection of God, which was the theist's initial liability, turns out to be his only hope of explaining how the human race will ever learn from its mistakes (i.e., learn how evil never pays). The infinity of God lends probability to the thesis that the world is profiting by its abuse of freedom. It is profiting from it because God is storing the lessons for men. All the lessons of why free choice with evil is better than free choice without evil are being preserved by God and will ultimately be applied by him to the whole race in order to convince it of the wrongness of evil. Then, when the infinitely persuasive good of God's nature is revealed, it will not violate but perfect the freedom to do good that free choice to do evil has shown is the only proper good for free creatures.

The biblical theist has a further evidence for the probability of his thesis, namely, the supernatural intervention of God in world events.[26] The om-

---

26. See Bernard Ramm, *Protestant Christian Evidences* (Chicago: Moody, 1953); C. S. Lewis, *Miracles* (New York: Macmillan, 1947).

nipotence of God makes miracles possible; the omnibenevolence of God makes them probable in view of our evil condition; but only human history shows that they are actual. But according to biblical theism, God has manifested himself in human history (the incarnation of Christ). Furthermore, he did do something to defeat evil (the atonement of Christ) and he did provide assurance—historically verifiable assurance—that this is true (the resurrection of Christ).[27] It is not our purpose to develop these arguments here; others have done so adequately enough to indicate a probability in favor of the fact that God has moved in the time-space world against evil. Furthermore, there is evidence in the history of the believing community that evil is being overcome in the lives of all those who avail themselves of this overcoming power.

And the assurance to the biblical theist that the final perfect end will come is the prophecy of Scripture. The Bible was correct in its supernatural prediction that Christ would come and defeat sin (his first advent). This fact lends probability to its predictions that Christ will come again (his second advent) and destroy evil. It is not our task here to prove this is true nor to persuade all skeptics that it is so but merely to indicate the probability that rational persons have seen in this kind of verification. The evidence is available for others who want to know both from history and from Christian experience.

The Attainability of a Theistic Answer to Evil

So far we have argued for the possibility of a theistic solution to moral evil on the grounds that there is no apparent contradiction in affirming that this world with evil in it is the best of all possible ways to achieve the best possible world, there is confirmation in human experience that the presence of evil is the occasion for achieving greater moral virtues, and there appears to be no way to disprove our thesis in the strict sense without engaging in a purely a priori type of argument. We then defended the probability of our solution that an evil world is the best way to achieve a perfect world in three ways. The nature of God as absolutely perfect demands that whatever he undertakes is done perfectly. Of the alternatives open to God this present world is the best kind of world to achieve the maximum moral perfection demanded by his nature. The final verification of our "best way" will be in the future when a perfect world is achieved. Now we turn briefly to the third and final aspect of our case for a "best way" theodicy—its attainability.

Is it really possible to bring good out of evil? In view of the persistence and power of evil down through the centuries, is it possible that evil will ever

27. See Frank Morrison, *Who Moved the Stone?* (London: Faber and Faber, 1958).

really be vanquished completely? Even granting that some good can be achieved out of some evil, how can the greatest good be derived from the great evil that has occurred in the history of free moral beings? It seems logistically implausible that every specific act of evil counts for some specific good. Surely much unnecessary and wasteful evil has occurred in the process of achieving this supposed greater good. And further, no explanation is provided via the "best world" hypothesis to anything but moral evil; what about all the evil that does not result from the abuse of human freedom, such as sickness, death, and natural disasters?

There are really three separate questions here. How is it logistically possible to achieve the maximum moral good out of the abuse of moral freedom such as our world has experienced? How can we account for the moral evil that never brought about any greater good? What explanation is offered for the many evils not resulting from the abuse of freedom such as natural disasters? The third question is the subject of the next chapter. The first two will be dealt with here.

1. *Maximum moral perfection can be achieved.* How God can bring good out of evil is not a serious problem for theism. An omnipotent God can do anything that is not impossible. And the possibility of this solution has already been defended. An all-powerful Being can accomplish anything necessary and an all-loving Being will accomplish it. As a matter of fact, the theistic God is the only kind of God who could possibly solve the problem of evil. As William James put it, "The world is all the richer for having a devil in it, so long as we keep our foot upon his neck."[28] But the only assurance that we really have our foot on his neck is the infinitely powerful God of theism. Hence, the infinite perfection and power of God, which at first appeared to be the theist's greatest liability, turns out in the end to be the only hope for a solution to the problem of evil. Only an all-powerful Being can guarantee the defeat of evil without destroying freedom. Only an omniscient Being can utilize the various strains of good and evil into the long-range plan for the greatest good. And only an all-loving God would permit creatures the freedom to reject even him.

Our argument can be stated briefly as follows:

1. It is logically possible for evil to turn out for a greater good.
2. An all-powerful God has the ability to bring the greatest good out of evil.
3. An all-loving God has the desire to bring the greatest good out of evil.
4. An all-knowing God has the wisdom to bring the greatest good out of evil.

28. William James, *The Varieties of Religious Experience* (New York: Mentor, New American Library, 1958), p. 55.

5. Therefore, the greatest good will be brought out of evil.

Since the antitheist has already granted theism the truth of premises 2, 3, and 4, his only hope lies in showing that it is impossible to use evil as a means of achieving a greater good. And, as we have just seen, there seems to be no way of doing this. Evil does sometimes produce a greater good and there is no reason why it could not always produce a greater good, especially if there is an all-perfect, all-powerful God to guarantee that it will.

2. *All moral evil is a necessary condition to achieving a greater good.* Many antitheists will accept the fact that some evils lead to greater goods, but the problem for them is explaining the seemingly exorbitant waste of human lives in the pursuit of this supposed greater good. Surely the same goal could be achieved without this much suffering. Why does God allow unnecessary moral evil? Certainly he could intervene miraculously and stop just the unnecessary evil without jamming up the mechanism that is working to accomplish this greater good.

Here again the theist's answer to the economy of God's use of evil in the plan to achieve the greatest good is that only a theistic God can guarantee to humanity that unnecessary evil will not occur. For only an omniscient God can devise a plan to maximize good and minimize the evil necessary to this greater good. And only an omnibenevolent God can assure us that this world is the best plan to achieve the most good. And only an omnipotent God can make the outcome certain. In brief, *only* the theistic God can provide an answer that is both actually adequate for achieving the greatest good and is also existentially adequate for those who believe that there is an answer to evil. Theism holds out the only sure hope to solve the problem of moral evil. The achievability of the answer is guaranteed by the infinity of God.

The theist need not defend all the specifics of the history of evil as they have unfolded in the universe as the exact acts and the exact amounts of evil necessary to achieve the greatest moral good possible.

Many theists do believe that each single evil is somehow part of God's plan. But such a belief is not needed in this context. All that is necessary to an adequate theodicy is this:

1. That this kind of world be permitted where free humans actually do evil.
2. That all evil be given a full opportunity of occurring, whether it ever occurs or not. This will give full assurance that God has not violated the creature's free choice.
3. That some evil actually occur—at least enough to provide the occasion for the achievement of the greater moral virtues not possible without evil.

4. That the total amount of evil that does occur be no more than is necessary to the achievement of the overall plan to obtain the greatest good possible.

Now 1, 2, and 3 are the case with the world we have, and 4 could be known only by an infinite mind. Although the human mind still cannot show how all specific evils contribute to the greater good, it is unnecessary to defend the specific amounts of evil that specific people suffer (sometimes seemingly unnecessarily large amounts) because they can be justified as part of a total amount of evil that is justifiably allowed. We can argue from the whole to the part: Since we accept the whole as necessary, we must believe that all of the particular parts must somehow be necessary (or there would be no totality).

Not everyone in the universe has to commit every sin to learn from it. God is recording all the lessons of sin that any free creature has ever learned. And God will make this fund of human experience available to people throughout eternity as a human witness that evil is always wrong. This fund of proven experience with evil will be humanity's own testimony to humanity that true freedom is only the freedom to do good, and that free choice to do evil is really destruction of true freedom. The choices of good and their consequences will be a testimony to the truth of what is good of this truth, and the choices of evil and their consequences will be a witness to what is evil.[29]

But how can theists justify the fact that much evil never does in fact bring this alleged greater good either in this life or the supposed life to come? Suffering makes some people better but it makes others bitter. Fear occasions courage in some but cowardice in others. Tribulation produces patience in some but frustration in others. And what is even more severe from the point of view of biblical theism is that the world to come does not turn out to be a universally perfect world. There are Saint Pauls, to be sure, but there are also Judases. And did not Jesus say it would have been better for Judas if he had never been born?

There are several important things to recognize about a world capable of optimal moral perfection. First, this implies a world of optimal moral freedom, for only a free world is a moral world and only a world of greatest moral freedom is a world of greatest moral perfectibility. Second, only a moral world where evil actually occurs is one where the greatest moral good is achievable. For the highest moral perfection is dependent on the presence of evil obstacles. With this in mind, we can see why the best possible moral world must have both a permanent heaven (where evil will nevermore be done) and a permanent hell (where evil can evermore be done but nevermore spread).

29. See Geisler, *Roots of Evil*, p. 80.

First, in the game of life, as in other games, some must win and some must lose.[30] When people are given the opportunity freely to choose either to do good or to do evil, they must be given the opportunity to follow through with their own choices. For God to coerce humanity to do the good would be both unworthy of his nature and a violation of their freedom. Likewise, for God to snuff out the freedom of all who misuse their freedom would be beneath the dignity of the Divine. It would be tantamount to saying, "If you do not freely choose to love me, I will take away your freedom." No, it is more befitting an absolutely perfect Being that he allow people to freely reject him if they desire. As Lewis pointed out, there are only two kinds of people in the universe: "those who say to God, '*Thy* will be done' and those to whom God says, in the end, '*thy* will be done.'"[31] The former constitute those in heaven and the latter, those in hell.

Here, contrary to what Lewis himself thought, Calvinism constitutes no exception at all, not even in its strong forms. For no one will be in heaven or in hell against his will. Calvinists agree with all Christians that no one will be in hell who would rather bow his knees before Jesus Christ. God's demonstration of his grace and sovereignty would be meaningless if in the end the rebels against him did not have to live with the consequences of their significant choices against God.

But what if a person, upon arriving in hell, changes his mind? What if a few more chances here on earth would help persuade a person to change his mind? Again the theist's answer is based in the infinity of God. An all-loving God will surely give every opportunity possible for a human being to choose to submit his will to God's will. If one more chance or a hundred or a

---

30. See C. S. Lewis, *The Problem of Pain* (New York: Macmillan, 1944), p. 106. Just why God did not create a world where all men would ultimately learn from the misuse of their freedom is answerable along the following lines. First, in every game some must lose. The game of life is no exception. Secondly, a world where everyone ultimately turns to God is logically possible, but God by foreknowledge may have seen that it was unachievable. That is, he may have seen that some men would never willingly love him. Thirdly, God could not guarantee such a world against human choice without violating both his own perfect love and man's full freedom, both of which are necessary for a morally perfect universe. Fourthly, a world where it just so happened that every single free creature turned out to freely love God would be morally suspect. Was everyone really loving God freely or had he pulled some invisible puppet strings to accomplish this? Finally, both human freedom and divine love—essential components of a morally perfect world—are magnified when some creatures finally reject God. The fact that God will not force himself on anyone and the fact that he created some men who he knows will never go his way shows just how loving God is. Also, the fact that some men will never change their will indicates just how free man is. Hence, the Christian doctrine of hell that teaches that some men will remain eternally impenitent and reprobate is compatible with a morally perfected universe. Since eternal rejection of God will diminish neither God's love nor man's freedom, neither can it in any way diminish a morally perfect world.

31. C. S. Lewis, *The Great Divorce* (New York: Macmillan, 1946), p. 69.

thousand would elicit the decision to do God's will freely, then surely God would give it.

On the other hand, an all-knowing God who sees that the choice to do his will will never come, no matter how many more opportunities are given, will not force a person against his will.[32] God will permit a human the free choice to do his "thing" eternally just as he will permit others to do their "thing" forever. Only those persons will be permitted in heaven who God knows would never change their will; and only those will be pronounced reprobate and eternally separated from God who God knows will never change their will. In brief, the omniscience of God guarantees that the decisions are eternal (Luke 16:26; Heb. 9:27).

The finality of the decisions is the only way to guarantee the ultimate perfection of the universe. Sin cannot be allowed to be on the rampage forever. This present world is not the best possible world. And the best possible way to end this world is by a "great divorce." Just as it is true on earth that one partner's irreconcilable unfaithfulness leads to a final separation, even so those who do not will to be married to God must be granted a divorce. Love is perturbing to one who does not desire to be loved by a certain person or to love that person. In fact, there comes a time when the gifts of love and love itself must be finally rejected by the one who is in love with another. And, as Lewis forcefully wrote, "The only place in the world where one is free of the perturbations of love is hell."[33] Those in love with themselves will be permitted to live forever with this choice; those in love with God will likewise be permanentized in this choice. But up leads up and down leads down and never the twain shall meet (Matt. 25:34, 41; 2 Thess. 1:7–9; Rev. 20:10–15).

Secondly, it is better to allow failure, with the opportunity for a greater good, than not to give the opportunity at all. The objection that God should not have created a world with people (like Judas)[34] who he knew would

32. Jesus' statement that Tyre and Sidon "would have repented" if the mighty miracles he performed elsewhere had been performed there (Matt. 11:21) may be only a hypothetical hyperbole. The parallel phrase says, "It would be more tolerable . . . for you." Or, Jesus may be referring only to the national existence of these cities and not to the destinies of the individual souls in them.

33. C. S. Lewis, *The Four Loves* (New York: Harcourt, Brace, 1960), p. 139.

34. Jesus said, "It would have been better for the man [Judas] if he had not been born" (Matt. 26:24). But the word *better* may mean only "desirable" and surely Judas's judgment was undesirable to him. Even if "better" is taken to mean "beneficial," the context implies only that this would have been better for Judas as an individual, not necessarily better for the whole world. Further, it says only that it would have been better for Judas not to have come into being; it does not say that, once he is in being, it would be better to go into nonbeing. Once he exists as a free creature, it is better that he be given the full choices of his freedom. However, it seems best to take it as a hypothetical hyperbole of severe judgment.

choose their own way is not justified for many reasons. First, the door of hell is locked on the inside.[35] It is locked, to be sure; the decision is final but the decision was free. People may not want to be there but they have willed to be there and will be eternally unwilling to will the conditions of their own release (viz., to will to do God's will). The results of drug addiction are no doubt undesirable but they are chosen. The drunk undoubtedly is displeased with his hangover but becoming drunk is what he decided to do, little by little. Further, it is better to offer something better, knowing it will be refused, than not to offer it at all. For instance, it is better to try to transcend racial barriers by love, even if one knows he will be misunderstood in his attempt, than not to love at all. The kind of love which forgives one's enemies is the greatest kind of all. It is better that God loves persons, even if they reject this love, than for God not to love them at all. Love, despite the anticipated rejection, actually magnifies God. It is in this sense that even the wrath of man shall praise God. For no love is more worthy than the love that loves while being rejected. There is a sense in which it is better for freedom to fail to achieve the good than that it be forced to do good. John Stuart Mill said, "It is better to be an unhappy man than a happy pig."[36] A pig has no moral freedom; a human does. And even if a person does not achieve his own highest good, it is better that he be allowed to live with his own free choice to do evil than to force him to do good. Heaven would be worse than hell for those who do not will to be there. For to force a man to praise forever the one he hates would be worse than allowing the man to curse him. Demanding that a man consent to love God against his will would be a divine rape. It is better that each person be given the free choice to love or not to love God.

Third, the world where not all humans love God and do his will is not a failure. It is not less than the best possible moral world. For love succeeds even when it is not received. It succeeds in two ways. First, it succeeds in manifesting its highest expression. Where sin abounds, there grace does much more abound. The true nature of love is more obvious where it is rejected. And God so loved human beings that he gave them the choice to reject his love. Second, it is better to have loved and lost than not to have loved at all. It is better for God to have loved all and lost some than for him not to have loved at all. It is better, because the only worthy way for love to elicit a response is to elicit it freely. It is unworthy to demand love; one must never love because he has to love but only because he wants to love.

For this reason God does not usually miraculously intervene in the basic moral process of the world. Miraculous prevention of evil consequences would not eliminate moral evil; people could still think moral evil. Evil is in

---

35. See Lewis, *Problem of Pain*, chap. 8.
36. John S. Mill, *Utilitarianism* (1863; New York: Meridian, 1962).

the will, not only in actions. Further, destroying all evil action would eliminate the lesson that evil is providing for free creatures. Humans would never really learn anything from their experiment with evil if all the consequences of evil acts were intercepted by God. In short, a world where evil never happened is not logically impossible but it would be morally unproductive.

In brief, evil is a necessary condition and a necessary by-product of a maximally perfect moral world. Evil is a necessary condition because without it certain higher moral perfections could never be accomplished and without the experience of evil, humans could never learn for themselves that evil is wrong (and it is a higher good that free humans learn the lesson for themselves). Evil is a necessary by-product of a moral world because in a serious game of life's choice between good and evil some must win and some must lose, and even those that lose do so only by their free choice that, by the rejection of God's way, magnifies the love of God which permits men's rejection of himself.

The theistic God is absolutely perfect. Such a God need not create anything, let alone a world with moral beings in it. But if he decides to make a world with free beings, it must be the best he is capable of producing. For doing less than his best would be an evil for God. But an optimally perfect moral world should contain four components: the process leading to the final achievement of a world where humans are free but never will do any evil; a world wherein is permitted the full and final uncoerced exercise of moral freedom; a world in which there is permitted the presence of enough evil to provide both the condition for the achievement of higher moral virtues and a comprehensive lesson of the wrongness of evil for free creatures; a world where free creatures learn for themselves why evil is wrong.

Now, a world where sin never occurred certainly could not fulfill the requirements for an optimally perfect moral world. In fact, it is difficult to conceive of a world that would better suit these conditions than the world we now live in. And the absolutely perfect and powerful God of theism is both the only hope and the ultimate assurance that the greatest moral perfection will be finally achieved from this present world.

17 ✳

The Physical
Problem of Evil

Evil is a three-dimensional problem for theism. First, the metaphysical problem is how to account for the reality of evil. Theists answer this problem by noting that evil is not a real thing but a real privation in things. God created only the possibility of the privation; finite freedom is responsible for actual privations in things (see chap. 15). This leads to the moral problem of evil: Why God created even the possibility of evil by making free creatures who would sin. Theists answer this by pointing out that only by permitting the possibility of evil can God produce a moral world, let alone the best possible world. In short, permitting an evil world is the best possible way to obtain the best possible world (see chap. 16). This leads us to the problem of physical evil: What about all the evil that is not connected with human freedom? That is, what about the apparent gratuity of much human suffering? Why does an absolutely perfect Being allow unnecessary and unredeemable human suffering, such as sickness, pestilences, and hurricanes?

In this chapter we will continue to elaborate the "best way" theodicy. Once again, where reference is made to the free acts of free creatures, in most cases the strong Calvinist can be accommodated simply by thinking of the significant choices of creatures instead, though at times individual divergencies need to be noted.

The Problem of Physical Evil for Theism

It would appear that not all evil results either directly or indirectly from the abuse of human freedom. Even granting that free choice is the cause of some physical evil, it seems clear that at least some physical evil is not the direct consequence of human choice. How can theism account for this apparently gratuitous evil? Why is there so much useless suffering and pain that is unconnected with the abuse of human freedom?

Posing the Problem of Physical Evil

Perhaps the best known statement of the problem of physical evil is in Albert Camus's *Plague*. Speaking about a plague of rats visited upon the city of Oran at the beginning of the Second World War, Camus insisted that

1. Either one must join the doctor and fight the plague or else he must join the priest and not fight the plague.
2. Not to fight the plague is antihumanitarian.
3. To fight the plague is to fight against God who sent it.
4. Therefore, if humanitarianism is right, theism is wrong.
5. Humanitarianism is right.
6. Therefore, theism is wrong.

The theist denies the truth of the third premise, but just how he can make a case for his point remains to be seen. The severity of the dilemma for theism in the face of the problem of physical evil is evident from H. J. McCloskey's statement of it:[1]

1. The theist is morally obligated to promote the greatest good.
2. The greatest good cannot be achieved by eliminating suffering (according to theism), for
   a. if the necessary condition for achieving something is eliminated, then the possibility of achieving that something is eliminated,
   b. and eliminating evil would (according to theism) eliminate the necessary condition for achieving a greater good;
   c. hence, the greatest good cannot be achieved by eliminating suffering.
3. Therefore, the theist is morally obligated (in accord with his own thesis) not to work to eliminate all evil.

We may summarize this argument against theism from physical evil in the following way:

1. If suffering is justifiable, it is wrong to work against it.
2. It is not wrong to work to eliminate suffering (it is right to do so).
3. Hence, suffering is not justifiable.
4. But if evil is not justifiable, then the theistic God does not exist.
5. For God's existence is incompatible with unjustifiable suffering.
6. And there is unjustifiable suffering (from premise 3).
7. Therefore, the theistic God cannot exist.

The dilemma is this: if suffering is the condition of a greater good, then one should not work to eliminate suffering lest he be working (indirectly) to

---

1. H. J. McCloskey, "God and Evil" in *God and Evil: Readings on the Theological Problem of Evil*, ed. Nelson Pike (New York: Prentice-Hall, 1964).

eliminate the greatest good. If God sent the plague to punish us, then we are working directly against God when we fight it. Hence, whether suffering is a condition for achieving a greater good or a consequence of doing evil, one is working against the greater good by working against suffering. Theism is unhumanitarian.

Proposed Theistic Solutions to Physical Evil

Theists have replied in various ways to the problem of suffering. These theistic answers will now be examined in the light of antitheistic objections to them. In one way or another all of the theistic solutions contend that physical evil is a necessary condition to the greater good that the theistic God is committed to achieving. But each particular solution is attacked by antitheistic objections.[2]

1. *Evil is a necessary contrast to the good.* One learns and appreciates the good only by contrast with evil. If everything were pleasure without contrasting pain, one would not fully appreciate pleasure. For example, without the pangs of hunger one would not fully appreciate the delights of food.

Antitheists point out three problems with this position. At best it explains only some kinds of physical evil (viz., those connected with pain). Further, much less pain would accomplish the same result. Also, the appreciation of health and sanity does not necessitate that one has been previously sick or insane. Even if evil depends on good, experience shows that one can know the good without participating in evil.

2. *Evil is a necessary by-product of laws that bring good results.* Some theists believe that God created a world in which natural laws work for the overall benefit of the world and man but which involve some necessary by-products that are evil.[3] For instance, what is evil for the worm is good for the bird that eats it; evil for the lower forms of life is a necessary by-product of a world in which good is possible for the higher forms of life.

There are three basic problems with this view from the antitheistic standpoint:

It explains only some kinds of evil, especially those connected with animal pain.

An omnipotent God could have created a different kind of world without these evil by-products in it.

2. Edward H. Madden and P. H. Hare give the most comprehensive list of objections in *Evil and the Concept of God* (Springfield, Ill.: Charles C. Thomas, 1968), chap. 4; also see Pike, *God and Evil,* pp. 67–83.

3. See F. R. Tennant, *Philosophical Theology* (Cambridge: Cambridge University Press, 1930), 2:197–205.

An omnipotent God could miraculously intervene in this kind of world and stop (at least some) evil by-products without disturbing the overall moral fiber or without upsetting the regularity and predictability of the laws of nature.

In brief, the by-product theory tries to exonerate God by capitulating his sovereign control over the world he has created. It implies that God's hands are tied by the laws he has made.

3. *Evil is necessary to punish the wicked.* Theists often propose natural calamities (including sickness, earthquake, tornadoes, and death) are sent as a judgment of God on wicked persons. The punishment may be for sins committed either publicly, secretly, or in a previous life.[4]

The objections to this position from the antitheistic point of view must be divided into two parts. The first reply will treat sins committed publicly or privately. This view is contrary to the biblical teaching on Job who suffered innocently. Jesus, too, indicated that sin is not the cause of all suffering (Luke 13:4). It does not explain the apparent unjust distribution of suffering, which includes many innocent adults and children and even babies born with deformities.

The suggestion that such suffering can be explained by sins committed in a previous life has several problems. Biblical theism denies the truth of the reincarnation theory: people have only one physical birth and death (Heb. 9:27). Even if one accepts the concept of reincarnation, it does not explain why God would permit sin in the first incarnation. It would also amount to a systematic delusion as to why God would punish people for sins that no one, even the person suffering, is conscious ever occurred.

4. *Evil is a necessary example to others.* Theists sometimes claim that God inflicts evil on a man like Job precisely because God knows that he will be steadfast in his faith and serve as a good example to others. Suffering is in effect substitutional in that the patient suffers as a pattern for others to emulate.

This explanation of physical evil has several serious problems. It would account for only a small amount of suffering at best. It definitely does not account for mass disasters. Not everyone is a Job, and the purpose backfires when the sufferer renounces God rather than praises him.

5. *Evil is necessary as a warning to the wicked.* Theists often point out that pain serves to prod the wicked into a recognition of God. It is a kind of

4. See W. H. Sheldon, "God and Polarity," in *Basic Problems in Philosophy,* ed. Daniel J. Bronstein, Y. H. Krikorian, and P. P. Wiener, 3d ed. (Englewood Cliffs, N.J.: Prentice-Hall, 1964), p. 513. Although some aberrant forms of theism suggest this, preincarnation and reincarnation are generally associated with pantheistic views. See Norman L. Geisler and J. V. Amano, *The Reincarnation Sensation* (Wheaton: Tyndale, 1986).

divine megaphone to arouse morally insensitive persons to God's purposes for their lives.[5] The awful powers of nature stir people from religious indifference to reverence.

Antitheists see several loopholes in this hypothesis about physical evil. Physical suffering and natural catastrophes often turn people away from God rather than to God. Further, the evils would not need to be nearly so deadly to evoke the awe in those who are positively affected by them. An omnipotent God has less deadly but equally effective methods of stirring up religious sentiment in people, such as miracles and special revelation. Such evil demonstrations of power as hurricanes and earthquakes are inconsistent with the omnibenevolent nature of the theistic God. In short, the goodness of God would be much more effective than the power of God in turning men to himself.

6. *Evil is a necessary part of the best possible world.* Some theists claim that this world with evil in it is the best of all possible worlds because evil is an integral part of the total picture of good.[6] Even God could not have made it better. Finite worlds cannot be perfect, but this finite world has the minimal amount of evil for the maximal amount of moral good. Just as one piece of a mosaic may be ugly but yet be an essential part of a beautiful whole, so evil fits into the total picture of good as an essential ingredient.

From the point of view of nontheists there are a number of flaws in this explanation of physical evil. An all-powerful God could have made a world without any evil in it. Even a minimal amount of evil is incompatible with an absolutely perfect God. Even granting evil as part of a total picture of good, still a better total picture could be made than this world. For there is an unjust distribution of evil in the world. The theistic God is like the old schoolmaster who punished the whole class because of what a few individuals did.

7. *Evil is necessary for ultimate harmony.* Some theists have suggested that just as a musical chord heard in isolation may sound dissonant but when heard in context sounds harmonious, so it is with evil. An event seen in isolation from the finite human perspective is really good when seen from the infinite perspective of God. Hence, the problem of evil disappears when it is seen from God's perspective.[7]

This solution to suffering is open to a number of serious objections from antitheists. It makes all evil only prima facie and eliminates the need for reform, since any change may affect the ultimate harmony. It makes God a systematic deceiver, since what appears evil to us is not really evil in his eyes.

5. See C. S. Lewis, *The Problem of Pain* (New York: Macmillan, 1944), chap. 6.

6. Gottfried Wilhelm Leibniz, *Theodicy*, trans. E. M. Huggard (Indianapolis: Bobbs-Merrill, 1966).

7. This view is similar to the previous one, but it is listed separately by Madden and Hare, *Evil and the Concept of God*, pp. 60ff.

The so-called higher morality has no meaning to humanity because it is completely different from our concept of what is moral. It requires that what we ordinarily call wrong is right when God does it. This double standard of morality is unjust.[8] Why, for example, is murder right simply because God does it to human beings in natural disasters?

8. *Evil is a necessary condition for achieving the best world.* Some theists insist that present evils eventually lead to long-run goods. All is well that ends well, and in the end a greater good will be achieved via physical suffering than without it. First-order evils are a necessary condition for achieving second-order goods. For instance, pain, misery, and disease are necessary to bring into being the more noble virtues of courage, endurance, and benevolence.[9]

The antitheistic objections to this view are five. It does not explain why God permitted the first-order evils; God could have achieved the same end without such ghastly means. The price for the long-run goods is too high to pay; the good end does not justify the evil means necessary to attain it. Furthermore, some long-run consequences are not good but evil; sometimes evil only produces more evil. How long is the long run? Either the theist does not know or else he tells us that the long run means when good appears, which is tautological. Immortal bliss does not really compensate for any evil suffered. A torturer consoling his victim by telling him of the bliss that will follow does not explain why the victim had to suffer any torture to begin with.

9. *Evil is a necessary conflict among natural systems.* A more recent theistic innovation suggests that natural evil results from the mutual interference of natural systems.[10] In just being itself, everything interferes of necessity with the movement of other systems. The organic, for instance, conflicts with the functioning of the inorganic world. This mutual conflict is indigenous to any world of genuine natural forces. Ridding the world of this conflict would eliminate the natural world altogether. And eliminating this kind of world would be contrary to the intent of divine goodness to make all possible kinds of excellences, including physical ones.

The antitheist offers several objections to this thesis. God could have created another kind of world without conflicting natural forces. Even a natural world could have much less interference in it than ours has. It implies that all kinds of existence (including physical existence) is a necessary value, a premise disputed by both Arthur Schopenhauer and many Oriental philoso-

8. See John Stuart Mill, *Nature and Utility of Religion,* reprinted in *The Existence of God,* ed. John H. Hick (New York: Macmillan, 1964), pp. 114–20.

9. See *Encyclopedia of Religion and Ethics,* ed. James Hastings, 13 vols. (New York: Charles Scribner and Sons, 1955), s.v. "Good and Evil," by W. D. Niven.

10. See Austin M. Farrer, *Love Almighty and Ills Unlimited* (New York: Doubleday, 1961), pp. 71–94.

phies. It implies that evil is an ugly patch that somehow makes the whole beautiful (this is subject to the same criticisms leveled against the "best world" view); satisfying God's desire to create all kinds of excellences at the expense of all this human agony is not compatible with the morality of God (nor is it worth it to humans).

10. *Evil is necessary to build character.* According to this view, the rough edges of the world are necessary to produce spiritually significant beings. A world without tears would not produce charity or sympathy. A world without suffering would be morally bland. It is the pressure on coal that forms diamonds. Pain is a perfecting process.[11]

As a solution to the problem of physical evil, this view is subject to many antitheistic criticisms. First, the character-building argument obviously does not apply to some kinds of evil, such as insanity or brainwashing. At best, it can account for only small amounts of evil, which would not include mass disasters or maiming of character. Again, the price is too high for the yield. God could have produced spiritually significant beings without allowing physical evil. If some goods depend on evils, then we should not work to eliminate these evils; otherwise, we are working against the greater good that can be achieved by them.

Since theists have sometimes used a number of these ten arguments in combination, one more antitheistic objection should be noted here. Edward H. Madden and P. H. Hare refer to the theistic move to combine the arguments into one overall answer to the problem of evil as the "ten-leaky-buckets-tactic." "It amounts to saying," they insist, "that while one cannot carry water far in a leaky bucket, with ten of them he can."[12] Certainly if one solution does not hold water, then nine more that do not hold water are not going to provide the answer.

A Theistic Solution to the Problem of Physical Evil

In response, it should be noted that many of the antitheistic criticisms gain their weight on the basis of several assumptions that we have already shown to be wrong: that an all-powerful God could have achieved the best possible moral world without permitting physical suffering; that a greater good does not result from the presence of evil; that all physical evil cannot be explained as necessary to human freedom (i.e., by moral evil); and that the best world possible is not worth the price in evil that must be paid to achieve it. First we

11. Several theists have used this kind of argument, including Irenaeus, Schleiermacher, and William Temple. See Temple's work, *Nature, Man and God,* partly reprinted in *Philosophy of Religion: A Book of Readings,* ed. George L. Abernathy and Thomas A. Langford, 2d ed. (New York: Macmillan, 1968), pp. 451–62.

12. Madden and Hare, *Evil and the Concept of God,* p. 53.

will lay out the proposed solution to the problem of physical evil, and then we will examine again the remaining criticisms of this kind of solution.

Each of the proposed theistic solutions is correct in making physical evil somehow necessary. For unnecessary evil of any kind would certainly be incongruous with an absolutely perfect God. If there had been any way God could have achieved the greatest moral good without evil, then he should have done it. But we have already argued (in chap. 16) that this kind of world with free beings who do sin is the best of all possible ways of obtaining the best of all possible worlds, and that no other world or nonworld would have been morally better than this world. Building on this conclusion, then, it remains for us only to indicate just how it is that physical evil fits into the necessity of this kind of moral world.

Several obvious ways and some other possible ways combine to explain the presence of physical evil as an essential part of the kind of world that is the best way to produce the best world. Each of these points is not a "leaky bucket" trying to help other leaky buckets hold water. Rather, there is so much water (evil) to account for and each argument accounts for so much of it. The buckets are not leaky; each is solid, but each holds only so much water. All the buckets together, however, hold all the physical evil in this world necessary to produce an optimally perfect world.

Before we list the various ways that physical evil can be accounted for, we must set forth the characteristics of an optimally perfect moral world. It must be a world such that a greater than it could not be achieved; since God is the best possible Being, it follows that if he makes a moral world at all, it must eventually be the very best possible moral world. Since freedom is the essence of a moral world, the highest moral world must permit the greatest exercise of moral freedom possible; to curb moral freedom would be to limit the free moral potential of the world. The amount of evil permitted must be justifiable in view of the moral good achieved. In an optimally perfect moral world evil should ultimately be defeated. In brief, if evil can be defeated without destroying freedom, then a perfect moral world will be achieved.

It is our contention that this is precisely the kind of world that the theistic God is producing through the world that we now have, as was shown in the preceding chapter. All that remains here is to show how physical evil is a necessary part of this morally "best way" to obtain the morally best world. The logic of our argument can be outlined this way:

1. The kind of world where human beings freely do evil is the best way to produce a morally perfect world.
2. This present world is the kind of world where human beings freely do evil.

3. Hence, this present evil world is the best way to produce a morally perfect world.
4. But physical evil is a necessary part of this kind of present evil world.
5. Therefore, physical evil is a necessary part of the best way to produce a morally perfect world.
6. But it is necessary for God to permit whatever is necessary to the production of a morally perfect world.
7. Therefore, it is necessary for God to permit physical evil in order to produce a morally perfect world.

The sixth premise is supported by the fact, previously established, that doing less than his best is an evil for God. It is the fourth premise that carries the burden of our theodicy. How can it be demonstrated that all physical evils that happen in this world are really necessary to a morally free world? Even if some physical evil is necessary, is there not an exorbitant and unfairly distributed amount of physical evil in this world? The necessity of all the physical evil in this world is defended by theism in the following ways.

1. *Some physical evils are necessary conditions for moral perfection.* First, there are higher second-order goods that cannot be achieved without the presence of first-order evils. Sympathy is not achievable without misery or patience without tribulation. Courage is not obtainable without fear, and endurance is occasioned only by hardship. In brief, some virtues would be totally absent from a world without physical evil.

Second, the highest degree of other virtues is unobtainable without the presence of physical evil. For instance, the highest appreciation of pleasure is impossible without pain. The greatest recognition of the value of health comes only after one has been sick. Indeed, justice is more fully appreciated after one has suffered injustice. Love is more appreciated if one has been hated, and so on with almost all the virtues. In short, the highest moral achievements in almost any virtue are conditioned (at least in part) on the presence of physical evil, and some virtues are completely unobtainable without this precondition.

It is not sufficient to retort that a morally significant world is obtainable without these. Of course it is, but that is not the point under discussion. The question is not whether God has produced a morally significant world, but whether he is producing a morally perfect world. After all, if God is the best possible Being, then he must do his best, not merely what is good.

The antitheist cannot withdraw his insistence that God must do his moral best, for if he does, his case is defeated. If God does not have to do his best, why is the antitheist complaining that there were morally better alternatives open to a theistic God? The full force of the antitheistic argument is dependent on the thesis that we have admitted: that doing less than his best would be an evil for an absolutely perfect God. But if God is absolutely perfect and must do his best, it follows that it is necessary to permit physical evil as the occasion for obtaining the highest moral perfection possible. We may summarize the argument in this manner:

1. It is necessary for God to do his moral best (i.e., if he chooses to do anything moral).
2. A world without the attainment of all the virtues possible or without the highest attainment of each virtue would not be the morally best world possible.
3. It is necessary to have physical evil in order to attain some virtues and in order to obtain the highest degree of other virtues.
4. Therefore, it is necessary for God to permit physical evils (as the condition) by which he can produce the morally best world.

The nontheist could object, of course, that it would not take so much evil to accomplish this task; the theist can respond by pointing out that the positing of evil as a necessary condition for a greater good is not intended to account for all physical evil but only some. The rest of the evil is a necessary part of the best kind of world for producing the best possible world in other ways. Further, the theist has good reasons (see chap. 9) for believing God is all-knowing. And an infinitely wise God is in a much better position than finite persons to know just how much evil is necessary to produce the best possible world.

2. *Some physical evils are a necessary consequence of human free choice.* We have already established that the free choice to do evil is a necessary part of the "best way" theodicy. But in a physical world where one creature is free to do evil, certain kinds of physical evil follow. First of all, people freely bring some physical evil on themselves. If a person is free to get drunk, the evil of hangovers will result. Those who are free to take drugs will be subject to the evil of bad trips and addiction. Where people are free to smoke, disease and death may follow. And if people are free to eat all they want, the evils of obesity will also be present.

In a world of free choice some physical evil to other persons will result directly from the abuse of one person's freedom. For example, if people are free to get drunk and drive, they will be able to inflict injury and death on others. If cruelty is a possibility within freedom, it will be possible for someone to suffer torment. If the pleasures of swimming and boating are possible, the pain of drowning is also possible. A world with the freedom to invent will produce implements that will be used for both good and evil. There is no way for God to prevent all physical suffering without tampering with the full exercise of human free choices. And we have already agreed that the full exercise of free choice is a necessary part of a maximally moral world.

Some physical evil to others results indirectly from the abuse of freedom. A careless man can cause himself a physical disability (e.g., maiming or blinding himself) which can occasion suffering both for himself and others. In the same way, an abuse of one's body can pass on deformities to future generations. Indeed, the Bible declares that Adam's abuse of free choice brought the evils of sorrow and death on all persons.[13] This abuse of freedom accounts for a vast amount of physical evil. Some have estimated that between 80 and 95 percent of physical evil results from moral free choice.[14]

The antitheistic move to insist that divine intervention could prevent physical evil is insufficient for several reasons. It would hinder the full exercise of freedom. For part of the exercise of freedom is not merely to think evil but to actually do some evil. If all evil actions were prevented by divine miracle or persuasion, then human beings could not really freely do what they want to do. And this kind of limitation upon freedom would be less than the optimal moral freedom called for in an optimally moral world.

If God prevented all physical evil from actually happening, he would be eliminating the possibility for people to learn the lesson from doing evil. And since in the long run it is the lessons that people learn from the abuse of free choice that guarantee the defeat of evil, it is necessary for God to allow human beings to learn the lessons for themselves. (God is storing the lessons of human experience for later and eternal application in destroying evil without destroying freedom. See chapter 16.)

The elimination of physical pain would also eliminate physical pleasure. In a nonphysical world all the pleasures of the senses would be entirely absent. No one could ever enjoy food, sex, or sports.

If the antitheist insists that God could at least intercept some evil consequences without disrupting the plan, then he must be reminded that according to the Bible and human history God has sometimes intervened to intercept evil consequences. Preventative miracles have been experienced by Christians. If it would seem that God could do more of this kind of thing, we must remind ourselves of two things: An infinite mind is in a better position to know just how much is too much for optimal moral perfection, and even a finite mind can see that too much divine interruption would upset the regularity and predictability of nature upon which our human lives depend in crucial ways. Indeed, moral activity is dependent on a universe that operates by regular natural laws. Otherwise, one could not reasonably anticipate the consequences of his actions.

Also, the antitheistic attempt to contend that God could have created a nonphysical world that would have eliminated any kind of physical evil will

13. See Genesis 3:15–19; Romans 5:12.
14. See Hugh Silvester, *Arguing with God: A Christian Examination of the Problem of Evil* (Downers Grove: Inter-Varsity, 1971), p. 32.

not suffice. As long as there are free beings doing evil there will be evil consequences, whether they are physical or spiritual consequences. Making the world purely spiritual would not eliminate evil consequences but would merely make them wholly spiritual consequences. Neither the theist nor the atheist lives in this nonphysical world. Both must account for what they have—a physical world. Now there is nothing incongruous with the nature of God to create a physical world with physical evil, providing that physical evil be a necessary part of producing a morally perfect world. According to biblical theism, there is a spiritual world of evil finite beings. Angels, like human beings, abused their free choice and brought evil into their non-physical world. A physical world may be necessary to occasion the kind of moral effort needed to achieve optimal moral perfection. Presumably, purely spiritual beings have no need of food and they move with effortless ease. If so, physical conditions occasion some effort essential to achieving higher moral good that angels are unable to attain. Thus, this kind of physical world, with its concomitant evil, is a necessary condition of achieving the maximally perfect moral world possible.

3. *Some physical evil is a necessary consequence of the free choice of demons.* Biblical theism proposes a solution that would easily account for all of the other physical evils in the world. Fallen angels are demons who inflict suffering on even the innocent.[15] Job was attacked by Satan (Job 1). Paul said, "A thorn was given me in the flesh, a messenger of Satan, to harass me . . ." (2 Cor. 12:7). In the New Testament both some insanity and some sickness are attributed to evil spirits (Mark 5:1–20).

In view of the existence of evil spirits who are opposed to God and his plan, all manner of physical evils, including "natural" disasters, can be explained. And the plausibility of this solution is supported by the fact that part of the tactics of these supernatural evil beings is to deceive humans into believing lies, including the lie that evil spirits do not exist (2 Thess. 2:10–11). For the Christian, the fact that Christ was tempted by, talked with, and cast out, evil spirits is sufficient to verify their existence and evil activity in this physical world (Matt. 4:1). But if such free evil beings exist, then it is possible that their free choice accounts for much (if not all) of the physical evil in this world.

If the theist is asked why God does not destroy the demonic powers, he answers that God already has defeated them and will one day finally destroy them. God is defeating them in the most just way possible (viz., by permitting them the maximal moral freedom necessary with the minimal evil essential to achieve the optimally moral perfect world). The best way to defeat evil is to let it express itself; it is ultimately self-defeating. Another response would be

15. See Revelation 12:9; Jude 6; 2 Peter 2:4.

morally unworthy of God. An infinitely perfect Being does not react impatiently or impulsively to the appearance of opposing forces. God readily concedes battles in order to win the war. One who is in sovereign control and motivated by infinite love is neither threatened nor intimidated by the finite forces of evil. Christ has already defeated evil (Heb. 2), and God will destroy it in due time (Rev. 20–22).

4. *Some physical evil is a necessary moral warning.* Physical pain is a blow in a person's moral solar plexis. It hits morally lethargic people where it hurts. When a person is down physically, there is a greater chance that he will look up morally and spiritually. As C. S. Lewis succinctly stated it, "God whispers to us in our pleasures, speaks in our conscience, but shouts in our pain: it is His megaphone to rouse a deaf world."[16]

True, not all persons are aroused positively by pain, but the opportunity is there for all. God is calling, whether all people are responding or not. Some do respond, and it is better that the others be warned than that they meet their doom unawares. It certainly would not be morally right for the medically informed not to warn smokers of the evils of lung cancer and heart disease. In fact, the cough and shortness of breath are God's way of warning smokers of physical evils to come. A toothache warns us of something worse coming, and a pain in the side or in the chest may be a warning of impending sickness. Surely God would be less than moral not to provide warnings of moral disaster to come. Physical evils often serve this role very effectively.

5. *Some physical evils are necessary components of a physical world.* There are instances of evil that are constitutive of the very processes of a natural world. Natural evil is a component of a physical world in several ways. Some evil is a result of lower forms being used to sustain higher forms. A natural world is one in which certain higher forms of life are dependent on lower forms. Animals feed on plants and minerals, plants feed on minerals, and a human being feeds on all of them. In such a world, the pain of the lower is necessary for the life of the higher.

Other natural evil results from the overlap of systems in the spatio-temporal continuum. Wherever two or more things vie for the same place at the same time, there will be conflicts. Such is indigenous to a world of physical forces.

Other evils result as by-products of a process that produces the overall balance of nature. If there is to be a sun to warm the earth for life and growth, it will also burn other things that are exposed to it too much. If there is air to breathe and water to drink, then it will be possible for people to suffocate in water. None of these evil by-products is the purpose of the natural process, but they are a necessary result of the achievement of other natural goods. It is

16. Lewis, *Problem of Pain*, p. 81.

possible that floods, droughts, earthquakes, tornadoes, and other natural disasters are all necessary by-products of a physical world. And since we have already ruled out regular miraculous intervention into the physical world (and the alternative of a nonphysical world), it follows that the kind of physical world we have with natural evils in it is compatible with the "best way" to obtain the best possible world. Indeed, since it is necessary for God to do his best, then such a world is necessary in order for God to achieve the best possible world.

It should be added that the present world with natural evil, even though it serves well as a condition to achieving the best possible world, is not the best kind of physical world possible. In contrast, an immortal resurrection body and a new heaven and a new earth without sickness, sorrow, and decay will be perfect.[17] And the reason God did not create the perfect physical world first is that the greatest moral perfectibility is not obtainable in any other kind of world than the natural type of world we have. The characteristics of a natural world are necessary constituents of a world that is the necessary condition for achieving the best world possible. These essential physical characteristics include the following factors found only in a physical world like our own: the presence of pleasure to encourage man to do what is good; the presence of pain to warn him of moral consequences; the existence of sex by which he can reproduce his kind and enlarge his physical joy; a material medium by which he can express his appreciation for God (e.g., art); and an environment in which struggle and effort are possible in order that higher goods can be achieved. All of these things are made possible by a material world. And each one contributes to the process of freedom and serves as part of the condition for achieving the greatest moral good possible.

In summation, many different functions are served by physical evil. But all physical evil is necessary to the moral conditions of free creatures (human or angelic), which conditions are necessary for the achievement of the best possible world. Natural evils are necessary to a natural world and a natural world is essential to (or at least not incompatible with) the conditions of full freedom that are necessary for the achievement of the best possible world.

A corollary of our view is that this is the worst of all possible worlds. Surprising as it sounds, Gottfried Wilhelm Leibniz was not only wrong in calling this the best of all possible worlds; he asserted the very contrary of what has to be true, given this theodicy. This world must be the worst of all possible worlds.

A bit of reflection will demonstrate the truth of this assertion. We have shown that this present evil world is not only God's way of bringing about the best of all possible worlds; it must be the best way of bringing about the best

17. See Romans 8:18–25; Revelation 21–22.

world. In order to do this God has permitted evil to occur. Some evil has to be tolerated in order to achieve the highest goods. But how much evil will an omnipotent, omniscient, and omnibenevolent God allow to happen? Clearly the answer is that God will allow all the evil necessary to achieve his ends, not a bit less. Thus the actual amount of evil in the world must be the upper limit. If the evil in this world is the necessary condition for bringing about the best of all possible worlds, then we must be experiencing the maximal amount of evil necessary.

Several observations can help us to appreciate this point.

1. *The worst possible world is not the worst conceivable world.* In pure modal logic, any world conceivable without contradiction is a possible world. But some worlds that are logically possible are metaphysically (actually) impossible. For example, there is a logically possible world where finite beings are uncaused, but metaphysically such a world is impossible. Similarly we are now also considering metaphysical possibilities. It is certainly possible to imagine a world that contains far more evil than the present one. But, unless the theist wants to let his talk degenerate into mere rote, not just any amount of evil is justifiable in a world governed by an omniscient, omnipotent, and omnibenevolent being. No evil beyond that required by God to carry out his plan to bring about the best world can exist. Thus all conceivable (and perhaps logically possible) worlds in which there is more suffering, more cancer, or more natural disasters are impossible because such worlds could not coexist with their omnibenevolent creator and sustainer.

2. *There is no gratuitous evil.* Michael Peterson is certainly right in claiming that we experience much evil as gratuitous.[18] But experience is an inadequate measure. In view of our theodicy, evil that we experience as gratuitous is a component of the total amount and kind of evil allowed by God to bring about the best of all possible worlds. Alvin Plantinga has invented the whimsical unit of "turps" to measure the amount of evil in the world.[19] He states that there might 10^{13} turps of evil in the world. If this is so, then this theodicy holds that even though God has seen fit to allow that many turps of evil in the world, he will not allow one fraction of a turp more than is necessary.

3. *We can accept the reality of suffering.* This theodicy does not need to make evil look good. It tries to understand why God has permitted evil without attempting to pass off the notion that pain does not really hurt or death does not really bereave. Instead it reconciles itself to the fact that in

18. Michael Peterson, *Evil and the Christian God* (Grand Rapids: Baker, 1982), pp. 89–93.
19. Alvin Plantinga, *God, Freedom, and Evil* (New York: Harper Torchbooks, 1974), p. 63.

bringing about the best world allowing this much pain to occur is integral to God's plan.

4. *We can appreciate the amount of good in this world.* If this is the worst possible world (though far worse worlds are conceivable), we can be thankful for all the good that is found even in the metaphysically worst world. There is so much good in the worst possible world that Leibniz could mistake it for the best possible world. This world, containing the horrors of genocide, diseases, and natural disasters, also contains beauty, love, and happiness. And this is only a stage on the way to a world in which there is no more evil and only good!

Objections to the Theistic Solution to Physical Evil

We must face some residual problems with our theodicy that have not been explicitly answered in the foregoing discussion. Each objection will be stated and answered in the context of the solution we have proposed, even though the objections were sometimes originally leveled at different theodicies than the one suggested here.

1. *This theodicy implies that the end justifies the means.* The first objection to the "best way" solution implies that an evil means is the best way to obtain the best end. The view that a good end justifies performing evil means to reach it is an ethic rejected by most theists and many nontheists. How, then, can the theist justify this apparently utilitarian approach?

In response the theist makes an important distinction. He does not say that a good end justifies God's performing evil acts, but it only justifies God's permitting such acts. God cannot perform any evil, but he can permit evil in order to perform the good of bringing good out of evil. God is interested in bringing the greatest good for the greatest number, but not by performing or promoting any evil.

God will, however, refrain from preventing some evil (i.e., he will permit humans to use their freedom to do evil), only because he knows that he can achieve a morally perfect world in this way. In brief, God has utilitarian goals (the greatest good for the greatest number in the long run), but he does not use utilitarian means (doing evil that good may come) in order to achieve them.

Ultimately, only God can permit evil in order to accomplish a greater good, since only God is omniscient and can foresee what the long-range results will be, and only God is omnipotent and can guarantee that permitting evil means will help achieve the greatest good in the long run.

In brief, it is true that God works on an end-justifies-the-means philosophy but with two important differences than the way this is normally conceived. The end of the greater good only justifies permitting evil as a condition for achieving this end, not promoting or performing any evil. God merely permits free creatures to exercise their free choice to do evil, knowing that he can bring a greater good out of it than if they were not permitted to do evil at all. Permitting evil to gain the long-run good is ethical for God but not necessarily for human beings because only an infinite God can guarantee that a greater good will come from permitting evil. In permitting free choice in order to achieve the highest moral good, God is acting in accord with the norm of his own absolutely perfect nature in order to determine what is the long-range good. That is, the means is good, not simply because it accords with the end (or brings the greatest good) but because this end is in accord with the norm of God's nature. In other words, God not only commands others to act in accord with his nature but he, too, in determining what is the greatest good in the end, is complying with the moral demands of his own nature.

2. *This theodicy does not account for the large amount nor the unequal distribution of physical evil.* Even granting that some or even much physical suffering can be accounted for along the lines already suggested, the amount of human suffering seems exorbitant. It would appear that much less suffering and a little more divine intervention would have been the case if there were an infinitely perfect and powerful God.

Several observations are relevant to this criticism. First, certainly no finite mind is in a position to press this point. Only an infinite mind could calculate the precise amount of human suffering essential to obtaining a morally perfect world. Second, the theistic argument for an infinitely perfect God and the historical and experiential arguments that he does miraculously intervene in the world lend credibility to the belief that the right amount of evil is being allowed to accomplish the greatest good. As we already stated, this is the worst possible world. Third, the theodicy suggested here does not require weighing exact amounts of evil or measuring the degree of distribution present in the world, for two reasons. In specific circumstances a person is rewarded in the afterlife according to what he does in this life, and knowing specific amounts and degrees of evil is not essential to our theodicy. We need only know about a certain kind of world where all kinds of evil are freely permitted; enough evils do occur to occasion the greatest moral achievements and the complete moral lesson (for all people) that all kinds of evil are always wrong. However, it would be incongruous with what we know about the nature of God to assume that a greater amount of evil than necessary is permitted.

Ultimately, it is necessary for theism to demonstrate only that more good than evil results from permitting freedom. That this "more" is not the "most" good achievable is what the antitheist must prove. And without superior knowledge it would seem that there is no way to actually prove that more good is possible without diminishing free choice, which would be a lesser good.

In brief , knowing the exact amounts and distribution of evil is not crucial to our theodicy. We do need to recognize that God allows full opportunity for freedom and evil and for learning the lesson that all kinds of evil are wrong. Nevertheless, we believe that God does not permit any excess evil.

3. *This theodicy entails a double standard.* If God declares good the process of evil that achieves a greater good but declares it evil for men to promote this evil, then there are two standards of good, one for God and another for humans. For God condemns humans for operating on an end-justifies-the-means ethic which he employs himself.

Several misconceptions are entailed in this objection. First, as was just pointed out, God does not employ an end-justifies-the-means ethic; God does not perform or promote evil in order that good may come. He merely permits evil because he can achieve a greater good with it than without it. Second, permitting evil is not an evil for a Being who can achieve a greater good from it, and only God is such a Being who can guarantee the achievement of the greatest good in the long run from permitting evil. Third, both the end and the means must be morally right for both God and humanity; permitting the full exercise of finite freedom is the morally right means to the morally best end. Fourth, God does not pronounce the evil process good for either himself or anyone else; it is only the end that is pronounced good, not the evil means.

The experience of pain from an operation is not really a pleasure; it is pain. But it is the means to the greater pleasure of good health after the operation. Thus our theodicy is not declaring evil good; evil as such is evil. But evil as a means to a greater good is not evil as such. A parent does not will his sick child the pain of treatment but the pleasure of restored health. Likewise, God does not will the performance of the evil but only the production of the good end obtained from permitting the evil.

Fifth, the same moral principle can be applied to God and creatures only analogously. For example, both God and human beings must love (i.e., will one's own good and the good of the other) but God must will his own good infinitely and the creature's good only finitely, because of the differences in their mode of being. This is not a double standard but the analogous application of the same standard to different objects. An everyday example will help. It is wrong for a man to uproot bushes out of his neighbor's yard but not out of his own yard. One is sovereign over the plants of his own yard, but he has no rights over the shrubs in his neighbor's yard. God is sovereign over all life. Hence, what would be murder for humans is not murder for God. God gives life and has the right to take it, but people do not.

Sixth, there is only one standard for both God and human beings, and that is the nature of God. When God justifies the end (e.g., the greatest good for the greatest number) and the means of attaining that end (free choice), he is judging both in terms of the norm of his nature. There is only one standard

(God's nature) by which God determined whether the end to be achieved (a finitely perfect moral world) would be justified. And it is only in view of the norm of his nature that God can justify the end of producing a perfect world and the means of permitting evil to achieve such a world.

Seventh, a non-Calvinistic theist can add: When God permitted evil means to produce a good end, he was not thereby encouraging the world to be evil. God did not load the dice of life in favor of evil means to achieve good ends. God created the world in full awareness of what people would freely choose to do. And foreknowledge does not imply forced action.[20] God knew how human beings would exercise their freedom but did not tilt the scales of freedom one way or the other. God foreknew what humans would decide and so he created this kind of world in accordance with his foreknowledge (Rom. 8:29; 2 Peter 1:3). In brief, God wills directly the good end; he wills only indirectly the evil means necessary to produce that good end. The reader has no doubt found himself willing the relief from a toothache directly but the painful means of obtaining this relief only indirectly as a necessary means of attaining relief.

In brief, no double standard is involved in God's action to permit an evil means to obtain a good end, even though humans are not permitted to do exactly the same thing. Humans experience similar situations on a limited scale (e.g., parents giving more freedom to mature young people than to children), yet only God can achieve good ends by permitting evil on the long range, and both God and human beings are committed to performing acts and producing ends that are in accord with the norm of their respective natures.

4. *This theodicy implies that it is wrong to alleviate human suffering.* The most pointed criticism of this theodicy is that it would seem to necessitate an inhumanitarianism. For if suffering is the condition for a greater good, then in working against suffering one is eliminating the possibility of achieving the greater good. It is God's plan to use evil to bring about a greater good. Hence, if one works to eliminate all evil, he is working at cross-purposes with God.

This objection is built on three mistaken notions. First, it assumes that God is promoting evil or at least that he is not working to alleviate it. As was already affirmed, God is not promoting or producing any evil in the world.

---

20. If God can foreknown a world where men freely choose not to sin (which the antitheist suggests), then there is no reason he cannot foreknow a world where men freely do evil, which he will then use as a condition for a greater good. And if the antitheist wishes to withdraw the possibility of God foreknowing a sinless world without foreordaining it, then he has thereby withdrawn his main argument against theism. For in that case, it was not really possible to create free beings who would simply never choose to sin. And if this is so, then the antitheist cannot object to God creating free beings who do sin, on the grounds that a sinless free being was possible.

God is permitting evil only because it is a necessary condition to producing the greatest good. *If there were any other way to obtain optimal moral perfection, God would not even permit evil.* Further, God is working against evil. His moral law urges us not to do evil. He sends warnings against doing evil, and he sends evil consequences for doing evil. The biblical theist holds that God sent Christ to defeat evil and will send him again to destroy evil (Heb. 2:14). God's efforts on this planet have been an all-out attack on evil.

Second, when man works against evil, he is not frustrating the purposes of God but fulfilling them. It is a misunderstanding of God's foreknowledge of free acts and God's commands to do good that misleads the antitheistic argument. Human duty, like God's duty, is not to promote the evil means to good ends; the human's role is to work against all evil. In so doing, he is not working against God, because God is not working to promote evil means. God knows what evil means will be available for the achievement of the greater good, because God knows what every free creature will do with his free choice before he ever does it. Both God and humans must be against the production of evil means as well as evil ends. But only God can guarantee that a greater good will result from permitting evil.

The third mistaken notion is that since God sent the plague of evil, it follows that people should not work against it lest they be fighting God. First of all, God did not cause the plague; human free but evil choices did. God did not send the plague; he merely allowed it because he knows that through it he can bring a greater good. Further, the Christian does not work merely against the result of the plague which is death; he works against the cause of the plague which is sin. Or, in other words, the plague results from the misuse of the creature's freedom, and the Christian is working most earnestly to correct this source of evil. For by getting persons to submit their will to God through Christ who died for the willfully evil, the Christian offers a cure for sin. Christianity fights sin at its source—the only truly effective way to fight the plague. Every other effort will be nothing more than a treatment of symptoms. This is not to say that Christians should not treat symptoms; they should. But what evil needs is a cure, not a cover-up. And every effort is being made by God, and should be made by humans also, to eliminate the plague at its source. Thus, theism is not antihumanitarian. In fact, it is the only truly humanitarian view, for it alone permits persons full free choice and yet guarantees a morally perfect world.

5. *This theodicy exalts human freedom at the expense of divine sovereignty.* Another set of objections to our theodicy is that it both makes human freedom indeterminate and robs God of his sovereignty. It is claimed that human actions are not determined by God or by anything else. God, who is allegedly the cause of all, turns out not to be the controlling cause of human actions. Thus, the sovereign God is not really sovereign over the universe,

because the creature can sovereignly determine his own destiny in opposition to what God desires for him.

There are two ways of replying to this objection. First, a strong Calvinistic theist can reiterate that this theodicy does not require a commitment to significant freedom for human beings at all. Even though such a Calvinist denies that human beings have free choice beyond divine control, he does not deny that the human being has a will with the capacity for making choices and assuming moral responsibility. Thus this theodicy, which is premised on God working through his creatures and teaching his creatures, can be maintained in this context. Consequently the strong Calvinist could simply retreat before this objection without losing the battle.

But other theists can continue the war without any such concessions. They can point out that there are two problems here: the nature of human freedom and its relation to divine sovereignty. First, as to the nature of freedom, we hold the view of moral self-determination. No moral action is externally determined nor is it indeterminate. Hence, moral actions are self-determined. Every moral action would have to be either caused from without, not caused, or self-caused. But to cause a moral action from without would be a violation of freedom, would be determinism, and would eliminate individual responsibility for the action. Ultimately, it would make God directly responsible for performing evil acts. And not to be caused at all would make the act gratuitous, arbitrary, irresponsible, and unpredictable. But human acts are responsible. God knows what persons will do with their freedom and holds them responsible for it. Hence, human moral acts must be self-caused or self-determined. Now self-caused acts are not a contradiction (as self-caused beings are contradictory). For it is not impossible for someone to cause his own becoming (which is what free choice does), but it is impossible for someone to cause his own being. Humans freely determine to become this or that, but they never determine their own *be*-ing. God alone is the Cause of the being of everything that exists (see chap. 9). Hence, self-determination is neither contradictory nor irresponsible. A person is responsible for what he by moral choice comes to be. That is to say, he is responsible for his own free moral self-determination.

Secondly, how can God be in sovereign control of the world if a human being has the final say about his own destiny? Is it not an infringement on divine sovereignty to invest a person with the ultimate decision about anything? Our reply is that God sovereignly willed human free choice. God determined that a human would be a morally self-determining creature. God caused the person to have self-causality of moral thought and action. Human free choice is delegated sovereignty. The Sovereign made the human sovereign over his own moral choices. Nevertheless, God is in control over the whole process because God is operating through the process of free choice in accordance with his own foreknowledge; God sees what free choice will do and that he can bring a greater good out of it; God is in sovereign control of the end in which humans' free choices will be permanentized according to their own will so that free choice to do evil will bring eternal bondage to the autonomy of one's own evil will, and the freedom to do the good will bring eternally liberation to an infinite good. In brief, God (the primary Cause) is working in and through the self-causality of human freedom (the secondary cause) to produce the greatest good for the greatest number (the final cause) in accordance with the absolute perfection of his own nature (the exemplar cause).

As a matter of fact, this view of human self-determination enhances not only divine sovereignty but also human dignity. God is not threatened by the full exercise of human free choice. He knows that ultimately people will say either, "*Thy* will be done" or "*my* will be done." A God who would permit only the former is less than magnanimous. The fact that God will allow the creature to bite his gracious hand exalts his love in the highest moral degree. And the fact that God does not coerce anyone to love and obey him but withholds the infinite persuasion (of the beatific vision) until a person has willed to be captivated by his love indicates, too, that he has elicited love from men in the most morally worthy way conceivable. Infinite Love will receive love from finite men only if it is freely given. Heart-twisting, like arm-twisting, is beneath the dignity of the Divine. Only those who will to do his will know the true and eternal Good that God is.

Physical evil is essentially connected with moral evil. Moral evil is the best way to produce the optimally perfect moral world, and physical evil is a necessary part of this kind of evil world. Physical evil is necessitated in several ways: it is a condition, consequence, component, and concomitant of a morally free world. The evil that is not directly or indirectly traceable to human freedom is attributed to evil spirits. Physical evils are a necessary condition and concomitant of the best kind of world for achieving the best of all possible moral worlds. And since God is the best of all possible beings, it is necessary that he use the best way to achieve the best world.

Bibliography

Abernethy, George L., and Thomas A. Langford, eds. *Philosophy of Religion: A Book of Readings*. 2d ed. New York: Macmillan, 1968.

Ahern, M. B. "The Nature of Evil." *Sophia* 5 (1966): 40–42.

Aiken, Henry D., ed. *The Age of Ideology*. New York: Mentor, 1956.

Altizer, Thomas J. J. *The Gospel of Christian Atheism*. Philadelphia: Westminster, 1966.

———, and William Hamilton. *Radical Theology and the Death of God*. New York: Bobbs-Merrill, 1960.

Anglin, Bill, and Stewart Goetz. "Evil Is Privation." *International Journal for Philosophy of Religion* 13 (1982): 3–12.

Anselm, Saint. *Basic Writings*. Translated by S. N. Deane. 2d ed. LaSalle, Ill.: Open Court, 1962.

Aristotle. *Basic Works of Aristotle*. Edited by R. McKeon. New York: Random, 1941.

Augustine, Saint. *The City of God*. Edited by Vernon J. Bourke. Translated by G. G. Walsh et al. New York: Image Books, Doubleday, 1958.

———. *Confessions and Enchiridion*. Edited and translated by A. C. Outler. Library of Christian Classics, vol. 7. Philadelphia: Westminster, 1955.

———. *The Fathers of the Church: The Retractions*. Vol. 60. Translated by Sister M. I. Bogan. Washington, D.C.: Catholic University of America Press, 1968.

———. *The Nicene and Post-Nicene Fathers*. Vols. 2, 4, 5. Edited by Philip Schaff. Grand Rapids: Eerdmans, 1956.

Ayer, A. J. *Language, Truth, and Logic*. New York: Dover, 1946.

———. *Metaphysics and Common Sense*. San Francisco: Freeman, Cooper, 1970.

Barrett, William. *Irrational Man*. New York: Doubleday, Anchor Books, 1958.

Beller, E., and Lee M. Beller, Jr., eds. *Selections from Bayle's Dictionary*. Princeton: Princeton University Press, 1952.

Bergson, Henri. *The Two Sources of Morality and Religion*. Translated by R. A. Audra and C. Brereton. New York: Doubleday, 1935.

Black, Max. *Models and Metaphors*. Ithaca, N.Y.: Cornell University Press, 1962.

Bréhier, Emile. *The Philosophy of Plotinus*. Translated by Joseph Thomas. Chicago: University of Chicago Press, 1958.

Bronstein, Daniel J., Y. H. Krikorian, and P. P Wiener, eds. *Basic Problems of Philosophy*. 3d ed. Englewood Cliffs, N.J.: Prentice-Hall, 1964.

Buber, Martin. *The Eclipse of God*. New York: Harper Torchbooks, 1957.

———. *The Writings of Martin Buber*. Edited by Will Herberg. New York: World, 1956.

Bultmann, Rudolf. *Jesus Christ and Mythology*. New York: Charles Scribner's Sons, 1958.

——. *Kerygma and Myth*. Vol. 1. Edited by Hans W. Bartsch. New York: Harper and Row, 1953.

Burrell, David. *Analogy and Philosophical Language*. New Haven: Yale University Press, 1973.

Burrill, Donald R., ed. *The Cosmological Arguments: A Spectrum of Opinion*. New York: Anchor Books, Doubleday, 1967.

Buttrick, George A. *God, Pain and Evil*. Nashville: Abingdon, 1966.

Cajetan, Thomas. *The Analogy of Names and the Concept of Being*. Pittsburgh: Duquesne University Press, 1953.

Camus, Albert. *Camus: A Collection of Critical Essays*. Edited by Germaine Bree. Englewood Cliffs, N.J.: Prentice-Hall, 1962.

——. *The Plague*. Translated by S. Gilbert. New York: Modern Library, 1948.

Carnell, E. J. *Introduction to Christian Apologetics*. 3d ed. Grand Rapids: Eerdmans, 1950.

Clark, Gordon H. *Religion, Reason and Revelation*. Nutley, N.J.: Craig, 1961.

Clark, R. E. D. *The Universe: Plan or Accident?* London: Paternoster, 1949.

Collins, James. *God in Modern Philosophy*. Chicago: Regnery, 1959.

Corduan, Winfried. *Handmaid to Theology: An Essay in Philosophical Prolegomena*. Grand Rapids: Baker, 1981.

——. "Hegelian Themes in Contemporary Theology." *Journal of the Evangelical Theological Society* 22 (1979): 351–61.

Cornford, F. M. *From Religion to Philosophy*. New York: Harper and Row, 1912.

Craig, William Lane. *Apologetics: An Introduction*. Chicago: Moody, 1984.

Cusanus, Nicholas. *Of Learned Ignorance*. Translated by G. Heron, O.F.M. New Haven: Yale University Press, 1949.

D'Arcy, M. C. *The Pain of This World and the Providence of God*. London: Longmans, Green and Co., 1936.

Descartes, René. *Meditations*. Translated by L. J. Lafleur. New York: Liberal Arts, Bobbs-Merrill, 1951.

——. *Selections*. Edited by Ralph M. Eaton. New York: Charles Scribner and Sons, 1927.

Dewart, Leslie. *The Foundations of Belief*. New York: Herder and Herder, 1969.

Dewey, John. *A Common Faith*. New Haven: Yale University Press, 1934.

Dostoevsky, Fyodor. *The Brothers Karamazov*. Edited by A. Yarmolinsky. Translated by Constance Garnett. New York: Heritage, 1968.

Durbin, Bill. "A Scientist Caught Between Two Faiths: Interview with Robert Jastrow." *Christianity Today* 26, no. 13 (August 6, 1982): 14–18.

Edwards, Paul. "Professor Tillich's Confusions." *Mind* 74 (1965): 197–206.

Eliade, Mircea. *Myth and Reality*. Translated by Willard R. Trask. New York: Harper and Row, 1963.

——. *The Myth of the Eternal Return*. Translated by Willard R. Trask. New York: Pantheon, 1954.

——. *The Sacred and the Profane*. Translated by Willard R. Trask. New York: Harcourt, Brace and World, 1959.

Emmet, Dorothy. *The Nature of Metaphysical Thinking.* London: Macmillan, 1946.

Eslick, Leonard J. "The Real Distinction: Reply to Professor Reese." *The Modern Schoolman* 38, no. 2 (January 1961): 149–61.

Evans, C. Stephen. *Philosophy of Religion: Thinking About Faith.* Contours of Christian Philosophy series. Downers Grove: Inter-Varsity, 1985.

Farrer, Austin M. *Finite and Infinite.* 2d ed. Naperville, Ill.: Allenson, 1959.

_____. *The Glass of Vision.* London: Dacre, 1948.

_____. *Love Almighty and Ills Unlimited.* New York: Doubleday, 1961.

Feinberg, John S. "And the Atheist Shall Lie Down with the Calvinist: Atheism, Calvinism, and the Freewill Defense." *Trinity Journal* 1 (1980): 142–52.

_____. "Noncognitivism: Wittgenstein." In *Biblical Errancy: An Analysis of Its Philosophical Roots,* edited by Norman L. Geisler, 161–201. Grand Rapids: Zondervan, 1981.

_____. *Theologies and Evil.* Washington, D.C.: University Press of America, 1979.

Ferré, Frederick. "Analogy in Theology." In *Encyclopedia of Philosophy,* edited by Paul Edwards, 1:94–97. 4 vols. New York: Free Press, 1973.

_____. *Basic Modern Philosophy of Religion.* New York: Charles Scribner's Sons, 1967.

_____, and Kent Bendall. *Exploring the Logic of Faith: A Dialogue on the Relation of Modern Philosophy to Christian Faith.* New York: Association, 1962.

_____. *Language, Logic and God.* 1961. New York: Harper Torchbooks, 1969.

_____. "The Logic of Our Current Opportunity." *The Philosophy Forum* 8 (June 1970): 61–87.

_____. "Mapping the Logic of Models in Science and Theology." *The Christian Scholar* 46, no. 1 (Spring 1963): 9–39.

_____. "Metaphors, Models and Religion." *Soundings* 51, no. 3 (Fall 1968): 327–45.

_____. "Science and the Death of God." In *Science and Religion: New Perspective on the Dialogue,* edited by I. Barbour, pp. 134–56. New York: Harper and Row, 1968.

Ferré, Nels F. S. *Evil and the Christian Faith.* New York: Harper, 1947.

Feuerbach, Ludwig. *The Essence of Christianity.* Translated by George Eliot. New York: Harper and Row, 1957.

Flew, Antony, and Alasdair MacIntyre, eds. *New Essays in Philosophical Theology.* London: SCM, 1963.

Freud, Sigmund. *The Future of an Illusion.* Translated by W. D. Robson-Scott. New York: Doubleday, 1957.

Fromm, Erich. *The Art of Loving.* New York: Harper and Row, 1956.

_____. *Psychoanalysis and Religion.* New Haven: Yale University Press, 1959.

Garrigou-Lagrange, Reginald. *God: His Existence and His Nature.* Translated by Dom. B. Rose. Saint Louis: Herder, 1934.

Geisler, Norman L. *Ethics: Alternatives and Issues.* Grand Rapids: Zondervan, 1971.

_____. *False Gods of Our Time: A Defense of the Christian Faith.* Eugene, Ore.: Harvest House, 1985.

_____. "God Knows All Things." In *Predestination and Free Will,* edited by David Basinger and Randall Basinger, pp. 61–98. Downers Grove: Inter-Varsity, 1985.

————. *Miracles and Modern Thought.* Grand Rapids: Zondervan, 1982.

————. "The Missing Premise in the Cosmological Argument." *The Modern Schoolman* 56 (1978): 31–45.

————. "The Missing Premise in the Ontological Argument." *Religious Studies* 9, no. 3 (September 1973): 289–96.

————, and J. Kerby Anderson. *Origin Science: A Proposal for the Creation-Evolution Controversy.* Grand Rapids: Baker, 1987.

————, and William D. Watkins. *Perspectives: Understanding and Evaluating Today's World Views.* San Bernardino, Cal.: Here's Life, 1984.

————, and J. V. Amano. *The Reincarnation Sensation.* Wheaton: Tyndale, 1986.

————. *The Roots of Evil.* Grand Rapids: Zondervan, 1981.

————. "A Scientific Basis for Creation: The Principle of Uniformity." *Creation/Evolution* 4 (1984): 1–6.

Gilkey, Langdon. *Naming the Whirlwind: The Renewal of God-Language.* Indianapolis: Bobbs-Merrill, 1969.

Gill, Jerry H. "Ian Ramsey's Interpretation of Christian Language." Unpublished doctoral dissertation. Duke University, 1966. Ann Arbor: University of Michigan Microfilms, 1967.

————. "The Meaning of Religious Language." *Christianity Today* 9, no. 8 (January 15, 1965): 16–23.

————. *On Knowing God: New Directions for the Future of Theology.* Philadelphia: Westminster, 1981.

————. *Philosophy and Religion: Some Contemporary Perspectives.* Minneapolis: Burgess, 1968.

Gurr, John E. *The Principle of Sufficient Reason in Some Scholastic Systems, 1750–1900.* Milwaukee: Marquette University Press, 1959.

Hackett, Stuart C. *The Reconstruction of the Christian Revelation Claim: A Philosophical and Critical Apologetic.* Grand Rapids: Baker, 1984.

————. *The Resurrection of Theism.* Chicago: Moody, 1957.

Hartshorne, Charles. *Man's Vision of God.* New York: Harper and Row, 1941.

————. *Omnipotence and Other Theological Mistakes.* Albany: State University of New York Press, 1983.

Hastings, James, ed. *Encyclopedia of Religion and Ethics.* 13 vols. New York: Charles Scribner and Sons, 1955.

Hegel, Georg W. F. *The Philosophy of Hegel.* Edited by Carl J. Friedrich. New York: Modern Library, 1953.

————. *Science of Logic.* Translated by W. H. Johnston and L. G. Struthers. 2 vols. New York: Macmillan, 1931.

Heidegger, Martin. *Being and Time.* New York: Macmillan, 1967.

Henle, Paul. "A Reply by Paul Henle." In *The Ontological Argument: From Saint Anselm to Contemporary Philosophers,* edited by Alvin Plantinga, 171–80. Garden City, N.Y.: Anchor Books, Doubleday, 1965.

Hick, John H. *Evil and the God of Love.* New York: Harper and Row, 1966.

————. *Faith and the Philosophers.* London: Macmillan, 1964.

————, ed. *The Existence of God.* New York: Macmillan, 1964.

————, and Arthur C. McGill, eds. *The Many-Faced Argument: Recent Studies in the Ontological Argument for the Existence of God.* New York: Macmillan, 1967.

Hospers, John. "What Is Explanation?" In *Reason and Responsibility,* edited by Joel Feinberg, 181–91. Belmont, Cal.: Dickenson, 1965.

Hume, David. *Dialogues Concerning Natural Religion.* Edited by Norman Kemp Smith. Indianapolis: Bobbs-Merrill, 1962.

_____. *Enquiry Concerning Human Understanding.* Indianapolis: Bobbs-Merrill, 1955.

_____. "A Letter of Hume to John Stewart." In Ernest Campbell Mossner, *The Life of David Hume,* 2d ed., p. 259 (Oxford: Clarendon, 1980).

_____. *The Letters of David Hume.* Edited by T. Greig. Oxford: Clarendon, 1932.

Huxley, Julian. *Evolution in Action.* New York: Harper and Brothers, 1953.

James, William. *Pragmatism, and Other Essays.* New York: Washington Square, 1963.

_____. *The Varieties of Religious Experience.* New York: Mentor, New American Library, 1958.

Jaspers, Karl, and Rudolf Bultmann. *Myth and Christianity.* New York: Noonday, 1958.

Jung, Carl. *The Portable Jung.* Edited by Joseph Campbell. New York: Penguin, 1971.

_____. *Psychology and Religion.* Vol. 2 of *Collected Works of C. G. Jung.* Translated by R. F. C. Hull. Princeton: Princeton University Press, 1970.

Kane, G. Stanley. "Evil and Privation." *International Journal for Philosophy of Religion* 11 (1980): 43–58.

Kant, Immanuel. *The Critique of Practical Reason.* Translated by Lewis W. Beck. New York: Liberal Arts, Bobbs-Merrill, 1956.

_____. *The Critique of Pure Reason.* Translated by Lewis W. Beck. New York: Bobbs-Merrill, 1956.

_____. *Prolegomena to Any Future Metaphysics.* Introduction by Lewis W. Beck. New York: Liberal Arts, Bobbs-Merrill, 1950.

_____. *Religion Within the Limits of Reason Alone.* New York: Harper Torchbooks, 1960.

Kaufmann, Walter. *Critique of Religion and Philosophy.* New York: Doubleday, 1961.

Kierkegaard, Søren. *Concluding Unscientific Postscript.* Translated by D. F. Swenson and W. Lowrie. Princeton: Princeton University Press, 1944.

_____. *Either/Or.* Translated by W. Lowrie. New York: Doubleday, 1959.

_____. *Fear and Trembling* and *The Sickness Unto Death.* Translated by W. Lowrie. New York: Doubleday, 1954.

_____. *Philosophical Fragments.* Translated, with introduction, by David F. Swenson. New introduction and commentary by Nels Thulstrup. Translation revised and commentary translated by H. V. Hong. Princeton: Princeton University Press, 1967.

_____. *Stages on Life's Way.* New York: Harper and Row, 1954.

King, Winston L. *Introduction to Religion.* New York: Harper and Row, 1954.

Kirk, G. S., and J. E. Raven. *The Presocratic Philosophers.* Cambridge: Cambridge University Press, 1964.

Klubertanz, George P. *St. Thomas Aquinas on Analogy.* Chicago: Loyola University Press, 1960.

Küng, Hans. *Does God Exist? An Answer for Today.* Translated by Edward Quinn. New York: Vintage, 1981.

Kushner, Harold S. *When Bad Things Happen to Good People.* New York: Schocken, 1981.

Leibniz, Gottfried. *Monadology and Other Philosophical Essays.* Translated by Paul Schrecker and Anne Schrecker. Indianapolis: Liberal Arts, Bobbs-Merrill, 1965.

_____. *Theodicy.* Translated by E. M. Huggard. Indianapolis: Bobbs-Merrill, 1966.

Lewis, C. I. *Mind and the World Order.* New York: Charles Scribner and Sons, 1929.

Lewis, C. S. *The Great Divorce.* New York: Macmillan, 1946.

_____. *Mere Christianity.* New York: Macmillan, 1953.

_____. *Miracles.* New York: Macmillan, 1947.

_____. *The Problem of Pain.* New York: Macmillan, 1944.

McInerny, Ralph. *The Logic of Analogy.* The Hague: Nijhoff, 1961.

McTaggert, J. M. E. *Some Dogmas of Religion.* London: E. Arnold, 1930.

Madden, Edward H., and P. H. Hare. *Evil and the Concept of God.* Springfield, Ill.: Charles C. Thomas, 1968.

Maimonides, Moses. *The Guide for the Perplexed.* Translated by M. Friedlander. New York: Dover, 1904.

Maritain, Jacques. *St. Thomas and the Problem of Evil.* Milwaukee: Marquette University Press, 1942.

Marty, Martin E. *Varieties of Unbelief.* New York: Doubleday, 1964.

Marx, Karl, and Friedrich Engels. *On Religion.* Introduction by Reinhold Niebuhr. New York: Schocken, 1964.

Mascall, Eric L. *Existence and Analogy.* New York: Longmans, Green and Co., 1949.

_____. *He Who Is.* London: Longmans, Green and Co., 1943.

_____. *Words and Images: A Study in Theological Discourse.* New York: Ronald, 1957.

Maurer, Armand A. *A History of Medieval Philosophy.* New York: Random, 1962.

_____. "St. Thomas and the Analogy of Genus." *New Scholasticism* 29 (April 1955): 127–44.

Mill, John Stuart. *Utilitarianism.* 1863. New York: Meridian, 1962.

Mondin, Battista. *The Principle of Analogy in Protestant and Catholic Theology.* The Hague: Nijhoff, 1963.

Moreland, J. P. *Universals, Qualities, and Quality-Instances: A Defense of Realism.* Lanham, Md.: University Press of America, 1985.

Morrison, Frank. *Who Moved the Stone?* London: Faber and Faber, 1958.

Nielsen, Kai E. *Contemporary Critiques of Religion.* New York: Herder and Herder, 1971.

_____. *An Introduction to the Philosophy of Religion.* New Studies in the Philosophy of Religion series. New York: St. Martin, 1982.

_____. *Scepticism.* New York: St. Martin, 1973.

Nielsen, Niels C., Jr. "Analogy and the Knowledge of God: An Ecumenical Appraisal." *Rice University Studies* 60 (1974): 21–102.

Nietzsche, Friedrich. *The Portable Nietzsche.* Edited by Walter Kaufmann. New York: Viking, 1954.

Novak, Michael. *Belief and Unbelief.* New York: Macmillan, 1965.

Ockham, William. *Philosophical Writings.* Translated by Philotheus Boehner. Indianapolis: Liberal Arts, Bobbs-Merrill, 1964.

Onions, C. T., ed. *Shorter Oxford English Dictionary.* 3d ed. Oxford: Oxford University Press, 1932.

Otto, Rudolf. *The Idea of the Holy.* Translated by J. W. Harvey. New York: Oxford University Press, 1967.

Owens, J. P. *The Christian Knowledge of God.* London: Athlone, 1969.

Packer, J. I. "The Adequacy of Human Language." In *Inerrancy,* edited by Norman L. Geisler, 197–226. Grand Rapids: Zondervan, 1980.

Penelhum, Terence. *Religion and Rationality.* New York: Random, 1971.

Peterson, Michael. *Evil and the Christian God.* Grand Rapids: Baker, 1982.

Phillips, D. Z. *Religion Without Explanation.* Oxford: Blackwell, 1976.

Philo, Judaeus. *Works of Philo.* Translated by C. D. Yange. London: Heinemann, 1854–55.

Pike, Nelson. *God and Timelessness.* Studies in Ethics and the Philosophy of Religion series. New York: Schocken, 1970.

_____, ed. *God and Evil: Readings on the Theological Problem of Evil.* New York: Prentice-Hall, 1964.

Plantinga, Alvin. *God and Other Minds: A Study of the Rational Justification of Belief in God.* Contemporary Philosophy series. Ithaca, N.Y: Cornell University Press, 1967.

_____. *God, Freedom, and Evil.* New York: Harper Torchbooks, 1974.

_____. *The Nature of Necessity.* Oxford: Clarendon, 1974.

_____, ed. *The Ontological Argument: From Anselm to Contemporary Philosophers.* Garden City, N.Y.: Doubleday, Anchor Books, 1965.

Plato. *The Collected Dialogues.* Edited by Edith Hamilton and H. Cairns Huntington. New York: Pantheon, 1941.

Plotinus. *Six Enneads.* Chicago: Encyclopedia Britannica Press, 1952.

Polanyi, Michael. *The Tacit Dimension.* Garden City, N.Y.: Doubleday, 1966.

Ramm, Bernard. *Protestant Christian Evidences.* Chicago: Moody, 1953.

Ramsey, Ian T. *Christian Discourse: Some Logical Explorations.* London: Oxford University Press, 1956.

_____. "History and the Gospels: Some Philosophical Reflections." *Studia Evangelica,* vol. 3 (Berlin: Akademie Verlog, 1964).

_____. *Models and Metaphors.* London: Oxford University Press, 1964.

_____. *Models and Mystery.* London: Oxford University Press, 1964.

_____. *Prospects for Metaphysics.* London: George Allen and Unwin, 1961.

_____. *Religious Language.* New York: Macmillan, 1963.

Rand, Ayn. *For the New Intellectual.* New York: New American Library, 1961.

Reichenbach, Bruce R. *The Cosmological Argument: A Reassessment.* Springfield, Ill.: Charles C. Thomas, 1972.

Robinson, John A. T. *Honest to God.* Philadelphia: Westminster, 1963.

Ross, James F. "Analogy as a Rule of Meaning for Religious Language." *International Philosophical Quarterly* 1, no. 3 (September 1961): 468–502.

Russell, Bertrand. *The Basic Writings of Bertrand Russell.* Edited by Robert E. Egner and Lester E. Denonn. New York: Simon and Schuster, 1957.

_____. *Why I Am Not a Christian*. New York: Simon and Schuster, 1957.

Sargants, William. *Battle for the Mind*. London: William Heinemann, 1957.

Sartre, Jean-Paul. *Existential Psychoanalysis*. Translated by H. E. Barnes. New York: Philosophical Library, 1953.

_____. *Existentialism and Humanism*. Translated by P. Mairet. London: Methuen, 1955.

_____. *The Words*. Translated by B. Frechtman. New York: Braziller, 1964.

Schaeffer, Francis. *The God Who Is There*. Downers Grove: Inter-Varsity, 1968.

Schleiermacher, Friedrich. *The Christian Faith*. Translated by H. R. Macintosh and T. S. Stewart. Edinburgh: T. and T. Clark, 1928.

_____. *On Religion: Speeches to Its Cultured Despisers*. Translated by John Oman. New York: Ungar, 1955.

Scotus, John Duns. *Philosophical Writings*. Translated by Allan B. Wolter. Indianapolis: Liberal Arts, Bobbs-Merrill, 1962.

Shedd, W. G. T. *Dogmatic Theology*. Vol. 1. New York: Charles Scribner and Sons, 1868–94.

Silvester, Hugh. *Arguing with God: A Christian Examination of the Problem of Evil*. Downers Grove: Inter-Varsity, 1971.

Siwek, Paul, S. J. *The Philosophy of Evil*. New York: Ronald, 1951.

Smart, Ninian. *Philosophy of Religion*. New York: Random, 1970.

_____. *The Religious Experience of Mankind*. New York: Charles Scribner's Sons, 1969.

Smith, Wilfred C. *The Meaning and End of Religion*. New York: New American Library of World Literature, 1964.

Spiegelberg, Frederic. *Living Religions of the World*. Englewood Cliffs, N.J.: Prentice-Hall, 1956.

Spinoza, Benedict. *Epistola 50 (Opera)*, 4. In *Chief Works*, translated by R. H. M. Elwes. New York: Dover, 1955.

_____. *Ethics*. Translated by Andrew Boyle. New York: Dutton, 1963.

Stace, W. T. *Mysticism and Philosophy*. Philadelphia: Lippincott, 1960.

Taylor, Alfred E. *Plato: The Man and His Works*. New York: World, 1956.

Teilhard de Chardin, Pierre. *The Divine Milieu: An Essay on the Interior Life*. New York: Harper Torchbooks, 1960.

Temple, William. *Nature, Man, and God*. New York: Macmillan, 1935.

Tennant, F. R. *Philosophical Theology*. Vol. 2. Cambridge: Cambridge University Press, 1930.

Tertullian. *The Ante-Nicene Fathers*. Vol. 3. Edited by Philip Schaff. Grand Rapids: Eerdmans, 1956.

Tholfsen, Trygve R. *Historical Thinking: An Introduction*. New York: Harper and Row, 1967.

Thomas Aquinas, Saint. *Compendium of Theology*. Translated by C. Vollert. Saint Louis: Herder, 1949.

_____. *On the Power of God*. Translated by the English Dominican Fathers. 3 books in 1. Westminster, Md.: Newman, 1952.

_____. *St. Thomas Aquinas: Philosophical Texts*. Edited by T. Gilby. London: Oxford University Press, 1951.

_____. *Summa contra Gentiles*. Vols. 1, 2. Translated by the English Dominican Fathers. London: Burns, Oates and Washbourne, 1923, 1924.

_____. *Summa Theologica*. Translated by the English Dominican Fathers. Chicago: Benziger Brothers, 1947, 1948.

Tillich, Paul. *Christianity and the Encounter of the World Religions*. New York: Columbia University Press, 1963.

_____. *The Dynamics of Faith*. New York: Harper Torchbooks, 1957.

_____. *Morality and Beyond*. New York: Harper and Row, 1963.

_____. *Systematic Theology*. Vol. 1. Chicago: University of Chicago Press, 1951.

_____. *Ultimate Concern*. Edited by D. Mackenzie Brown. London: SCM, 1965.

Trueblood, Elton. *Philosophy of Religion*. New York: Harper and Row, 1957.

van Buren, Paul M. *The Edge of Language: An Essay in the Logic of Religion*. New York: Macmillan, 1972.

_____. *The Secular Meaning of the Gospel*. New York: Macmillan, 1963.

Voltaire, Francois M. A. *Candide*. Translated and edited by Peter Gay. New York: St. Martin, 1963.

Watts, Alan. *The Supreme Identity: An Essay on Oriental Metaphysic and the Christian Religion*. New York: Random, 1972.

Whitehead, Alfred North. *Process and Reality*. New York: Harper and Row, 1929.

_____. *Religion in the Making*. New York: World, 1960.

Wittgenstein, Ludwig. *Philosophical Investigations*. 3d ed. Translated by G. E. M. Anscombe. Oxford: Blackwell, 1967.

_____. *Tractatus Logico-Philosophicus*. Translated by D. F. Pears and B. F. McGuinness. London: Routledge and Kegan Paul, 1961.

Wolter, Allan B. *The Transcendentals and Their Function in the Metaphysics of Duns Scotus*. St. Bonaventure, N.Y.: The Franciscan Institute, 1946.

Xenophon. *Memorabilia of Socrates*. I, IV, 4f. Boston: Allyn, 1894.

Yaeger, Werner. *Aristotle: Fundamentals of the History of His Development*. 2d ed. Translated by R. Robinson. Oxford: Clarendon, 1934.

Yandell, Keith. "The Problem of Evil." Paper presented at the Wheaton Philosophy Conference, Wheaton, Ill., October 1980.

Index of Names

Index of Subjects

Made in the USA
Lexington, KY
20 March 2019

3 4711 00230 8148